SOUTHERN MOUNTAIN REPUBLICANS
1865–1900

SOUTHERN MOUNTAIN REPUBLICANS 1865–1900

Politics and the Appalachian Community

Gordon B. McKinney

THE UNIVERSITY OF NORTH CAROLINA PRESS
CHAPEL HILL

© 1978 by
The University of North Carolina Press
All rights reserved
Manufactured in the United States of America
ISBN 0-8078-1300-1
Library of Congress Catalog Card Number 78-2888

Library of Congress Cataloging in Publication Data

McKinney, Gordon Bartlett, 1943–
   Southern mountain Republicans, 1865–1900.

   Bibliography: p.
   Includes index.
   1. Applachian region, Southern—Politics and government. 2. Republican Party—History. I. Title
F217.A65M23   329.6'00975   78-2888
ISBN 0-8078-1300-1

To Martha

CONTENTS

	Preface	xi
1	Mountain Republicanism: The Context	3
2	The Civil War and the Origins of Mountain Republicanism	12
3	Reconstruction in the Mountains	30
4	The Mountain Republican Party-Army	62
5	Emergence of the Party-Army	75
6	The Party-Army in Control	110
7	Racial Policy, Industrialization, and Violence	124
8	Destruction of the Bosses and New Republican Leadership	142
9	Reaction, Defeat, and Disfranchisement	183
	Appendix	205
	Notes	223
	Selected Bibliography	257
	Index	271

TABLES

Text

1	Mountain Counties Voting Democrat and Whig, Presidential Elections, 1836–1848	14
2	Counties Voting Democrat, Whig, and Opposition, Presidential Elections, 1852 and 1856	15
3	Counties Carried by, and Popular Vote for, Candidates, Presidential Election, 1860	16
4	Popular Vote and Percentage of Total Vote, Presidential Elections, 1868, 1872, and 1876	33
5	Gubernatorial, Congressional, and Legislative Races, Kentucky, 1867	51
6	Votes for and against the Constitutional Convention by Race, Selected Virginia Counties, 1867	58
7	Sample Voter Information Form	72
8	Republican Votes for Federal and State Offices, Anderson County, Tennessee, 1900	73
9	Qualified and Not Qualified Readjuster Voters by Race, Selected Virginia Counties, 1881	103
10	Popular Vote and Percentage of Total Vote, Presidential Elections, 1876, 1880, 1884	111
11	Popular Vote and Percentage of Total Vote, Presidential Elections, 1884 and 1888	120
12	Negro Population and Total Population of Mountain Counties, 1870 and 1900	135
13	Voter Registration by Race in Knoxville, Tennessee, 1894	140
14	Percentage of Republican Vote in Mountain Counties, Upper South, 1896, 1898, and 1900	196

Appendix

1	Illiteracy in the Upper South, 1870	206
2	Illiteracy and White Republican Voting, Presidential Election, 1876	207
3	Church Membership, 1890, and Party Vote, Presidential Election, 1876	208
4	White Republican Vote and Negro Population in Five States, 1876	209
5	White Republican Vote and Negro Population in Mountain Counties, 1876	209
6	Population Having at Least One Foreign-born Parent, 1870	210
7	Antisecession Vote, 1861, and Republican Vote, 1876, Eastern Tennessee	212
8	Antisecession Vote, 1861, and Democratic Vote, 1876, Selected Northwestern West Virginia Counties	212
9	Republican Vote from 1876 to 1896 in the Mountain Counties	215
10	Increase of Republican Vote in the Mountain Counties	215
11	Republican Vote in Thirty-one Mountain Counties with Urban Populations, 1900	216
12	Increase of Republican Vote in Twenty-eight Mountain Counties with One Million Dollars of Manufacturing Capital, 1900	217
13	Democratic Percentage for Presidential Election, 1876, and Increase of Republican Percentage, 1876–1888, All Mountain Counties	220

PREFACE

The study of the history of the people of the Appalachian mountains must be written with great care. The rediscovery of poverty in West Virginia in the early 1960s has created a widespread stereotyped image of the region and its inhabitants. The result is that the historian is tempted to concentrate on those events that help to explain the present situation. This approach to the period between 1865 and 1900 would distort seriously the contemporary southern mountain people's view of their own times and would obscure some important developments. These years were a time of hope for the mountain people, for the promise of industrialization hid many of its consequences. At the same time, the historian must be aware of the developments in the twentieth century and, where appropriate, point out the origins of the tragic social and economic problems that have plagued the area.

All efforts to achieve a balanced approach to Appalachian history are hampered by the absence of scholarly studies of the region's past. Much of the material on the mountain people has been written by advocates who were more concerned about proving a point than about understanding the complexity of the situation. This study itself has changed drastically since it was first conceived. The original outline of the project envisioned a largely statistical study of the political developments in the region. That plan had to be modified because much of the fundamental background of mountain politics remained undiscovered. In addition, few historical investigations of the social life of the mountain people have been undertaken—although Ron Eller at Mars Hill College will shortly complete one. Thus, it was necessary first to construct the basic narrative. Subsequent statistical tests revealed that the mountain people formed a relatively homogeneous ethnic and religious group. This part of the work showed little unexpected information, and much of it became an appendix to the manuscript, rather than its core. As a result the present text represents an effort to relate the political

xi

history of one segment of mountain society and explain the wider implications of these developments.

Defining what constitutes Appalachia, particularly in the late nineteenth century, is a difficult task. Each author who deals with the region has used different criteria and the result is confusion. For this study I have included the following counties as being part of Appalachia on the basis of geographical location and economic characteristics. Kentucky: Bell, Boyd, Breathitt, Carter, Clay, Clinton, Cumberland, Elliott, Estill, Floyd, Greenup, Harlan, Jackson, Johnson, Knott, Knox, Laurel, Lawrence, Lee, Leslie, Letcher, Lewis, McCreary, Magoffin, Martin, Menifee, Morgan, Owsley, Perry, Pike, Powell, Pulaski, Rockcastle, Wayne, Whitley, Wolfe; North Carolina: Alexander, Alleghany, Ashe, Buncombe, Burke, Caldwell, Catawba, Cherokee, Clay, Cleveland, Gaston, Haywood, Henderson, Lincoln, McDowell, Macon, Madison, Mitchell, Polk, Rutherford, Swain, Transylvania, Watauga, Wilkes, Yancey; Tennessee: Anderson, Bledsoe, Blount, Bradley, Campbell, Carter, Claiborne, Cocke, Cumberland, Grainer, Greene, Hamblen, Hamilton, Hancock, Hawkins, James, Jefferson, Johnson, Knox, Loudon, McMinn, Marion, Meigs, Monroe, Morgan, Polk, Rhea, Roane, Scott, Sequatchie, Sevier, Sullivan, Unicoi, Union, Washington; Virginia: Alleghany, Bath, Bland, Botetourt, Buchanan, Carroll, Craig, Dickenson, Floyd, Giles, Grayson, Highland, Lee, Montgomery, Pulaski, Roanoke, Russell, Scott, Smyth, Tazewell, Washington, Wythe; West Virginia: Barbour, Braxton, Brooke, Cabell, Calhoun, Clay, Doddridge, Gilmer, Hancock, Harrison, Jackson, Kanawha, Lewis, Lincoln, Marion, Marshall, Mason, Monongalia, Nicholas, Ohio, Pleasants, Pocahontas, Preston, Putnam, Randolph, Ritchie, Roane, Taylor, Tucker, Tyler, Upshur, Wayne, Webster, Wetzel, Wirt, Wood. The major difference between this list and many of the others is the exclusion of some West Virginia counties. Richard O. Curry argues persuasively in *A House Divided: A Study of Statehood Politics and the Copperhead Movement in West Virginia* (1964) that there were two distinct groups of counties in that state. I have followed Curry's division and limited most of my work to the original Unionist counties in the northwestern part of the state.

These counties in the five-state area formed the population base for the statistical analysis of the mountain people and their politics. Several individuals and institutions have offered me assistance with the preparation and analysis of the quantitative data used in this study. The National Science Foundation gave me a grant that allowed me to attend a summer session at the Inter-University Consortium for Political Research in Ann Arbor, Michigan. The classes at the consortium were of great assistance to me in preparing the study. In addition, the consortium made available a great deal of election and census data, which form the basis for that part of this manuscript. All of the conclusions are mine, however, and the consortium is not responsible for any of the assertions made in the statistical analysis of their data. John Curtis of Valdosta State College and John Blydenburgh of Clark University aided with crucial advice at several points in the data analysis process.

I am also indebted to a number of libraries and research institutions for their assistance in locating manuscript collections dealing with mountain politics. The staffs of the following institutions have greeted me with courtesy and extended professional advice about their holdings: Chattanooga Public Library; Duke University Library; Filson Club Library; Kentucky Historical Society; Lawson McGhee Library and the East Tennessee Historical Society; Library of Congress; New Hampshire Historical Society; North Carolina Department of Art, Culture, and History; Northwestern University Library; University of Kentucky Library; University of Louisville Law Library; University of North Carolina Library; University of Tennessee Library; University of Virginia Library; West Virginia University Library; Valdosta State College Library; West Virginia Department of Archives and History; and the College of William and Mary Library. Miss Pollyanna Creekmore, formerly of the East Tennessee Historical Society and Lawson McGhee Library and now at East Tennessee State University, introduced me to the field of Appalachian research and provided me with insights I could have gained in no other way. The late Dr. Virginia Gray and Dr. Mattie Russell were of especial assistance to me during my long stay at the Duke University Library. Miss Joy Trulock and the Reference Department at the Valdosta State College Library have worked with unfailing dedication and ingenuity to find and secure copies of rare documents and newspapers for me.

A number of individuals also helped with the final preparation of this manuscript. I wish to thank the editors the following journals for permission to use material from my previously published articles: "The Mountain Republican Party-Army," *Tennessee Historical Quarterly* 32; "The Rise of the Houk Machine in East Tennessee," and "Farewell to the Bloody Shirt: The Decline of the Houk Machine," East Tennessee Historical Society's *Publications*, No. 45 and No. 46; "Mountain Republicans and the Negro, 1865–1900," *Journal of Southern History* 41; "Racism and the Electorate: Two Late Nineteenth Century Elections," *Appalachian Journal* 1. I wish to thank the editor of the *Appalachian Journal* for permission to quote from "Industrialization and Violence in Appalachia in the 1890's," which was delivered at the Cratis Williams Symposium at Appalachian State University. Professor George Fredrickson of Northwestern University, Professors Richard McMurry of Valdosta State College, E. Stanly Godbold of Mississippi State University, and the late Stanley Folmsbee of the University of Tennessee all read and commented on parts of the manuscript. Mrs. Ethel G. Schmitt edited the manuscript with care and improved it substantially. Mrs. Tommye Miller, Mrs. Shirley Adair, and Mrs. Gail Champion typed the final drafts with precision and sharp editorial eyes. The Graduate School at Valdosta State College gave me two grants to expedite the completion of the project. Professor Robert H. Wiebe of Northwestern University guided me through the periods of doubt and frustration for this entire enterprise. His insight, compassion, and honesty have greatly improved both the writing and the interpretive framework of the manuscript. I deeply appreciate his willingness to offer encouragement and advice without attempting to assume control over the work itself.

I owe my greatest debt to my wife, Martha McCreedy McKinney. She edited one draft of the manuscript with skill and rooted out many of the errors. But, much more important, she has given me the support needed for a long project, and at the same time she has refused to allow me to neglect more important things. Finally, I thank my dog Boozer for waiting patiently during all these years for me to spend more time with him.

SOUTHERN MOUNTAIN REPUBLICANS
1865–1900

CHAPTER 1

MOUNTAIN REPUBLICANISM: THE CONTEXT

One of the most persistent stereotypes in American history has been that of the independent, ignorant, violent, and poor southern mountaineer. This image, created by novelists, scholars, and politicians in the late nineteenth century, has persisted in such diverse parts of American society as federal poverty programs and the comic pages of daily newspapers. Despite the efforts of a number of writers who have demonstrated the mythological nature of this picture of the mountain population, the people of Appalachia are still regarded as different from all other Americans.[1] At the same time, a second school of interpretation has suggested that the mountain people can best be understood as "victims" of predatory outside capitalists, who destroyed the mountain economy and culture.[2] Popular acceptance of these mental constructs has discouraged rigorous investigation into the history of the mountain region.

Instead, most observers have been content to point out the qualities and experiences that helped to create the stereotype. The seemingly unusual political history of the mountain people offers an opportunity to test the validity of this image.[3] Unlike most southern whites in the years between 1861 and 1865, the mountain men resisted secession and often fought against the Confederacy. After 1865, many mountain voters joined the Republican party and remained the only large group of white southerners in the party until the 1950s.[4] A number of interpretations have been offered to explain this phenomenon, but they have all shared the common idea that there was something unique about the mountain people. These unusual character traits or patterns of loyalty were generally regarded as unchanging. Thus mountain republicanism became almost an inherited physical abnormality, similar to possessing six fingers.

This type of explanation of the creation and persistence of mountain republicanism denies the complexity of historical developments in Appalachia. Equally significant is the fact that the two major interpretations of Appalachian history are contradictory. First, there is the conflict between the representation of the mountain people as living in a static and isolated society and the claim that the Applachian people can best be understood as being crushed by the dynamic changes brought by industrialization. Clearly, one cannot have revolution and an unchanging society at the same time. Another set of images maintains that the mountain people were passive actors on the stage of history, who were plundered by outsiders; at the same time, they were the independent and courageous people who overcame southern nationalism and racism to maintain their own identity. Again, this paradox cannot be resolved within the bounds of the traditional mountaineer stereotype. Thus, it is necessary first to present a narrative of the events surrounding the appearance and growth of mountain republicanism. Only after that process has provided information for analysis can explanations of mountaineer political behavior be attempted.

Ironically, one of the significant features of politics in the Gilded Age was the prominent role played by self-constituted geographical communities that tried to create an appealing image for themselves. In fact, the organization of local groups is one of the most consistent themes in United States history.[5] Even in the midst of national crises, such as war and economic collapse, Americans have sought to preserve local traditions. This tendency has been encouraged by the religious diversity, racial and ethnic heterogeneity, and the geographical dispersion of the American people. Each small segment of society has sought to protect its autonomy. These efforts to retain local hegemony have been reflected in many American institutions and practices. The innumerable independent Protestant congregations, the splintered public school system, and the ubiquitous social and service clubs attest to the power of local interests in the United States. In politics this situation has been institutionalized in the division of power among national, state, county, municipal, and township governments. Few other nations in the world have such a complex federal system.[6]

Another important attribute of these communities was that they often appeared in response to outside pressure. In many cases, people would not recognize common characteristics until they became involved in resisting a challenge to their normal routine. An excellent example of this process, and one that had an impact on southern mountain politics, was the debate over slavery. Forced by racial prejudice and economic self-interest to defend a common labor and social system, the inhabitants of the slave states discovered a common heritage. By 1861 many southerners were willing to leave the Union and to fight against the national government in order to defend what appeared to be local rights. Thus, the creation of local groups not only was a matter of geographical proximity, but also indicated a recognition that a community of interests existed.

The Civil War and Reconstruction provided a number of instances of centralized power that encouraged local political organizations to be more conscious of local interests during the Gilded Age that followed. The fighting required a greater concentration of military, economic, and political power than Americans had ever experienced before. The creation and provisioning of two great armies required that many citizens accept government direction in their lives for the first time. Some recognized the opportunities and seized economic and political advantages that depended upon a strong national government for sustenance. A relatively well-disciplined group of Republicans was able to continue the program of central direction through part of Reconstruction, but by 1869 local groups were reasserting themselves.[7]

Most Americans were not favorably impressed by their brief experience with a strong federal government. The war had brought economic problems and death to every town in the country, and Reconstruction brought government-imposed changes in the daily lives of a large number of citizens. When the war ended, the suffering continued for many. Widows, disabled veterans, and the financially ruined were constant reminders of the price paid in defending national causes. Probably more important was the growing realization that despite the sacrifices, the effort had been in vain. This was most apparent in the South, where the slaves were freed and military units helped to determine who would govern. Northern communities discovered, however, that they could not escape the demands of the more powerful national government, either. Blacks had to be allowed to vote in the North as well as the South; unwilling consumers in every state paid high prices caused by tariffs and were forced to underwrite corrupt financial arrangements with the nation's railroads. Many Americans turned to local leaders to defend them against these changes in their life.

The events of the Civil War and Reconstruction helped to forge a particularly strong bond among southern white voters. Political coalitions made up of members of all antebellum political parties joined together to resist programs imposed by the federal government and to prevent blacks from gaining political power. Mountain whites were attracted by this appeal to their regional pride. On the other hand, many of them were repelled by the glorification of the Confederacy that also became a part of the Democratic party's campaign rhetoric. Despite this qualification, the South was once again defining itself as a single region and calling on the whites of the area to indicate their support of this idea by voting for Democratic candidates.

Political parties in the United States had to adapt to these same historical developments. All politicians had to reconcile disparate demands made upon them by local, state, and national organizations. Since the parties had to deal with conflicting community demands, they made no attempt to make their policies ideologically consistent. In fact, Gilded Age party platforms were notorious for saying nothing specific. Henry Adams captured the essence of the successful politician in this era when he wrote, "Ratcliffe was a great statesman. The smoothness of his manipulation was marvelous. No other man in politics . . . could—his admirers said—have brought together so many hostile interests and made so fantastic a combination. . . . The beauty of his work consisted in the skill with which he evaded questions of principle."[8] Adams was voicing his criticism of contemporary politics, but many Americans felt that Ratcliffe and similar real-life politicians were a necessity. These men were required to give their primary loyalty to local concerns, no matter how much these activities might conflict with the national party platform. The guiding principle during the years between 1872 and 1892 was not an ideology but the defense of the community.

Another result of the federal government system in the United States was the decentralized party structure that evolved. Since each party had to appeal to voters on three levels, each segment of the organization had to be allowed great flexibility in its own sphere. The state parties have always maintained their independence from the national organization. Any attempt by the national leadership of the party to dictate to state leaders has always been fiercely resented and has often led to open revolt. There was no way for the national chairman or committee effectively to discipline recalcitrant underlings. The state party had its own independent constituency, and as long as it pleased these voters national leaders could not challenge the dissenters. Robert D. Marcus has delineated this process in great detail in his study of the Republican party in the Gilded Age. He showed the lack of continuity in national leadership between presidential nominating conventions, and the great importance of local considerations in the decisions made at these gatherings.[9]

The place of local groups in the party structure was also secure, as indicated by studies of politics in the last quarter of the nineteenth century. Party affiliation was strongly influenced by such demographic variables as the ethnic and religious backgrounds of the voters.[10] These self-defined units could not be coerced into conforming to partisan dictates; instead, the political organizations sought to make concessions to them. When a community did become identified with a party, it supported that political group loyally, particularly in the Gilded Age when most eligible voters cast ballots and did not split their tickets.[11] Local leaders, therefore, had a firm base with which to work as long as they retained community approval. State leaders who tried to replace the local men found that they risked alienating a group of voters needed by the party. The result was that the local leader protected the community, in part to preserve his own independence.

However, other powerful forces, the new ideas and groups created by the industrial revolution in the United States, threatened the autonomy of the community in the Gilded Age. Antebellum inventions, such as the railroad and the telegraph, invaded almost every part of the country. News and products from distant cities competed with local happenings and goods for public attention. Conversely, the natural resources and products of each locality had a greatly expanded market, and it seemed as if fortunes were there for the taking. Thus, every town eagerly sought to be connected to these new national transportation and communication systems.

What followed was not the expected riches, but the disintegration of the geographically based community. Local businessmen and farmers suddenly found themselves part of a national, and in some cases an international, economy. Profits were determined by forces beyond the control and understanding of the local merchant. Even during good times farmers and rural businessmen found that railroads were not necessarily their allies, since corporations and urban communities paid lower rates and enjoyed other significant competitive advantages. Frequently, local business concerns were absorbed or replaced by units of large industrial empires whose decisions on such crucial matters as plant location and employment levels were not influenced by the needs of the local population. The relationship between workers and factory owners was more likely to be strictly economic instead of personal. A feeling of alienation and impotence swept through whole towns and destroyed their cohesion.[12]

The search for order amid the chaos of the industrial revolution quickly spread to all parts of American society.[13] Corporations needed standardized procedures that would allow them to produce, transport, and merchandise their goods throughout the country. Uniform gauges for railroads and common accounting practices were different aspects of the same movement. The new industrialized society needed people trained to run the new system, and national standards were soon applied to these professional workers. Doctors, lawyers, educators, engineers, and, increasingly, government officials were required to earn college degrees and pass specialized examinations to be certified. To insure that only a small group of qualified persons entered the professions, each specialty organized a governing body to protect its self-proclaimed standards. The result was, for example, that the village doctor owed his primary allegiance to the American Medical Association and the practice of medicine rather than to the values of the community.

Unlike the battle between national and local levels of political parties where rural groups retained power, the local groups could not defeat these new nationalizing forces. In fact, new communities—based no longer upon geography but on occupation and economic interest—were being formed. The older leaders found that the local community itself was disintegrating. The needs and desires of their constituents now transcended local jurisdictions and required policies and decisions that could be made only at the national level. Not unexpectedly, American politics reflected these changes.[14] The new professionals and businessmen demanded that the parties recognize their concerns. They attacked the political machines dedicated to community interests, and beginning in the 1890s the nationally oriented middle class began to challenge for control of the nation's politics. The old bosses fought back fiercely, but many were eventually overwhelmed. The political organizations created to act as community spokesmen could not survive the destruction of the local interest groups that had supported them.

One of the most widely perceived geographical communities during the Gilded Age was that formed by the inhabitants of the mountain regions of the upper South. Significantly, this grouping together of the mountain population was a new development. Before the Civil War, there was no recognition that the mountain people represented a distinct segment of the American people. Antebellum journalist Frederick Law Olmsted interviewed a mountain farm owner and related his impressions in a chapter entitled "Tennessee Squire."[15] Olmsted pictured the man as ignorant and lazy—characteristics that would contribute to the later stereotype—but referred to him as a southerner rather than a mountaineer. In politics much the same situation prevailed. None of the political leaders or voters in one mountain region claimed any special relationship with those in other states.

The events of the secession crisis and the Civil War served as the starting point of the mountaineer community identity. As early as 1869, novelists began to create a national image of the mountain people as unusual and cut off from the main developments in American life.[16]

Virtually all mountain people rejected this description of themselves and defiantly maintained that they were simply Americans. This reaction against the literary image did not prevent Republicans in the mountains from attempting to create a community feeling based on the events of secession and the Civil War. While few denied the significance of these experiences, many mountain men refused to agree that they had made the highland population into a distinct group. Most of these dissenters preferred to view themselves as southerners and to support the Democratic party.

The Republican party during Reconstruction, in fact, did not seem to offer a satisfactory alternative to the Democrats for many mountaineers. The party was associated with federal laws that freed the slaves and gave blacks the right to vote—programs that were intensely unpopular among mountain whites and kept many of them from joining the party. When the Republicans passed legislation in 1875 that extended civil rights to blacks, the highlanders deserted the party in large numbers. Only the fact that the Republicans were regarded as the defenders of the Union allowed them to retain a following among those mountain men who had opposed the Confederacy. The only question that remained to be answered was which party represented the lesser evil.

The end of Reconstruction settled the issue for many mountain voters. As long as the Republicans did not use the power of the federal government to attempt to secure greater rights for blacks, the mountain men ignored the issue. At the same time, Republicans made a concerted effort to emphasize local issues and to sponsor candidates representative of the highland population. When lowland Democrats continued to slight the demands of the mountain people of their states, increasing numbers of mountaineers found the Republican party attractive. Forming their political organization into a structure reminiscent of the Union army, Republican leaders recalled Civil War memories to counter Democratic appeals to mountain voters to remain southerners on racial matters. Soon Republican leaders began to act as regional advocates, defending the mountaineers against the slanders of outsiders and trying to attract outside investors to the region.

Although the Republicans gained strength in the mountain counties, there were serious limitations to their advances. Just as most other community political organizations in the Gilded Age, the mountain Republican leadership formed a centralized machine to insure their personal control. The bosses that dominated local politics, however, did so with the support of the voters. Defending the mountain community was paramount to these mountain politicians, and they had little patience with those calling for a greater diversity of ideas within the party. Although strengthened, the Republicans remained a minority at the state level. They were forced to forge alliances with lowland blacks and dissident lowland whites in attempts to gain power. Since the groups in these coalitions were not compatible, the Democrats were ultimately able to beat back all efforts to unseat them. Despite the handicap of being divided into five states and being unable to win state elections, the Republicans did continue to act as spokesmen for the mountain region throughout the 1880s.

Two developments in the 1890s weakened and finally destroyed the mountain Republican community machines. The first factor was the reintroduction of the racial issue into mountain politics. As George Fredrickson has explained in detail, the 1890s saw the rise of southern Negrophobia.[17] When the Republican Congress threatened to enact a federal elections bill in 1890, the hatred just boiled over. Mountain Republican bosses found that many of their most loyal supporters had deserted them. In the following decade Democratic leaders whipped lowland whites into a frenzy, leading to laws that disfranchised blacks and crippled the Republican party in the upper South. One condition necessary for mountain Republican success—absence of federal pressure for black rights—had disappeared, and the party leaders could no longer claim to speak for the community.

At the same time that racial hostility was weakening the old machines, the industrial revolution came to the mountain region. The area's extensive coal deposits were being exploited for the first time. Improved transportation encouraged outside commercial interests to invest in the mountains. As a result, urban population increased rapidly, and large numbers of mountain men began to adopt a more nationally oriented outlook. The changes bewildered some of the highland population, who sensed that their secure world was disappearing and reacted with violence. Their irrational attacks and feuds, actually symptoms of a disintegrating society, did no damage to the corporations that dominated the new economy. As they did elsewhere in the United States, the businessmen and the professional middle class sought to bring order to mountain society, by challenging the old mountain Republican machines within the party itself. Although the bosses resisted briefly, they found that they were no match for the forces ranged against them. A new Republican party appeared in the mountain counties of the upper South. The local parties were now part of a national political organization that pursued policies even at the expense of specific geographical interests.

The continued allegiance of the mountain voters to the Republican party masked the momentous change that had taken place. The highland people no longer viewed local matters as the leading political issues. Just as nationally oriented people and institutions were taking over control of the Appalachian economy, they came also to dominate the local Republican parties. The Republican organization would no longer act as the spokesman for this region and its people. In the battle to assert their independence after Reconstruction, the mountain voters had helped to create a significant political organization in the Republican community machines; but as the mountaineers' society and their perception of it were dramatically altered, so were their political institutions.

These historical developments make manifest several significant points about the Republican party in the southern mountains between 1865 and 1900. First, the party was not built on a preexisting tradition or community. The image of a distinct mountain political heritage was deliberately created by Republican politicians in order to appeal to mountain voters. They used the events of the Civil War period to document their assertions. Although their motive was undoubtedly political, the politicians did build this identity on the memory of events experienced by the mountain people. Republican victories in the 1880s further indicate that many mountain voters found this alternative more attractive than the sterile racist appeals offered by the Democrats. When the harsh economic realities of the 1890s forced Republican politicians to deal directly with questions of policy, however, party bosses discovered that the image of the party as community protector was less persuasive than they had thought.

Despite their efforts, local Republican leaders failed to isolate their constituents from outside influences. Mountain political developments were constantly shaped by pressures from outside the region. Reconstruction, civil service reform, industrialization, racism, and depressions all had a much greater impact on mountain politics than did any condition that was peculiar to the highland region. In fact, with the presence of a competitive two-party system, the mountain counties were much more typical of the national political pattern than was the rest of the South. Ironically, these profoundly ordinary reactions to political events have often been cited by observers as evidence that mountain Republicans were a unique and peculiar people.

CHAPTER 2

THE CIVIL WAR AND THE ORIGINS OF MOUNTAIN REPUBLICANISM

As late as 1865 the Republican party still had not been established in the southern mountains, but the Civil War had produced a number of conditions that could be used thereafter by ambitious politicians to create Republican organizations. Perhaps the most significant of the opportunities was the pattern of loyalties developed by the war. Before the conflict, there had been no recognition by the people of the region that they had common interests to defend. The fierce guerrilla war that developed in all five mountain regions changed this outlook. In combination with the presence of hostile armies and personal military service, the local fighting forced the mountain people to extend their loyalties to a greater cause. By the time the war ended, most mountain men either identified with the Union government or at least were very bitter toward those who had led the South into the war. The Republicans, as the party that claimed to have saved the Union, could appeal directly to these new broad attachments developed by the mountaineers.

In the antebellum period, the possibility that the Republican party would be successful in the southern Appalachians seemed remote. The highlands were part of the slave states, and the people there did not accept the new party when it appeared in 1854. They associated the party with the abolitionists and feared it as a radical movement. One contemporary, writing in 1875, stated that "thirty years ago, Western Virginia was almost totally and emphatically pro-slavery. A large majority of the people traditionally voted the Democratic ticket, and the Whig minority were almost a unit with them against human freedom."[1] In Rockcastle County, Kentucky, large numbers of mountain men attempted to kill or drive away antislavery speakers in 1857.[2] When John Brown's raid was launched in 1859, the stunned reaction of mountain whites was to increase the allegiance to slavery as a system of social control.[3] Even when the difficult choice of defending either the Union or slavery faced the mountain men, most felt the necessity to defend the "peculiar institution." Mountain whites agreed with Tennessee Unionist William G. Brownlow when he stated in 1861 that "if we were once convinced in the border Slave States that the Administration at Washington . . . contemplated . . . the *abolishing* of slavery, there would not be a Union man among us in twenty-four hours."[4] Thus the mountain men were part of the South, defending the slave system and rejecting the Republican party.

Some conditions in the upper South were favorable to the creation of the Republican party at a later time. The most significant of these was the fact that each of the five mountain areas needed capital to develop its resources. One historian, describing the mountain counties of western North Carolina, observed, "In 1860 it still had many of the characteristics of a frontier region—scarcity of capital, sparsity of population, little contact with other areas, and lack of social advantages."[5] He supported these assertions with census data showing that the western counties had a per capita income of less than half of that for the entire state.[6] While conditions varied in details from state to state, there was little question that the mountain regions were less economically advanced than the lowlands.

Also setting the mountain region apart was a legacy of political discrimination against the area in all the states of the upper South. In North Carolina constitutional reforms in 1835 and 1857 had helped to improve the situation somewhat, but much hostility remained.[7] It was particularly galling for the mountaineers to watch the richer lowland region receive all the benefits given by the state governments. After the Civil War one West Virginia resident commented that "the complaints of West Virginians were directed . . . against taxation for which they . . . felt they were being made to pay more than a legitimate share. Old Virginia was systematically keeping for herself all the public institutions, railroads, and canals our money helped to build up."[8] Sectional conflict resulting from these feelings was an important part of state politics in each of the five states until the Civil War.

Despite the evidence of sectional economic and political discrimination in each state, mountain voters refused to perceive themselves as a separate group before 1860. Voters in eastern Tennessee and northwestern Virginia saw no reason to belong to one of the major parties as opposed to the other. This attitude was not surprising, since Appalachia was not yet recognized as a unique region. Most of the area was not settled until 1800, and the experiences necessary to create the self-conscious unity of the mountain people had not occurred.[9] Thus the mountain voters' allegiance to the two parties was based on personal considerations such as local leadership and opposition to the dominant lowland party rather than on a deep loyalty to one particular organization. This stance would be an important factor in the rise of the Republican party after the Civil War. The absence of shared partisan attachments made joining a new party much easier.

These impressions of partisan flexibility are documented in table 1. The voters in eastern Kentucky, eastern Tennessee, and western North Carolina were usually Whigs. In each case, however, the general pattern showed important variations. For example, Tennessee mountain voters viewed Martin Van Buren with great suspicion in 1836, and the Democrats won only three of the twenty-one highland counties that year. Eight years later Tennessean James Knox Polk was able to attract twelve of the region's twenty-six counties to the Democratic side. The reverse was the case in northwestern and southwestern Virginia, where

TABLE 1. Mountain Counties Voting Democrat and Whig, Presidential Elections, 1836–1848

	1836 Democrat	1836 Whig	1840 Democrat	1840 Whig
Eastern Kentucky	6	9	3	16
Western North Carolina	4	5	1	9
Eastern Tennessee	3	18	9	16
Southwestern Virginia	12	—	13	2
Northwestern Virginia	11	5	8	9
Total	36	37	34	52

	1844 Democrat	1844 Whig	1848 Democrat	1848 Whig
Eastern Kentucky	8	14	6	14
Western North Carolina	3	9	2	11
Eastern Tennessee	12	14	9	17
Southwestern Virginia	15	1	11	6
Northwestern Virginia	14	8	15	12
Total	52	46	43	60

SOURCE: W. Dean Burnham, *Presidential Ballots, 1836–1892*, pp. 186–88, 205–7, 215–17, 223–27.

the Democrats were the dominant party. However, the candidacies of popular military heroes William Henry Harrison and Zachary Taylor on the Whig tickets in 1840 and 1848 substantially reduced the Democratic majorities in these two mountain regions. Like much of the rest of the United States during this period, the mountain counties of the upper South were divided into pockets of Whig and Democratic strength. As Richard P. McCormick noted, these loyalties were often negated by the personalities and records of the particular presidential candidates.[10]

The intrusion of the slavery issue dramatically altered the partisan alignment in the mountain counties. The disruption of the Whig party in 1852 was reflected in the results of the presidential election of that year. Table 2 reveals that the Democrats gained substantial support, and the party won a majority of the counties in eastern Kentucky for the first time since the creation of the Whig party. By 1856 the Whig party was gone, and the Democrats were left in complete control. The Republican party's position on slavery prevented it from becoming the new party in the Appalachian highlands. Instead, opposition to the Democrats came from the Know-Nothings and self-styled opposition parties. Only in eastern Tennessee where William "Parson" Brownlow and his popular newspaper, the *Knoxville Whig*, served as a rallying point did these new parties offer any real challenge to the Democrats.[11] This confused situation made it easier for Republicans to create a new organization opposed to the Democrats after the war was over.

The critical election of 1860 served only to confuse further the political situation in the mountain counties. In the border states three of the four national candidates ran aggressive campaigns. Both John Bell of

TABLE 2. Counties Voting Democrat, Whig, and Opposition, Presidential Elections, 1852 and 1856

	1852 Democrat	1852 Whig	1856 Democrat	1856 Opposition
Eastern Kentucky	11	10	14	5
Western North Carolina	3	10	14	7
Eastern Tennessee	11	15	15	13
Southwestern Virginia	15	3	18	—
Northwestern Virginia	21	9	25	6
Total	61	47	86	31

SOURCE: W. Dean Burnham, *Presidential Ballots, 1836–1892*, pp. 186–88, 205–7, 215–17, 223–27.

Tennessee and the Constitutional Union party and Stephen A. Douglas of the National or Northern Democratic party stressed the danger to the Union. John C. Breckinridge of Kentucky, the candidate of the southern Democrats, also supported the Union but was nevertheless widely viewed as the candidate of the proponents of secession. Table 3 shows the confused result of the voting. Somewhat surprisingly, John Bell, the spokesman for border state Unionists, carried only the mountain counties in his own state of Tennessee. The 1860 election returns in Kentucky, analyzed in the appendix, shows that no candidate could be viewed as the sole Unionist candidate. In fact, one of the most obvious conclusions that can be drawn about these returns was that the mountain people failed to express a clear preference. The vote for Douglas indicated that even the Democratic party was beginning to splinter under the pressure of the debate about secession.

Another significant observation that can be drawn from table 3 is that the mountaineers rejected the Republican party as a viable alternative in this crisis period. In northwestern Virginia, Republicans were

TABLE 3. Counties Carried by, and Popular Vote for, Candidates, Presidential Election, 1860

	Breckinridge	Bell	Douglas	Lincoln
	Number of Counties Carried			
Eastern Kentucky	17	10	—	—
Western North Carolina	10	10	—	—
Eastern Tennessee	12	17	—	—
Southwestern Virginia	13	5	1	—
Northwestern Virginia	18	12	2	—
Total	70	54	3	0
	Popular Vote			
Eastern Kentucky	11,270	9,016	1,231	373
Western North Carolina	9,271	8,745	190	—
Eastern Tennessee	18,800	22,134	1,619	—
Southwestern Virginia	9,413	7,338	936	—
Northwestern Virginia	16,335	13,567	4,551	1,765
Total	65,089	60,800	8,527	2,138

SOURCE: W. Dean Burnham, *Presidential Ballots, 1836–1892*, pp. 458–84, 646–68, 742–62, 818–38, 852–64.

constantly threatened with violence. Republican G. P. Smith was mobbed while making a speech in August 1856 in Wheeling and escaped serious injury only by brandishing and using a knife.[12] A month later, only the intervention of the Wheeling city government allowed the Republican state convention to be held.[13] In 1860 difficulties continued, and a Republican parade in Wheeling was fired upon from the crowd.[14] The Virginia tradition of viva voce voting made election day difficult for Republicans, and several were assaulted when they tried to vote. While the collapse of the other party organizations had given the Republicans an opportunity to play a role in mountain politics, the party's stand on the slavery issue was intensely unpopular and prevented any real growth of support.

As the secession crisis deepened, the question of partisan alignment became less important to the mountaineers than their overriding concern about the future of the Union. Their initial reactions were to preserve the Union, to avoid fighting, and to be left alone. The inhabitants of the upper South recognized the strategic position they occupied and were faintly aware of the consequences of becoming the battlefield when the war came. Eastern Kentucky mountain men enthusiastically endorsed the policy of neutrality and noninvolvement advocated by the Unionists in that state.[15] Spokesmen for the Unionists of eastern Tennessee stated their position as follows: "That we do earnestly desire the restoration of peace to our whole country, and most especially that our own section of the State of Tennessee shall not be involved in civil war."[16] All evidence indicates that most mountaineers agreed with this position at least until Lincoln's call for troops in April 1861.

The special elections held in the spring of 1861 to determine the future of the upper South states gave further evidence of a growing community of feeling among the mountain men. In the northwestern counties of Virginia the vote to remain in the Union was 30,637 and for secession 10,087.[17] The overwhelming Union vote came from all segments of the region's political life. In Wetzel County, which Breckinridge carried with more than 70 percent of the ballots, the pro-Union vote in 1861 was about 81 percent. In Ohio County, where the 1860 presidential returns were Bell 1,202, Breckinridge 912, Lincoln 771, and Douglas 716, the vote in favor of the Union was 3,268 to 157.[18] It is clear that in this area members of all parties joined together against secession.

Much the same reactions were being expressed in eastern Tennessee. Two elections were required in that state before the secession forces were able to gain a majority in favor of their program. In February 1861 eastern Tennessee voted 33,299 to 7,070 against holding a secession convention; in June the vote was 32,205 to 14,095.[19] Greene County, a

Democratic stronghold and the home of Democratic United States senator Andrew Johnson, voted 2,648 to 377 for the Union in February and 2,691 to 744 for the Union in June. One Johnson partisan later wrote, "When he [Johnson] declared for the Union, his followers in that district with only a few exceptions, did the same."[20] Sevier County, which had a strong Whig tradition and gave Bell more than 80 percent of its votes in 1860, also overwhelmingly supported the Union. The anticonvention vote in that county in February was 1,243 to 69; in June it increased to 1,528 to 60.[21] In the February contest for a delegate to the proposed secession convention from Sevier County, the pro-Union delegate won 1,301 out of 1,302 votes cast.[22] While there was some correlation between support for Breckinridge in 1860 and the prosecession vote in 1861 in both northwestern Virginia and eastern Tennessee, the Union effort was both essentially nonpartisan and very popular.

Kentucky Unionists were also strong in the mountain counties. Unlike their counterparts mentioned above, the mountaineers of eastern Kentucky found themselves part of a coalition that controlled the state. The secession forces, or the States-Rights party as it was called, were such a minority that they did not attempt to run candidates in the state election in May 1861 for delegates to the Border State convention.[23] In the special congressional elections held six weeks later, the Unionists won nine of Kentucky's ten seats. In the Ninth and Tenth districts in the mountain region, the Unionists received 20,603 votes to 8,246 for the opposition.[24] As in northwestern Virginia and eastern Tennessee, party labels disappeared as mountain voters rallied to the defense of the national government.

The situation in western North Carolina and southwestern Virginia was not as clear. Opposition to secession was apparent in both regions, but it was not as dominant as in the other three mountain areas. Although the antisecession voters were in the majority in the North Carolina mountains, they won a rather unimpressive total of twelve of twenty-one counties.[25] In southwest Virginia they also won a large share of the vote but could claim little more than parity with their opponents. The antisecessionists did win a decisive victory in Washington County by a 1,465 to 576 vote, and this area would remain an anti-Confederate stronghold during the war.[26] These expressions of opposition to the coming of the Confederacy were not necessarily votes in support of the federal government. When the war came, the majority of the men in these two regions served in the Confederate army. Thus, the votes in western North Carolina and southwestern Virginia should be interpreted as a desire to avoid change rather than as a positive statement of some kind.

Despite the reservations just stated, the secession crisis did produce one important result. Both mountaineers and other southerners came to realize that the highland population had some shared interests. For the first time these people were acting in similar manner to a common problem. Although this new unity was brief and uncertain, it was an episode upon which the mountain Republican parties were built. The Republicans later claimed to be the major opponent of secession and therefore friends of the mountain people. The Republicans' assertion that they defended the mountaineers' interests did not take place until after the fighting was over; the events of the war also had a profound effect on the relationship between the mountaineers and politics as well. Nevertheless, the secession crisis of 1861 still was the starting point in the development of mountain republicanism.

Despite their strenuous efforts to prevent the conflict, the mountain people of the upper South found themselves in a war that was fought with great bitterness in their own region. The impact of the war on the mountaineers was overwhelming. These rural people were suddenly drawn into a great national crusade; mountain men who had never extended their loyalties much beyond their families and a local political leader now were called on to defend their section or nation. The highlanders' perception of the world often led them to think of the conflict in personal terms. Therefore, they often attacked the nearest family that supported the other cause and had to defend themselves against retaliation by other neighbors. Although most of them made only a partial adjustment to the new demands, the destruction and death brought by the war would impress the new loyalties into the minds of the mountain dwellers.

By the early summer of 1861 most mountain people had decided which government they would support. For many of them expediency played an important role in the final choice. Geographical location was a particularly significant element in most mountaineers' calculations. Those living in southwestern Virginia and western North Carolina had no alternative but to acquiesce in the establishment of the Confederate government. Trapped deep within the Confederacy, these mountaineers could expect no assistance from the federal government. The change was not made without some reluctance, for as the wife of one farmer related, "The Union is gone and all these things follow it, as the shadow steals after a great strong man who goes out from your door forever! How quietly we drift out into such an awful night into the darkness, the lowering clouds, the howling winds, and the ghostly light of our former glory going with us 'to make the gloom visible' with its pale glare."[27]

Unionists in Washington County, Virginia, even attempted open resistance. There John A. Campbell raised a regiment of two hundred men in the town of Abingdon and tried to encourage other mountain men to follow his example.[28] Few did, and the anti-Confederate movement was quickly suppressed. As a demonstration of their loyalty, mountaineers in both sections volunteered for the Confederate army in large numbers. For example, nearly nine thousand North Carolina mountain men had joined the Confederate army by the end of 1861, and more than twenty thousand would serve in some way before the war was over.[29]

Kentucky mountain men also had relatively little difficulty choosing sides. Most of them supported the Union, and they worked vigorously to keep their state out of the Confederacy. Mountain county representatives were among the Unionist majority in the state legislature that guided Kentucky into a position of neutrality between the warring sections. The mountaineers eagerly accepted weapons from the federal government and joined the Union Home Guards.[30] This militia group organized by the state legislature proved to be an effective counterweight to the prosecessionist State Guard directed by Gov. Beriah Magoffin and Gen. Simon B. Buckner.[31] The result was that Kentucky remained in the Union, and the mountaineers could transfer their attention to the national scene. By August 1861 many Kentucky mountain men had made their way to Camp Dick Robinson in Garrard County and joined the Union army.[32]

The mountaineers of northwestern Virginia and eastern Tennessee were in a much more difficult position than those located in the other three regions. Determined to support the Union at all costs, these men were faced with hostile Confederate state governments. Northwestern Virginia Unionists anticipated the confrontation and began to organize at the April 1861 Virginia convention that authorized the vote on secession.[33] About twenty delegates from the northwestern counties decided to call a convention to meet in Wheeling in early May. The Wheeling convention took no action, however, because the Unionists wanted to see what the popular reaction to the secession referendum held later that month would be. As the referendum approached, one observer reported, "The Union men of Northwestern Virginia are becoming more firm every day."[34] The overwhelming Union vote in the May 1861 election confirmed the opinion. The new-state men then called a second convention to meet in June. This meeting in Wheeling formed the Reorganized Government of Virginia under the leadership of Gov. Francis H. Pierpont. Soon thereafter the Union army under George B. McClellan cleared the region of opposition forces; and, when a later Confederate invasion failed, the Unionists felt free to act. In

August a convention of Unionists met in Wheeling and, after enlarging the state to include eleven lowland counties in order to placate conservatives, adopted a resolution calling for a separate state. This proposal was almost unanimously approved by the voters in the northwestern counties.[35]

Then the statehood movement had to deal with the problem that had stifled the growth of the Republican party in the region. The Unionist leadership, which included some Republicans, refused to add a provision to the state constitution abolishing slavery. While the mountain voters enthusiastically supported this position, Congress and President Abraham Lincoln objected to the slavery provision. When Waitman T. Willey, one of the new state leaders, proposed a scheme that gradually emancipated slaves in the region, the House and Senate approved the amended constitution.[36] Lincoln signed the statehood bill, and in February 1863 the constitutional convention reconvened to amend the state charter as required by Congress. After a heated discussion, the Willey Amendment was added to the constitution by a vote of 28 to 26.[37] Opposition to the emancipation continued, but in March the voters once again sustained the Unionist leaders.[38] In June 1863 Lincoln proclaimed the creation of the new state of West Virginia. The people of northwestern Virginia had secured a state government favorable to their ideas by manufacturing their own state.

The Unionists of eastern Tennessee attempted to follow the example of their counterparts in West Virginia. Soon after Tennessee joined the Confederacy, they met in convention at Greeneville. On 19 June 1861 they resolved, "That in order to avert a conflict with our brethren in other parts of the State, and desiring that every constitutional means shall be resorted to for the preservation of peace, we do therefore constitute and appoint . . . commissioners, whose duty it shall be to prepare a memorial and cause the same to be presented to the General Assembly of Tennessee, now in session, asking its consent that the counties composing East Tennessee, and such counties in Middle Tennessee as desire to co-operate with them, may form and erect a separate State."[39] The Confederate state legislature in Nashville refused the petition. In the elections held in August 1861 the Unionists ran their own candidates against those supporting the Confederacy. One candidate for the legislature promised, "If elected, I shall vote against any and every proposition that favors directly or indirectly this most ungodly Rebellion!"[40] The election returns confirmed the continuing unionism of eastern Tennessee voters, for Horace Maynard and other supports of the national government swept to victory.

Alarmed by the continued unionism in east Tennessee, the state government sent an army to occupy the region. Gen. Felix K. Zollicoffer attempted to conciliate the local population but soon found that he would have to use force to disarm Unionists in several counties.[41] Zollicoffer was only partially successful, and federal military officers trained a number of Union guerrilla units in the fall of 1861.[42] On the night of 8 November a number of these groups attacked five railroad bridges linking Virginia with the lower South.[43] Moving swiftly, Zollicoffer dispersed the two major groups within ten days, and the rebellion was crushed.[44] The remainder of the pro-Union men of eastern Tennessee fled through the mountains to Kentucky and enlisted in the federal army.[45] Despite the collapse of armed resistance, the Tennessee mountaineers continued to be loyal to the Union.

These commitments made by the mountain people in 1861 were severely tested in the next four years. Not only were the men in the regular army exposed to hardship and danger, but, more than any other American civilians, mountain women and children were victims of the war as well. The presence of large hostile armies was a significant problem, and one campaign in eastern Tennessee was particularly destructive. After repeated requests from Tennessee Unionist leaders, Gen. Ambrose E. Burnside and a federal army entered the mountain region of the state, captured control of the city of Knoxville, and drove the smaller Confederate force into the hills. Then Confederate general James Longstreet and a large army advanced and laid siege to Knoxville.[46] Both armies attempted to live off the land, and supplies were soon depleted.[47] One Union commander complained that his men were on quarter rations and were in no condition to fight.[48] The Confederates suffered a great deal as well, especially after Gen. William T. Sherman advanced from Chattanooga and forced Longstreet to retreat into the mountains. One southern soldier wrote home, "What a Christmas our soldiers are enjoying with their bare feet and ragged clothes."[49]

The deprivation of the soldiers was less than that of the people who were forced to give their food to the troops. Longstreet noted that in the area where his troops were located he saw "farms destroyed and foraged and subsistence consumed" to the point that he was apprehensive about the welfare of the civilian population.[50] A Union officer reported that the people were "absolutely starving" and told of feeding the mother of five children who had not eaten in three days.[51] Leaders of both armies were aware that abuses by their own men were largely responsible for the difficult situation. Irregular troops such as the partisan rangers connected with Longstreet's army were constant offenders and were charged with profiteering by Confederate officials.[52] The regular forces were not much better. An eastern Tennessee Unionist leader was forced to complain to a federal officer that "the Union Army is more destructive to Union men than the rebel army ever was. Our fences are burned, our horses are taken, our people are stripped in many instances of the very vestige of subsistence, our means to make a crop next year are being rapidly destroyed, and when the best Union men in the country make appeals to the soldiers, they are heartlessly cursed as rebels."[53] With both armies remaining in the area during the winter of 1864, the situation became critical.

Eastern Tennessee Unionist Nathanial G. Taylor recognized that immediate action was necessary and toured the northern states soliciting supplies and money for the relief of the destitute mountaineers.[54] Encouraged by the success Taylor had in his appeals, Unionist leaders formed the East Tennessee Relief Association in February 1864.[55] By March a system of purchase and supply had been created, and appeals to people of Boston brought contributions of more than $40,000. Hungry mountaineers were receiving food and other supplies by April, although only Unionists were allowed access to the goods.[56] Despite the presence of a large number of refugees in Knoxville and the end of provisions from the federal army, the worst was over. The relief association continued its work, collecting more than $139,000 by the end of 1864 and providing at least a minimum existence for the civilian population of eastern Tennessee.[57]

As if the Tennessee mountaineers did not suffer enough from the presence of regular armies, that region was also a center for guerrilla operations. Before the arrival of Burnside's army in 1863 it was the Unionists who had operated in clandestine bands and plundered Confederate sympathizers.[58] By the summer of 1864, however, the situation was reversed, and the pro-Union majority was under attack.[59] Despite the capture and killing of the most effective of the Confederate raiders, John H. Morgan, Unionists were not freed from the depredations of bands protected by the isolation of the mountains.[60] Another development that meant hardship for mountaineers on both sides was the appearance of independent or robber bands that preyed on Unionists and Confederates alike.[61] Partisan attachments were being etched deeply into the bodies and the minds of the mountain people. Those who survived the ordeal used these memories to help them choose political parties after 1865.

As in eastern Tennessee, the mountain population of eastern Kentucky and the Union counties in northwestern West Virginia was plagued by a large number of Confederate guerrilla groups. Because both areas were under Union control from the beginnings of the war, the loyal population had to endure such attacks for nearly four years. In eastern Kentucky a local Union militia leader warned that there were more than one thousand Confederate partisans in a three-county area by the fall of 1862. He continued, "Unless you order a force of mounted men, supported by some infantry to clear out the region . . . all this part of the State will be infested and plundered all fall and winter."[62] Events soon confirmed the assessment, for Unionists were murdered, public buildings were burned, and property was stolen.[63] The state and federal authorities tried to suppress the guerrillas through retaliatory taxes and troop drafts, but to no avail; Kentucky mountain Unionists were subjected to sudden and violent attacks until the end of the war.[64] As might have been expected, many Unionists retaliated by destroying the property of, and sometimes killing, known Confederate sympathizers in the area.[65]

Much the same pattern was found in West Virginia. In the spring of 1862 Gov. John Letcher of Virginia organized a guerrilla group known as rangers and sent them to harass Unionists.[66] Although the rangers were quickly disbanded at the request of Gen. Robert E. Lee, Confederate sympathizers in the region soon organized their own units. Local Unionists fought back as effectively as they could, but the absence of adequate armaments made the task difficult.[67] The most effective means of control were occasional expeditions by regular federal forces, which often captured or dispersed the most troublesome guerrilla groups.[68] Still, one Unionist leader observed in 1863, "After you get a short distance below the 'Pan Handle' it is *not safe* for a loyal man to go into the interior out of sight of the Ohio River."[69] Even more difficult were the raids of organized bands of Confederate troops. The most significant of these episodes was the attack by Gen. John Imboden and Gen. William Jones in April and May of 1863. For three weeks these two men terrorized West Virginia Unionists without being effectivley opposed by a federal force.[70] As a result, West Virginia mountain Unionists were destitute and living in constant fear.

Guerrilla warfare and its attendant animosities developed much more slowly in southwestern Virginia and western North Carolina. In both regions large numbers of men volunteered for Confederate service. The few remaining Union sympathizers found it difficult to mount a military movement. During the first year of the war, when the Confederate army was often victorious, there was little overt violence. When the Confederate government introduced the military draft in 1862, however, hostility directed toward the Jefferson Davis administration grew rapidly. As the South began to face certain defeat and as economic hardship began to press on the highland population, many mountain soldiers deserted and joined paramilitary groups to avoid continued military service. Many of these organizations became centers of anti-Confederate activities that disrupted the southern war effort.

Dissatisfaction with the war began as early as 1862 in the mountains of western North Carolina. One observer in the spring of that year said there was a truce between Unionists and Confederates but that the situation could lead to violence at any time.[71] The gubernatorial election later in the summer showed continued resistance to the Confederacy. William W. Holden, editor of the *Raleigh Standard*, strongly backed western North Carolina politician Zebulon B. Vance for governor and demanded that the state attempt to make peace with the national government. Although Vance never endorsed Holden's platform, part of the new governor's majorities in the mountain counties undoubtedly wanted peace.[72] By the end of September guerrillas were active in Haywood County.[73] The major source of dissatisfaction was the Confederate government's successive conscription acts that blatantly discriminated against the poor and nonslaveowning farmers of the mountains.[74]

Vance, remaining a loyal Confederate, tried to suppress the opposition to the government in Richmond. Unfortunately, attempts to subdue some men in Madison County resulted in the slaughter of thirteen unarmed civilians, including several boys.[75] The incident was resurrected by Republicans when Vance ran for governor in 1876. Increasingly, men from western North Carolina began to make their way across the mountains to Kentucky, where an estimated forty-five hundred joined the Union army.[76] Those who remained behind became bolder and more open. For example, a hundred-man squad raided a Cherokee County town in the middle of the day.[77] After the southern defeats at Gettysburg and Vicksburg, the situation deteriorated even further. Through his newspaper Holden began to call for immediate peace, and in response nearly one hundred meetings were held in the western part of the state.[78] The most significant development was that the meetings were controlled and directed by a pro-Union organization called the Heroes of America. When the federal army began to commission raiders to disrupt Confederate activities in western North Carolina, the region nearly degenerated into anarchy.

The North Carolina gubernatorial election of 1864 offered the anti-Confederate forces an opportunity to test their strength. Holden became the peace candidate against Vance; the governor accepted the challenge and spoke in several mountain counties during the canvass.[79] Holden's campaign was hampered by the unpopular raids conducted by Union guerrilla leaders George Kirk and Montreval Ray in the spring and summer of 1864.[80] Any remaining hope that Holden had of a victory was destroyed in July when Vance was able to demonstrate that the

Heroes of America were part of the federal war effort. Consequently, Holden won only one-fifth of the votes and even lost in many mountain counties.[81] Despite Holden's defeat, anti-Confederate feeling remained strong in the mountain counties, and the vicious guerrilla war continued. As in other mountain areas, the civilian population suffered greatly, food becoming so scarce that one group of housewives attacked a government storehouse and carried away the supply of grain.[82]

The course of events in southwestern Virginia was somewhat the same as that in North Carolina, but never developed as completely. By July 1862 there was widespread opposition to the Confederate draft in the southwestern counties, and heavy-handed enforcement by military authorities greatly upset the local population.[83] In the congressional elections of 1863 the voters of the region generally rejected candidates closely related to the war effort.[84] By the fall of that year the Heroes of America had been imported into the state to organize the anti-Confederate forces.[85] As in North Carolina, this organization enjoyed enormous success. By November 1864, the Heroes had created a state government of southwest Virginia with a governor and other officials.[86] Concerned Confederate authorities found themselves virtually powerless to deal with the threat posed by the clandestine organization. Guerrilla bands roamed unmolested and the civilian population there, as elsewhere in the mountains of the upper South, suffered as food became scarce.

In the midst of the bushwhacking, starving, and dying, the Republican party made its first serious appeals to mountain voters. The unsettled conditions made normal political activities difficult to pursue. The party was thus forced to work within limits created by the military situation. In eastern Tennessee, eastern Kentucky, and northwestern West Virginia, Republicans depended on the army for protection. In addition, the military often became involved in matters concerning the civilian population, and Republicans found that they had to defend themselves as the party of the Union army. The party also had to sacrifice partisan advantage to maintain unity within the Union coalition in each of these three states.

The Kentucky Republican party remained a passive part of that state's Union party until the presidential election of 1864 approached. In January of that year the state union committee issued a call for a convention to send delegates to the Democratic national convention. A group of Unionists who wanted to identify with the national administration called their own convention. In May more than one hundred delegates from fifty-six counties, led by Benjamin H. Bristow and Robert J. Breckinridge, met in Louisville and selected delegates to the Union party national convention.[87] The delegates were instructed to vote for Lincoln, and the emancipation of slaves—very unpopular in Kentucky—was supported. These Unconditional Unionists, as the Republicans were called by their opponents, were weakened when the army interfered in the local elections in August 1864.[88] Further violations of the civilian population's civil rights continued to hamper the new party's efforts to carry the state for the president. For example, a Lexington newspaper was suppressed for not supporting Lincoln, and Kentucky hog farmers were coerced into selling their livestock to the federal government at reduced prices.[89] In each case the Republicans were linked with the objectionable action taken by the federal authorities.

Despite these handicaps and their acceptance of the end of slavery, the Republicans did very well in the mountain counties. Because of unsettled conditions, only twenty counties recorded votes; the party carried twelve of these. Lincoln's share of the mountain vote was 55.9 percent. In two of the counties, Jackson and Whitley, the president won more than 90 percent of the ballots.[90] Mountain men in the army were also conspicuous in their support of Lincoln.[91] The result in the state, however, was far from satisfactory, for Democratic candidate George McClellan easily carried Kentucky. Undaunted by this failure, the Republicans called a convention to prepare for the 1865 legislative session. They demanded that Kentucky ratify the Thirteenth Amendment and that the army engage in "retaliatory warfare against all guerrillas, raiders, and predatory bands of robbers and assassins."[92] The party thus established itself as the advocate for racial moderation and provided the uncompromising Unionists with a platform that would continue to appeal to mountain voters after the war had ended.

West Virginia Republicans did not emerge as clearly from the Unionist coalition. Undoubtedly prompted by the experience of the recent battle for statehood, the Unionists of northwestern West Virginia refused to divide into recognizable political parties. The leading Republican in the region, Archibald W. Campbell, who was editor of the *Wheeling Intelligencer*, was frustrated when he tried to secure office after the new state government began to organize in the summer of 1863. When the state legislature met to select United States senators, Campbell was passed over, moderates Waitman Willey and Peter Van Winkle being chosen instead.[93] At one point Campbell led the balloting, but his Republican affiliation did him little good.[94] In the early fall of 1863 Campbell's candidate for Congress in the First District was defeated at the Union party convention, again demonstrating the absence of an organized Republican party. The election of 1864 did little to differentiate the various elements in the Unionist coalition. Although all of the groups supported Lincoln to some degree, many Unionists strongly opposed the growing radicalism of the national Republican party.[95] Only the active leadership of moderates like Senator Willey and Gov. Arthur I. Boreman prevented the Union party from splitting into conservatives and Republicans. The result was an overwhelming victory for Lincoln, in which the president won in every county except one and carried seven unanimously.[96] Any temptation for the Republicans to operate independently was removed by the small turnout and the realization that the Unionists did not have a safe majority in the new state. The Union party was dependent on the Lincoln administration and the army for support, and many moderate members were drawn reluctantly toward the Republican party. This trend developed slowly, however, as Willey's easy victory over Campbell in the 1865 senatorial contest demonstrated.

The unusual and significant position occupied by Andrew Johnson in Tennessee also delayed the formal development of the Republican party in that state. In 1862 Lincoln had appointed Johnson, well-known Unionist and Democrat, as the military governor of the state, and Johnson became the recognized leader of the Unionists' struggle to gain control of the state's civil government. Although military uncertainty prevented a full restoration under Johnson, his selection as the vice-presidential nominee on the Union ticket with Lincoln in 1864 served to reaffirm his position as the leading Unionist in the state. Therefore, any attempt to create a separate Republican party in Tennessee would have been rejected by both local Unionists and the national administration.

An Unconditional Union party was formed, however, to allow the state to take part in the election of 1864. Supporters of McClellan were excluded from the party and, since the party controlled the franchise, from the electorate.[97] That action alienated many conservative Unionists and forced the Tennessee Unconditional Unionists to become more dependent on the national government. The result was that, as in West Virginia, this party was slowly being transformed into a Republican party organization by its relationship with the federal army and government. In late 1864 the Unionists called a party convention that was later transformed into a constitutional convention. This meeting created a new civilian government for Tennessee and nominated William Brownlow for governor. Again, events paralleled developments in West Virginia. The new constitution was overwhelmingly approved in February 1865, but the small number of voters who took part was disappointing to party leaders.[98] Within two months state elections were held, and Brownlow and the Unconditional Union party started to govern Tennessee.

The opportunity to develop a Republican party organization never appeared in southwestern Virginia and western North Carolina. The most significant problems here were that the party had no legal standing in the Confederacy and was also the party of the military enemy. In addition, the Republicans were now identified as the party of emancipation, a situation that further alienated the mountain people of these two areas.[99] As the fortunes of the Confederacy declined, such aggressive organizations as the Heroes of America became in these areas centers of protest against government policies. In some counties these organizations functioned as political parties and elected men to local offices.[100] While it would not be accurate to equate these groups with the Unconditional Unionists of eastern Kentucky, eastern Tennessee, and northwestern West Virginia, they were nevertheless often the starting point for the Republican party in these two mountain areas after the war.

Thus, the impact of the Civil War on the development of the Republican party in the mountains was mixed in April 1865 when Lee surrendered. Only in Kentucky had the party emerged distinct from other political organizations. Even in that region the Republicans had been only recently organized in response to the presidential campaign of 1864. Unionists could be found in all five mountain sections, but significant developments already indicated that support for the Union could not be equated with allegiance to the Republican party. In addition, the party was greatly weakened in its attempts to appeal to the mountain people by its associaton with the movement to gain greater rights for blacks. By the end of the war, mountain whites accepted the end of slavery but resisted any proposals to extend greater rights to the former slaves.

Equally important positive elements were available to Republican political leaders. For the first time, most mountaineers were forced to adopt a wider pattern of loyalties than their local communities. These commitments had been further impressed into the minds of the mountain people by the war's hardships. The devastation and financial chaos left by the fighting also provided the Republicans with an opportunity to appeal to mountain voters. The inhabitants recognized that they lived in poverty in a region of potentially great mineral wealth. The Republican program of government grants and protective tariffs to help business develop the country was therefore attractive to many in the mountains. Finally, for the first time, the mountain people self-consciously recognized that they shared a common historical background and many of the same concerns. Their opposition to the Confederacy had marked them as a distinct group in the South, and the events of the war had confirmed this impression. The mountain Republican parties that developed during Reconstruction would try to build on this tradition.

CHAPTER 3

RECONSTRUCTION IN THE MOUNTAINS

A mountain Republican politician reflecting in 1876 on the party's experience in the previous ten years would have had difficulty determining whether the party had profited from the events of that turbulent decade. The intervention of the federal government had insured that the Republican party would have some support in all of the five mountain areas. Yet this very intervention was resented by many potential supporters and stunted the growth of the party. The newly enfranchised black voter usually voted Republican, but this practice alienated the majority white population. Especially in the mountain counties, where blacks numbered less than one-tenth of the population, Republican racial policies were a liability.[1] The history of the party in the highlands during Reconstruction was one of trying to avoid the implications of the national platform while securing the benefits of federal assistance.

The problem that mountain Republican politicians faced was that they rarely had control over their own destiny. At one time during the Reconstruction period the army, the Congress, and the federal executive all dictated to local leaders what actions they would take. In the immediate aftermath of the war, the policies of President Johnson seemed to preclude the possibility of creating a strong Republican organization. Johnson worked with conservative Unionists, and in most states the Unconditional Unionists were either excluded from power or forced to submerge their ambitions and join a coalition. Thus, in all five states of the upper South the Republican party still had no independent life of its own. In addition, there were no local conditions that could counteract conservative control.

The emergence of radical Republican leadership in the Congress in 1866 dramatically changed the political conditions of the upper South. The Congress refused to seat the delegations sent by the reconstructed states. Then, taking the offensive, the radicals passed the Civil Rights

Act in April 1866 that extended citizenship rights to the former slaves. Two months later the Republicans framed and submitted the Fourteenth Amendment to the states, a constitutional provision designed to insure that local jurisdictions could not circumvent the national policies recently enacted by Congress. The radicals on the Joint Committee on Reconstruction also demanded that (1) blacks be given full civil rights before a southern state be restored; (2) southern financial claims be voided; (3) suffrage be returned to Unionists; and (4) suffrage be denied to at least some former Confederates.[2] The battle lines between Congress and President Johnson were now sharply drawn. Southern Unionists were forced to choose between the conservative Unionist president and the Republican Congress.

The Unconditional Unionists, finding themselves in the minority on the local level, discovered that they had only one course of action. Since most of the opposition backed the president, the mountain politicians aligned themselves with the Congress. For many Unconditional Unionists this decision was made with great reluctance. The radicals' racial policies were widely opposed by Appalachian whites, and deep resentment was directed toward the Republican party for using outside power to impose these changes. These attitudes were further strengthened when Congress passed the first Reconstruction Act of 1867. In Virginia and North Carolina blacks were immediately added to the electorate. Congressional pressure had already accomplished the same result in Tennessee in 1866. Two supplementary Reconstruction Acts passed in 1867 brought the army to Virginia and North Carolina as well. In 1868 Kentucky and West Virginia mountaineers faced a similar situation when the radicals introduced the Fifteenth Amendment. When ratified in 1870, the amendment imposed black suffrage on the entire nation. Thus, all of the mountain whites were forced to accept black political participation despite their own aversion to the new policies.

Ignoring their personal reservations about federal racial policies, most Unconditional Unionist political leaders joined the Republican party. Several considerations persuaded them that this was a practical course of action. First, the black voters proved to be loyal Republicans and formed the bulwark of the state parties in Virginia, Tennessee, Kentucky, and North Carolina. Ambitious mountain politicians who sought state offices were happy to receive the backing of the new black voters. In addition, the congressional radicals were willing to offer political and financial aid to southern Republicans during critical campaigns. The ties between national and local levels were unusually strong during this period, and the inexperienced mountain Republican leadership often solicited advice from party leaders.[3] Finally, mountain Republican politicians were able to retain the loyalty of many mountain whites because of the demographic factor that most distinguished the mountains from the rest of the South—the relative absence of blacks. Not confronted by a large black population, mountain whites reacted more favorably than lowland whites to Republican appeals. For all these reasons the Republican party was established in the mountains in spite of the hostility its national Reconstruction policy created.

At the same time local Republican leaders were trying to find ways to stay in power when direct federal intervention ended. This desire, combined with racial conservatism, led to the liberal movement within the party in each region. The objective of these mountain politicians was to adjust the party platform to local conditions and appeal to more white voters. Two further actions by the Congress, however, frustrated this attempted reconciliation. In 1870 and 1871 laws directed at the Ku Klux Klan and similar organizations again brought federal intervention into southern politics. While few mountain counties were directly involved, this action kept fears of change alive. Such concerns surfaced again in 1874 when Senator Charles Sumner introduced a comprehensive civil rights act that guaranteed equal rights on juries and in public accommodations to blacks. Charging that this legislation promoted social equality, mountain whites, including many Republicans, opposed the bill. When the act passed in 1875, the Republican party seemed on the verge of extinction in the highlands.

The decline of the Republican party in the mountain counties during Reconstruction can be traced accurately in the presidential elections of that period. Table 4 documents the dramatic decrease in the Republican proportion of the total vote from 1868 to 1876. While several unusual conditions prevailed in 1868—the disfranchisement of former Confederates in Tennessee and West Virginia and no election in Virginia—there was no question but that the Republican party had lost public support by 1876. They were in the minority, and, if the downward trend continued, the party could not compete even in the mountain counties.

The result was that even after ten years in existence the future of the Republican party in the mountains of the upper South was uncertain. The local leadership had been unable to solve the dilemma of its dependence on the national party and at the same time avoiding association with legislation that forced changes in the relationship between the races. National issues had helped to create the party in the mountain region— unionism and the dispute between Johnson and Congress; national racial intervention could also destroy the party. Within every mountain region were conditions that made the Reconstruction experience unique in each

TABLE 4. Popular Vote and Percentage of Total Vote, Presidential Elections, 1868, 1872, and 1876

	All Counties			Mountain Counties	
Democrat	Republican	Other	Democrat	Republican	Other
	1868			1868	
246,925	222,138	0	46,688	75,987	0
52.64%	47.36%	0.0%	38.06%	61.94%	0.0%
	1872			1872	
413,466	402,709	0	74,956	86,443	0
50.66%	49.34%	0.0%	46.44%	53.56%	0.0
	1876			1876	
614,505	432,761	4,097	137,510	108,834	1,406
58.45%	41.16%	0.39%	53.50%	43.93%	0.57%

SOURCE: The returns for the 1868 and 1872 elections were compiled from the *Tribune Almanac, and Political Register, 1869*, p. 83; ibid., *1873*, pp. 62, 74, 83; ibid., *1874*, pp. 64–65; ibid., *1876*, p. 81. The returns for 1876 were compiled from ICPR Election Data.

state. The differences only emphasized the depth of the problem that mountain Republican politicians faced. Despite all of the varied conditions and personalities involved, no one was able to solve the riddle of the party's relationship to the national government.

The appearance of the Republican party in eastern Tennessee was the work of one man. William Brownlow directed the party's destinies during this critical period, and his personality left a powerful imprint on Tennessee politics. Brownlow was a physically imposing man of six feet, with abundant, unruly black hair and enormous energy. A former Methodist circuit rider, the "fighting Parson" had become a well-known newspaper editor in the pre-Civil War years. A violent partisan at all times, Brownlow's antebellum career had been marked by violent physical confrontations and bitter attacks on the Catholic church.[4] During the secession crisis and the Civil War he was an outspoken defender of the Union cause. He was placed in a Confederate Prison for several months before being paroled to the North.[5] There he compiled the extremely popular anti-Confederate tract, *Sketches of the Rise, Progress, and Decline of Secession*. For many in the North and in Tennessee, Brownlow was the chief spokesman for southern Unionists. After Andrew Johnson was elected vice-president on the Union ticket, Brownlow helped continue Johnson's efforts to return Tennessee to civilian control. As a reward for his work, Brownlow was elected governor under the new constitution early in 1865.

Brownlow's personality dominated Tennessee politics for the next four years. He was a radical, but not an ideologue. In 1858 he had toured the North defending slavery; in 1866 he forced the Tennessee legislature to adopt Negro suffrage. His radicalism was more one of assuming that all who disagreed with him were enemies and that violence directed toward them was acceptable. When returning Confederate soldiers found it difficult to settle in eastern Tennessee after the war, a group of Knoxville Unionists requested that Brownlow calm the situation. He issued a proclamation that said in part:

> When the Federal soldiers who survive after an absence of three years of hard figting [sic] return to their homes from which they were driven, and find their homes desolated, find their wives and children have sunk into poverty and starvation, crying for bread—when these wan and weary men, many of themselves crippled for life or reduced in health, with their constitutions broken, and their prospects in life blasted, I am not among those who would restrain their vengeance against their oppressors, so long as their vengeance is kept within reasonable bounds and sought through legitimate channels.[6]

It is doubtful that even Brownlow knew what "reasonable" vengeance was, but it is important to note the venom in his words. His actions and speeches led the mountain men through the first years of Reconstruction and encouraged other Republicans to deal harshly with the opposition.

Presidential Reconstruction proved a disappointment for Brownlow. Although the legislature in 1865 passed a franchise law that required proof of Union sentiments before and during the war, the conservative Unionists or Democrats won many contests in the first elections held after the return of civil government.[7] This unexpected result encouraged Brownlow to repudiate Johnson and align himself with Congress and the Republican party. When the March 1866 county elections showed continued conservative strength, Brownlow demanded harsher registration laws to insure that only "true" Unionists—Republicans—would be able to vote.[8] To pressure the legislators, Brownlow encouraged eastern Tennessee Unionists to call a convention and demand that the mountain region be allowed to become a separate state.[9] The threat of dismemberment was effective, and a second franchise bill was passed in May 1866. This measure provided for the perpetual disfranchisement of all voters except Union soldiers and those who could take an ironclad test oath.[10] The Republicans demonstrated their willingness to enforce the new law by arresting men who tried to vote without meeting the requirements.[11]

Attempting to cement his alliance with Congress and to allow Tennessee's readmittance into the Union, Brownlow next proposed that Tennessee blacks be given the right to vote. This proposal was extremely controversial and actually ran against what Brownlow himself had been saying. In October 1865 Brownlow and other Unionist leaders had specifically rejected black suffrage.[12] The next May the legislature gave blacks limited civil rights but specifically forbade them to serve on juries or to attend school with whites.[13] Brownlow experienced the greatest difficulty in convincing the mountain Republican legislators of the political necessity of suffrage. Only the implied threat by Congress not to recognize the new government prompted the Tennessee Republicans to pass a bill allowing blacks to vote. The mountain politicians were careful to add a provision, however, that prohibited blacks from holding office.[14]

The results of the gubernatorial campaign of 1867 seemed to justify Brownlow's strategy. Union League chapters were organized throughout the state, and both blacks and white unionists joined in large numbers.[15] The organization was particularly strong in the mountain counties and provided the party with an assured base of support.[16] Brownlow also encouraged the legislature to create a state militia, which had the task of insuring that only Unionists voted. During the 1867 campaign the militia was used to protect black voters from violent attacks and to harass Brownlow's opponent, Emerson Etheridge.[17] The new black voters cast their ballots as expected, and Brownlow was elected to a second term by a vote of 74,484 to 22,584.[18]

Brownlow's methods, which polarized the entire state politically, also divided the people of eastern Tennessee in many areas besides politics. An excellent example of the pervasiveness of the political conflict generated by Reconstruction in Tennessee was the split in the Methodist Episcopal church. As in politics, Brownlow and his newspaper, the *Whig*, were in the center of the controversy. The parson-turned-politician justified his intervention with the following explanation: "But as this great conflict has grown out of the late Rebellion, and as one of these Churches is emphatically a rebel organization, dangerous to the peace of the country, and at war with the spiritual interests of the people, it will be the duty of the journal to notice its movements, expose its fallacies, and vindicate the right."[19] This was essentially the same argument that Brownlow used against his political opposition. Despite the unnecessary harshness of the terms used, Brownlow's analysis was correct.

The split in the Methodist Episcopal church in eastern Tennessee had begun during the war and continued for many years thereafter in the political arena. Until 1860 the Methodists of the Tennessee mountains were firm supporters of the southern branch of the church, formed in

1844. The secession crisis and the coming of the war prompted the southern Methodists to align themselves politically with the Confederacy. Unionists like Brownlow were outraged. Their anger increased as the Holston Conference, which included eastern Tennessee, began to expel clergymen for supporting the Union.[20] The obvious dissatisfaction of many eastern Tennessee Methodists encouraged the national organization to attempt to win back congregations that had left in 1844. With the aid of the army, Bishop Mathew Simpson came south to promote Union Methodism.[21] Brownlow backed Simpson's efforts completely, charging that the southern Methodist clergy "are false to the principles of their church, to the teachings of the Holy Scriptures, to their country, themselves, posterity, and their God."[22] By the late spring of 1864, the decline in Confederate military fortunes had seriously weakened the southern conference.[23] In July a loyal or Unionist Holston Conference was formed in Knoxville and, led by Brownlow, claimed control of all Methodist property in the region.[24]

The end of the war brought no end to the fighting among Methodists in eastern Tennessee. The Unionist state legislature passed a series of laws directed at clergymen who had supported the Confederacy. They were forbidden to conduct marriages and, unlike loyal ministers, were required to work on the roads and serve in the militia.[25] The missionary work of the Union Methodists and Brownlow's propaganda campaigns were very effective, and by 1866 a majority of the Methodists belonged to the new conference. At first the southern church reacted mildly and agreed that it had not acted responsibly in expelling Unionists during the war. Northern observers hoped that Brownlow and his associates would moderate their position and work with the now-contrite opposition.[26] However, the appointment of Thomas H. Pearne as presiding elder of the Knoxville district of the Unionist Methodists made this reconciliation highly unlikely. Pearne, like Brownlow, was a Republican politician, having been a delegate to the 1864 convention that nominated Lincoln.[27] His appointment meant that there was no real moderating of the conflict.

Slowly regaining confidence, the southern Methodists began to fight back. They accused Brownlow and Pearne of having a political and "Negro Equality" church.[28] Both charges were accurate enough to help weaken the appeal of the Union Methodists. Their church was political; Brownlow was a partisan newspaper editor and governor; Pearne was a member of the Union League, a delegate to the national convention, and president of a state Republican convention in 1869. Nor could Pearne deny the fact that black Methodist clergymen had been served communion in the same service with white ministers.[29] A series of confrontations took place between the competing churches. In Washington County a southern Methodist minister interrupted and took over a burial service that a Union Methodist had started.[30] In Blount County Henry C. Neal invaded a Unionist church and preached a "rebel" sermon and was severely beaten for his trouble.[31] Undaunted by the opposition, the southern Methodists recruited a large group of young and energetic preachers and by the 1870s had a strong organization again in eastern Tennessee.[32] As late as 1888 the controversy was still quite bitter, but with the decline of the Republican fortunes the battles became confined to local Methodist congregations.[33]

The bitterness created by congressional Reconstruction and Brownlow's method of applying it undermined Republican efforts to stay in office. Democrats, including those in the mountains, were turning to violence as a means of regaining power.[34] Even more important for the revival of the Democrats was the return of Andrew Johnson to the state in 1869. Johnson became a symbol around which to rally, and the Democrats prepared to take advantage of any Republican weakness.[35] Within months of the former president's arrival in Tennessee, the Republicans were swept from power. Racism and personal ambition had combined to tear the Republican organization into competing factions. Brownlow's dominance was so complete that other ambitious men in the party had to suppress their natural inclinations. Brownlow constructed a personal machine of mountain politicians that largely excluded blacks, carpetbaggers, and lowland whites from positions of leadership. All of these groups were looking for an opportunity to challenge his position.

The conflict came out in the open when Brownlow announced that he was a candidate for the United States Senate seat that became vacant in 1869. Congressman William Stokes tried to challenge the governor and unite all the the dissatisfied elements behind himself. The vote in the legislature was quite close, and Brownlow was forced to make a political deal with the speaker of the state senate, DeWitt C. Senter.[36] Brownlow agreed to back Senter for governor in the special election to be held when the office became vacant. Brownlow was elected to the Senate and Senter became acting governor and immediately called a special election. The opposition once again backed Stokes. Despite Brownlow's support, Senter had great difficulty in securing delegates to the state convention,[37] primarily because Stokes was able to win the support of most black Republicans.[38] The convention in Nashville in May became a two-day riot that split the party in half. Order could not be maintained on the convention floor; on the second day the Senter forces walked out, and each man was nominated by his own convention.[39] Stokes made an immediate appeal to black voters, who formed the majority of the restricted electorate.

This action, placing Senter and the Brownlow forces in a difficult position, led to a decision that returned the Democratic party to power. Senter was a fairly typical mountain political leader, described as a "good-natured fellow, who can drink, ride, speak, and play poker with any man of his age and build in Tennessee."[40] Senter's proximity to the average mountain Republican in lifestyle was matched by his agreement with the racist attitudes of this group. He had been an early opponent of Negro suffrage and had accepted it only reluctantly. One of his first acts as governor was to disband the state militia that had been used primarily to protect black voters.[41] At the same time, a number of Republican party leaders began to demand that all white voters in the state be allowed to vote. Two weeks after the convention Senter endorsed the idea of universal suffrage and said that war-inspired legislation should be abolished.[42]

This announcement changed the nature of the entire campaign. As acting governor, Senter had the power to change the registrars in every county in the state, and he appointed men who allowed most of the disfranchised white voters to register for the August election. Although somewhat dubious of the advisability of Senter's strategy, Brownlow continued to back him.[43] It also became clear that the newly enfranchised Democrats would support him.[44] Senter gained an overwhelming victory, but the Democrats won enough local elections to gain control of the state legislature. The shock of losing power continued the split within the Tennessee Republican party.

Chagrined at the result, a number of mountain Republican leaders tried to secure federal intervention to prevent the Democrats from seizing control of the state. Congressmen Random R. Butler, Horace Maynard, and William Stokes, all from eastern Tennessee, were leaders in the movement to have the state reconstructed.[45] President U. S. Grant sympathized to the extent of removing Senter's followers from office and putting in those who had supported Stokes.[46] In December 1869 Senator Brownlow demanded that Senter prevent the meeting of a constitutional convention that the Democrats had called.[47] In January 1870 Butler introduced a bill to apply the Fourteenth Amendment very strictly in Tennessee and thus nullify Democratic control of the state legislature.[48] The bill never was reported out of committee, however, and this effort and others to draw the federal government into Tennessee failed. Butler and the other Republican leaders found that Senter's winning a majority of the vote in the mountain counties made it difficult for them to claim that he was not a Union Republican candidate.[49] When the Democrats finished their work in the constitutional convention, therefore, the mountain Republicans were a minority in Tennessee politics, without hope of a rapid change of fortune.[50]

Other mountain Republican leaders, recognizing that Reconstruction tactics and policies would not work now that the party was in the minority, began to appeal on a more liberal platform. The 1870 Republican gubernatorial candidate, William H. Wisener, was considered an "unusually mild Radical" by a Democratic newspaper.[51] The 1872 Republican gubernatorial nominee, A. A. Freeman, followed the same pattern. He explained his strategy in the following manner: "There are thousands of honest men in Tennessee who were never Democrats at heart[;] men who are Conservative in their feeling and have been driven to act with that party by what was regarded as the proscriptive policy of our party[.] Happily all these causes of differences among the opponents of Democracy have been removed and these men will act and vote with us."[52] Freeman's campaign proved quite successful. He received more votes than did any Republican candidate for governor during Reconstruction and amassed more than 46 percent of the vote.[53] In 1874 Horace Maynard attempted to strengthen his chances for the governorship by introducing a bill into the House of Representatives to remove all political disabilities from former Confederates.[54]

This new Republican strategy in Tennessee was brought to an abrupt end in the summer of 1874 by the debate over the Civil Rights Bill in the national Congress. During the spring and summer of that year Tennessee Republicans tried to avoid being identified with the legislation that extended many social rights to blacks.[55] The section of the act that was most repugnant to the mountain men was the requirement for integrated schools; even Horace Maynard, a formerly staunch defender of all Reconstruction measures, attacked this proposal. The local elections in August confirmed that the Civil Rights Bill was extremely unpopular, as Republicans lost throughout eastern Tennessee.[56] The tension created by the political debate may in part explain the particularly brutal lynching of a Negro in the heavily Republican mountain county of Carter during this period.[57] Significantly, Senator Brownlow now moved in complete opposition to the civil rights legislation, calling the integrated schools section "the sum of villainy and the quintessence of abominations."[58]

The Republican state convention that met in September 1874 to nominate a gubernatorial candidate faced gloomy prospects. Mountain Republicans wanted to make no nomination in order to save the party from a humiliating defeat. But black delegates from middle and western

Tennessee demanded that the party acknowledge its debt to them by running a candidate and supporting the Civil Rights Bill in the party platform. Horace Maynard was finally nominated because he was the only leader of the party who would support the legislation as a whole—this despite his opposition to integrated schools.[59] The civil rights plank of the platform was a complete evasion that maintained that blacks should have full rights but Congress should not pass legislation to force compliance.[60] Eastern Tennessee Republicans continued to run away from social rights for blacks, incumbent Congressman R. R. Butler being particularly vigorous in his denunciation of the measure. Brownlow continued his record of inconsistent positions by publicly condemning the bill, yet supporting Maynard for governor.[61] The election was an absolute disaster for the Republicans. Maynard polled nearly thirty thousand fewer votes than Freeman had in 1872, and the Republican share of the vote declined to only 35 percent of the total. Maynard did not even win a majority of the votes in eastern Tennessee—the only time between 1865 and 1900 that a regularly nominated Republican did not carry the region, and the Democrats won ninety-three of the hundred seats in the legislature.[62]

The demoralization of eastern Tennessee Republicans extended into the presidential election year of 1876. Some individuals, sensing the destruction of the party, even tried to revive the Whig Party, but that scheme generated little enthusiasm.[63] The state convention refused to instruct the national convention delegates to vote for a particular candidate, a very unusual practice for southern Republicans, although there is some evidence that this refusal may have been a maneuver to help the candidacy of Rutherford B. Hayes.[64] At a second state convention in late August, the Republicans failed to nominate a gubernatorial candidate, and the expectation was that Dorsey B. Thomas, an Independent Democrat, would receive most of the Republican votes.[65] One Democratic paper was moved to exult that the "Radical party of Tennessee committed suicide," and the statement seemed quite accurate.[66]

The bankruptcy of the party was further demonstrated by the failure of two independent Republican candidates. One, William Yardley, caused a sensation. Yardley was black, and his campaign, coming so soon after the passage of the Civil Rights Bill in early 1875, was viewed by most mountain Republicans as a disastrous reminder of the party's dependence on black votes. Although Yardley lived in Knoxville, he was received with great hostility by both black and white Republicans in the mountain counties.[67] The second candidate, George Maney, a former Confederate general, withdrew from the race when he found that he could not unite the party behind him. The party even failed when it tried to organize a soldiers' reunion to generate support for Republicans seeking local positions.[68] The results of the voting were not surprising: Thomas was slaughtered, and Maney and Yardley won fewer than thirteen thousand Republican votes.[69]

Thus, in the decade of Reconstruction the Republican party of eastern Tennessee had failed to develop a strong organization or a consistent platform. The harshness of congressional Reconstruction under Brownlow alienated many potential allies among the more conservative Unionists. The Reconstruction Acts, the Fourteenth and Fifteenth amendments, and the Civil Rights Act only confirmed the suspicions of many mountaineers about the racial policies of the Republican party. Consequently, during the 1870s mountain voters left the Republican party in large numbers. The party leadership were unable to resolve the conflict between their dependence on Congress and the opposition of many mountain men to the radical Republican program. By 1876 these failures seemed to doom the Republican party in an area where thousands had died supporting the Union war effort. To survive, the party would have to find a way to appeal directly to mountain voters.

Reconstruction was equally disastrous for the Republicans in West Virginia. Like their counterparts in eastern Tennessee, party leaders in West Virginia were forced to deal with the reality that the majority of the voters were not Republicans.[70] This problem did not arise until after the Civil War ended. While the fighting continued, conservative Unionists had worked with Republicans to insure that West Virginia remained a state. In addition, many potential voters served in the Confederate army and were unable to cast their ballots. As the war drew to a close, Governor Arthur Boreman secured passage of a voters' test oath, which was designed to limit the political power of the returning Confederates. Like Brownlow in Tennessee, Boreman hoped to limit restrictions to the Confederates and to unite all of the Unionists into one political organization. Almost immediately, however, the racial policies of the national Republican party caused conservative Unionists to withdraw from the wartime coalition and to oppose Republican policies.[71]

The mountain Republican leaders responded to this loss with a conscious effort to punish the conservative Unionists. By 1866 the legislature had passed a series of acts that momentarily silenced the opposition. The most effective piece of legislation allowed the governor to appoint boards of registration in each county. Operating much as the same officials did in Tennessee, the West Virginia boards eliminated approximately one-half of the potential Democratic vote.[72] Encouraged by the example of the radical Republicans in Congress, northwestern

West Virginia Republicans willingly used undemocratic methods to maintain their power. For a short period these expedients worked. In the 1868 elections the Republican candidates won nearly 60 percent of the vote and sixty of the seventy-eight seats in the state legislature.[73] Despite this success, the harsh policies alienated many mountain Republicans and there was an increasing desire to loosen the controls.[74]

This feeling was strengthened when it became obvious that the Fifteenth Amendment was going to be ratified. That eventuality would mean that blacks would soon be voting in West Virginia. Mountaineers who had resented the forced abolition of slavery in the state were appalled by this second intrusion by the federal government in West Virginia's race relations. From the beginning of the party in the northwestern section of the state, mountain Republicans had strenuously opposed Negro suffrage.[75] Many white Republicans could not justify allowing blacks to vote when many whites were still disqualified. When the federal government withdrew the army from the state in the spring of 1869, there were already signs of a revolt within the party against the Republicans' Reconstruction policies.[76]

Considerable discussion went on concerning the advisability of removing the voting restrictions in the summer of 1869, and soon a well-defined group of Republicans was identified as favoring more liberal election laws. These people first took action on 1 September when they issued an "Address to the Republican Voters of Ohio County," which said in part, "We believe that the test oaths that were adopted in this state during, and at the close of the war, were in the main necessary, if not absolutely indispensable . . . as regards the safety of our loyal people at this time, even in the most exposed counties, our information impresses us with the belief that we can afford to inaugurate the necessary steps for discontinuing everything known as war legislation."[77] The result was that the Republican organization was split in two, with great bitterness on both sides.[78] Because of that split the Democrats made dramatic gains in the legislative elections in 1869, and, although still a minority, they combined with liberal Republicans to control the state legislature.

The division between Republicans who supported congressional Reconstruction and those who favored universal suffrage widened in 1870. In January William H. Flick, a liberal Republican, introduced a resolution into the state legislature calling for universal suffrage.[79] The liberal Republican-Democratic majority passed it for the first of two required successful readings necessary to amend the state constitution. Conservative impatience with present conditions was emphasized by an outbreak of Ku Klux Klan activity directed at blacks and white Republicans.[80] Trying to rally support to their cause, radicals called for a state Union veterans convention. However, complete lack of interest in reviving the hatreds generated by the war led to the cancellation of the event.[81] Despite deep splits in the party, the state convention was held in June, and Governor William E. Stevenson was renominated. The Republican campaign was disorganized, and many local offices were uncontested.[82]

The Democrats were strengthened by the actions of federal judge John J. Jackson, who interpreted the Fifteenth Amendment in a novel manner. He maintained that the amendment undermined any restrictions on suffrage and instructed the United States commissioners under his jurisdiction to replace the local registration boards.[83] One man by the name of C. A. Sperry was particularly zealous, and several Republican election officials were arrested through his efforts.[84] The combination of enforced loosening of registration requirements in many counties and the failure of the Republican campaign to inspire the party to continue proscription resulted in a Democratic victory. John J. Jacob was the new governor, and in early 1871 the legislature passed the Flick universal suffrage amendment again. On 27 April 1871, the Flick amendment was submitted to the voters and passed overwhelmingly, 23,546 to 6,323.[85]

Out of power, the West Virginia Republican organization rapidly disintegrated. In 1871 the Democrats won absolute control of the legislature and succeeded in securing a constitutional convention, which produced a new plan of government that dismantled the Reconstruction structure of political control created by the Republicans. The next year the Republicans decided not to nominate a gubernatorial candidate, but to back incumbent governor John Jacob, who was running as an independent. Instead, they attacked the proposed constitution and attempted to convince the voters that the old form of government should be retained.[86] The election results were essentially a defeat for the Republicans. Jacob won, but the Democrats remained in power and the new constitution was adopted by the voters.[87] The presidential canvass did provide a bright spot, for Grant won the state. A close inspection of the returns revealed, however, that this Republican victory was the result of the tremendous unpopularity of the Democratic candidate, Horace Greeley.

The debate surrounding the Civil Rights Bill in 1874 completed the collapse of the party in northwestern West Virginia. As one mountain Republican newspaper stated, "We consented willingly to granting political and legal rights to . . . the colored men, but we will *never* favor forcing social equality upon us."[88] Because of the hostile reaction of the mountain people to direct federal intervention in racial matters, Republican politicians were reluctant to become candidates in 1874. Instead, the party's state convention endorsed the policy of supporting Independent Democrats for the state legislature.[89] In the Second Congressional District former senator Waitman Willey refused to accept the Republican nomination for Congress.[90] Only young Union veteran Nathan Goff, Jr., ran a respectable race among West Virginia Republicans. Goff came within 168 votes of being elected to Congress in the First District.[91] Thus, except for a few stalwart individuals, the party was reduced to a wing of the Democratic party. The overwhelming Republican defeats in West Virginia in 1876 confirmed the results of two years before.

Both Tennessee and West Virginia mountain Republicans had failed to create a majority party in their states. The obvious cause was the destruction of the Unionist coalition by racial issues. Although the mountain politicians dominated the state organizations, they were still at the mercy of outside events. The debate over the Civil Rights Bill of 1874 demonstrated how fragile the Republican support was in the strongest Unionist regions.

North Carolina mountain Republicans played a much less significant role in the party during Reconstruction. Western North Carolina Unionists were a minority and therefore did not control their own section. The majority of mountain men had served in the Confederate army and were inclined to ignore their earlier reluctance to leave the Union. Even the committed Unionists in the mountain counties were poorly organized, with deep divisions in their ranks.[92] In addition, lowland Unionists under the leadership of William Holden were recognized as the leading anti-Confederate spokesmen in the state. The Republican party in North Carolina was directed by these lowland politicians, particularly after blacks were allowed to vote. The western North Carolina Republicans, therefore, had very little control over their own destiny. Not only did they face the intervention of the federal government, but they were forced to defend the actions of the lowland leadership of the state party.

The Republican party did not appear in North Carolina until after presidential Reconstruction had ended. In 1865 President Johnson appointed William Holden provisional governor and ordered him to call a convention to prepare the state for reentry into the Union. This process went smoothly until October 1865, when a number of the members of the convention requested that Holden become a gubernatorial candidate under the new constitution.[93] Holden, a successful Raleigh newspaper editor, agreed; however, he was a controversial figure and immediate opposition to his candidacy appeared. Holden had been denied the 1858 Democratic nomination for governor in part because of his undistinguished social background, and he had been defeated in 1864 by Zebulon Vance because of his call for immediate peace. Those who viewed Holden as a traitor and upstart ran Confederate state treasurer Jonathan Worth as their candidate. The campaign was bitter and the voting close, but Worth won despite Holden's strong showing in the mountain counties.[94] Because both candidates asserted that they were Unionists, the campaign split this group beyond hope of reconciliation. Thus the Republican party, when it appeared, could not claim to be the only political home for North Carolina Unionists.

Worth's administration saw the steady growth of hostility between the two political organizations that had been created. The Conservative Unionists who supported President Johnson's Reconstruction policies were soon joined by the former Confederates who claimed no connection with unionism. This coalition clearly had a majority of the votes and sought to discourage the opposition, their principal concern being to reclaim the mountain counties where Holden had done well in 1865.[95] The campaign was largely successful; the Holden forces ran only an unofficial candidate for governor in 1866, and he was decisively defeated by Worth.[96] Recognizing that unless the situation were radically changed they would remain a hopeless minority, Holden and some political allies went to Washington to convince Congress to reconstruct North Carolina.[97] Holden soon endorsed Negro suffrage and placed himself in line with the Reconstruction policies being adopted by Congress. Then, by adapting the Heroes of America to peacetime and starting Union Leagues, Holden prepared for the launching of a new political party.

At a convention held on 27 and 28 March, 1867, the Republican party of North Carolina was born. The debt it owed to congressional Reconstruction was immediately apparent. A large number of the delegates were black, and the party endorsed biracial voting.[98] Some white Unionists opposed this course, but their protests were brushed aside.[99] The Union League, an effective organizing agency once again, in two years claimed a membership of seventy thousand voters.[100] The league was quite effective in the mountain counties despite the fact that it was racially integrated.[101] A second state convention held in September 1867 nearly split the new party in two. Reflecting the numerical composition of the party, black delegates were in the majority. In addition, a significant number of northern Republicans were present for the first time, and they, along with the blacks, dominated the proceedings.[102] Among the proposals accepted by the convention was one calling for the confiscation of the property of former Confederates.

Native white Republicans of North Carolina were aghast at what had taken place. David R. Goodloe proposed that the North Carolina

Unionists meet and form a constitutional Union party separate from the Holden Republicans.[103] Nothing came of this plan, but mass meetings of Republicans, particularly in the mountain counties, objected to the confiscation plank in the platform. One Republican undoubtedly caught the despair of the Unionists when he reported:

> Such men as you, Dick, Settle, Fowle, Warren, Barnes & myself are very greivously [sic] threatened with political ruin. I did all I could to get some justice for us, & some prudence in our counsels. But to no purpose. We are badly treated, & that for the purpose of accomplishing the personal ends of men who have come among us under the hope of so controlling the negro vote as to dominate the whole government of the state. These who assist to put our government in the hands of strangers will be odious forever. Holden admits the injustice & danger, but says he must obey the authority of the Convention, having accepted the chairmanship of the Executive Committee.[104]

The position of the native Unionists was weak in most parts of the state because of the dominance of black voters. Only in the mountain counties did the Republican organization remain in white Unionist hands.[105] Thus, unlike mountain Republicans in West Virginia and Tennessee at that time, those in North Carolina were a powerless minority in their state organization.

As North Carolina Republicans prepared for their first electoral tests in 1868, the party leaders in the mountain counties tried to reconcile the party's platform with the conservatism and racism of their constituency. The Republican state convention aided them by nominating prominent mountain Unionist Tod R. Caldwell for lieutenant governor.[106] When respected mountain state supreme court justice Richmond M. Pearson also announced his support of the Republican ticket, the party found that it could appeal successfully to former Unionists.[107] The first test of voting strength in April 1868 resulted in Republican victories in both the state and the mountain counties. The vote for the Republican ticket and the new Republican-sponsored constitution in the mountain region was approximately 53 percent.[108] It was obvious that the party was attracting a significant number of white voters in the region. For example, Holden won 73 percent of the vote of Wilkes County as the Republican gubernatorial candidate, while blacks made up only 11 percent of the voting population.[109] The November elections were not as favorable to the Republicans in the mountain counties; both Republican candidates for Congress in that region were defeated.[110]

Once again the weakness of the party centered around racial conflicts. The immediate problem had been a riot between blacks and whites in Asheville on election day, but mountain Republicans were troubled by other considerations as well.[111] As in Tennessee and West

Virginia, there were many whites who could not vote, while blacks could. The fact that it was a congressional act rather than state legislation that disfranchised these whites did not seem to make much difference to the racially conservative mountain Republicans.[112] By August of 1869 when county elections were held, Republicans were losing elections in their strongest areas, with the party split between native Unionists on one side and carpetbaggers and blacks on the other.[113]

Complicating efforts of the divided Republicans to stay in power was the rise of a widespread Ku Klux Klan organization in the state. The carpetbag wing of the party convinced Governor Holden that the solution was the creation of a state militia.[114] The militia was severely criticized by the Democrats for its aggressive methods, but it was an effective agency for protecting Republican voters and candidates in a number of counties.[115] For the white population of the mountains, the idea of protecting black political rights while whites could not vote was unacceptable.[116] Holden and the Republicans had come to expect the support of mountain Unionists, but the events of Reconstruction drove them from the party in large numbers. In the gubernatorial election of 1868, Holden had won majorities in twelve of the twenty-four western counties and received 53 percent of the vote. The Republicans in 1870, in contrast, were able to carry only four counties and saw their proportion of the vote fall to 40 percent.[117] This disastrous performance was partially responsible for the Democrats' regaining control of the legislature and subsequently impeaching Holden. With Holden gone, many of the carpetbaggers left the state or dropped out of politics.

Almost by default the Republican organization fell under the control of the new governor, mountain Republican Tod Caldwell. Caldwell and mountain Republican leaders faced an immediate problem of defeating a Democratic attempt to call a constitutional convention and thereby put an end to suffrage restriction. The Republicans centered their campaign around the lack of concreteness of Democratic proposals, which could lead to unexpected changes and the end to certain advantages the old constitution gave to the western part of the state.[118] Unlike the 1870 fiasco, the Republicans were now well organized and working effectively, as the results confirmed. The movement against holding the convention won a substantial victory throughout the state; and, although the mountain counties voted for the convention, the Republicans were able to increase their share of the vote to 44 percent.[119]

In the midst of their campaign against the constitutional convention, the Republicans in western North Carolina became the targets of the only extensive Klan violence experienced in the five mountain regions during Reconstruction. The activity centered in the counties along the

South Carolina border, and events in that state apparently influenced North Carolina Klan leaders.[120] Both federal and state governments sent troops and legal help to local Republican leaders. Despite this assistance, a Republican newspaper office was destroyed in Rutherford County, although the local Klan leader was quickly arrested.[121] This quick action did not prevent the spread of the organization to other mountain counties. It was not until a group of Klansmen raped the wife of a white Republican leader and outraged the public that the organization finally collapsed.[122] Generally speaking, this episode did the Republican party little damage in the mountain counties; in fact, the senseless violence may have even hurt the Democrats.

Having survived the events of the previous two years, the mountain Republicans began to organize for the critical gubernatorial election of 1872. Caldwell, as the representative of the white Unionists and the western counties, was one of the two leading Republican candidates. His chief opponent was Thomas Settle, who had been a state supreme court justice and minister to Peru and who was a personal friend of President Grant.[123] Settle quickly became the candidate of the carpetbag wing of the party.[124] Caldwell, however, swept the delegations from the mountain counties and was popular enough in the remainder of the state to win the nomination on the first ballot.[125] Caldwell's campaign against Democratic candidate A. S. Merrimon was directed at disassociating the Republican party from the policy of proscripting its political opponents. The Republican state convention had called on Congress to pass a general amnesty bill for all former Confederates, and Caldwell emphasized the fact that his administration had not sought to punish Democrats.[126] Caldwell, recognizing that the state organization could not carry the load alone, appealed for help from national party leaders, requesting twelve thousand dollars to finance his campaign.[127] The exact extent of outside aid that was provided is unknown, but there was some. The result was a very narrow victory for Caldwell at the state level and little change in the vote in mountain counties.[128] In the presidential vote four months later, when Greeley's unpopularity allowed the Republicans to sweep the state, Grant won a majority in the mountains.

These Republican victories were nevertheless deceptive, and by May 1873 one Democratic paper observed that the North Carolina "Republican party is fast dying out."[129] One cause for the party's decline was the extremely unsettled situation in the Internal Revenue Service. The taxes on whiskey were unpopular among mountain farmers, and as collectors of the tax the Republicans suffered accordingly.[130] But an even more important factor in weakening the party was the battle within

Republican ranks to control the patronage of this agency. The vast majority of federal appointees in western North Carolina were employed in the Internal Revenue Service, with the man who was the head or collector in the region usually controlling the party organization. Throughout 1873, 1874, and 1875 a major battle raged between the collector, Dr. John J. Mott, and James G. Ramsay for control of the patronage.[131] The result of this battle was to split the party in the mountain counties into two competing and antagonistic groups.

Another factor in the rapid decline of Republican fortunes was the debate over the Civil Rights Bill in 1874 and 1875. The Democrats immediately charged that the law would provide for "negro social equality,"[132] and Republicans all over North Carolina quickly moved to disassociate themselves from this unpopular piece of legislation.[133] The party's efforts to maintain itself were also greatly weakened when Governor Caldwell died in July 1874. His death caused complete Republican disorganization in the western counties. The party failed to nominate congressional candidates in two mountain districts and backed Independent Democrats instead.[134] In one district, Republicans finally supported a man who was widely recognized as a former leading member of the Klan. The election returns for state superintendent for public instruction demonstrated how seriously the Civil Rights Bill had weakened the party in the mountain counties. In this race the Republican candidate was forced to answer attacks directed at the integrated school section of the bill, and his share of the mountain vote fell to 31 percent of the total.[135]

During the 1875 campaign for delegates to a constitutional convention, the Civil Rights Bill continued to plague the Republicans. In fact, it was the only issue that Democratic speakers discussed.[136] The Republican federal district judge of the western section of the state tried to alleviate the pressure by announcing that all the act called for was separate but equal facilities.[137] This argument was apparently unconvincing to most mountain Republicans. At the state convention in June, delegates from the western counties were the leaders in the fight to have the party ignore the civil rights controversy.[138] Despite these problems the Republicans nearly won a majority of delegates. The blacks helped the party carry the majority of the lowland districts. In the mountain counties, however, dissatisfaction with the party's racial policies was overwhelming. The Republicans won only eight of the twenty-eight contests in the highlands, and the Democrats were able to gain control of the convention.[139]

The elections of 1876 in North Carolina demonstrated that these trends would continue. Unlike the situation in Tennessee and West Virginia, the collapse of the party in the mountain counties did not destroy the state organization. The mountain Republicans had formed only part of the party's leadership group. They were also a distinct minority among Republican voters; thus, the party remained competitive in 1876. Thomas Settle ran a strong race for governor against popular war governor Zebulon Vance. In the mountain region, Republican speakers tried to weaken Vance by reminding voters of his use of the state militia against Unionists during the war. Despite this strategy, the Republicans were in serious trouble in the mountain counties. Federal intervention in racial matters was deeply resented, and mountain voters deserted the Republicans in large numbers. Only if the Republican party could avoid this association with black civil rights could it expect to prosper in western North Carolina.

Kentucky mountain Republicans seemed to be working under even greater handicaps than those in western North Carolina. Like their counterparts in that region, eastern Kentucky Republicans did not dominate their state party organization. At no time during Reconstruction did a mountain politician play a prominent part in determining what party policy would be. In addition, Kentucky mountain Republicans never enjoyed the luxury of being part of the party that controlled the state government, as those in the other states did. Because Kentucky, as a loyal state during the Civil War, did not have to be reconstructed by Congress, the Unconditional Unionists, or Republicans, found that they formed a hopeless minority. The August elections of 1865 gave the first indication of the party's status. By order of the civilian governor and the commanding federal army officer in the state, those who had served in the Confederate army were not allowed to vote.[140] The Unionists continued to be split into Conservatives and Republicans, and the Conservatives won a major victory, capturing five of the nine congressional seats and gaining complete control of the legislature.[141] Only in the mountain counties were the Republicans in control of the former Unionist coalition.[142] Thus the party was in the minority even among supporters of the union. By December 1865 former Confederates were given back their franchise, and they united with the Conservative Unionists to protect Kentucky from political interference by the Congress.

Recognizing their minority position, Kentucky Republicans began to search for a way to detach the Conservative Unionists from the opposition. The opening move, however, was made by the Conservatives, who established a group in the legislature that called on Kentucky to forget slavery and to support President Andrew Johnson's Reconstruction policy.[143] On 30 May, 1866, the Conservative Union Democrats formed a separate organization and tried to create a party organization opposing both southern Democrats and Republicans. The new party nominated former Union general Edward H. Hobson for clerk of the court of appeals; the Republicans made no nomination and supported Hobson.[144] When Hobson was decisively defeated by the regular Democratic candidate, it was obvious to all that this third-party movement could not draw sufficient Union Democratic support to defeat the party organization.

The gubernatorial, congressional, and local elections of 1867 gave further evidence of the failure of the Republicans. The Republican and Conservative Unionist coalition fell apart, and a Union Democratic party emerged as a separate organization.[145] The Republicans still attempted to appeal to Conservative Unionists by adopting a very conciliatory party platform.[146] The Union Democrats and Republicans both ran gubernatorial candidates. Table 5 indicates the extent of the Democratic victory. It was obvious that, even if the Republicans did attract the Union Democrats, they would still be the minority party. Probably the most encouraging part of the returns was the fact that in the heavily Unionist mountain counties the Republicans won more than 53 percent of the vote.[147]

Finding that conciliation did not work as a strategy in the state as a whole, Republicans began to follow policies more in keeping with the national party in Congress. In August 1867 a meeting of former Union soldiers demanded that the Confederates on the recently elected Democratic ticket be excluded from office and that the federal government intervene if necessary.[148] Because Congress did not act on this request, the new regime took over without incident. This militant action, however, helped break up the Union Democrats, and by early 1868 the party's central committee called on its members to join the Democrats.[149] Most of them did so; but, fortunately for the Republicans, John M. Harlan, one of the third party's most articulate spokesmen, joined their ranks. The

TABLE 5. Gubernatorial, Congressional, and Legislative Races, Kentucky, 1867

	Governor	Congress	State House	State Senate
Democrat	90,225	9	85	28
Republican	33,939	0	10	7
Union Democrat	13,167	0	5	3

SOURCE: E. Merton Coulter, *The Civil War and Readjustment in Kentucky*, p. 325 n.

accession to the party of a number of the more prominent conservatives in the state encouraged the 1868 Republican state convention to adopt a conciliatory platform.[150] In the mountain counties, however, many Republican Unionists refused to follow the party line. Union Leagues were formed, and political opponents were treated violently in Harlan County.[151] The continued Democratic success only increased the discontent of those in the party who favored more radical policies.

The more aggressive Unionists seized control of the party in 1869. A group of them sent to the United States Senate a protest against removing disabilities from Kentucky Democratic leaders under the Fourteenth Amendment.[152] In addition, the party's state convention supported the Fifteenth Amendment and black suffrage.[153] Many Republicans found this new party platform unacceptable, and, as a result, in many parts of the state Republicans failed to contest local and legislative contests.[154] The revolt against the more radical program was particularly strong in the mountain counties. The Republican vote declined to only 44 percent of the total, and a number of supposedly safe Republican counties supported Democratic candidates.[155] The party was further weakened by a series of petty fights over patronage.

The final ratification of the Fifteenth Amendment at the national level meant that, no matter what their position on Negro suffrage had been, Kentucky Republicans now had to work with black voters. Despite previous divisions, after ratification the party moved as a single unit to encourage the new voters to join the party.[156] The state committee even requested that federal troops be dispatched to the state to protect black voters.[157] Yet the congressional election results in 1870 were somewhat disappointing to the Republicans. Although blacks generally voted with the party and the Republican vote more than doubled in the state over 1869, the Democrats still won all nine seats. The Republican vote in the mountain counties rose to a little more than 48 percent, which was a slight increase over the year before but still left the party a minority in this heavily Unionist region.[158] The brief experiment in radical policies was an obvious failure and had even weakened the Republicans in the one part of the state where they had been strong.

The Republican gubernatorial campaign in 1871 would decide the future course of the party. Many in the party were critical of its recent actions and desired a more responsive party leadership.[159] In addition, many Republicans, including those in the mountain county of Estill, faced Klan violence and wanted to avoid issues raised by Reconstruction.[160] The Republican state convention in May accomplished both objectives. John M. Harlan, the former leader of the Union Democrats, was unanimously nominated as the Republican gubernatorial candidate.[161]

The party adopted a liberal and progressive platform at the convention, emphasizing amnesty for all former Confederates, internal improvements, and improved educational opportunities.[162] Even highly partisan Democratic editor Henry Watterson was forced to comment favorably on the "nomination of General Harlan, the conciliatory tone of the resolutions and speeches, the respectability and moderation of the gathering."[163]

The campaign speeches of Harlan, George M. Thomas, who was candidate for lieutenant governor, and Benjamin Bristow all emphasized the progressive party platform and encouraged liberal Democrats to join them.[164] Harlan's efforts in the mountain counties were regarded by local Republicans as particularly effective.[165] The election returns gave the Republicans the answer to the question of what course they should pursue. Although Harlan lost decisively, he won more votes than had any previous Republican candidate in Kentucky. Clearly the party in Kentucky would have to follow a conciliatory policy if it hoped for future success. Harlan's proportion of the vote in the mountain counties, 52 percent, encouraged mountain Republican politicians to follow the policy adopted by the state convention.[166]

Kentucky Republicans continued to follow a liberal course and managed to minimize the effects of federal interference in racial matters. Unlike Republicans in the other three states, the Kentucky party suffered no important split between radicals and moderates. Part of this outcome was due to the program the party had followed and the electoral results that confirmed the wisdom of the policy, but there was an additional practical political reason for the unity. President Grant had appointed Kentucky Republican leader Benjamin Bristow to the new post of solicitor general of the United States.[167] From this position Bristow was able to assist other Kentucky Republicans in their efforts to gain patronage positions.[168] Since Kentucky party members rarely won elective office, they did not want to weaken Bristow's position in Washington. Thus, when a party revolt against Grant's renomination threatened to break out in 1872, it was quickly and thoroughly crushed.

Opposition to Grant in Kentucky was concentrated in Louisville and the city of Covington in Kenton County. The major problem in Covington was the fact that Grant had appointed his father, Jesse Root Grant, postmaster. The old man was incompetent, and his presence alienated many local Republicans.[169] Black voters in Louisville were also dissatisfied. Anti-Grant leaders in the state's largest city included state Republican committee secretary M. H. Bland and therefore represented a real threat to the unity of the party.[170] In an effort to prevent the growth of opposition, party leaders scheduled the state convention in

March, which was much earlier than usual. In February the Louisville primary election was held, and the regular leadership was able to gain the support of a majority of the blacks. Consequently, the anti-Grant forces elected few delegates to the state convention.[171] At that meeting the president's backers were in complete control and easily selected delegates who were instructed to vote for Grant for president and Kentucky's John Harlan for vice-president. When the convention demanded that all party members pledge their loyalty to Grant, only the Kenton County delegates walked out.[172]

Mountain Republicans refused to take part in the revolt at all. They were satisfied with the leadership provided by Harlan and Bristow at the state level and accepted Grant as the party's logical candidate. This unity resulted in a particularly strong showing by the Republicans in the mountain counties in 1872. In the three congressional districts containing mountain counties, the Republicans won at least 45 percent of the vote, although they lost all three seats. Particularly significant was the effective campaign run by William O. Bradley of Garrard County in the Eighth District.[173] Bradley was not a mountain man, but the large number of highland counties in his district gave him an opportunity to identify with mountain voters.

Despite the absence of strong factions within the party, the Civil Rights Bill made the 1874 campaign difficult for Republicans in Kentucky. Blacks were demanding a share of the patronage for the first time, and Kentucky party leaders faced the difficult task of reconciling these demands with the racism of their white candidates. Republicans, including those in the mountains, refused to run for local offices and risk identifying themselves with the Civil Rights Bill.[174] The party backed Independent Democrat John B. Cochran for the statewide election for clerk of the court of appeals and saw the party vote decline by 30,000 votes from the level Harlan had reached in 1871.[175] In the Eighth Congressional District, where the party never really got organized, the Republican vote dropped from 10,063 in 1872 to 382 in 1874.[176] Thus, Kentucky Republicans did suffer from many of the problems created by the civil rights legislation that other southern Republicans faced.

The Ninth Congressional District in the heart of the mountains did offer a great deal of hope to the party, however. In August, Republican W. H. Randall won more than 80 percent of the vote in the election for state district judge in counties in the Ninth District.[177] Inspired by this success, the party turned to a new man to make the congressional race. John D. White was a lawyer from Clay County and only twenty-five years old. Despite his heavy beard, his supporters had to admit he resembled a "mere boy," but this was an advantage since he "will go to

Congress untrammeled by old political prejudices."[178] White spent most of his campaign attacking the Civil Rights Bill and promising to secure federal aid to bring railroads into the mountain counties.[179] White's opponent, Harrison Cockrill, was as aggressive and partisan as White was moderate. In 1871 Cockrill had been the leader of the Estill County Klan organization, and in the 1874 congressional campaign he continued his violent opposition to black civil rights.[180] Cockrill also hurt his chances by being drunk at several campaign appearances, provoking criticism from a number of Democrats.[181] The result was a close but very significant victory for White and the Kentucky Republicans. The mountain voters had rejected extremism again, and the party could only conclude that its policies were following the proper path.

The gubernatorial election of 1875 showed both the strengths and the weaknesses of the strategy adopted by Kentucky Republicans. Trying to take advantage of White's success, the party once again nominated John M. Harlan for governor and concentrated much more of its campaign in the mountain counties.[182] White carefully organized the party in his district and warned Harlan to visit the region early in the campaign because in the mountains "we have only the grapevine for telegrams."[183] Harlan announced his opposition to racially mixed schools and attempted to campaign on the same progressive platform that he had four years before.[184] For the first time, the Republican campaign was adequately financed. Bristow was able to secure money from northern Republicans, and even in the remote mountain counties the party had money to run its activities.[185] By the first week in July the Democrats, realizing that the Harlan campaign was effective, began to bring in prominent Democrats from other states and to emphasize the Civil Rights Bill to counteract the Republicans.

The highlight of the Republican campaign was Harlan's speaking tour of the mountain counties in mid-July. As one Republican politician reported to Bristow, for the first time Republicans were getting a fair hearing from Kentucky campaign crowds.[186] Harlan emphasized the need for state aid for the region, particularly in education.[187] Despite the Civil Rights Bill, Harlan could report, "I have just returned from my joint discussions in the mountain portion of the state with Col. McCreary. I find everything in the best possible condition there. Our friends have never been so hopeful and so far from my losing votes I received in 1871 in that section, we will largely increase them."[188] Harlan did in fact gain votes in the mountain region, but the gains were smaller than he had hoped. Out of approximately 35,000 votes in the region, Harlan's majority increased only 142 over 1871.[189] Thus, the limitations of the Republican strategy in Kentucky were clearly revealed. While the party held its own—not a minor achievement when compared to other Republican organizations of the upper South—it was still a minority that had little hope for immediate success.

The Republican party's inability to control the state government seemed to be an advantage among mountain voters. Since the state was not under congressional Reconstruction and the Democrats dominated the state, mountain voters had few direct grievances with the local Republican organization and the party emerged in 1874 with its organization still intact, despite the controversy surrounding the Civil Rights Bill. No other party structure in the highlands could make that claim.

Mountain Republicans in southwestern Virginia were uniformly unsuccessful in their attempts to construct a viable party. As in Kentucky, the highlanders in Virginia were not part of the state leadership of the party. In addition, the absence of large numbers of Unionists gave outside politicians little opportunity to create an organization in the mountains. Virginia Republican leaders, therefore, ignored the mountaineers and followed policies that insured the party's continuing weakness in the southwestern part of the state. Even when local mountain Republicans began to organize, the party platform alienated too many voters to allow these men to strengthen the party.

The confused political conditions in Virginia in 1865 retarded the development of the Republican party. When the war ended, President Andrew Johnson recognized the reorganized government of Francis H. Pierpont as the legal government in Virginia. Pierpont, who was from the area that had become West Virginia, was interested in trying to build a strong conservative Unionist party to help him rule the state.[190] In June of 1865 the Union Association of Alexandria was formed, a group that proposed a more radical course, including giving the right to vote to "loyal male citizens without regard to color."[191] This basic split in the Unionist party and the later Republican party remained throughout the Reconstruction period. In the mountain counties there were no Unionist organizations of either variety at all. The October 1865 elections were a great disappointment to Unionists, for the Conservative party won virtually every contest.

Recognizing that organization would be important if the Unionists expected to win in the future, the Republican party was officially established in May 1866. Calling for free public schools and restricted black suffrage, the party convention also demanded that Confederates be temporarily disfranchised to allow Unionists an opportunity to gain control of the state government.[192] Finally, in January of 1867, there were some meetings in the mountain counties of southwestern Virginia that supported the Republicans.[193] Further efforts to strengthen the party organization were thwarted by the 17 April 1867 Republican convention held in Richmond. The majority of the delegates were black, and the convention was dominated by white radical leader James W. Hunnicutt. The platform that was adopted included demands for equitable taxation, free schools, and racial equality.[194] Hunnicutt, as the state leader of the Union League, was now in complete control of the formal party organization.

The program espoused by the Virginia Republicans alienated most of the whites in the state and led to an attempt to replace Hunnicutt as party leader. John M. Botts, a well-known Virginia Unionist, suggested another convention to encourage more white membership in the party. Botts and a number of conservative Virginians formed a cooperative movement to return the party to white control. The second convention, August 1867, was largely a repetition of the April convention, leaving Hunnicutt in complete control of the black vote recently enfranchised by Congress.[195] The Botts faction was forced to call its own meeting and state its own position without the benefit of the official machinery of the party. Despite all the factional bitterness in the party, the Union League was operating with some success in a number of mountain counties, although it seemed to be attracting only a small number of white mountaineers.[196] Thus the Republican party organized but alienated most Virginia whites in the process.

The election for the constitutional convention required by congressional reconstruction, held in October 1867, simply confirmed Hunnicutt's dominance. Not only did delegates representing his wing of the party defeat Conservatives, but also they defeated candidates representing the Botts section of the party.[197] Generally, the voting followed racial lines, and only in the mountain counties did the Republicans get much support from white voters. The returns from four mountain counties illustrate this point (see table 6). A combination of congressional disfranchisement of a number of former Confederates and a high black voter turnout left the convention under radical Republican control.

The constitutional convention of 1868 completed the process of alienating most of Virginia's white voters from the Republican party. The new constitution disfranchised a large number of former Confederates and required an ironclad test oath be taken to establish eligibility to vote. Another controversial section stipulated free public schools, with no provision for racial separation.[198] At the same time Governor Pierpont was removed and carpetbagger Henry H. Wells installed in his position.[199] Wells moved quickly to replace Conservative Unionists with other carpetbaggers, further angering white native Republicans. The process was completed in May 1868, when Wells rather than Hunnicutt

TABLE 6. Votes for and against the Constitutional Convention by Race, Selected Virginia Counties, 1867

	White		Black	
	For	Against	For	Against
Grayson	447	106	170	0
Lee	307	491	51	0
Scott	767	346	76	1
Washington	422	1,154	500	5

SOURCES: *Knoxville Whig*, 13 Nov. 1867; Lewis P. Summers, *History of Southwestern Virginia, 1746–1786*, pp. 551–52.

became the Republican gubernatorial candidate.[200] The Conservative party then met and nominated a ticket headed by former Confederate colonel R. E. Withers. Wells requested a delay in the election when the congressional act that provided for the voting included a section calling for a new registration.

As the delay lengthened, forces in the state began to assemble a political coalition that would defeat Wells and the Republican radicals. One part of the opposition came from railroad president and former Confederate general William Mahone, who was fighting with the Baltimore and Ohio system for control of the state's railroads. Much to his disgust, he discovered that neither Wells nor Withers could be relied on to support his plans.[201] In early 1869 a group of prominent Virginia Conservatives went to Washington and proposed a familiar compromise: universal suffrage.[202] They were able to persuade the Grant administration to give Virginia voters an opportunity to vote separately on the franchise and test oath sections of the constitution. Thus the constitution would be approved and the state would be readmitted to the Union without the Confederate disfranchisement that had been effected in other reconstructed states.

The election campaign that followed this compromise was a disaster for the Republicans. At the party's March 1869 convention, Wells was renominated and a black man, Dr. J. D. Harris, was nominated for lieutenant governor. Although Harris's nomination was opposed by Wells, conservative white Republicans with black votes overwhelmed Wells and, as his opponents hoped, greatly weakened the ticket among white voters.[203] Mahone and the conservative white Republicans held a meeting and nominated moderate carpetbagger Gilbert C. Walker, a Mahone business associate, for governor and white Unionist Republican John F. Lewis for the second spot on the ticket. The Conservatives withdrew the

Withers ticket and backed the moderate Walker, who was extremely popular among white voters in the mountain counties and made a successful campaign tour of the region.[204] The election results showed a complete defeat for the Wells ticket. Wells lost to Walker by eighteen thousand votes, disfranchisement and the test oath sections of the constitution were defeated by forty thousand votes, and the Conservative party captured complete control of the state legislature.[205] Walker carried every mountain county, winning 72 percent of the vote and establishing beyond any question the mountaineers' dissatisfaction with radical policies.[206]

The Republicans did not recover from this defeat for more than a decade. Its effects were particularly evident in the mountain counties where J. B. Rives, collector of internal revenue, dominated a patronage machine that wanted a small Republican party in order to reduce competition for jobs. The Republicans who had supported Wells for governor demanded that Congress intervene; when it did not, the radicals were left with few alternative policies.[207] Most of the Republicans who had supported Walker were forced out of the party by the angry radicals, further weakening the party. In the 1870 congressional elections Republican victories in three congressional districts in the black belt of the state confirmed the leadership of the state organization in its course. The party in the mountains had few white supporters. In the Ninth, or mountain, District the Democratic party split; additionally, the regular Democratic candidate, William Terry, had taken a very unpopular stand on the major issue of the campaign.[208] The Republicans ran their most attractive candidate, Robert W. Hughes; yet Hughes drew only 21 percent of the vote.[209] Since blacks usually voted Republican and the black proportion of the district's population was approximately 15 percent, the party's appeal to mountain whites was obviously quite limited.

Hughes's career for the next three years paralleled that of the party's rejection of the radical course it had followed. The former Confederate colonel found himself unable to secure a good federal patronage position because of his moderate position in the party.[210] He continued to work in the party and was rewarded when the moderate wing of the party seized control of the state organization at the state convention in September 1871.[211] Hughes followed this success with another congressional race in the Ninth District in 1872, at which time he increased the Republican percentage of the vote.[212] By the summer of 1873, he was recognized as the leading Republican in the state and was easily nominated for governor at the state convention.[213] Hughes's campaign was extremely conciliatory toward Virginia whites; he rejected social equality among the races and demanded a more progressive state government.[214]

While his campaign was received favorably in the mountain counties, it did not win the party many new members, as Hughes received only 29 percent of the mountain vote.[215] Apparently recognizing the hopelessness of creating a strong party organization in southwestern Virginia, Hughes accepted a federal judgeship and retired from active politics.

The departure of Hughes signaled the collapse of the Republicans' organization, both at the state level and in the mountain region. As in the other four states, the Civil Rights Bill alienated most of the white voters and left the party greatly weakened.[216] Despite another bad split among Democrats in the Ninth District, the Republicans never had a chance, and their share of the vote fell to less than 11 percent.[217] The Conservative party insured its continued dominance by passing a poll tax and other measures designed to restrict black voting. The new measures worked quite well, for the Virginia Republican party was completely demoralized by 1876 and seemed headed for extinction.[218] The party had never been strong at any point. From the very beginning it had been dominated by competing factions that often alienated both loyal party members and potential allies. This situation was especially true in the mountain counties, where the Republican party as it was known in the other four mountain regions of the upper South never really developed.

Despite a decade of intensive work in the Appalachian highlands, the Republican party faced an uncertain future in that region. Although the party received considerable assistance from the national government, it was unable to establish itself among white voters as a legitimate alternative to the Democratic party. Even in those areas where support for the Union had been strong, the Republican share of the vote declined dangerously in the 1870s. The biggest problem was that the party's leaders seemed to have few ideas about how they could improve the situation.

Two obvious problems had to be solved if the Republicans were not to be relegated to oblivion in the mountain counties. The first one centered around the policy of federal interference into the racial situation in the South. The first Reconstruction Act of March 1867, the Fifteenth Amendment, and the Civil Rights Bill of 1875 all drove southern whites, including mountaineers, out of the Republican party. The addition of blacks to the electorate provided a loyal base on which Republicans could build, but whites refused to support the party that was forcing them to accept new racial policies. The situation was particularly critical in the mountain counties where there were few blacks and the party was dependent on poor white voters.

The Republicans had to do more, however, than erase the negative image created by their association with blacks. They had to find a means to appeal directly to mountain voters as a specific constituency. Some efforts were made in this direction during Reconstruction. Although not specifically directed at mountaineers, the Republicans' efforts to improve education and to support industrial development were popular in the highlands. Thus, the task that faced the party was to find the precise combination of policies and political strategies that would be most attractive to mountain whites. Despite the gloomy prospects facing the party in 1876, the mountain Republican leaders were able to revitalize the organization in a remarkably short period of time.

CHAPTER 4

THE MOUNTAIN REPUBLICAN PARTY-ARMY

The defeats that the mountain Republicans suffered during Reconstruction caused them to reexamine their party structure. One North Carolina Republican probably spoke for the whole party when he observed, "The old organization has accomplished its purpose. Something new, calculated to popularize the organization, must be adopted at the next State Convention."[1] Not only was there general agreement among mountain Republicans as to the nature of the problem, but, even more significant, there was general agreement about what was the proper solution. The party had to adopt a better organized, more military structure. As one mountaineer stated, it was time to put "the party in fighting trim"[2] or improve the "party drill and discipline."[3] Thus the story of mountain republicanism in this period after 1876 was that of growth, dominance, and decline of the party as a military organization.

The mountaineers' experience was certainly not unique in American history. The military had long served as a model for political organizations. James Parton described early political leader Aaron Burr's thoughts on the necessity of martial organization in the following passage: "A party, he would maintain, in order to carry elections, must submit to discipline; must execute faithfully, and even blindly, the decrees of its leaders. Whatever is decided upon in the conclaves of the legitimate and recognized chiefs is *Law* to the rank and files, which they must execute to the letter, on pain of proscription."[4] The party-army of the highlanders, then, was not singular in American politics. This new organization did have one added feature that made it even more significant to mountain Republicans. Military structures functioned as a reminder to mountain voters of war-related experiences and loyalties. For the Republican party, these memories encouraged mountain voters not only to accept political discipline but also to remember events that separated them from other southerners. Thus, the party-army emphasized a common opposition to the Confederacy as well as a type of political structure.

The great impact of the Civil War on the mountain region was responsible for the mountaineers' preoccupation with a military type of political organization. Of course, most mountain men had served some time in either the Confederate or the Union army, where they had learned directly the demands of discipline and organizational loyalty. As indicated earlier, however, the Civil War in the mountains involved the civilian population as much as it did the soldiers. There was no escape from the discomforts, starvation, and sudden death brought by the disruption of transportation and guerrilla warfare. The entire mountain population, therefore, had been deeply affected by the Civil War and was acutely aware of the army's principles of organization. During the Reconstruction period, the leading roles played by military organizations such as the United States army and the state militias and by paramilitary organizations such as the Ku Klux Klan and the Union League made the connection between politics and the army seem a natural one.

The disorganized condition of the Republican party in these five states in the early 1870s made the martial type of organization even more appealing. Union loyalties during the war had created a predisposition among the mountaineers to favor the Republicans, but the failures of Reconstruction had left the party organization unsettled and ineffective. The army plan of organization in politics was recognized and accepted by almost everyone in the region. Quickly, each level of authority in the party was identified and labeled. Once clarified, this chain of command allowed coordinated planning and provided for maximum utilization of resources. By 1880 the mountain Republicans were ready once again to offer a challenge to the Democrats.

At the top of these new party structures in Virginia, Kentucky, Tennessee, West Virginia, and North Carolina were individuals recognized as dominant leaders in their areas. The leader of Kentucky mountain Republicans was a youthful lawyer, John D. White. White was elected to Congress three times between 1874 and 1884 and controlled the party patronage in the southeastern section of the state. The North Carolina boss was Dr. John James Mott, son of the leading Episcopal divine in the mountain area of the state. Mott held the leading federal patronage position in western North Carolina, that of district collector of internal revenue, and used it to build his organization. Another federal official, Nathan Goff, Jr., dominated West Virginia Republicans. Forced out of his position as United States district attorney by the Arthur administration in 1882, Goff was elected to Congress for three terms from West

Virginia's First District. Another Congressman was Leonidas Campbell Houk, the leader of east Tennessee Republicans. Like Goff, White, and Mott, Houk used federal patronage to construct his machine.

The situation in the hills of southwestern Virginia was somewhat different. In the late 1870s and early 1880s there was virtually no Republican party organization in that area. Republican leaders and voters had joined William Mahone's Readjuster party in an effort to defeat the dominant Conservatives. Mahone effectively centralized all the Readjuster organization's power in his own hands, and since the Readjusters controlled the Republican party structure, Mahone was the real leader of all Virginia Republicans, including those in the mountains. When the Readjusters formally joined the Republican party in the spring of 1884, Mahone's leadership of Republicans in southwest Virginia was officially recognized. Mahone, like the other four men, used his official position as United States senator to manipulate federal patronage and strengthen his organization.

Despite the fact that these five men held several different positions, the creation of the party-army followed the same general pattern in all five mountain regions. Party leaders relied heavily on war-related terms to explain the necessity for a highly disciplined organization. They maintained that an election was a battle, and that the party was like an army in that conflict. Few highland Republicans, recalling the need for discipline in the army, found fault with this reasoning. Thus, when Republican leaders extended the argument and said that the party had to be organized as a military organization, there were few objections. While the process of reaching this consensus was going on, the centralization of organization was continuing. It should be pointed out that these arguments for change in the party were never offered as a definite program by any individual leader. Mott, Goff, Houk, White, and Mahone reacted to events, using military organizing principles as the need arose.

In order to understand the line of argument that Republican leaders employed, it is necessary to become acquainted with their terminology. The vocabulary of the battlefield had always been a part of political jargon. Early in the history of elections, the word "campaign" was borrowed from warfare to describe a political contest. After the Civil War, other military terms were added to the political vocabulary in all parts of the United States. So many of the candidates and such a large part of the electorate had served in the war that these terms were a natural means of communication. The southern mountaineers differed little from their fellow countrymen in the use of such language. Military titles were retained as a form of address by mountain Republicans, and their campaign rhetoric was dominated by military phrases.

Not confined to politics alone, the war analogy found expression in all aspects of mountain life. Mountain Republican John W. Mason used it in 1877 in a college commencement address: "You are now entering the great battlefield of life. Whether or not you will be successful, will depend to a very large extent upon the fact, as to whether you now appreciate the magnitude of the conflict. If you go into the fight fully armed and equipped with a full knowledge of the ground to be taken possession of, and with determined souls, you will succeed."[5] Descriptions of mountaineers' private lives also showed the influence of the war on their speech. One Virginian, describing his financial condition, said, "Now I have carefully looked over my larder and find I have not enough provisions to stand a siege of that length."[6] All personal enemies became "rebels"[7] and one had to go to "battle"[8] to prosper in the business world.

Politics offered even greater opportunities for the use of military terms. Each part of the electoral process came to have a martial phrase attached to it. Party workers were told that it was as important for them to supply their organization with funds as it was for the government to supply the army with weapons. Election day tactics and political infighting were so vividly described in combat terms that one would have thought bullets and bayonets, instead of ballots, were being used to settle the issue. The aftermath of the election called for analysis of victory or defeat in terms that would have explained a similar verdict after armed conflict. To illustrate the role played by military terminology and principles in mountain Republican organizations, the following typical campaign has been constructed.

The beginning of a political campaign meant preparing the party for the battle to follow. One North Carolina Republican observed, about some early campaign strategy, that it was time "to throw out the skirmish forces preparatory to the gigantic struggle which must ensue later on."[9] Houk, in an 1884 address, began his campaign by telling the nominating convention, "We are here for the purpose of taking action toward organizing our forces, of beginning a great battle—and I wish to emphasize that word and call your attention to the fact that I mean all it implies, that we are here today for the purpose . . . of engaging in a great political battle, and it is mete that we should buckle on our whole armor to go forth and engage in this struggle."[10] The convention, like the army camp, was the place to bring the "enlisted"[11] men together. As one West Virginian reported to Goff, "I told my wife I had enlisted for the war."[12]

Soon it was time for the mountain Republicans to prepare to march to battle. The party members were alerted to the beginning of the campaign by a signal or "Call to Arms,"[13] which usually consisted of a parade to "the tap of the drum"[14] and the "bugle call."[15] The military procession, followed by a cookout, was a standard and successful method of gathering large crowds for Republican speakers. The largest of these extravaganzas held in the mountains took place in Knoxville, Tennessee, on the evening of 1 November 1884. More than eight thousand people participated in a procession that was viewed by an estimated forty thousand. These elaborate preparations cost Congressman Houk thirty-five hundred dollars.[16]

There were other matters to attend to before the party was ready to meet the enemy in full battle array. The opposition had to be tested to see how hard they would fight in the coming election. Since the Democrats controlled the election machinery, the Republicans could tell how vigorously the dominant party was going to campaign by the amount of resistance they showed to registering prospective Republican voters. As one Republican leader phrased it, "Our first battle is in the registration."[17] Another matter that had to be decided, with the help of local leaders, was the proper "fighting ground."[18] Decisions had to be made about where the campaign activities would be directed and what issues would be discussed. After checking with local leaders to determine the morale of the Republican troops, the party was ready for battle.

Military terms also proved useful in explaining the need for campaign contributions. The Republican leaders told their followers that before the battle could begin, "the sinews of war must be first raised."[19] "Ammunition"[20] in the form of money, pamphlets, broadsides, circulars, banners, and buttons had to be supplied to party workers. Then the "implements of war"[21] had to be manufactured. The most notable of these items was the party ticket. This document, which resembled a long postcard, was said to be as important to the voter on election day as a gun to the soldier in combat. The ticket listed the offices to be contested as well as the party's candidate for each place. In many instances, all the voter had to do was to deposit this piece of paper in the ballot box.

In the last week before the election, the party-army attacked the enemy. Their first move was to have "bombs . . . thrown into the [opposition] camp"[22] by a Republican newspaper. When the newspaper editor was sure the Democrats would not have time to respond to his charges, he would publish a story designed to discredit the opposition. Often these stories were even more explosive than bombs. An excellent example of this campaign technique was the "Danville Circular" distributed by Virginia Democrats in November 1883. This pamphlet described Danville race riots in lurid terms and is generally credited with playing a decisive part in the Democrats' subsequent victory. Often Republicans were warned, "One vote less in this election is one bullet less hurled against the enemies of freedom."[23] By election eve, the party workers were "drawn up in a regular line of battle,"[24] prepared to serve as poll watchers, to hand out tickets, and to transport the party faithful to the polls. "A truce for the night . . . Mahone's Brigade at sunrise will charge"[25] and ride forward to "go through the Democratic camps like a whirlwind."[26]

The portrayal of the election as a cavalry charge was not much exaggerated. In the Virginia gubernatorial election of 1885, Democratic candidate Fitzhugh Lee toured the mountainous southwestern section of the state at the head of mounted military processions.[27] These parades were designed to be vivid reminders of the Confederate cavalry. And John C. Houk maintained that he could have two thousand men on horseback on election day.[28] The practice most similar to an armed charge, however, was the manner in which people cast their ballots. The voting was usually done in large groups or well-organized small squads, which approached the election officials in a solid phalanx.[29] The purpose was to decrease intimidation of Republican voters and to make sure that they voted the party ticket. West Virginia Democrats became so concerned about the effectiveness of the Republican tactic that they tried to outlaw it in the early 1890s.[30]

Another compelling reason for using combat terminology was that physical violence often occurred during the campaign and at the polling places. The violent activities of mountain Democrats were not organized terrorist assaults, but more often individual acts of intimidation.[31] Republican speakers were sometimes subjected to personal assaults. At the end of a campaign in Richmond, Mahone was badly roughed up and nearly killed by a supposedly friendly mass meeting.[32] The North Carolina Republican candidates in 1876 were threatened by hostile mobs when they tried to speak.[33] In east Tennessee, Houk was attacked by a Democratic newspaperman at one of his speaking engagements.[34] All of these incidents reinforced the mountain Republicans' view of elections as battles and of the party as an attacking force.

The few times when the Republicans did control the offices and election machinery, they viewed themselves as being an army on the defensive. Mahone was warned to be "on your guard for the attack, which I expect you to *meet* and *repulse* in your usual, vigorous old style. Have every man in position, *ammunition ready*, for a *war of no ordinary character*, as *far as I can learn*, is going to be declared against you and your party."[35] The party in control was described as being positioned behind "breastworks"[36] and ready to meet any offensive. Although the mountain Republicans were rarely incumbents, even this unlikely event could easily be described in military language.

Specific elements of electioneering also became identified with combat counterparts. Since an important news story was called a "bomb," the newspaper often was described as a "battery"[37] or "big gun."[38] A speaker who attacked the entrenched party was said to be firing "shell and shot into the ranks of the enemy."[39] The rebuttal to an attack by the opposition was often characterized as a "counter charge."[40] Even a simple declaration of party loyalty seemed to be the same as "carrying the Republican banner into the thickest of the fight."[41]

Once the election was over, war analogies were used to explain the voting returns. No analyses could begin until the "smoke"[42] of battle had cleared away. Then it was time to count the "killed and wounded"[43] and to determine the exact result. Unfortunately for mountain Republicans, the result was often defeat. The reason, however, always seemed to be attributed to Democratic fraud and not to Republican failures. One Virginian blamed a loss on a restrictive Democratic election law, saying, "The battle has been fought and through the Anderson McCormick Gun we have been slaughtered."[44]

Not only did the party have to explain the setbacks, but it also had to find encouragement in what was left. One Kentucky Republican was lauded because he "made a gallant fight and has been defeated with his face to the foe."[45] The inevitable frustrations suffered by the minority party were often relieved by seeking revenge. Congressman Houk was instructed by one irate Republican "not to sheath his sword, until the head of the *rebel, democrat*, Chambers falls."[46] At times, however, a simple admission of the facts was the only avenue open to the Republicans. As one Virginian was forced to observe, "There is no disguising the fact Capt. Gaines was completely driven to the rear."[47] For the Republican party-army, the greatest threat was not defeat, but demoralization. Yet even though there were usually some who wanted to "abandon their guns,"[48] the party always continued the struggle.

Perceiving the election as a battle made it easy for mountain Republicans to picture the party as an army. For many highlanders who had remained loyal to the Union during the war, the Republican party was the logical successor to the federal army. The *Knoxville Republican* expressed this feeling by saying, "We are still true to the flag, and the forces of Lincoln, and Grant and Blaine will march on forever."[49] One east Tennessee Republican reformer gave the following account of the party's history: "The great army of Republican patriots have vanquished slavery and put to rights divers heresies of a hot bed of treason in the south." Things had changed, he lamented. "In the first decade of republicanism we had Donelson, Vicksburgh [sic], Gettysburg and Appomattox—in the second decade—spoils."[50] It seemed logical to the mountain people that Garfield, Blaine, and their local leaders were carrying on the work of Sherman and Grant. President Grant offered a very effective transition figure for this idea, having been both commander of the federal army and civilian leader of the Republican party. As one North Carolinian stated, "I was a Union soldier born in N.C. and this is my home. Gen. Grant was my commander and I will do my level best for him at all hazards."[51]

The Unionist sentiments were carefully nurtured by the Republicans, especially when the party was dealing with veterans of federal army service. Some politicians, including Houk and Goff, owed much of their success to their ability to appeal to the old soldiers. Party leaders found that the soldiers' reunion was the most effective way of strengthening the alliance between veterans and the party. One such reunion evoked the following comment: "if the soldiers of other Counties were like ours, the reunion will be the largest assembly since the war, and don't you forget it, there is a large amount of enthusiasm on the subject, and if properly conducted will be one of the best things imaginable for our party."[52] This close working relationship between party leaders and war veterans had disadvantages as well. For one thing, the Grand Army of the Republic and other veterans' groups felt that all patronage should start with them, a belief that quite often generated friction within the party.[53]

The former federal soldiers from southwestern Virginia and western North Carolina posed a special problem for the Republicans. Few of them had enlisted in the federal army at the beginning of the war. To do so would have required them to leave their families at the mercy of hostile neighbors and cross the mountains to Kentucky. Most of those who eventually fought against the South were first conscripted into the Confederate army and later deserted to federal lines. After the war, these men found that they were excluded from enjoying the benefits offered veterans because of their previous disloyalty.[54] Republican politicians in both mountain regions who felt handicapped by these restrictions worked actively for a change in the pension law.

These same Virginia and North Carolina mountain Republicans had to contend with another problem involving war veterans. How could the Republican party appeal to those constituents who had served in the Confederate army? The Republicans found a rather simple solution. Since many party leaders in these states had been in the Confederate service themselves, they emphasized this connection. The technique proved to be quite effective, as the following letter to Mahone shows: "Having served in the Conf Army from May 61 to Appomattox (at the latter place and for a long time then, in your command) . . . I write to ask your influence in the Congress of the United States to get me a position."[55] Mahone regarded former Confederate soldiers as so important for the success of his machine that he directed the Readjuster administration of Governor William Cameron to pass a state pension act for the benefit of those who had served the South.[56] The Republican leaders did not seem to sense the contradiction manifest in their appeals to the veterans of opposing armies. Apparently the voters did not either, because their letters reveal no criticism on this point.

The party as an army was forced to serve as more than an electoral organization. It was expected also to act as a barrier between party members and a hostile community. As Republican governor Daniel L. Russell of North Carolina observed in 1898, "the irritations incident to being a Republican and living in the South, are getting too rank to be borne."[57] The party, then, had to protect its members and to prevent a "reign of terror"[58] from being directed against them. Since economic discrimination was frequently used to intimidate individual Republicans, the party had to become an employment agency. Patronage was offered to those who suffered discrimination nearly as often as it was used to reward those who had performed services for the organization.

The same ideas that caused men to regard the party as an army greatly influenced actual party structure and organization as well, a fact recognized by perceptive observers at the time. In Virginia, in 1888, former congressman John Wise attacked Mahone's leadership of the state Republican organization and described the military form of organization quite accurately:

After careful study of our situation I am satisfied that the deep-seated source of the present dissatisfaction in our party is a feeling among the voters that the present plan of organization does not give them any rights or voice; that it is too military, and that it places too much power in the hands of the chairman. . . . If we had a war going on in which we might *conscript* soldiers that plan might make soldiers *efficient*. But being unable to *conscript voters* . . . [59]

Political leaders used military titles to emphasize their power as well as to show the subordinate position of others around them. Politicians often continued to use military ranks attained during the Civil War. In 1886, more than twenty years after commanding a Confederate army and after having served five years in the Senate, Mahone was addressed as "General" by more than half of his correspondents. Of the 159 letters he received in February of that year with salutations or inside addresses, 96 of them addressed him as "General."[60] Fewer than 10 percent of the letters used the formal title of "Senator." The durability of the Mahone title undoubtedly was aided by his predominant political position. Goff of West Virginia also was usually referred to as "General."

Though he was only a major during the war, he was given the title of general by his political followers.[61] By 1870, when he was clearly regarded as the leading Republican in the state, Goff's new title was completely accepted by all. Kentucky Republican leader Benjamin H. Bristow even protested being called "General."[62] Maintaining that he had never earned the title, Bristow demanded that his friends stop using it in reference to him.

Lesser party officials were assigned military rankings in line with their party positions. One respected party leader in Tennessee earned the rank of major.[63] Occasionally, a group of subordinate party officials was assigned a single rank for convenience. A newspaper, noting the defeat of a congressional candidate, reported, "Even his own lieutenants have thrown up their commissions and are fighting against him."[64] Mahone used titles to designate specific positions within the Virginia Republican party. In the Mahone plan of organization, voters were divided into groups or squads, and their election day activities were directed by a squad captain.[65] The party official at the precinct level was officially designated a lieutenant.[66] The military rating system proved to be very effective in defining the relationship of officials to each other, to the leaders, and to the voters.

The voter was not excluded from membership in this stratified model. He proudly asserted his claim as "a private in the army of Loyal Republicans of East Tennessee."[67] Privates were expected to follow officers' orders. Kentucky mountain Republicans were reminded that it "is only the cowardly and unpatriotic soldier who deserts his post in the heat of battle."[68] Much to their chagrin, party leaders found that the privates often refused to come to the party's aid because their lowly position did not require them to do so.[69]

The structure of the party organization also showed the impact of military experience. The lines of authority were clear and carefully graded. Each party level was responsible to the next and all were responsible to the state chairman. Occasionally, there were variations in the basic structure. In North Carolina, the state chairman and the executive committee were replaced by the revenue collector as the final authority in the mountains. In Virginia in 1889, the split between Mahone and James D. Brady removed the federal patronage positions from the state chairman's control. As a result, the patronage of the revenue collector and the United States marshal were not available to the state organization.

The plans of organization make clear the dominant position of the state chairman. A North Carolina plan of organization defined the chairman's position. "The chairman of the respective county, district, and state executive committees shall call their conventions to order and act as temporary chairman until a permanent organization is effected."[70] In Virginia, Mahone, as state chairman, was given the power to appoint county chairmen.[71] These provisions and others allowed the state chairman to control the state convention. Since these meetings nominated candidates, selected delegates to the national convention, wrote the party platform, and named the state committee and state chairman, control of them meant control of the party. The only party members who were able to resist the power of the state chairman were federal patronage holders like Mott and Brady, who had their own organizations, and popular congressmen such as Houk. Houk controlled his district so completely that the state chairman was powerless to discipline him. In the case of Mott and Houk, there was little conflict since these two men usually dictated who was to be state chairman.

The influence of the military was found in even the most routine of party activities. The following Mahone plan of getting voters to the polls is an excellent example.

I. Resolve members of [Republican] club into squads of ten (10) composed of these who live nearest together.
II. Let each squad, so composed, elect its own Captain.
III. Each squad must agree on some common place of meeting Tuesday morning, the 3rd of November—election day—at sunrise, and thence proceed in charge of its Captain, to the polls.
IV. On arriving at the polls, the Captain, with his squad, will report immediately to the President of his club. The President of the club will check off on his roll . . . members of the squad who may be absent. The balance of the squad will be . . . sent off right away to bring up any absent member or members of his squad.[72]

TABLE 7. Sample Voter Information Form

Voter's Name	Color	Age	Party	Politics	Residence
S. L. York	W	59	D	G[ibson]	PO for all
A. Harrell	W	71	D	G	Bull Run
H. J. Davis	W	63	R	H[ouk]	
J. E. Webber	W	41	R	G	
J. F. Ward	W	32	R	G	
R. N. Bishop	W	27	D	H	
Jno. A. Kelley	W	83	D	Doubtful	

SOURCE: J. M. Homer memorandum, 22 Sept. 1894, Houk Papers.

Voter report forms provided another example of military thoroughness. Since in many parts of the mountains there was no voter registration, the report forms were sent to local party officials to help the party leadership obtain information about the voters. The form shown in table 7 was compiled in eastern Tennessee in 1894. With the help of practices such as these, the mountain Republican machines became very adept at organizing the party's vote.

The efficient organization of the mountain Republican party-armies was further reflected in the high percentage of straight-party voting. One Kentucky Republican editor warned specifically against "those guerrillas who forage between the two parties."[73] This precaution was unnecessary in most elections because the only tickets available were printed by the two parties, and each ticket contained only one party's candidates. The advent of the nonpartisan ballot, however, did not seem to affect the party-army's ability to secure straight-ticket voting. Table 8 shows the Republican returns from Anderson County, Tennessee, in 1900, illustrating that few ballots were split. Although table 8 shows only national and state votes, the party-army produced almost the same number of votes for local candidates.

TABLE 8. Republican Votes for Federal and State Offices, Anderson County, Tennessee, 1900

District	President	Governor	Congress	R.R. Commissioner	State Senate
1	101	101	100	101	101
2	102	102	102	102	102
3	88	88	88	88	88
4	145	145	145	145	145
5	260	260	260	260	260
6	224	223	224	223	225
7	134	132	132	132	132
8	105	104	104	104	104
10	101	101	101	101	101
11	57	57	57	57	57
12	126	126	126	126	126
13	275	275	275	275	275
14	167	167	167	167	167
Totals	1,997	1,993	1,994	1,993	1,995

SOURCE: *Clinton Gazette*, 21 Nov. 1900.

The success of the party-armies insured the survival of the mountain Republican parties. After Reconstruction, the mountain Republicans had been hopeless minorities in their own states. They faced an aggressive and resourceful opponent in the Democratic party, an opponent willing to resort to extralegal methods to sustain its supremacy. Despite these obstacles, the Republican share of the vote in West Virginia, east Tennessee, southeastern Kentucky, southwestern Virginia, and western North Carolina increased substantially between 1876 and 1888. Largely responsible for this growth was the superb organization of the mountain Republican parties, and this party structure was created by men drawing primarily on their military experience as a source of inspiration.

CHAPTER 5

EMERGENCE OF THE PARTY-ARMY

The party-army was the vehicle used by the mountain people to reassert local control over their political life. For more than a decade and a half a series of crises including secession, Civil War, and Reconstruction forced the mountaineers to accept outside direction for their lives. Competing armies and revolutionary racial policies had altered mountain society substantially during that period. These outside demands made on the mountaineers were not favorably received. In every highland village there were constant reminders of the impact of the war and federal policies. The presence of maimed men, poor widows, and enfranchised blacks were only the most obvious examples of the changes. Equally important, many mountaineers were required to extend their loyalties to causes that fulfilled none of their immediate needs. Thus, for fifteen years national concerns were a prominent part of highland politics.

As a consequence, mountain political leaders were men who emphasized national issues. Andrew Johnson, William Brownlow, Tod Caldwell, Waitman Willey, and Zebulon Vance were examples of this type of nationally oriented politician. Each of these men, and many other less prominent officials, became identified with a particular national issue. While they were careful to explain their actions in terms that the mountain voters would understand, they could not avoid emphasizing programs and events that extended beyond the mountains. Mountain voters were proud of the accomplishments of these men and maintained them in office during Reconstruction. For all of their success, however, these political leaders were unable to satisfy the needs of their constituents in one area.

By 1876 the mountain population was tired of national issues. They wanted political leaders who would be less concerned with great national issues and would worry about providing individual services to their constituents. Former federal soldiers wanted pensions; farmers needed the improved seed developed by the Department of Agriculture; local governments and businesses expected their representatives to secure subsidies for their benefit. In addition to these specific requirements, the mountain population wanted their political leaders to justify the sacrifices made during the Civil War and Reconstruction. At the same time, forces created by the rapid industrialization of the Gilded Age threatened to continue the paramount position of national concerns in mountain politics. The highland population reacted quickly to protect itself from what it perceived as a challenge to its local autonomy.

The Republican party was able to take advantage of this sentiment to strengthen its position in the mountain region. The disastrous influence of the Civil Rights Bill on the elections of 1874 and 1876 had convinced many party leaders of the necessity for a change in party strategy. In addition, a new generation of political leaders was appearing in the mountain counties and demanding a share of the power. These men appealed to the local interests of the mountain people and challenged the authority of the older leaders. The younger men, often veterans of the Civil War, found the military experience useful for principles of organization and helped develop the party-armies of the late 1870s. The combination of organizational ability and local appeals allowed these men to seize control of the mountain Republican organizations from the more nationally oriented leaders.

The new leadership had solved half the problems faced by the Republican party in Appalachia in 1876. They had found a positive way to appeal to mountain voters. These men now became community spokesmen, defending the mountain people both from lowland detractors who claimed that they were traitors to the South and from the stresses of the modern industrial order simultaneously. Mountain voters responded by joining the Republican party in ever-increasing numbers throughout the 1880s. By the latter part of that decade the Republicans had the loyal support of a clear majority of mountain voters. The sequence of events varied from state to state, but the election returns made it clear that the Republican party was attractive to mountain voters.

Mountain Republican politicians still faced the problem of how to avoid association with federally sponsored racial policies. This concern was solved by the events surrounding the disputed presidential election of 1876. The compromise that allowed Rutherford Hayes to become president included the withdrawal of federal forces from the southern states. The end of Reconstruction removed a major Democratic issue from mountain elections. In addition, Hayes pursued a policy of trying to reconcile southern whites and attempted to encourage conservative white businessmen and social leaders to join the Republican party.[1] Although these efforts to revive the Republican party's appeal failed in the lowland South, many mountain men viewed the party with renewed interest. Republican leaders did not like the fact that some of the president's appointments went to Democrats, but the new party leaders found it easier to win converts to the Republican cause in the more relaxed atmosphere.

The situation remained unchanged until 1889. During the short presidency of James Garfield there was little deviation from policy. Garfield had been in office four months when he was shot, and when he died two months later a new southern strategy was launched. President Chester Arthur was even more persistent than Hayes in his efforts to attract southern whites into the Republican party. Arthur encouraged dissatisfied whites to leave the Democratic party and form independent political organizations.[2] The president offered federal patronage and the support of local Republicans as an inducement to the dissident Democrats. This strategy failed, as the Democrats retained control of the South. For mountain Republican politicians Arthur's policy did mean a continuation of federal noninvolvement in racial matters. The election of Democrat Grover Cleveland in 1884 insured that the policy would be maintained for four more years.

The two major barriers to Republican success in the mountain counties had been removed. The party no longer could be accused of trying to regulate local racial relationships through federal power. In the mountain counties where there were few blacks the small number of black Republicans encouraged many whites to consider joining the party. The new mountain Republican leadership offered an appealing program of local services that attracted many of these individuals. As the Republican party became the majority party in the highlands, it became the creator and defender of a community identity. The party acted as a shield against the outside world and protected the mountaineers against attacks made on their willingness to violate southern political traditions.

The changes in the Republican party in eastern Tennessee after 1876 were brought about by the persistent efforts of Leonidas Houk. Houk seemed to sense his constituents' need for "home rule" and was able to identify himself as one of the people. He was in every way a typical rural mountain man. In personal appearance he was short and spare, with an expressive face dotted by a small mustache—his only concession to the fashion of the times. His unconcern with dress was described by a sympathetic observer. "The truth is that he is so careless in his attire and so indifferent to his personal appearance that a single new outward garment is an event in Houk's life; the donning of an entire new suit at once marks an epoch."[3] His personal life appears to have been beyond reproach, although there are indications that Houk drank heavily on occasion.[4] Houk's campaign style can most accurately be described as aggressive and abrasive. He attacked people directly on the stump and was often called on to defend himself from physical attack.[5] In a letter in the *Knoxville Whig* in 1866 Houk remarked, "It is not desirable to encumber the columns . . . with the technical denunciations which I defiantly hurled against these political Lepers. I was much more offensive in my oral than in my published remarks."[6] Houk was taught few of the basic social graces and remained to the end of his life an aggressive spokesman for mountain people who were unable to secure formal education and training.

If his crude manner allowed many rural constituents to identify with Houk, then his early life made him even more appealing. Born in isolated Sevier County in 1836, Houk received virtually no formal education as a youth. He tried earning a living as a clergyman, a carpenter, and a teacher, before studying law and passing the bar in 1859.[7] He became locally prominent in Anderson County politics and served as a delegate to both the Knoxville and the Greenville Union conventions in 1861.[8] When the Civil War started, Houk escaped through the mountains to Kentucky and enrolled as a private in the First East Tennessee Infantry Volunteers.[9] He was later promoted to lieutenant and on 5 February 1862 was named colonel of the Third Tennessee Infantry Volunteers.[10] On 17 August 1862, Houk's regiment was surrounded by a much larger Confederate force at London, Kentucky.[11] Facing overwhelming defeat, Houk led his men in a successful retreat, described by Houk himself in the following journal entry: "We were from Sunday till Friday making our way from London to this point. Having ascertained the strength of the enemy to be such as to require extreme caution on our part, we traveled what is known as the Hog Road to within twelve miles of Barboursville, when we took to mountain byways, and after traveling over 100 miles, subsisting on green corn, we reached camp Friday, 2 o'clock."[12] This brutal trip ruined Houk's health, and in April 1863 he was forced to resign his commission and return to civilian life. Despite the brevity of his active military career, Houk later used it to identify himself with the thirty-three thousand Union veterans in eastern Tennessee.

Houk's commitment to the Union cause soon found an outlet in Tennessee political activities. In December 1863 Houk spoke to an eastern Tennessee audience in defense of Lincoln's Emancipation Proclamation.[13] The effectiveness of that address and others led Houk to be chosen as elector of the Lincoln-Johnson Union ticket in 1864. In this capacity Houk spent a number of days in the fall of that year speaking in defense of the Lincoln administration. In January 1865 he was one of the members of the state constitutional convention that not only gave Tennessee a new constitution, but also helped organize the Brownlow government that would dominate the state for the next four years. As a delegate from Anderson County, Houk was a leader in the movement to insure that only "true" Union men were seated at the convention.

Emboldened by his recent political successes, Houk challenged former congressman Horace Maynard for the seat in Tennessee's Second Congressional District. Maynard practiced an entirely different style of politics from that of Houk. Born in Massachusetts in 1814, Maynard had graduated from Amherst College in 1838, moving to Knoxville shortly thereafter. After six years as a professor of mathematics at East Tennessee University, he passed the bar and soon was widely acknowledged as the most brilliant lawyer in the region. He entered politics and was first elected to Congress in 1854. Although a highly effective public speaker, Maynard's scholarly presentations were quite unlike Houk's. A sympathetic observer reported, "As a man . . . he was rather admired and respected than popular, for in manner he was austere and cold."[14] The contrast between the polished and aloof Maynard and the untutored and crudely gregarious Houk could not have been greater.

Maynard's strength was his ability to articulate for his unsophisticated followers their loftiest ambitions. He drew around himself a group of men who appreciated his eloquence and concern for national issues. One of these followers was Jacob M. Thornburgh, son of a prominent Jefferson County attorney, and a minor war hero whose association with Maynard led to his being named district attorney for the Third Judicial District from 1866 to 1871. William Rule, another member of the Maynard circle, was a prominent newspaper publisher in Knoxville. Rule had served with distinction in the army during the Civil War and was a Republican mayor of Knoxville during the Reconstruction period. These men perceived themselves to be "the real Representatives of the intelligence, respectability and honesty of the people of the Second Congressional District of Tennessee."[15]

Maynard's political power lay in Brownlow's control of the Republican organization in Knoxville and Knox County. Aided by federal patronage at the Knoxville post office and the Knoxville custom house, Brownlow had constructed a seemingly unbeatable machine. Although Maynard "could not lead or manage" his own political forces, his national stature and the backing of the Knox County organization maintained him in power.[16] So successful was the Brownlow-Maynard combination that its Republican opposition pinned on it the name of the

Custom House Ring. The only successful way to attack it would be to organize all the sparsely populated rural counties into a well-disciplined opposition.

The special election held in August 1865 was completely issueless, and there seems to have been little personal antagonism between Houk and Maynard. Although Maynard had been nominated by the Unionist party convention, he found that he faced five opponents, including Houk. Houk's slogan was "I am opposed to negroes and rebels voting!"[17] Since this platform was shared by all the other candidates, the election became a matter of personalities. Although he lost, Houk did relatively well. He finished third with 13 percent of the vote. In addition, he won decisively in two of the rural counties, with 51 percent of the Morgan County vote and 55 percent of the ballots in his home county of Anderson.[18] Maynard was easily elected, in large part because of the Custom House Ring's control of populous Knox County. Since only Unionists could vote in the election, it could be regarded as a party primary. In that context, the five anti-Maynard candidates won 45 percent of the vote. Even in the immediate aftermath of the Civil War, Maynard's position as the leader in the Second District was not secure.

Whatever bitterness Houk felt over the election results was completely assuaged in March 1866 when he was elected a state circuit judge.[19] Houk worked in harmony with the Custom House Ring for the next two years, but that relationship came to an abrupt end in 1868. Houk and two other candidates challenged Maynard for the Republican nomination for Congress in the Second District. Houk's appeals appear to have been fairly conventional, and it seems obvious that he was relying on the contacts he had made as judge to win the nomination. His platform included promises to aid Union veterans and a demand that the new congressman not come from Knox County, which had dominated the district for twenty years.[20] He also promised to support the candidate nominated by a "fair convention."[21] Houk received the backing of the only black-owned newspaper in the district and quickly gained control of six delegations in rural counties.[22] The machine rallied its forces, however, and Maynard won several important delegations.

The convention, meeting in early September, was confused from the start. A fight over who was to be the temporary chairman led to a momentary walkout of the Houk forces.[23] A compromise was reached, however, and the balloting began. On the first four ballots Maynard's control of Knox County assured him of 31 convention votes. Houk was second with 22 votes, and he was followed by Peter A. Cooper with 15 and John Williams with 9.[24] On the fifth ballot Williams released his delegates, allowing Maynard to be nominated under what Houk considered suspicious circumstances.[25] Angered by the actions of the convention, Houk announced that he would challenge Maynard as an Independent Republican in the general election.[26] Although Houk won three counties and lost another by only 3 votes, he was slaughtered. Maynard won over 75 percent of the ballots in the district and overwhelmed Houk in Knox County by a vote of 2,943 to 612.[27]

Houk's quarrel with Maynard and the Brownlow wing of the Republican party spilled over into state politics. Houk backed Governor DeWitt Senter against William Stokes and Maynard when the Republicans split in Tennessee in 1869. Houk refused to support efforts to have Congress intervene. When the Democrats regained control of the state, Houk became so disillusioned with the party's leadership in eastern Tennessee that he suggested that the Republican party be disbanded.[28] Houk opposed Maynard's nomination for statewide offices in 1872 and 1874, but his efforts were in vain in both cases. The campaign of 1874 seriously weakened the nationally committed leadership of the party, however. Over the protest of the local leadership wing of the party, Maynard was nominated for governor and the Civil Rights Bill was endorsed.[29] The unpopularity of these maneuvers was confirmed in the fall elections when Maynard was humiliated at the state level and failed to carry eastern Tennessee.

Any satisfaction that Houk derived from the defeat of his chief rival was tempered by another failure on his part to win the congressional nomination in the Second District in 1874. Apparently new district lines concerned Houk in 1872, and he did not challenge the candidate of the Maynard faction, Jacob Thornburgh. Despite all Democratic attempts to manipulate the Second District, it was still Republican and Thornburgh was elected by a small majority. By 1874, Houk was ready for another try at the nomination. Emphasizing local issues and the unfair share of federal patronage that went to Knox County Republicans, Houk began his campaign six months before the district convention assembled.[30] Houk's efforts were not as successful as he expected, and none of his adherents attended the district convention. He then announced that the delegate selection process had been unfair and that he was running as the legal Republican candidate.[31] The machine, feeling threatened, used its last resource to counter Houk's announcement. Senator Brownlow announced that he was entering the Second District race as a candidate to heal the party split.[32] Not wishing to challenge this legendary hero of his mountain followers, Houk withdrew from the race on 7 October.[33] The strategic nature of Brownlow's entry was emphasized when he withdrew the day after Houk did, allowing Thornburgh to win his second term.

As the 1876 congressional elections approached, Houk apparently was ready to challenge the machine again. Maynard had been appointed minister to Turkey, Brownlow was seriously ill, and the regular organization seemed greatly weakened. There were indications that Houk was prepared to run again, and the incumbent Thornburgh braced for the battle.[34] It never came. Apparently Houk reached a patronage agreement with the machine that required him to drop his race for Congress. All opposition to Thornburgh now centered on Oliver P. Temple, who refused to make the race, allowing Thornburgh to win his third term.[35] In the spring of 1877 Houk tried strenuously to be appointed United States district attorney for east Tennessee.[36] Despite widespread support, however, Houk did not receive the appointment.

Houk was ready once again in 1878 when he received some welcome news: Thornburgh was retiring. Although the machine had an available candidate in William Rule, Houk for the first time was not facing an incumbent. He moved rapidly to consolidate his hold on the rural counties and largely succeeded, despite Rule's best efforts.[37] The Knox County convention was still to be the crucial test. The Houk men, finding themselves outnumbered in Knoxville, withdrew from the convention, held their own convention, and named a competing delegation.[38] When the district convention met, neither delegation from Knox county was seated. Rule soon realized that this action left Houk with a majority of the uncontested delegates and control of the convention. He and his followers withdrew, and Houk received the nomination.

After thirteen years of seeking the nomination, Houk's candidacy must have been anticlimatic. Rule fumed for a short time and then officially withdrew from the race. The Democrats, trying to capitalize on the split in the Republican party, declined to name a candidate and instead supported Independent candidate Albert G. Watkins. Despite an extensive joint speaking tour, Houk appeared to make no special effort in the campaign. His judgement was justified when he carried the district by a 2,381-vote majority.[39] Only in the city of Knoxville did Houk do poorly. The results there indicated that the Custom House Ring was waiting for Houk to make a mistake to allow them to defeat him. Although Houk had won, it was obvious that to remain in office he would have to work hard to retain his followers' loyalty.

Houk sought to appeal to his constituents by virtually ignoring issues of national rather than local significance. Two prominent issues, the Blair Education Bill and the Pendleton Civil Service Act, best illustrate Houk's approach to national subjects. In all his surviving correspondence there is only one reference to the Blair Bill. It is a memorandum that determines to the penny what each county in eastern Tennessee would receive in grants under the Blair proposal.[40] This was the only point that interested him, and it was the only one he noted. Houk voted for the Pendleton Act when it passed in the House, but at no time did he indicate any support for the measure in his papers.[41] His letters, instead, suggest a politician who used many of the techniques outlawed by the civil service law. For example, the following excerpt from some political correspondence indicates Houk's willingness to use salary assessments:

> We must control Loudon and Campbell counties. It takes money to run the machine. I have spent all I had—about six hundred dollars. We must have another hundred for Campbell, and two more for Loudon, and we must have it at once.
> And I submit that the *three offices*,—Pension, Revenue, and Post Office—are interested in the matter quite as much as myself.
> The head of either makes more money than I do after deducting expenses. . . . If the money can be raised it should go to Loudon to-night or by the morning train. That to Campbell should go by the morning freight.[42]

This was not the action of a committed reformer.

The only national matter that Houk responded to at all vigorously was the selection of delegates to the Republican national convention. In 1880 Houk backed the third-term candidacy of Ulysses S. Grant. Despite a powerful effort on the part of supporters of James G. Blaine, Houk was able to secure a majority for Grant and was himself one of the 306 delegates to the convention who refused to change their vote for Grant, staying with him from the first ballot to the last.[43] Even this course of action can correctly be interpreted primarily for local considerations. Houk believed that a hostile state party would be a threat to him in the Second District, and he moved to forestall that possibility.

Houk's lack of concern with national issues left him plenty of time to look after the particular needs of his constituents. One major group of rural voters whose support Houk especially wanted was the farmers. The federal government provided the best seed in the country, and each congressman was allowed to distribute some to his constituents. Houk was so zealous in procuring the seeds that the chief clerk in the Department of Agriculture wrote, "By reference to our books we find you have exhausted your entire quota of all seeds standing to your credit."[44] This occurred only halfway through the two-year term! The Second District farmer could be assured that he had a friend in Congress.

Those seeking to settle property claims arising from the destruction and depredations of the Civil War also found a strong supporter in Congressman Houk. Eastern Tennesseans were not reluctant to press their claims against the government. An extreme example of the desire of Houk's constituents to be reimbursed was provided by the inhabitants of Anderson County. The 1860 census evaluated the property in the county at $45,545, but when all the damage claims from the county were added, the sum was $57,860.[45] The claim of $12,000 more damage than property failed to impress the Southern Claims Commission, which approved only one claim from Anderson County.[46] The only alternative left to those disappointed by the commission was to have their congressman introduce a special relief bill for them as individuals. Houk was overwhelmed by requests for special relief bills.[47] He introduced them all and worked hard for them. One of his first major speeches in Congress dealt with the claims of southern loyalists, and this issue became his major concern.[48]

A related constituent concern that occupied much of Houk's time was the question of veterans' benefits. Because of the backlog of pension cases, many Tennesseans' pension claims were seriously delayed. Again, the only solution for most people was the direct intervention of the congressman with a request that their case receive special handling. Houk was especially adroit at this intervention and was soon known as the soldiers' candidate. By 1887, 1,834 of Houk's constituents were receiving pensions giving a total of $220,455.48 in benefits annually.[49]

Houk also worked actively to secure federal assistance for local governments and businesses. In 1880 he was able to secure an appropriation to improve navigation on the French Broad River, which satisfied a significant constituent demand.[50] He helped local companies secure patents and tried to work out a solution for the problem of a discriminating North Carolina tax law.[51] Houk was asked to support a bill calling for a custom house in Chattanooga.[52] The Second District congressman also had a very close working relationship with E. B. Stahlman of the Louisville & Nashville Railroad. Houk consistently supported the L. & N. in Congress, and in return Stahlman "loaned" Houk more than nineteen thousand dollars in small amounts over a period of ten years.[53] While this arrangement certainly was corrupt, it must be said in Houk's defense that he never used the money for personal enrichment. Once again, Houk emerges as the champion of local interests, even if his involvement was tainted.

Racial, national, and religious groups found their new congressman especially concerned about their needs. Houk felt that it was excellent politics to distribute patronage positions to as many groups as possible. Houk's political ally, Postmaster Oliver P. Temple of Knoxville, found positions for Germans, Irishmen, and Negroes.[54] The following excerpt from a letter by Houk to an official in the Army Quartermaster

Corps illustrates his whole approach: "The 'half breeds' have been very much demoralized these 'peculiar people,' in this County where they are strong by the use of Garfields [sic] name, and in order to counteract "the enemy" I desire to give a prominent position to one of their number, and have selected Hon. James F. Beales, as the man. . . . It is all important to me, as my own renomination may turn upon this county."[55] The mixture of self-interest and help for local groups seen in Houk's dealings with business emerged once again. While Houk definitely expected to benefit from his appointments, there was little question that the concerned interest groups felt that the recognition accorded them was significant. Everyone was satisfied.

This contentment with the job that Houk was doing made Republican opposition to him very difficult. When Houk announced his intention of seeking a second term in 1880, he found that only one Republican —Dr. J. Nat. Lyle of Dandridge—entered the primary field. Although Lyle campaigned actively, Houk was never in serious danger.[56] His operatives in the rural areas assured him that he would control their counties as usual.[57] Houk's identification with Union veterans and his diligent efforts to organize at the local level had succeeded in creating an effective party-army structure. His control over the party organizations in the rural counties was complete; Lyle failed to win a single vote at the district nominating convention. The campaign in the fall was equally untroubled, and Houk even managed to carry Knoxville.[58]

Opposition was building, however, from a very predictable source. The old Custom House Ring was systematically being eliminated from leading patronage positions in the Second District. John A. Cooper, collector of internal revenue, was the first to go, and, although Cooper protested to President Hayes, Houk prevailed.[59] All of these forays were a prelude to the major battle over the Knoxville postmastership in 1881. William Rule, Houk's 1878 opponent, had been appointed to the position when Horace Maynard had been named postmaster general late in the Hayes administration. By 11 April 1881, Houk had secured more than nineteen hundred signatures on petitions opposing Rule.[60] In May, Houk used his congressional prerogative to bury the Rule nomination in committee.[61] By October Houk had secured the confirmation of his own candidate for the position, Oliver P. Temple.[62]

The enraged Rule and his followers were now determined to unseat Houk in 1882.[63] Rule, using his position as editor of the *Knoxville Daily Chronicle*, carried on a continuous attack against Houk. The congressman responded by beginning his campaign early. In April, Houk emphasized his strength in the state party organization by securing the position of temporary chairman of the Republican state convention.[64]

Rule began to threaten Houk's hold on black voters, and the congressman reacted by gaining the active support of black leader William Yardley.[65] Houk's quick action apparently preserved his position among the blacks. In July the reports from the rural counties indicated Houk's continued domination. The August district nominating convention was nearly a riot, with practically every delegation challenged by one of the candidates. The outcome was that both Rule and Houk claimed the nomination. Both men ran; the Democrats nominated no one.

Houk moved quickly once again to assure himself strong party support. A week after the convention, the National Republican Congressional Committee recognized Houk as the regular Republican nominee.[66] Despite his protests to the contrary, Rule was branded as a party traitor. Houk carried every county and won by a 14,535- to 8,821-vote margin.[67] Rule managed to carry the city of Knoxville, but the rural voters affirmed their support for Houk's style of politics. Rule recognized the futility of further resistance when he sold the *Knoxville Daily Chronicle* to Houk on 29 November 1882.[68]

Several years later a Republican reformer, John M. Bishop, commented on the change in politics in the Second District. "The grand republican party . . . sprang into existence to alleviate human misery. At its birth were congregated the noblest band of all the Noble men of this country. . . . In the first decade of republicanism we had Donelson, Vicksburgh [sic], Gettysburg and Appomattox—in the second decade— spoils. Then we adored Wendell Phillips, Geritte [sic] Smith, Horace Greely [sic]—now R. R. Butler, L. C. Houk."[69] Bishop was not completely fair to Houk. Houk was indeed a spoilsman who did nothing to raise the level of politics in the Gilded Age. He did, however, fill a need in the political life of Tennessee's Second Congressional District. Eastern Tennessee voters for nearly twenty years had been asked to sacrifice immediate needs for long-range goals. By 1878, these voters wanted a change. Houk offered them an alternative of service to local interests and personal involvement in their individual problems. With increasing enthusiasm, the voters supported Houk and his party-army organization. Until his sudden death in 1891, Houk remained the unchallenged boss of the Republicans in Tennessee's Second District.

Houk's counterpart among West Virginia Republicans was Nathan Goff. Goff was able to assume power more quickly than Houk, but the process was similar in both cases. Goff worked carefully to develop a strong local organization and avoided taking controversial positions on national political issues. Although born in the mountains like Houk, he did not share Houk's lifestyle. His family was wealthy; he was educated at a private academy and spent a year at Georgetown University.[70] Like Houk, however, he did serve in the Union army with distinction, eventually achieving the rank of major. One of his experiences during the war broke the social barrier between Goff and his many rural and poor constituents. Taken prisoner by the Confederates, he suffered greatly at their hands.[71] He described his situation in a letter that became public knowledge, and from it Goff's reputation as a defender of the Union was created. Although Goff was rich and wellborn by mountain standards, the voters appreciated that he had suffered willingly for the cause most mountain Republicans supported completely. No other political leader in the state could boast of a comparable record.

Using a combination of influence with veterans and family connections, Goff entered politics after the war, achieving immediate success. In February 1866 he was chairman of the Committee on Organization of the Soldiers' and Sailors' State League and later that year was selected as a delegate to the organization's national convention.[72] On this base Goff would build his career. Goff exploited it immediately. When his uncle refused renomination to the state legislature in August 1866, Goff became the candidate and won election from the restricted electorate imposed by the Republican state government.[73] Goff was reelected the following year on a platform that was uncompromisingly pro-Union, but his relationship with the old guard in the party must have been somewhat unusual. In June 1868, when most West Virginia Republicans were supporting congressional Reconstruction, Goff was appointed United States district attorney for West Virginia by Andrew Johnson.[74] While the appointment does not appear to have been made to reward Goff for siding with the president politically, the rapidity of his rise in the party did alienate older members of the party's radical wing.[75]

Goff next decided to challenge incumbent Republican congressman Isaac H. Duval for the First District nomination. Duval had supported congressional Reconstruction, thereby alienating conservative Republicans in the West Virginia mountains. Hoping to take advantage of Duval's weakness, Goff and former Union general Thomas M. Harris announced themselves as Republican candidates. Goff campaigned as the friend of the Union veteran and avoided commenting on national issues as much as possible. The convention balloting was close, but on the third ballot Goff won the nomination.[76] He could not overcome the handicap of Republican Reconstruction policies and was defeated in the general election. Widespread opposition to the Fifteenth Amendment allowed the Democrats to win most of the West Virginia elections in 1870. Thus, Goff's failure to win did not weaken him within the party; in fact, he emerged from the elections strengthened. As the state United

States district attorney, Goff was one of the few Republicans in the state in a position to dispense federal jobs. The recently defeated officeholders were more dependent than ever on Goff.[77]

Four years later Goff again was a candidate for the Republican nomination for Congress. As in 1870 the question of federal intervention into local racial matters was the major issue. Goff faced considerable opposition from Republicans who had supported national Republican policies. Despite the efforts of the old leaders, Goff was nominated on the third ballot. The losing candidates accused him of stealing votes at the convention and of being the candidate of the Democratic machine.[78] Clearly, the resistance to Goff's advancement in the Republican party remained unabated. However, Goff simply ignored the criticism from his own party and organized his personal followers into a strong political organization. In the canvass that followed against Democratic incumbent Ben Wilson, Goff spent most of his time appealing to veterans, discussing local issues, and avoiding questions of national implication.[79] Wilson's constant references to the Civil Rights Bill undoubtedly encouraged Goff to follow this course. The strategy seemed to work, for Goff came within 168 votes of defeating Wilson, while other West Virginia Republicans lost by large margins.

Goff's vote-getting ability did not pass unnoticed, and he became the leading candidate for the Republican gubernatorial nomination in 1876. For the first time Goff played out a charade that would mark the rest of his career. Maintaining that he was not interested in the honor, he asked that the party not nominate him.[80] Then his well-organized friends nominated him anyway, and he gave in with the greatest reluctance.[81] This action left some of his opponents quite dissatisfied, but they really could not blame Goff.[82] It was a very successful strategy that prevented serious splits in the party. Goff then canvassed the entire state, going into heavily Democratic counties, and attacked Democratic mismanagement of state government.[83] Although this maneuvering helped Goff run well ahead of the Republican ticket, he still won only 43 percent of the vote.

This campaign served to emphasize the paramount position that Goff had assumed in the party. He was offered the position of solicitor for the Treasury Department by President Rutherford Hayes, but he declined, preferring to remain district attorney and to keep authority over the local organization.[84] His control of patronage and his close relationship with Hayes alienated many old-line Republicans, but they were powerless to attack their new boss.[85] Goff continued to dominate the distribution of patronage in his state and at the state convention in 1880 confirmed his control. The West Virginia delegates to the national convention supported Blaine, as Goff desired, and then endorsed Goff for vice-president.[86]

This action came at the same time that the political situation in West Virginia changed dramatically. A relatively strong protest movement under the aegis of the Greenback party appeared in the state. Victory-hungry Republicans made every effort to organize a joint ticket with the new party.[87] Goff, exploring the possibility, found the third-party men eager to reach some kind of agreement.[88] The result was that the Republican National Committee agreed to help finance this coalition campaign.[89] The party in West Virginia suddenly sprang to life. Speakers were scheduled in all parts of the state and paid for the first time; New York newspapers were distributed free to doubtful voters; the state committee organized local groups throughout the state.[90] As with the Houk machine in eastern Tennessee, Goff and the West Virginia Republicans emphasized the party's commitment to the former Union soldiers.[91] The strong Republican and Greenback party effort reduced the Democratic proportion of the vote to 51 percent. In the northwestern counties the mountain voters gave the Republicans 43 percent of the ballots and the Greenbacks 9 percent.[92] The Republican organization recognized that victory was within their reach if they could absorb the third party.

The opportunity for success in the future rekindled Republican political ambitions, and the party was torn by factional strife for the next two years. Groups dissatisfied with Goff's leadership once again challenged his position. In January 1881 Goff accepted an interim appointment as secretary of the navy. A mad scramble to fill Goff's vacated office resulted, and the contest became quite bitter.[93] The fighting was all in vain because, when James Garfield assumed the presidency, Goff once again became United States district attorney for West Virginia. A second major controversy erupted over who was to be named United States marshal for the state. Goff supported George W. Atkinson, who had helped coordinate the Republican and Greenback campaigns in 1880.[94] The other candidate for the position, George L. Patton, was supported by Pennsylvania business interests.[95] Goff successfully resisted the outside influence and was able to have Atkinson appointed. A number of the party's financial backers were upset by this maneuver and started to organize in opposition to Goff. In addition, some local controversies over postmasterships seemed to be weakening the party.[96]

As the lower part of his organization languished, Goff found himself threatened personally. After the assassination of Garfield and the elevation of Chester Arthur to the presidency, Arthur attempted to eliminate his political enemies from patronage positions. Particularly, he sought to break the hold that Senator James G. Blaine had on some

Republican organizations. Goff and his followers in West Virginia had strongly supported Blaine in both 1876 and 1880 and were thus prime targets of the Arthur purge. The axe fell in June 1882, and Goff found himself out of power.[97] He tried to secure the position he had lost for his closest political ally, John W. Mason, but the administration selected instead a leader of the old-line group, William Flick.[98]

Following the pattern that had marked his career up to this point, Goff's defeat led to his gaining strength in the party. Driven out of appointive offices, Goff and Mason both secured Republican nominations for Congress in West Virginia.[99] The party-army proved powerful enough to resist the patronage assaults of the president and to insure the nomination of its leaders. The Arthur administration continued to attack the two men, however, by refusing to allow West Virginia federal workers in Washington to return home to vote.[100] That action probably cost Mason his congressional seat, since he lost by less than one hundred votes. On the other hand, Goff's campaign went quite smoothly. Black Republicans enthusiastically backed him, and the Greenback party nominee withdrew in his favor.[101] The outcome was the first Republican victory in a West Virginia congressional race in more than a decade. Arthur and the old-line party members could not take this office away from Goff.

Just as Houk did in eastern Tennessee, Goff moved to consolidate his position by looking after local interests. He spent much of his time writing special claims and pension bills to help constituents caught in the federal bureaucracy. When the Ohio River overflowed its banks, causing widespread destruction, Goff worked diligently to obtain federal aid for the victims.[102] He also tried to protect the local federal patronage holders whom he had helped to secure their positions originally. One party worker observed that "the fight is on and that the question must now be settled, whether the young men who sustain the party are to be considered, or crushed by the old fossils [sic]."[103] In general, Goff was successful and was even able to defend the appointment of George Atkinson as United States marshal.

The battle over the national convention delegates in 1884 decisively settled the issue. Goff considered his position so secure that he even tried to get Mason named assistant secretary of the treasury, but, not unexpectedly, Arthur did not appoint him. Arthur continued the battle; just three weeks before the state convention, Collector of Internal Revenue Isaac Duval was forced out of office by political pressure.[104] The Goff organization backed Blaine completely and fought back against the administration. One young Republican was told that "Blaine is the 'Bread Winner' for West Virginia young men."[105] Blaine's popularity and the smooth-working Goff machine produced a 229- to 190-vote victory at the state convention.[106] The old-line Republicans had been decisively defeated, despite the full support of the national administration.

Again like Houk after the 1882 election in Tennessee, Goff was now in complete control in West Virginia. The first critical test came at the Greenback state convention in May. Working through Republican Greenbackers like Romeo Freer, Goff persuaded the convention to support fusion with the Republicans on the gubernatorial nomination and then to nominate Goff's old law partner, Edwin Maxwell.[107] Late in July a Goff-dominated Republican convention also nominated Maxwell and left the Republican boss in complete control of the state campaign.[108] Once again, Goff ostentatiously declined to run for office, but his friends easily had him renominated for Congress.[109] His campaign centered on the role that the protective tariff would play in developing the resources of West Virginia.

Goff's campaign appeals on the tariff issues were encouraged by the active participation of the Republican National Committee in the state campaign. In August the committee promised financial aid, and a representative from the national organization, Stephen B. Elkins, met with West Virginia Republicans.[110] Elkins was particularly interested in securing the labor vote that was growing rapidly in the state.[111] The effective combination of ample money and the efficient Goff machine enabled the party to reach into many areas that had been neglected before. Goff and Maxwell spoke all over the state; in October, when Blaine spent one day in West Virginia, he drew an enthusiastic response.[112] The national committee continued to send money, but the Republicans lost both the state elections held in October[113] and the federal elections in November. Goff, however, was reelected to Congress and had every reason to be satisfied with his position. The opposition to his leadership was disorganized and powerless; his own party-army was functioning smoothly; the Republican share of the vote had risen to 48 percent in 1884. The Republican party in West Virginia was on the verge of victory, and Goff was its master.

The most youthful of all the new Republican leaders was John White of Kentucky. White was only twenty-five years old when elected to Congress in 1874. Although a resident of the mountains of southeastern Kentucky, White did not fit the stereotype of the mountaineer. He was a graduate of the University of Michigan Law School, and surviving pictures and prints of him suggest that he was very aware of fashion and style. He was unlike most mountain politicians in another way as well. A political principle—prohibition of alcohol—was more important to

White than anything, including partisan and personal victory. In many ways White as a person was the complete opposite of a man like Leonidas Houk, but he proved to be nearly as effective a politician.

White faced a far more difficult task of organization than either Goff or Houk. Only three of Kentucky's thirty-four mountain counties were served by railroads in the 1870s, so that the party organization in the region suffered from a serious lack of communication. White's efforts to organize the party were further hampered by a campaign pledge he had made in 1874. At that time, in order to receive the congressional nomination, White had to agree not to run in 1876.[114] This promise meant that White would have no continuity in office and that his patronage power was severely limited. In addition, White had some personal and business problems in 1875 that kept him from becoming too involved in political affairs.[115]

Despite these problems, White followed the pattern established by Goff and Houk. Most of his legislation dealt with the problems faced by veterans of the Union army.[116] His efforts usually involved trying to secure some monetary claim that one of his constituents had against the federal government. White extended his work on behalf of other parts of the highland population as well. He introduced several bills to aid navigation improvements in the rivers of southeastern Kentucky in order to upgrade transportation in the region.[117] Bills designed to help the average voter, such as one that required a money-order post office in each county seat, were part of White's program.[118] All this time, White seems to have made a consistent effort to enhance his position within the state organization and to control patronage in his district.[119]

White's legislative proposals were not limited by these traditional ideas. His introduction of three significant reform measures during his first term made him a unique figure among mountain Republicans of this period. He submitted a bill calling for the national prohibition of the selling of alcoholic beverages.[120] Like his other attempted reforms, this one was not seriously considered. A second area that attracted White's attention was retrenchment and reduction of federal expenditures. His first bill proposed that all government salaries over fifteen hundred dollars be reduced by 20 percent; the second required that Congress be reduced to two hundred members.[121] Neither of these bills received serious consideration, even though they did offer alternatives to high taxes during a period of economic depression.

The result of White's hard work in building the party in his two years in Congress was impressive. In April and May of 1875, he persuaded mountain Republicans to back John Harlan for the Republican gubernatorial nomination.[122] Then White acted as coordinator of Harlan's highly successful campaign in the mountain counties.[123] White's activities were bolstered by a five-thousand-dollar allotment from the state committee in the closing days before the voting.[124] Despite his promise not to run again, White was urged to do so by many mountain Republicans. However, he refused to go back on his pledge;[125] instead, he worked hard to help Benjamin Bristow win control of the Kentucky delegation to the national convention in 1876. When Robert Boyd was nominated for Congress in White's district, the young congressman actively supported Boyd and made speeches in several counties.[126] After Boyd lost, White temporarily retired from politics and took an extended vacation in Europe.

At the same time that White was constructing an organization in the mountains, the leadership of the state party was disintegrating. Benjamin Bristow and John Harlan had worked as a very effective team since the early 1870s, Bristow on the national scene in a succession of offices culminating in his appointment as secretary of the treasury. In that position he received substantial publicity as a reformer and was a candidate for the Republican presidential nomination in 1876. Harlan served as the junior partner in this relationship and was responsible for directing state political activities. During both Harlan's gubernatorial campaign in 1875 and Bristow's presidential candidacy in 1876, the two men retained tight control over the party organization.[127]

This situation changed rapidly as the ambitions of the two men collided in 1877. Before this time considerable tension was already evident within the party. In the spring of 1876, Bristow had fired Kentucky Republican Augustus E. Willson as his chief clerk in the Treasury Department.[128] Since Willson was Harlan's law partner, Bristow's action undoubtedly created some ill feeling between the two men. Further pressure on the party's leadership came when an angry President Grant began to remove all of Bristow's friends from office.[129] Although Hayes's policy was more evenhanded in the spring of 1877, it was clear that Bristow had lost power.[130] At the same time, Harlan was working successfully to ingratiate himself with the new president. Harlan had swung the Kentucky delegation to Hayes at a critical point in 1876 and had served at Hayes's request on the Louisiana Commission that helped end Reconstruction.[131]

A vacancy on the United States Supreme Court precipitated a crisis in the relationship between Harlan and Bristow. At first Bristow was backed for the position by a number of prominent Republicans, including Harlan, who handled the political negotiations between his partner and the president. The opposition of James G. Blaine and Bristow's own coyness, however, led Hayes to look elsewhere.[132] Hoping to placate the Bristow wing of the party, Hayes offered the appointment to Harlan. Bristow felt betrayed by both Harlan and Hayes. Harlan himself recognized his awkward position, but he managed to rationalize it and actively pursued the nomination.[133] Enlisting the support of Kentucky Democrats as well as the Republicans, Harlan overcame Bristow's refusal to endorse him and was confirmed by the Senate.[134] Harlan was now removed from active participation in Kentucky politics. An angry and embittered Bristow moved to New York and also left politics.[135] Their departures set the stage for a struggle within the Kentucky Republican party for the vacated leadership positions.

John White was part of the new leadership that quickly appeared. One of the emerging party chiefs in the Louisville area was Walter Evans, Bristow's former law partner. At the 1879 state convention, Evans was selected as the Republican gubernatorial nominee. William Bradley of Garrard County became the primary spokesman for the party in the Bluegrass region. Weighing well over two hundred pounds, Bradley was an extremely entertaining and effective political speaker.[136] Bradley was the temporary chairman of the 1879 state convention and was nominated for attorney general, but was later forced to withdraw from the race. White was apparently regarded as the most impressive mountain Republican and was elected permanent chairman of the state convention.[137] White ran for the legislature in 1879 and, with the help of Bradley and Evans, was easily elected.[138] Although Evans lost his gubernatorial race, Kentucky politicians once again had a strong and established leadership.

White moved quickly to consolidate his position in the party in the mountain counties. He worked closely with Bradley and Evans to secure the Kentucky delegation to the 1880 Republican National Convention for Grant. In January of that year, White delivered an hour-long speech at a Grant meeting in the state capital.[139] Returning to the mountain counties, he was quite successful in obtaining a large number of Grant delegations.[140] Despite the widespread unfavorable publicity given to the openly partisan activities of White, Bradley, and Evans, Grant received more than 70 percent of the convention vote.[141] This outcome confirmed the position of the new party leaders once again. White's position of power was emphasized by the fact that he was able to cast more than one hundred proxy votes from the mountain region at the convention.[142] He was recreating with great effectiveness the organization that he had built up as a congressman.

In the midst of the campaign to select delegates to the convention, an incident occurred that made White a political hero in his region. On 10 February White attempted to commit a local bill to a state legislative committee, but his motion was not recorded by State House Clerk E. Polk Jackson. White verbally attacked Jackson, and after the session the clerk threatened White and warned him to end his criticism. The next day White related the events to the legislature and demanded to be vindicated. When the House refused to do so, White resigned his seat.[143] Then White returned home to Clay County and requested that his stand be supported. In a special election held in March, White won more than 90 percent of the vote and returned triumphantly to the state legislature.[144]

A cynical observer would be forced to conclude that this incident was only a prelude to White's congressional campaign of that summer and fall. White faced Andrew T. Wood from the Bluegrass county of Montgomery in the Republican primary.[145] Wood never really had a chance in the predominantly mountain Ninth District, and at the district convention White was unanimously nominated.[146] White's campaign against Democrat Tom Turner in the general election was a very quiet one. Because the state organization had almost no money, White had to rely on his party-army to pull him through.[147] His personal popularity and efficient political machine gave him more than 53 percent of the vote and his second term in Congress.[148]

White's congressional career continued to be a mixture of machine politics and reform. Once again veterans' benefits were his leading concern, particularly payment for those men who had served in state forces during the war.[149] He was also able to secure more than three hundred thousand dollars for navigational improvements in southeastern Kentucky rivers.[150] He was able to combine his concern for his constituents and his desire for reform by introducing legislation to supplement state and local funding of education with federal monies.[151] Like the more famous legislation originated by Senator Henry W. Blair of New Hampshire, White's plan proposed to distribute the funds according to the level of illiteracy in a given area.[152] As always, White introduced a prohibition bill that would have limited the use of alcohol to medicinal purposes.[153]

The mountain congressman's program was paying dividends as he gained more power in the party. In 1881 his candidate, George M. Thomas, was appointed United States district attorney for the state despite the protests of Walter Evans and James G. Blaine.[154] In the summer of 1881 White was one of fifteen party leaders who decided not to run a candidate against Democratic state treasurer "Honest Dick" Tate, but to concentrate instead on winning seats in the legislature.[155] Substantial Republican gains in the legislature vindicated this policy.[156] White now corresponded regularly with Republicans throughout the state, and the appointment of many mountain Republicans to office came as a result of his efforts.[157] In December 1881 White was the Republican candidate for the balloting for the United States Senate in the state legislature.[158] That this honor was often reserved for the leading member of the party in the state gave a clear indication of White's preeminence, in the mountain counties at the very least.

The Democrats now tested the strength of the White organization. They redistricted the state, removing White from the Ninth District and placing him in the Tenth District.[159] This classic maneuver, designed to eliminate undesirable incumbent congressmen, forced White to run in a district with a normal Democratic majority. The young political veteran met this challenge with a combination of guile and hard work. He defeated his Republican opponent for the nomination by the simple expedient of having his district committee not hold a district convention. Unable to confront White directly, the man finally withdrew from the contest.[160] White also refused to debate his Democratic opponent, feeling that debates would arouse partisan loyalties and strengthen the Democrats.[161] Then White distributed fifty thousand government documents, rode several hundred miles on horseback, spoke in every county, and directed his party workers in an extremely energetic campaign.[162] He was thus able to retain his seat and win approximately 52 percent of the vote.[163] Like Houk and Goff before him, White had met challenges posed both from within and from outside the party and had emerged as the Republican boss in his mountain section.

The boss of the Republican party in the mountains of North Carolina did not fit the pattern established by Houk, Goff, and White. Dr. John J. Mott was, first of all, not a mountaineer. He lived in the Piedmont county of Iredell and controlled the party in the mountains through his position as collector of internal revenue for western North Carolina. A mysterious figure who rarely emerged from the shadows of political intrigue, Mott managed to survive the upheavals at the end of Reconstruction and rebuilt the party in the early 1880s. Not only did Mott differ from the other bosses by being a survivor of the Reconstruction period, but he also tended to play down the debt the Republican party owed to the Unionists. The reason was obvious. The Unionists were a definite minority in the western counties, and a party that did not try to appeal to former Confederates was doomed to failure. In addition, the large patronage force under Mott's control provided a satisfactory substitute. Thus, although Mott differed in many respects from the other bosses, he was similar in that he was the director of a disciplined political machine. Mott's hold on the party organization was severely challenged at the end of Reconstruction. James G. Ramsay charged Mott with malfeasance and sought to line up support for himself.[164] Mott, fighting back, enlisted considerable support within the party.[165] By November 1874, however, Ramsay's campaign was successful, and Mott was removed from office.[166] Ramsay assumed that his nomination would be quickly acted upon and that Mott's influence would vanish. Eliminating Mott's influence was not that simple, however, for Mott was able to convince President Grant that Ramsay's charges were inaccurate.[167] Ramsay held a temporary appointment, but opposition to his tenure grew rapidly. Complaints by Republicans of interference by Internal Revenue Service workers in politics weakened Ramsay's position. Mott was soon reinstated and once more controlled the party organization in the mountain region.[168]

The fight directed by Ramsay chastened Mott so that during the period between 1877 and 1880 he limited his political involvement. The Internal Revenue Service workers were charged with being so obnoxious to the population that their conduct seriously weakened the party in the mountain counties.[169] Mott reacted to this complaint by restricting the activities of his agents and openly tried to recruit more responsible men.[170] When an official abused his position, Mott investigated and finally fired him.[171] In 1878 this nonpolitical campaign of Mott's carried over to the state committee, which decided not to contest any state offices that year. The Republicans nearly disbanded the party.[172] The only interesting feature of the election was the appearance of the Greenback party and the willingness of many Republicans to support it.[173]

Mott swung back into action in early 1880 in the battle for delegates to the Republican National Convention. Mott backed John Sherman and used all of his considerable power to support the secretary of the treasury. He was able to induce the state Republican committee to dispense with a convention and to elect Sherman supporters as at-large delegates.[174] This action aroused the men behind the attempt of former president Grant to secure a third term. Grant was apparently very popular among the party members, and Grant delegates formed a majority of the delegation.[175] Despite the counterattack of the Grant forces, Mott still retained his popularity in the mountain counties.[176] Mott also tried to secure the position of chairman of the state committee, but the Grant men temporarily blocked his path.

Looking for a new avenue to power, Mott seized on a seemingly nonpartisan vote on the question of prohibition in 1881. When the state committee met in May 1881, Mott was elected chairman in a move designed apparently to heal party wounds.[177] The former party chairman, Tom N. Cooper, then became part of the North Carolina Anti-Prohibition

Executive Committee and asked Mott and the Republicans to join the largely Democratic committee in the campaign.[178] Mott called a meeting of the state committee on such short notice several of his opponents could not attend it, and Mott's suggestion for an antiprohibition campaign was endorsed.[179] There was widespread opposition to Mott's action within the party, many members feeling they had been betrayed.[180] Sensing the unpopularity of his maneuver, Mott tried to justify his action with the following announcement:

Republicans in every township must organize and poll a full vote against this bill as the only means of condemning class legislation and to prevent the creation of a powerful monopoly of druggists, apothecaries and physicians, which is always dangerous in a government like ours, and should be prevented at the outset. When this has been done, Republicans will be ready to aid in regulating the sale of liquor in such manner as will remedy and correct as many abuses growing out of the use of liquor, as can be remedied and corrected by legislation.[181]

If Mott had been candid, a further reason for his opposition to the prohibition amendment would have emerged. Prohibition would have greatly reduced the need for revenue workers and thus seriously weakened Mott's political organization. Realizing this fact, Mott and his men worked vigorously to defeat the proposal.[182]

The election returns produced a resounding victory for Mott and led to an even more involved political alliance. More than two-thirds of the mountain voters voted against prohibition.[183] Mott moved quickly to encourage antiprohibition Democrats to join in a general liberal movement against the Bourbons who dominated the state.[184] To insure little opposition within Republican ranks, Mott sought and secured the support of President Arthur.[185] Mott then resigned as collector of internal revenue, to allow himself more freedom of action. Mott's ally in the antiprohibition campaign, Tom Cooper, was nominated to take his place. Former state chairman Thomas Keogh led the fight against Cooper, claiming that Cooper's appointment would make Mott unchallenged boss of the state organization.[186] Keogh even carried his case to the newspapers in Washington and seemed to have won, when the Senate rejected Cooper in March 1882.[187] Mott did not give up, however, and five weeks later Cooper's nomination was reconsidered and confirmed.[188] As Keogh had feared, Mott was left in complete control of the party organization.

Unchallenged in his own party, Mott now sought to attract many of the dissatisfied Democrats into the Liberal movement. Changing the issue from opposition to prohibition to opposition to the undemocratic county government system, Mott attracted some significant recruits. At the Liberal convention on 7 June, the new party nominated Republican Oliver H. Dockery for congressman-at-large and Liberal Democrat G. N.

Folk for state supreme court judge.[189] A week later, the Republican state convention accepted the Liberal nominations and worked out a fusion agreement that provided that the two parties would cooperate on races for the state legislature.[190] The coalition candidates centered their attack on the county government system, and it soon became obvious that many dissatisfied Democrats were going to support the Fusion candidates.[191]

Despite Mott's careful preparations, mountain Republicans in the Eighth Congressional District revolted against his policy. The district convention refused to nominate a candidate who would work with the coalition.[192] One of the leaders of the anti-Mott group, C. L. Cooke, who was fired from his position in the Internal Revenue Service at Mott's request, ran as an independent candidate.[193] Cooke's candidacy ended quickly when he received a letter from Washington informing him that President Arthur supported Mott's position.[194] In the meantime, Mott had been carefully organizing the Republicans in the state and by the middle of September had an accurate picture of the condition of the party.[195] The coalition candidates ran strong races and nearly unseated the Bourbons. Dockery came within five hundred votes of carrying the state, while popular Liberal Democrat, Tyre York, was elected to Congress from a mountain district.[196] Mott was completely vindicated. The Liberal movement had weakened the Democratic party and was supported by the president; Mott was in complete control of the state Republican organization. Although the Liberal Democrats were somewhat reluctant to join the Republican party formally, Mott knew his position was secure. There was no one in the mountain counties or any other part of the state who could challenge his authority.

The boss of the mountain Republicans in southwestern Virginia was perhaps the most dynamic political figure in the South during the Gilded Age. William Mahone was a master organizer; this talent made him a successful general in the Confederate army, the president of several railroads, and a political leader. An unusual, almost ludicrous, figure, Mahone stood five feet, five inches tall and weighed less than one hundred pounds. He had an unkempt foot-long beard and usually wore a tall hat to give the illusion of greater height. Perhaps because of his physical appearance, Mahone had a single-mindedness and a need to dominate those around him. Yet he appears to have been someone who was a natural leader. His presence, as odd as it was, was usually enough to inspire his followers, and among the rank and file of his partisans he generated great loyalty.

Mahone's relationship to mountain Republicans was not a direct one. Mahone lived in the city of Petersburg in the middle of the state and rarely visited the mountain counties. Instead, Mahone, like Mott, exercised his control through an organization that he directed. While federal patronage was used to hold this machine together, it was much more than a typical Gilded Age political organization. Mahone helped create a successful popular political coalition that overthrew the Conservative party in Virginia and liberalized state government during its four years in power. The mountain Republicans were submerged in this coalition in the late 1870s; when they reappeared in 1884, they had been strengthened and changed. Even the ultimate defeat of Mahone's movement did not diminish his impact on mountain Republicans.

The fact that Mahone was able to capture control of the mountain Republicans and add them to his coalition can be easily understood. For all practical purposes the Republican party had collapsed in Virginia by the mid-1870s, particularly in the counties of the southwest. By 1876 the plight of the party in this region was serious. Its most popular leader was a federal judge who could not help the organization directly. The Democrats in the Ninth District were splitting over the state debt question, yet the Republicans were too weak to take advantage of the situation.[197] The Republican candidate, George T. Egbert, polled only 24 percent of the vote. Egbert lost every county in the district, including Buchanan where he won only 6 of the 317 votes.[198] For all practical purposes, the Republican party did not exist as an effective political organization in the mountains on the southwest.

There was, however, tremendous opposition to the ruling Conservative party in these same counties. The question that split the Conservatives was the controversy over the state debt. Virginia, like most southern states, had an enormous indebtedness as a result of Reconstruction. Unlike most states, however, Virginia, or the Conservative party at least, was determined to repay the debt in full. Because of the unequal tax structure, this decision meant high taxes for the small farmers, including those in the mountains. In return, the Conservative leaders paid the debt first, to the neglect of the schools and other state services. By the time of the local elections of 1875 there was considerable unrest in the mountain counties, and anti-Funder, or antidebt payment, candidates did well.[199] These stirrings did not alert the Funder leaders to the necessity of compromise with the dissidents in their ranks. Instead, they continued to regard public schools as a "luxury" and demanded that the bondholders—many of whom lived in the north and in Europe—receive full payment.[200]

The gubernatorial election of 1877 in Virginia brought organization to this discontent. Mahone was a candidate for the Democratic nomination on a vaguely liberal platform and had substantial support at the state convention. He was not nominated, however, and sought a way to maintain his influence in Virginia politics. Mahone seized upon the antidebt movement as his vehicle.[201] He encouraged independent or Readjuster candidates to challenge regular Conservative party candidates for the party's nominations. In effect, Mahone was building a personal organization within the old party. Mahone's supporters did well throughout the state, and in the mountain counties in the southwestern part of the state they won fourteen of the eighteen legislative elections.[202] This success weakened the Republican party's position as the chief opposition spokesman to the Conservatives. In fact, the Republican candidate in the mountain congressional district won only 4 percent of the vote in 1878.[203] For all practical purposes, the mountain Republican party organization had disappeared in Virginia.

The political situation was perfect for a man with the organizing ability that William Mahone possessed. On 25 February 1879, the Readjuster party was formed at a state convention in Richmond.[204] Mahone and other Readjuster speakers toured the state, concentrating their efforts on the politically unsettled mountain region.[205] As the Readjusters prepared for the legislative elections in the fall of that year, they realized that the Republicans could well play a decisive role in the voting. The Readjusters moved cautiously, for any alliance with the Republicans would mean being branded as the "Negro party." The fierceness of the political battle forced both the Funders and the Readjusters to abandon any hesitation they had had and to appeal openly to the Republicans.[206] The Readjusters' promise to support the public school system seemed to have been the more successful in attracting both black and white Republicans. Mahone's careful planning was rewarded by the Readjusters' sweeping victory in November. The new party won control of both houses of the state legislature and quickly elected Mahone to the United States Senate when the legislature convened. The Readjusters fared even better in the mountain counties than in the rest of the state, winning all but one of the contests in the southwestern part of the state.[207] Significantly, at least two of the successful Readjuster candidates were Republicans, indicating that in this area at least the Republicans were full members of the new party.[208]

During the eighteen months following the election of 1879, national political developments shaped the Readjuster movement. As a local party, the Readjusters faced a serious problem with the presidential election of 1880. After much maneuvering, Mahone endorsed the Democratic candidate, Winfield Hancock, and ran a separate slate of electors. That strategy failed to satisfy most of his followers, and the Readjuster ticket finished a distant third in the voting. Only in the mountain counties, where Readjuster candidates John Paul and Abram Fulkerson were elected to Congress, did the new party do well.[209] The impact of this defeat was mitigated by the situation created when Mahone assumed his Senate seat in the spring of 1881. There were thirty-seven Republican senators, thirty-seven Democratic senators, and two independents, one of whom was Mahone. Since the other independent planned to vote with the Democrats, Mahone's vote would create a tie and the vice-president's vote would allow the Republicans to organize the Senate. In return for his vote, the Republicans offered to make Mahone chairman of the Agriculture Committee. The Readjuster leader accepted. When President James Garfield died in September 1881, the new president, Chester Arthur, gave Mahone complete control over federal patronage in Virginia.[210] The result was a close working relationship between the Republicans and the Readjusters at the national level.

Mahone, at the same time he was negotiating with Republicans at the national level, was in the process of capturing the Republican state party organization. At best, William C. Wickham and the Funders had shaky control of the party, and Wickham had come within eight votes of being deposed at the party's convention in 1880.[211] The first step was taken in February 1881 when Mahone's Republican allies, led by John F. Lewis, were able to delay the Republican gubernatorial nomination until after the Readjusters had met.[212] This delay gave Mahone enough time to perfect his plans. In March the Negro Republicans held a state convention in Mahone's hometown of Petersburg. The blacks endorsed Mahone and the Readjusters, calling on the Republicans to join forces with the Readjusters.[213] Despite a somewhat devisive fight between John Massey and William Cameron for the Readjuster gubernatorial nomination, the Mahone-dominated convention meeting in June offered a major office to the Republicans in return for their support.[214] Lewis, the leading Republican in the state, was selected as the Readjusters' candidate for lieutenant governor. A former United States senator and now chairman of the state committee, Lewis accepted the nomination.

Trying vainly to maintain the Virginia Republican party as an independent organization, Wickham called a meeting of part of the state committee and deposed Lewis from his position of leadership.[215] Lewis called a meeting of the full committee a week later and regained his position. The crucial issue at this meeting was the question of whether a Republican who had joined the Readjusters could still attend the Republican state convention. After a bitter debate, the Readjusters were allowed to go to the convention by a vote of fourteen to thirteen.[216] Although the vote was close, it was sufficient to allow Mahone to complete his plan.

On 10 August the Readjusters dominated the Republican convention and prevented the party from nominating a separate ticket.[217] Wickham and his friends withdrew and called their own meeting, but decided against running a Republican slate of candidates.[218] Instead, Wickham withdrew from the Republican organization altogether—leaving the Readjusters with a twenty-to-seven voting advantage on the state committee—and supported the Funder candidates.[219] Mahone had effectively removed the Republican party as a disruptive influence in Virginia politics. Equally important was the fact that most Readjusters and Republicans endorsed Mahone's course and accepted the biracial nature of the party.[220]

Having gained control of the Republican organization, Mahone was able to concentrate his attention on the 1881 gubernatorial election. Mahone's candidate William Cameron was nominated by the Readjusters to challenge Funder John Daniel for the office. The major problem that the Readjusters faced was the fact that many of their followers were too poor to pay the poll tax. In late September, Mahone requested that his local workers send him information about those Readjusters not qualified to vote.[221] The thoroughness of Mahone's organizational efforts was demonstrated by the representative sample of responses shown in table 9. Clearly, Mahone had to insure that the thousands of poor voters paid their poll taxes. After obtaining this precise information, Mahone sent money to local workers to pay the tax and, if possible, a little more money to encourage the newly qualified voter to vote correctly.

The Readjuster machine worked smoothly throughout the fall of 1881 and brought in an overwhelming victory. Mahone financed the campaign internally by requiring that all federal officeholders contribute at least 10 percent of their annual salary to the party.[222] These people

TABLE 9. Qualified and Not Qualified Readjuster Voters by Race, Selected Virginia Counties, 1881

	White		Black	
	Q	NQ	Q	NQ
Hanover	626	176	675	1168
Fauquier	469	145	475	480
Accomack	488	155	451	686
York	71	16	244	249
Madison	625	92	680	102

SOURCE: C. G. Hedwison to Mahone, 10 Oct. 1881, James D. Brady to Mahone, 13 Oct. 1881, Mahone Papers.

also served as the structure through which Mahone gave his commands for the canvass and election day. Once again the Funder response to Mahone's methods was weak and unimaginative. Thus, Cameron was able to carry the state by more than eleven thousand votes, and once again the Readjusters won control of the state legislature. The mountaineers of the southwestern counties cast 60 percent of their ballots for Cameron and sent a solidly Readjuster delegation to the legislature.[223]

To insure that this victory was not wasted, Mahone extended his dominance to the elected officials. The recently seated legislators agreed to the following pledge: "I hereby pledge myself to stand by the Readjuster party and platform, and to go into caucus with the Readjuster members of the legislature, and vote for all measures, nominees, and candidates to be elected by the legislature that meets in Richmond, as the caucus may agree upon."[224] Since the caucus attempted to distribute favors equitably, the pledge encountered little opposition. On 28 November 1881, the Committee on the Distribution of Patronage was formed by the Readjuster leadership and gave out the state offices on the basis of an equal proportion of offices for each congressional district.[225] For the first time, men from the mountain counties were given positions of authority in the state government. Only two controversies surrounded the patronage. Mahone had to suppress a revolt against his candidate for the United States Senate, Harrison H. Riddleberger,[226] and State Auditor John Massey was replaced when he refused to accept the caucus's recommendations for workers in his office.[227] Massey, in turn, attacked Mahone, saying that the little boss was betraying the principles of the Readjuster movement to satisfy his personal ambition.

The performance of the Readjuster legislature in 1882 and 1883 demonstrated without question that, in part, Massey's charge was not true. The disciplined Readjuster machine fulfilled most of the party's campaign promises and greatly liberalized state government in Virginia. First, through the Riddleberger Debt Bill state debt was scaled down in such a way that the United States Supreme Court refused to hold against the law.[228] Then the Readjusters restructured the tax system, raising the taxes on corporations and railroads and lowering them for farmers. With that revenue made available to the state government, the Readjusters rebuilt the public school system. The facilities for black students were particularly improved and included the first state-supported black college in Virginia. Other significant reforms included improved facilities for the mentally ill, a fairer mechanic's lien law, abolition of the whipping post and the poll tax, and suppression of dueling.[229] Mahone and the Readjusters were trying to modernize Virginia in two years. Initially, the magnitude of the changes stunned the opposition; then it galvanized them into action.

The conservative Republican leadership acted first. In the congressional elections of 1882 William Wickham and his allies attempted to resurrect the regular Republican party. Aiming their appeals at the black voters, the Wickham Republicans nominated a black man, John Dawson, as their candidate for the at-large congressional contest. The Funders attempted to confuse the Readjuster voters further by nominating former Readjuster John Massey as their candidate. Mahone replied by having popular John Wise nominated by the Readjuster convention. Then he forced white Readjusters to allow blacks to occupy prominent positions within the party and even encouraged the blacks to nominate their own candidate in one district.[230] These actions were quite effective, for there were few defections from the Readjusters. Then in September James G. Blaine endorsed Dawson and demanded that Republicans rejoin their own organization.[231] Mahone felt strong enough to ignore Blaine, and his confidence was vindicated when Dawson won only five thousand votes in the statewide contest. Wise was elected in a close race with Massey. The mountain counties were once again the stronghold of Mahone's coalition, and Wise won more than 60 percent of the vote there.[232]

Finally convinced of the durability of Mahone's coalition, his opposition tried its most dependable strategy to defeat the Readjusters. James Barbour became the party boss of the renamed Democratic party and planned a campaign designed to exploit the racial prejudices of the poor white members of the Readjuster coalition. William Royall, an extreme Funder, took a case to the United States Supreme Court in an attempt to have the state's miscegenation law declared unconstitutional. Royall hoped to be able to claim that the Readjusters favored mixed marriages. However, the court dismissed the case, and this avenue was closed to the Democrats.[233] Barbour finally decided to accept the Readjuster debt settlement and thus effectively eliminated the one issue that defined the two parties. The results of the local elections in the spring of 1883 showed continued Readjuster strength, indicating that the Democrats still had not convinced white voters. Most disturbing for Barbour was the fact that the Readjusters in the mountain counties had remained firm.[234]

Barbour and the Democrats redoubled their efforts and limited their campaign to the single issue of racism. Concentrating their work in the mountain counties of the southwest, they were rewarded by signs of disorganization in Readjuster ranks.[235] There is also a great deal of evidence to indicate that the Democrats were well financed and expected to use money to buy votes.[236] On 1 November Barbour unleashed the final weapon in his arsenal. Democrats began to distribute tens of thousands of the notorious political broadside, "Coalition Rule in Danville."[237] The pamphlet charged that blacks dominated the city council, the police department, and the city market in the south Virginia town of Danville.[238] This "Danville Circular," as it was called, pleaded with mountain voters, "We appeal to you by the sympathy which constitutes the bond of union between honorable men struggling in the cause of freedom, to help us throttle this viper of *Negroism* that is stinging us to madness and to death, *by voting against the Coalition-Radical candidates.*"[239] Racial tension reached a dangerous level throughout the state in the next few days.

On 3 November a major race riot erupted in Danville. The Democrats immediately seized on the situation and began sending thousands more documents into the southwestern counties.[240] Readjuster Governor William Cameron sent the state militia to Danville, but the damage had been done.[241] The Democrats now had a concrete example of what race relations were like under the Readjusters. The most complete study of the riot concluded that the Democrats may well have planned the violent outbreak. Shotguns loaded and stacked in a white bar where the riot took place and the fact the whites fired disciplined volleys indicated that considerable planning had occurred before the events took place.[242] Although there is no way directly to implicate Barbour and the Democratic leadership, it can be said that they certainly took advantage of the situation after it happened.

Barbour's strategy was successful throughout the state, particularly in the mountain counties. In the southwestern highlands the Readjuster share of the vote declined from over 60 percent to 48 percent. Some mountain political leaders wrote to Mahone and reported that they had been unable to hold their followers in line.[243] Others reported that voters in their area stood firm[244] This conflict can be settled by an inspection of the election returns, which reveals that in fact the Readjuster total vote did increase from 15,170 in the mountain counties in 1882 to 20,749 in 1883.[245] Thus, the Democratic victory was not caused so much by Readjuster desertions as it was by the Democratic party's ability to attract the voters recently enfranchised by the abolition of the poll tax. These new voters had no strong partisan attachments and were enticed by Barbour's racist appeals.[246] Rather than the mountain Readjusters, it was this peripheral voter, ironically enfranchised by Mahone's reforms, who destroyed the coalition majority in the mountain region.

The victorious Democrats moved swiftly to consolidate their success. United by a fear of what Mahone could accomplish if any divisions appeared in their ranks, the Democrats passed two pieces of legislation that virtually guaranteed their control of state government. First, they redistricted the state to insure a majority of safe Democratic seats.[247] Then the Democrats passed the Anderson-McCormick Act to regulate elections. Local election officials were to be appointed by the state and were given wide latitude in reporting and recording election returns.[248] These powers were often abused and constituted the real bulwark against defeat for the Democrats.

Mahone recognized that he needed outside help, and he moved quickly to secure it. At the state convention in April 1884, the Readjusters joined the Republican party and Mahone claimed to be the state chairman.[249] His claims were disputed by Wickham and the Funder Republicans, the controversy being complicated by the battle for the Republican presidential nomination. Mahone backed Arthur, while Wickham supported James G. Blaine. The Blaine men also held a state convention, which was poorly attended, and nominated a set of delegates to contest the seats claimed by the former Readjusters.[250] At the national convention the Mahone delegates found the Blaine forces in ascendancy, but they stated their case in terms that even their opposition could not ignore. "We speak for 127,000 voters—87,000 colored citizens and 40,000 of the best and truest white sons of Virginia, for two United States Senators, for six members of the House of Representatives, and for the executive and other branches of the State government."[251] The Readjuster argument was unanswerable, and they were recognized as the regular party organization in Virginia. Despite the Readjuster victory, Blaine was nominated, an event that complicated things for Mahone.

Mahone's dictatorial methods, which were acceptable to most Readjusters while they were winning elections, now became an irritant. Governor William Cameron revolted against a congressional nomination made in his own district and vigorously denounced Mahone for interfering.[252] Republicans in the mountain counties also acted independently. They refused to nominate incumbent Readjuster congressman Henry Bowen, who was a wretched campaigner, and instead selected Republican David Bailey as their candidate.[253] Bailey followed the lead of the Blaine campaign and centered his canvass around the tariff issue.[254] The clear identification of Bailey with the national campaign meant that mountain voters would be called on to vote for a serious Republican for the first time in a decade. No one was sure whether the former Democrats in the Readjuster coalition would follow Mahone and the party leadership into the new party.

The election returns in Virginia were watched closely in 1884 to determine how many voters would be lost to the party by affiliating with the Republicans. After the election was over, the answer was clear: very few. In the mountain counties the Republican vote was 47 percent of the total, which represented a loss of only 1 percent from 1883. Apparently, 1883 was the pivotal election. Those who withstood the racist onslaught in that year seemed to have no qualms about changing the party label. Two decades after the Civil War, white mountain Republican voters were a significant factor in Virginia politics for the first time. Because of their experiences during the Readjuster period, there was little chance that they would desert the party in the future. Despite the brief revolt in 1884, Mahone retained control over the party in the mountains and must be regarded, much like Houk or Goff, as the boss of the local organizations. Thus, by 1884 the mountain Republicans of southwest Virginia had reached about the same level of development as those in the four other mountain regions.

The position of the mountain Republican parties had improved dramatically between 1876 and 1884, largely because of the disciplined party-army machines. Under the leadership of shrewd bosses, these parties deployed party workers at election time to insure that all Republicans voted. The mountain Republicans also attracted new voters by shaping their platform to reflect the parochial interests of their constituents. Union army veterans, farmers, small businessmen, and patronage seekers were all satisfied by the Republican machines. In North Carolina and Virginia the party embraced popular state issues as well. The combination of local appeal and strong organization made the Republicans the majority party in the highland region.

However, a potential problem for both the leaders and the constituents of the party-army was obscured by this success. As the mountain Republicans became more concerned about local problems, men both inside and outside the mountains wanted to exploit the region's resources more completely. As the highland transportation and communication systems improved in the 1880s, these businessmen came to play more important roles in mountain life. They not only dominated the local economies, but soon challenged the bosses for control of the mountain Republican organizations in each state. The party-army leaders fought off their new rivals by trying to continue serving immediate constituent needs and emphasizing the mountain voters' pride in their Civil War heritage. The bosses' efforts were geared to defending community values rather than confronting changing conditions. Electoral victories had convinced them that their strategy did not need to be revised. Unfortunately for the mountain people, this failure of the political leaders to provide the transition to the new era helped to create the later tragedy of Appalachia.

None of these consequences was visible in 1884, however. Houk, Goff, White, Mott, and Mahone had only recently established their power and were looking for means to perpetuate themselves. For the remainder of the decade they were, to a large extent, successful. The Republican proportion of the mountain vote increased, despite the fact that the Democrats distributed federal patronage between 1885 and 1889. The fiscal conservatism and undemocratic party structure of the Democrats contributed greatly to continued Republican growth. Thus, Republicans found no incentive to rethink their own policies.

CHAPTER 6

THE PARTY-ARMY IN CONTROL

The strong mountain Republican local organizations continued to help the party grow for the remainder of the 1880s. Building on that firm foundation, the Republicans attracted increasing numbers of voters between 1884 and 1889. In both 1886 and 1888 the Republicans seriously challenged Democratic control in several states and won a majority of the vote in the mountain counties. At the same time, the rigid party structure was developing tensions among mountain men. Those men motivated by ambition or principle that opposed their local leader found themselves isolated from the sources of power. Success, like defeat, brought stresses that would test the strength of the party-army machines.

The irony of the situation was that the bosses had to function in this period without the benefit of their chief instrument of power. In the presidential election of 1884 Democrat Grover Cleveland was elected, and Republicans lost control of federal patronage. Since the Democrats also controlled the state government in all five states of the upper South, the Republican machines were left without any means to reward political workers. Under these circumstances, the general expectation was that the discipline of the organizations would break down and factionalism become rampant. Although this disintegration did occur in some cases, the general picture was one of continued loyalty to the boss and his machine. Mountain Republicans did not dwell on this point at length, and so any attempt to explain the continued loyalty cannot claim to be complete. One reason appears to be that mountain Republicans really did perceive their party as an army and that they were most reluctant to desert it in a time of trouble. There are also indications that the promise of future patronage is almost as effective in holding men to a party as patronage itself. Finally, the mountain Republicans remained loyal because they were winning. This last point was probably the most critical; as long as there was an opportunity for a Republican victory, party discipline could be enforced.

As table 10 demonstrates, Republicans in the upper South had every reason to be optimistic about the future in 1884. The pattern of steady Republican growth in the mountain counties and in all of the upper South was clear. The desperate situation of the party in 1876 had been rectified in 1880 by Republican unity and Democratic disunity. By 1884 the Republicans apparently had absorbed most of the Independent Democrats of four years before, and for the first time since Reconstruction, the party had a majority in the mountain counties. It was undoubtedly this pattern of constant growth that encouraged Republicans to remain loyal to their organizations.

The Republicans were strongest in eastern Tennessee. In 1884 the party had carried thirty of thirty-five mountain counties, winning 61 percent of the vote. Leonidas Houk, as the congressman from the Second District, remained in complete control of the situation. When an associate expressed concern over some opposition, Houk replied, "If the men you mention had all the news-papers in East Tennessee they could not run the politics of this District. There is no occasion for alarm on that score."[1] Houk was correct; he was unopposed for renomination. He even survived the failure of the party newspaper and personal financial failure without suffering politically.[2] Houk's strength in the state party came in part from the disunity of other prominent Republican leaders. In the First District four men—all of whom would be elected to Congress—contested for the Republican nomination. R. R. Butler, Alfred A. Taylor,

TABLE 10. Popular Vote and Percentage of Total Vote, Presidential Elections, 1876, 1880, 1884

| | All Counties | | | Mountain Counties | |
Democrat	Republican	Other	Democrat	Republican	Other
	1876			1876	
614,505	432,761	4,097	137,510	108,834	1,406
58.45%	41.16%	0.39%	55.50%	43.93%	0.57%
	1880			1880	
556,487	460,304	59,424	127,081	125,589	19,212
51.71%	42.77%	5.52%	46.74%	46.19%	7.07%
	1884			1884	
642,497	569,753	7,854	153,836	168,052	2,352
52.66%	46.70%	0.64%	47.44%	51.38%	0.73%

SOURCE: ICPR Election Data.

Augustus E. Pettibone, and Walter P. Brownlow were all so busy fighting each other that none of them could challenge Houk's leadership. In 1886 Butler was nominated in a bitterly fought campaign, and two years later Alf Taylor secured the victory in a Republican primary election that was marked by considerable recrimination.[3]

Houk's position was briefly threatened in 1887 by the intrusion of a referendum on prohibition. As noted earlier, Houk tried to avoid taking strong stands on issues unless absolutely necessary. His reluctance was especially evident in matters of a personal nature, and the congressman felt that drinking fell into this category. His own habits indicate that, although he went on an occasional binge, he was probably a moderate drinker.[4] To the leaders of the prohibition forces, however, Houk was a primary target. Houk felt it necessary to support the amendment favoring prohibition and denied that he "favored the use of strong drink as a beverage."[5] His statement seemed politically necessary, since many prohibition leaders were openly supporting Houk's campaign manager Henry R. Gibson because of Gibson's effective prohibition work.[6] Although the prohibition amendment lost at the state level, Houk's caution on the subject proved wise, for 57 percent of the mountain voters supported the amendment.[7] Any further threat that the prohibition campaign might have posed was removed when Gibson announced that he would not be a candidate for Congress in 1888.[8]

Houk's control of the party organization in the Second District was completed in 1888. The only real opposition left was centered around his old rival, William Rule. Even Rule did not seem to be much of a threat; a precinct worker in Loudon County reported that in a recent poll of voters Houk was favored over Rule seventy-two to eight.[9] At the county conventions held in early 1888 the Houk forces were in firm control.[10] Houk was renominated in May without any opposition. In July the last vestige of Republican opposition to the mountain congressman disappeared when William Rule spoke in support of Houk's candidacy.[11] The campaign now became more of a triumphal march than a political battle. The voters of the Second District confirmed the verdict; Houk carried 160 out of 168 precincts in the general election.[12] Thus the party-army was a successful vehicle not only for the party in east Tennessee, but also for the political ambition of a single man.

Nathan Goff, like Houk in Tennessee, kept firm control on the increasingly successful Republican organization in West Virginia. He was aided by a substantial family inheritance that he received in 1885, which meant that he no longer had to be concerned about his personal finances.[13] Goff's strong position in the party was illustrated by his continued success in playing hard to get. In 1886, when Goff announced he would not seek reelection to Congress, B. B. Dovener seemed assured of the Republican nomination. Then at the last moment Goff reentered the race, was unanimously nominated, and was elected again.[14] Two years later Goff resisted early efforts to nominate him for governor, and the uncertainty of the situation made it difficult for other Republican candidates to secure delegates to the state convention. Again at the last moment, Goff was drafted by the convention and became the party's gubernatorial candidate.[15] This tactic worked so long as Goff was the man who provided the party with some money and was the party's leading vote getter.

Goff was so secure that he was able to maintain his position despite the appearance of a formidable Republican rival. Stephen B. Elkins had long been a power in national Republican politics and now was looking for a base from which to launch a career in the United States Senate.[16] West Virginia—the home of his father-in-law, former Democratic senator Henry G. Davis—was Elkins's choice of his new political home. In February 1888, Elkins was introduced to the state at the Wheeling Boom Convention, where he pledged to help further the economic development of the state.[17] He also purchased a large share of the stock of the *Wheeling Intelligencer*, the leading Republican newspaper in West Virginia, which promptly published Elkins's Wheeling speech in five languages.[18] By October Elkins was working actively to aid Goff's gubernatorial campaign, although his speeches apparently were not too warmly received.[19] The election results were quite close, and Goff became involved in a long contest for control of the governor's office.

The ambitions of the two men could not be so easily contained, however. The West Virginia elections of 1888 reduced the Democratic majority in the state legislature to one vote and created the possibility that the Republicans could elect a United States senator.[20] Both Goff and Elkins sought the Republican caucus nomination despite the probability that the Democrats would unite behind one candidate and elect him. Trying to avoid an open break in the party, Goff and Elkins met on 5 December 1888 to resolve the impasse. Elkins gracefully acknowledged Goff's claim as the leading Republican in the state and withdrew from further consideration.[21] The maneuver by Elkins was a shrewd one. Goff had little chance of being elected, and if he did accept the Senate seat, he would have to abandon the contested gubernatorial election and disappoint all the Republicans who expected to receive state patronage positions. In fact, Goff lost the senatorial election and was unseated as governor by the Democratic legislature. Elkins had been successful in every way. Goff had not secured a major political victory, and, in addition, the party-army boss was now indebted to Elkins. Goff was still recognized as the leader of West Virginia Republicans, but he knew that he would be challenged at the first sign of weakness.

The bosses in the other three states faced even greater problems than did Goff. The pressure to conform to the dictates of the party machine irritated many mountain Republicans. John J. Mott managed to stay on top in western North Carolina, but he had to deal with a serious revolt against his leadership in 1886. Mott and the state executive committee refused to call a state convention in the summer of that year to nominate a state judicial ticket.[22] Mott's reasoning was that, although many Democrats were dissatisfied, they would not break away from the party if the Republicans continued to organize the black vote.[23] Led by J. C. L. Harris and Thomas Keogh, many Republicans refused to accept the committee's action and called for a state convention in September.[24] The focus of the battle soon became control of the party organization. The convention met and, although poorly attended and organized, nominated a state ticket. The convention also named a new executive committee to replace Mott and his friends.[25] The battle within Republican ranks continued until election day, with Mott announcing in October that he would not support the Republican ticket.[26]

The feud went on after the voting, but pressure from national leaders reunited the party in time for the 1888 presidential election. The election results generally supported Mott's strategy; many Independent Democrats were elected and the Republican state ticket suffered a resounding defeat. Harris and others opposed to Mott refused to acknowledge his wisdom, however, and North Carolina Republicans were still deeply divided throughout the year after the election. Finally, in December 1887, Mott called a reconciliation meeting.[27] Because the party had to present a united front at the Republican national convention, a compromise was worked out that left Mott in control once again.[28] The apparent harmony in the party was rewarded when the Republican National Committee sent financial and organizational aid to the local party.[29] With this help the western North Carolina mountain Republicans elected Hamilton G. Ewart to Congress—the first regular Republican elected from the region since Reconstruction. Ewart then worked with Mott to assume control of the party organization and to distribute the federal patronage.[30] Mott had survived and was once again the boss, but he must have recognized that his position was extremely insecure.

William Mahone's leadership in the Virginia Republican party also faced widespread opposition, although, significantly, very little of it came from mountain Republicans. As Virginia Republicans prepared for the gubernatorial election of 1885, resistance to Mahone's leadership organized. Governor William Cameron and Senator Harrison Riddleberger, along with former congressman James Brady, led the movement.[31] While some mountain Republicans joined the revolt, the vast majority seemed content with Mahone's control of the party organization.[32] The pressures of the campaign soon forced the rebels to reunite with Mahone and to support the candidacy of John Wise.[33] As in 1883, the Democrats directed their campaign at the white voters in the mountain counties. Their nominee, Fitzhugh Lee, toured the region on horseback and emphasized his allegiance to traditional southern values.[34] This tactic prompted many businessmen in the mountain counties to swing their support to the Readjusters and Wise.[35] The election results showed a few Republican losses in the region, but generally the organization remained intact.

The congressional elections of 1886 saw relative unity return to Republican ranks, and the result was an important victory. James Brady did attack Mahone for not allowing him to secure a congressional nomination, but no general revolt against the boss's authority followed.[36] Instead, Mahone seemed to grant local officials a little more autonomy, and harmony prevailed. The mountain Republicans emphasized the poor economic conditions under the Democratic administration.[37] This effective appeal, along with a continuing strong organization, gave the Republicans a majority of the mountain votes. In fact, the Republicans secured a majority of the vote throughout the state and won six of the state's ten congressional seats.[38]

The stunning Republican victory in Virginia did not, however, quiet opposition to Mahone's leadership. The local elections in 1887 would choose the legislature that would select a United States senator. Both Riddleberger and Mahone sought the support of Republican candidates, and their political controversy degenerated into a personal one. In September Mahone brought suit against Riddleberger to recover some money.[39] Riddleberger organized a small anti-Mahone convention that generated some publicity but did not deflect the energy behind the Republican campaign.[40] Mahone's authority was not seriously challenged by other Republicans, since he was able to raise a considerable campaign fund among northern Republicans to defray the party's election costs.[41] Mountain Republicans being particularly well organized, the Republicans won about half of the votes cast in the region and in the state.[42] However, a clever Democratic gerrymander of the state's legislative districts insured a Republican defeat, which only heightened tensions in the minority party.

The accumulating grievances against Mahone's ironhanded rule finally exploded in two major revolts that tore the party apart in 1888. The first was led by John Wise, who challenged Mahone's right to name

Virginia's national convention delegation. Mahone had traditionally had all of the delegation named at the state convention, but the national committee demanded that district conventions name the bulk of the delegates.[43] Although Mahone appealed to the committee to allow use of the old method, his request was turned down.[44] John Sherman—whom Mahone was supporting—cautioned Mahone not to weaken his position, but to accept the committee's ruling.[45] When Mahone refused, John Wise called on Republicans to repudiate their boss.[46] Although mountain Republicans were still Mahone's strongest supporters in the state and sent loyal delegations to the state convention, some of them joined the anti-Mahone delegates who walked out of the state meeting and organized district conventions throughout the state.[47] At the national convention many of Wise's district delegates were seated instead of Mahone's.[48] Significantly, the Mahone mountain delegates were seated, indicating once again that the Republican leaders in that section backed Mahone.[49] The split continued after the convention, and only the intervention of the national committee, which still recognized Mahone as state leader, ended the dispute.[50] Despite all the controversy, the mountain Republicans were very well organized and once again won about half of the vote in the fall election.[51]

The second rebellion was perhaps more important, but had even less impact on mountain Republicans. John Mercer Langston, an articulate, well-educated, and self-assured Negro, defied Mahone and ran for Congress in Virginia's Fourth District. Mahone worked effectively with black politicians when they remained in subordinate positions, but he was outraged by Langston's candidacy, fearing that it would arouse racial tensions like those in the 1883 campaign.[52] Mahone used every trick he knew to defeat his opponent, including having Frederick Douglass write a letter denouncing Langston.[53] None of his ploys worked, for Langston swept through the primary conventions in the predominantly black district and received the party's nomination in September.[54] Hoping to weaken Langston's candidacy, Mahone then ran a white Republican.[55] On election day in Mahone's hometown of Petersburg, blatantly fraudulent activities were directed at Langston's voters, and the black candidate lost the election to his Democratic opponent.[56] Langston was not daunted, appealed the election results to the House of Representatives, and was eventually seated. Mountain Republicans seemed to have sided completely with Mahone in this controversy and supported his efforts to prevent Langston from running.

The gubernatorial election of 1889 saw the continuation of the attack on Mahone's leadership of the party. The opposition, now led by James Brady and V. D. Groner, enlisted the support of the Harrison administration against Mahone.[57] Harrison tried to remain neutral, but he did appoint Brady to the powerful position of collector of internal revenue and Groner as head of the Norfolk navy yard.[58] While both men agreed to recognize Mahone as party leader, their actions indicated that they would continue to fight the little boss.[59] In fact, in August Mahone was unanimously nominated by the state convention, yet immediately a large anti-Mahone movement developed within the party.[60] In early October these men held a state convention, and, despite the efforts of the Republican National Committee, the break in Republican ranks was never healed.[61] Mahone was decisively defeated by Democrat Phillip McKinney, but once again mountain Republicans remained largely unaffected. They managed to maintain party unity during the factional fighting and gave Mahone relatively strong backing at the polls.[62] Thus, through all of the fighting within the Virginia Republican party, Mahone remained the party boss in the mountain counties.

Events in southeastern Kentucky, however, demonstrated that the local boss still had to respect local opinion. There the Republicans did win impressively in the mountain counties in 1884, gaining a majority of the votes in twenty-five of the thirty-six counties. The party's proportion of the vote rose to 53 percent, which represented the Republicans' strongest showing ever in this region.[63] At the same time, John White was forced out as the Republican leader in the mountain counties. White abandoned his position as spokesman for the mountain people and became an advocate of government control of alcoholic beverages. Since many mountain men considered drinking a basic right, White's stand was very unpopular. In addition, many highland Republican politicians were employees of the Internal Revenue Service and would have lost their positions if White's proposal were adopted. The resulting loss of local support temporarily ended White's political career. Despite the absence of centralized leadership, the party organization retained its discipline and the Republicans continued to gain adherents in the mountain counties.

White's fall from power resulted from personal decisions as well as political factors. He declined to run for reelection to Congress in 1884 and shortly thereafter moved to Louisville. One reason appears to have been his marriage in April 1883 to the daughter of a former Massachusetts congressman. The size and style of the Washington wedding indicated that White's bride was socially conscious and sophisticated.[64] The prospect of living in an isolated mountain hamlet of less than a thousand people must have appalled her, an attitude that undoubtedly encouraged White to leave the mountains. In addition, White apparently was embroiled in several personal controversies in the House that demanded that he constantly be on the defensive.[65] This situation must have made his life as a legislator difficult and made the decision not to run in 1884 much easier.

Equally important, however, was the fact that White found himself increasingly out of favor in the party. At the Republican gubernatorial convention in 1883, White threatened to repudiate the nominee unless the party adopted a temperance plank in the platform.[66] This stand alienated many of his former supporters. White continued his attack on alcoholic beverages and in the spring of 1884 came out in opposition to Arthur's nomination for president because Arthur's Kentucky supporters worked in the Internal Revenue Service collecting liquor taxes.[67] White was not alone in his opposition to the Arthur forces, but the extreme stand he took made alliances difficult to form.[68] At the state convention White addressed the delegates for more than two hours, demanding statewide prohibition and the seating of anti-Arthur delegates.[69] White's motions were easily defeated, and the election of delegates to the national convention that followed showed how deeply White had alienated members of the party. In the balloting Walter Evans, White's former ally and now the leader of the Arthur forces, received 718 votes, while White polled only 50.[70] One day after this crushing defeat White announced that he was leaving politics and moving to Louisville.[71]

Nevertheless, White remained on the edge of politics for the rest of the decade and did not cut himself off from mountain voters. He started a law practice in Louisville and became involved in real estate there.[72] Although records of his transactions have not survived, it appears that White prospered in his new ventures. This success allowed him to inject himself into the political situation at his leisure. In 1885, when the Republicans refused to nominate a candidate for state treasurer, White actively supported Prohibition party nominee Fountain Fox.[73] White's political activities became so numerous in 1886 that he twice had to deny that he planned to return to the mountains and run for Congress.[74] In 1887 he made a brief attempt to secure the Republican gubernatorial nomination before retiring to his law firm again.[75] Although White's political involvement was sharply curtailed in this period, he did manage to keep his name before the voters.

No one man was able to retain all the power that White had collected in the mountain counties, but one Republican did emerge as the leading figure in the region—party workhorse, H. Franklin Finley. Finley had become something of a martyr among mountain Republicans when he lost his patronage position to a lowland politician in 1878.[76] This image was further strengthened when, just before the election of 1880, his Democratic opponent circulated a forged letter attacking him.[77]

Despite this unfair campaign tactic, Finley was elected judge of a state judicial district. In June 1885 Finley announced that he would not hold court in several mountain counties unless the state militia provided him protection.[78] His stand was vindicated six weeks later by a serious outbreak of racial conflict in the town of Salyersville.[79]

The Democratic legislature in Kentucky also created circumstances that strengthened Finley's position in the Republican party. After White's victory in 1880, the legislature redistricted the state. Recognizing the growing Republican strength in the mountain counties, the Democrats created the Eleventh District and placed as many of the Republican voters as possible there, in an effort to weaken the Republicans in other parts of the state. The Republican congressional candidate in the Eleventh District of Kentucky, therefore, was virtually assured election. Finley won the congressional nomination in the district in both 1886 and 1888 and each time was easily elected.[80] The apparent security of his position and his long service to the party made Frank Finley the leading Republican in southeastern Kentucky after John White withdrew from active political participation.

The essential unity of the party-armies remained, despite the battles for party leadership, and the Republicans continued to gain votes in 1886 and 1888. In 1886 Republicans elected eleven congressmen from the five states of the upper South, including six from mountain congressional districts. That same year North Carolina Republicans, working with independents, captured control of the lower house of the state legislature. In Virginia Republican congressional candidates won a majority of the vote in the state. William O. Bradley, the Republican candidate for governor of Kentucky in 1887, reduced the normal Democratic victory margin of more than forty thousand votes to about seventeen thousand. Table 11 shows that Republican gains continued in the presidential election of 1888. The party, particularly in the mountain counties, exhibited growing strength. In 1888 Republicans elected twelve congressmen from these five states, including eight from districts in mountain regions. Overshadowing all of the accomplishments, however, was the election of Nathan Goff as governor of West Virginia. The desperate West Virginia Democrats contested Goff's election, and the Democratic legislature named Goff's opponent the winner. All these machinations could not hide the basic fact that, more than a decade and a half after the Republicans had lost power in West Virginia, they had elected a governor.

These victories were achieved by a combination of Democratic obtuseness and Republican responsiveness and organization. The Democratic party of the South was an alliance of a number of competing elements held together by the single issue of race.[81] In the period be-

TABLE 11. Popular Vote and Percentage of Total Vote, Presidential Elections, 1884 and 1888

	1884 Dem.	1884 Rep.	1884 O.	1888 Dem.	1888 Rep.	1888 O.
All Counties	642,497	569,752	7,845	721,085	657,509	18,690
	52.66%	46.70%	0.64%	51.61%	47.06%	1.34%
Mountain Counties	153,836	168,052	2,352	174,995	210,078	3,894
	47.44%	51.83%	0.73%	44.99%	54.01%	1.00%

SOURCE: ICPR Election Data.

tween 1870 and 1890 the Democrats of the upper South offered no program and made no real effort to develop a comprehensive platform. Their standard reply to Republican programs of improved education and government-assisted economic development was that these programs would raise taxes and might aid blacks. Democratic leaders also maintained tight control over their organization, forcing their increasingly dissatisfied followers to conform. The result was a continuing defection of white Democrats to the Republican party during the 1880s.

The events that took place in western North Carolina in the 1886 and 1888 elections provide an excellent example of this process. The Democrats had created a completely undemocratic county government system at the end of Reconstruction. The legislature named local officials rather than allowing them to be elected, and this power was used to suppress not only Republicans, but dissident Democrats as well. When the legislature passed an unpopular stock law, the farmers in the western counties protested vehemently.[82] The revolt was led by Richmond Pearson, son of North Carolina's chief justice during the Civil War, who attacked boss rule in the Democratic party.[83] Pearson and many other Independent Democrats were supported by the Republicans, and a temporary coalition formed.[84] The situation became so serious for the Democrats that they brought in popular United States senator Zebulon Vance to encourage party loyalty.[85] Democratic pressure only further alienated voters, and Republicans and Independents won 64 of the 120 assembly seats.[86] The coalition in the legislature tried unsuccessfully to repeal the county government system, but the electoral victory resulted only in the appointing of some Republicans to local positions for the first time in a decade.[87]

Even after the appearance of the Farmers' Alliance in North Carolina in 1887, the Democrats did not change their negative approach to state politics. In 1888 the Democrats resorted to their only unifying issue—race. Captain Buck Kitchen toured the mountain counties, demanding that mountain voters support the Democratic party and rescue whites in the eastern part of the state from "Negro Domination."[88] The nature of the party's campaign was unacceptable to numbers of the Independents in 1886, and many of them, including Pearson, joined the Republicans.[89] Taking advantage of the inept Democratic campaign, mountain Republicans elected Hamilton G. Ewart to Congress. Thus, one important element contributing to Republican gains in the 1880s was the failure of the opposition to respond to the changing needs of the electorate.

The Republicans did not just sit back and wait for dissatisfied Democrats to come to them, however; they made strenuous efforts to offer an attractive alternative. The gubernatorial campaign of Nathan Goff in West Virginia in 1888 illustrates the aggressive Republican technique. As soon as he received the nomination, Goff began an intensive discussion of the problems of economic growth facing West Virginia.[90] Maintaining that the state needed outside capital, Goff centered his talks on how the Republican protective tariff policy would encourage an influx of corporate money into the region. Looking back from the perspective of three-quarters of a century of exploitation of the mineral wealth and people of West Virginia, one may see that the desirability of Goff's policy is questionable. His Democratic opponent, however, did not feel capable of challenging the Republican boss on this issue in open debate.[91] Instead, West Virginia Democratic congressman William L. Wilson—the author of the 1894 tariff bill and the only constructive Democrat in the upper South—did debate Goff throughout the state.[92] The frightened Democrats received considerable help from outside the state, but seemingly to no avail.[93] When Stephen Elkins started to stump the state in the last two weeks of the campaign speaking on the protective tariff, Goff looked like a winner. The Democrats were reluctant to raise the race issue because it appeared that there might be a revolt of black voters against the Republicans.[94] The revolt never materialized; however, by the time the Democrats realized that, it was too late to change their campaign.

Goff's powerful appeal to West Virginia voters resulted in a narrow, 110-vote victory. The Democratic legislature then began a torturous, but successful, eighteen-month charade to award the election to their own candidate.[95] The entire contest of Goff's seat focused national attention on the plight of Republicans in the South. It was clear to all that, even if the Republicans won in the South, they would still be deprived of that victory. Many Republicans at the national level and most in the five states of the upper South became convinced that only fraudulent election practices by Democrats stood between the Republicans and victory in the region.

Another political matter deeply concerned the Republicans of this five-state region: how to distribute fairly the patronage provided by Benjamin Harrison's election to the presidency. Republican bosses like Houk and Mahone saw their political correspondence increase tenfold between January and April 1889 when the majority of the patronage decisions were under consideration. But the mountain Republican who was under the greatest pressure was Nathan Goff's chief assistant, John W. Mason. Mason had been appointed to the position of commissioner of the Internal Revenue Service, and in that position he was responsible for naming more candidates for office in the mountain counties than any other individual.[96] Mason found that most applicants felt, "I must get into some kind of employment and think this Government owes me a living if I am willing to work for it."[97] When a local newspaperman visited Mason's office after the latter's appointment, he found so many applicants that they were leaning against the walls in his waiting room.[98] From West Virginia alone 250 applications and 3,000 letters were received in less than seven weeks.[99] Mason found it necessary to send the following standard reply: "to obtain one of these places you would have to undergo a civil service examination and then take your chance on promotion."[100]

The situation was made worse by administrative changes that decreased the number of jobs available to untrained applicants. This is not to say that Mason did not let political and personal factors influence his decisions. He managed to appoint his Civil War commander to a substantial position and remained opposed to the new administration's naming Democrats when there were so few jobs available for Republicans.[101] In addition, Mason was called on to settle factional disputes among mountain Republicans in Tennessee and North Carolina.[102] The only satisfactory answer to the entire situation was to find additional sources of patronage. Once again, Republicans in the upper South were driven to the conclusion that they had to win control of their state governments. Republican control of some southern states would insure the party's control of the national government and that source of patronage as well.

These considerations led the mountain Republican leadership to make a momentous decision: they would embrace a nationally oriented political policy. They would tie their future not only to national action, but to the very idea they had rejected at the end of Reconstruction. Apparently convinced that their white followers would be loyal, the party-army leaders supported federal intervention to insure that blacks could vote and that their votes would be counted accurately. The success of this venture depended on the racial attitudes of the white voters of the upper South. The events of the next five years would reveal that the bosses had made a serious miscalculation, one that would cause them to lose power.

CHAPTER 7

RACIAL POLICY, INDUSTRIALIZATION, AND VIOLENCE

The economic, political, and social conditions that sustained the party-army were changing rapidly in the early 1890s. The mountain region of the upper South was experiencing the impact of industrialization. The vast mineral and timber resources of the region were being exploited, and many predictable disruptions of mountain communities followed. A new professional class of businessmen, lawyers, and engineers came to dominate Appalachian society and to replace the older leadership. At the same time, mountain men shared with other American whites a growing hostility toward blacks. Many of the racial compromises agreed to at the end of Reconstruction were being repudiated, and racial questions once more overshadowed all others. Thus the two conditions necessary for continued party-army success—the idea of the local community and relative racial harmony—were disappearing.

The advance of industry in the mountains was quite dramatic in the late 1880s and 1890s. In West Virginia, for example, the amount of capital invested in manufacturing doubled between 1890 and 1900.[1] The less developed areas showed even greater proportional increases. But the real impact of the change can be detected by considering individual counties, since the development of the region was unplanned and followed no predictable pattern. One example of rapid growth was Hamilton County, Tennessee—the city of Chattanooga. In 1870 there were 58 manufacturing concerns in Hamilton County with $475,155 invested in manufacturing; by 1900 there were 394 businesses in Hamilton with $9,254,228 invested in manufacturing.[2] Gaston County, North Carolina, center of the textile industry in the mountains, grew from an investment of $635,965 in 1880 to $4,035,958 in 1900.[3] Roanoke County, Virginia, had only $264,250 invested in manufacturing in 1880; ten years later, capital had increased to $3,828,177.[4] Obviously, these three counties were exceptional, but there can be no doubt that the economic and social structure of the mountain region was undergoing tremendous change.

One of the most spectacular of the new developments was the emergence of an industrial labor force. The summer of 1891 brought a series of violent confrontations between miners in Anderson County, Tennessee, and the state government over the use of convict labor in the mines.[5] The violence continued and escalated for three years until the state finally agreed to end the infamous convict lease system.[6] The depression of the 1890s brought a shorter but even more violent series of miners' strikes in West Virginia.[7] As organized labor tried to develop organizations in the mountain regions, the situation became even more tense. The problem at the root of most of the violence was the existence of inhumane working conditions. One mill owner who prided himself on his liberality said that he was gradually reducing the work week to sixty-six hours and had recently agreed not to lay off any laborers under the age of fourteen.[8] With this kind of liberalism, the only question is why there was not more violence as the mountain people submitted to the discipline of the industrial world.

The new industrialization had other effects on mountain society. By 1900 one out of every nine inhabitants of the highlands lived in a settlement of more than twenty-five hundred people.[9] Eight mountain cities now had a population of ten thousand or more.[10] Census reports indicate a similar rapid growth of towns and villages. The presence of increasing numbers of immigrant workers competing for jobs was attested to by the appearance of the American Protective Association (APA). This organization directed its attack toward the Catholic church in particular, although all "foreign" influences seem to have been its target. The APA appears to have been strongest in the cities of Kentucky and eastern Tennessee.[11] Even where there was no formal organization of antiimmigrant feeling, hostility toward the new inhabitants was quite evident.[12]

In areas where actual development was relatively slight, social conditions were nevertheless changing rapidly, as illustrated by southeastern Kentucky, where large capital investment was limited to only two of the thirty-five counties. Younger business and community leaders made every effort to secure a railroad connection to the lowlands. When the state government refused to aid the mountaineers with their transportation difficulties, one observer called on the mountain people to form a separate state.[13] Although their efforts were unsuccessful, the new leaders in southeastern Kentucky became the spokesmen for the region.

Thus, all of mountain society faced a period of rapid and unregulated change. Alternatives to the rural mountaineer lifestyle were available to the entire highland population. These developments were sometimes regarded as invasions and met with hostile resistance. Still, the encroachments continued and the mountain people were forced to react. Many welcomed new opportunities and flocked to the factories and the growing urban areas. The more enterprising secured capital and started their own businesses utilizing the resources of the mountains. After isolating themselves from national developments for more than two decades, mountain people were participating in wider concerns once again.

Some mountaineers were frightened by the new demands placed on them, fiercely resisting change and demanding that the outside world leave them alone. The culmination of this feeling was one of the most significant outbreaks of social violence in American history. By 1901 one observer of mountain life could comment, "It is the feud that most sharply differentiates the . . . mountaineer from his fellows . . . the feud means, of course, ignorance, shiftlessness, incredible lawlessness, a frightful estimate of the value of human life; the horrible custom of ambush, a class of cowardly assassins who can be hired to do murder for a gun, a mule, or a gallon of moonshine."[14] This stereotype of the southern mountaineer was created by a series of spectacular events that took place at the end of the nineteenth century. The first of the notorious eruptions was the bloody climax of the Hatfield-McCoy feud in 1888.[15] The nation was appalled by the ruthlessness of the family fighting and concerned over the implications of the near–civil war between Kentucky and West Virginia caused by the legal complications of the situation. Other incidents followed in quick succession.

Much of the lawlessness had obvious historical roots. For example, many incidents were a continuation of conflict generated by the Civil War, such as Kentucky's notorious Knott County "war," in which the two factions were led by opposing Confederate and Union guerrilla leaders.[16] As noted earlier, there were also direct labor-management conflicts that led to violent incidents. Finally, the increasing racial hostility often degenerated into open confrontations. At least fifteen lynchings occurred during the last decade of the century in the mountain counties, and a number of them involved several victims. These events were not unique to the mountain people, however. Many other parts of the country where similar conditions prevailed experienced the same turbulence.

Those who observed the highland people in the 1890s were painfully aware of another type of conflict in Appalachian society as well. Seemingly irrational acts of violence—feuds, homicides, and political assassinations—were a normal part of the mountaineer's lifestyle. It was this apparently unmotivated violence that was largely responsible for the creation of the enduring hillbilly stereotype. Contemporaries explained the eruption by the geographical isolation of the people, the absence of educational facilities, and the practice of sectarian religion.[17] These conditions, unfortunately present throughout the last third of the nineteenth century, do not explain the events of the 1890s. Several sociologists and social historians have offered more concrete explanations, however, and a more complete picture of the situation has emerged.

As early as 1887 German sociologist Ferdinand Tonnies discovered that industrialization produced a crisis in a predominantly rural and agricultural society. He noted that many people were forced to ignore traditional patterns of behavior and loyalty. They were unable to sustain themselves through their local interests but instead were required to identify with larger social groups. As a society underwent this transition, individuals resisted and serious social dislocation took place.[18] Recently, American historian Robert Wiebe has applied these insights to American society. Wiebe traces the rise of the progressive movement and documents how businessmen, lawyers, doctors, and educators transferred their loyalty from their communities to national standards of professionalism. For example, the medical doctor owed his primary loyalty to the American Medical Association rather than to the particular health needs of one location.[19] Wiebe also notes that the rapidity with which this transformation took place left many people behind—bewildered and bitter.

English historian Eric J. Hobsbawm has made a special study of those people left behind by industrialization. He discovered that the societies in his study had several points in common. They were rural, precapitalist, and "profoundly and tenaciously traditional,"[20] a description that would fit some southern mountain communities during the 1890s. Hobsbawm noted that these societies often were marked by irrational forms of violence. The people would strike out at those who threatened them without having any program to alleviate their problems. Hobsbawm noted that the following conditions often promoted conflict: "[Violence] is most likely to become a major phenomenon when their traditional equilibrium is upset: during and after periods of abnormal hardship, such as famines and wars, or at moments when the jaws of the dynamic modern world seize the static communities in order to destroy and transform them."[21] The southern highlands had recently suffered through the Civil War and faced the full impact of the American industrial revolution in the 1890s—a prime example of the conditions Hobsbawn cited.

Although no pattern to the conflicts emerged clearly to the people of the time, it is possible now to divide these events into two broad categories. The most obvious was an increase in attempted political assassinations. In the United States as a whole, political killings have been relatively rare. Between 1790 and 1968 only eight governors and nine congressmen were victims of attempted or actual murders.[22] Significantly, four of these crimes involved southern mountaineers in the 1890s. Three former congressmen were shot during the decade, and one died.[23] The most spectacular of the assassinations occurred in Kentucky in 1900 when William Goebel, Democratic contestant for governor, was killed by a mountaineer supporter of the Republican candidate.[24] This seemingly senseless string of political violence was evidence of a deeper malaise that infected mountain elections.

The 1890s was a period of political, as well as social, disruption in the mountains. In an effort to maintain themselves in office, Republican party-army leaders ignored larger issues and concentrated on immediate problems. When the depression of the 1890s struck the highlands, the mountain voters discovered that the old political bosses had few solutions to offer that would alleviate the suffering. New leaders appeared who preached the doctrines of the protective tariff and business leadership of society. These men—described effectively by Tonnies and Wiebe —seized control of the Republican organization and used it to begin the systematic exploitation of the people and resources of Appalachia.[25] The loss of local political control distressed many mountain people, and the violence that followed was a predictable response.

The second major strain of violence could be properly described as defense of community values, a rather broad category that includes many seemingly unrelated events. An underlying unity may, however, be discerned. All of the incidents reflected the inability of rural mountaineers to understand that their lifestyle would have to change. These mountain people viewed anything outside their families or local communities as a threat. The advent of industrialization insured that virtually every mountain dweller would have to make major adjustments in his life. As in politics, the huge corporations invaded the mountain economy and prevailed over it.[26] The rapidity with which these profound alterations in highland society took place left many of the inhabitants bewildered and fearful.

At the same time a new group of men appeared in the highlands. Part of the new professional middle class created by the industrial revolution, they soon came to dominate mountain society. Lawyers, bankers, and businessmen sought to bring the discipline and rationalized work processes of industry into the mountains. These new leaders and values threatened the individuality that many mountaineers prized. Often disagreement between the two groups seemed to have no immediate basis. To the professional middle class, the rural inhabitants and their lifestyle represented an anachronism that had to be reformed. The conflicts generated by confrontations between these two groups were based on the failure of either one to understand the motivations of the other.

The attempt to bring the order demanded by industrialization to Appalachian society was fiercely resisted. When one faction of a Virginia feud objected to the interference of the court in a dispute, the men shot to death the judge, the prosecutor, the sheriff, and three of the jurors.[27] Kentucky governor William O. Bradley was forced to send the state militia into Clay County in 1898 when a feud destroyed all semblance of law and order in the area.[28] In western North Carolina the sheriff of Mitchell County was killed in a street fight while trying to restrain a local troublemaker.[29] This case gained great notoriety because the officer was the brother of one of the state's United States senators. A large number of federal Internal Revenue Service officials were attacked as they attempted to enforce the tax laws.[30] Even the act of supporting the authorities was sufficient reason for some mountaineers to take offense. A newspaper editor in Pulaski County, Kentucky, J. R. Rucker, denounced lawlessness in an article in 1892. His reward for this editorial opinion was to be shot and killed by an irate reader.[31] The new middle class in the mountains was appalled by such reactionary violence.

The incident that best illustrates the conflict between these two groups in Appalachia is the lynching and riot that took place in Roanoke, Virginia, in September 1893. Roanoke was a predictable location for this type of confrontation. In the late 1870s the area contained a few hundred people and was named Big Lick. The convergence of railroad lines created a boom town that adopted the more dignified name of Roanoke. Mountain people from the surrounding counties came to work in the iron mills that formed the economic backbone of the growing community. By 1893 the population of the city had reached approximately twenty-five thousand, and Roanoke was ready to explode. With a much larger black population than most of Appalachia, the city experienced substantial racial tension. In addition, the severe financial collapse in the United States in 1893 struck Roanoke hard, and unemployed workers blamed the business leadership of the city for their plight.[32] All that was needed to set the city ablaze was an incident that would allow the mountain men to focus their fears on one object.

That spark was supplied on 20 September 1893 when an unemployed black worker beat a white woman. The predictable lynching did not immediately follow, however. The mayor, Henry S. Trout, was a local industrialist and banker and member of the new middle class. Trout was determined to insure that this case would be handled through the regular judicial process, and that a mob would not be allowed to take over the city. The mayor's objective ran counter to the desires of the disgruntled unemployed and the many rural inhabitants in the city that day. Once the prisoner was in jail, a mob gradually surrounded the building. Alarmed public officials called out the local unit of the state militia and ordered them to clear the streets. They were able to do so briefly, but by nightfall the crowd grew again until it numbered at least fifteen hundred people.[33] The mayor, the local judge, and the district attorney all assured the people that since the court was already in session, justice would be swift in this case.

The problem that these men faced, however, was that the mob was not interested in official justice. Frustrated by widespread joblessness and driven by racial fears, the angry whites demanded immediate execution. At this point a group of approximately fifty men who lived in the country near the injured woman's home began to attack an unprotected side of the jail. These men refused to believe that the authorities would use force against them and ignored repeated warnings issued by the militia leader. In the confusion that followed, the militia opened fire on the mob, which regrouped and charged again. The militia fired a second round, and the crowd quickly left the jail. Eight civilians were dead and more than a score were wounded, including the mayor.[34] Although driven away from the jail, the mob refused to disperse, and, indeed, their resentment only increased.

The object of their hatred turned from the Negro to the government officials who had demanded that due process be followed. The mayor became the particular focus of their wrath. Mob leaders searched his home and the major hotel in Roanoke in a vain attempt to locate Trout and lynch him. A state senatorial candidate who called for peace was shot at three times and forced to flee. The jail was left unguarded, and the militia was disbanded in an effort to placate the hostile population. Even after the police betrayed the prisoner the next morning and he was lynched, the mob remained in control of the city.[35] Personal revenge was still their major motivation, and only the most strenuous efforts prevented them from burying the lynched black man in the mayor's front yard.

Appalled by the events, the professional leadership of Roanoke sought to regain control of the city. Joseph H. Sands, vice-president of the

Roanoke Iron Works, spearheaded this effort, creating a special citizens' committee. Sands called together fraternal organizations and workers' groups and persuaded them to support efforts to suppress the existing anarchy. Resentment against the authorities still remained, as indicated by the following resolution, adopted by one meeting:

> Resolved, that, it is the opinion of this meeting, the firing upon the crowd assembled about the courthouse was not justified by existing circumstances and was in a great measure unprovoked, and we hereby demand from the proper authorities that a most rigid investigation be made of all the circumstances of the affair, and that, in case the guilt of any official, civil or military, be proved, that said officer shall be requested to resign, and that he be punished to the full extent of the law.[36]

The committee worked carefully and was able to avoid provoking further incidents. A week after the riot, Mayor Trout returned to town from his self-imposed exile, and the militia met without any outside interference.

The city officials moved swiftly to punish those who had led the mob. They realized that Roanoke's tarnished reputation would be a hindrance to further business growth, and they worked hard to restore the city's respectability. The thorough public investigation that was conducted served as a forum to vindicate the policies pursued by the public officials. A special grand jury was called, and nineteen indictments were handed down against the rioters. Significantly, two of those indicted were police officers who were charged with aiding the mob with the lynching of Smith. Unfortunately for the middle-class leadership, the cases were tried before juries made up of mountain men who accepted personal revenge as a routine practice. The outcome was that most of those indicted were convicted, but the jury's sentences were so light as to constitute no punishment at all. The local newspaper protested that the verdicts were "travesties upon justice."[37] The lack of understanding persisted between the two groups within the mountain society that created the conditions for the riot. The tension evident in Roanoke was found throughout Appalachia, and other violent outbreaks testified to the continuing conflict between the traditional mode of living and industrialization in the region.

Just as the community power base of the party-army was disappearing, the racial peace necessary for mountain Republicans' success was also coming to an end. Angered by increasing fraudulent counting of black votes in the South, the Republican party was determined to remedy the situation after they won control of both houses of Congress and the presidency in 1888. In his inaugural address and in his first annual message to Congress, President Benjamin Harrison called for legislation increasing federal power over elections.[38] Several bills were introduced, and in 1890 Congressman Henry Cabot Lodge submitted a proposal that incorporated most features of all of the other initiatives. Despite vehement southern and Democratic opposition, the Lodge bill passed the House. Most white southerners were outraged, claiming that federal investigation of election returns and federal interference with jury selection was the reimposition of Reconstruction. The South threatened violent reprisals if this "Force Bill" became law. A successful Senate filibuster prevented its passage, but the legislation remained a potent political issue in 1890.

The party-army bosses were trapped by the Lodge bill. They knew that it would alienate many white voters, but they also realized that an accurate count of the black vote would provide them with electoral victories. Their actions were determined to a great extent by their experience in working with black Republicans. Mountain Republicans had accepted blacks as political allies during Reconstruction very reluctantly.[39] When blacks proved to be loyal party members who often accepted a subordinate position meekly, mountain politicians relented and worked with the newly enfranchised freedmen.[40] In the lowland regions of every state except West Virginia, blacks formed the major portion of the party's voters, so that even if mountain Republican leaders had wanted to ignore the blacks they could not have done so. As Leonidas Houk, eastern Tennessee Republican leader, observed, "The more I have studied the matter, the more convinced I have become, that it would not only be good politics, but good Civil Service, and equitable Republicanism to distribute the appointments among all classes—Americans, Germans, Irish, and Colored People."[41]

The relationship between highland Republicans and blacks changed after Reconstruction. Both President Rutherford B. Hayes and President Chester Arthur sought to reduce the influence of blacks on the Republican party in the South. They hoped to attract whites through appeals designed to overcome their racial prejudices. One means used was to deny patronage to black Republicans and to grant it instead to white Democrats.[42] A result of this policy was that blacks became much more militant and demanded that local mountain Republican politicians protect them. Knoxville Negro Henry Casper spoke for the new black political leaders when he anounced "We not only want to be nominated, but we want some assurance, that those who help nominate us are sincere and intend voting for us at the polls. We will not suffer that trick any longer. There are enough colored voters in Knox County to demand one or two good county offices every year if the Republican party would but give us what our number entitled us to."[43] Not only did the black

Republicans make demands, but they also did something about the discrimination they felt. William Yardley, an east Tennessee black leader, shocked the party in his state by running as a gubernatorial candidate in 1876.[44] At the Republican state convention in Kentucky in 1883, black clergyman J. W. Asbury was nominated for the office of register of the land office. He was unpopular among white Republicans; many of them, including mountaineers, refused to vote for him.[45] In the 1880s black protest meetings in Tennessee, Kentucky, and North Carolina demanded more equal treatment from the party leaders.[46]

Two incidents involving blacks and mountain Republicans during this period illustrate the problems that the more aggressive black leadership created for white mountain Republicans. One difficulty was that blacks could act as the balance of power between competing white factions of the party. In 1882 in Tennessee's Second District a power struggle between Congressman Leonidas Houk and newspaper editor William Rule resulted in a desperate bargaining for black votes by both men. In 1881 Houk had induced blacks to protest Rule's appointment as postmaster of Knoxville.[47] This protest was successful, and Rule was replaced with a Houk man. Incensed by this action, Rule announced that he was going to unseat Houk in 1882. His campaign was based in part upon an attempt to control the black vote.[48] Houk reacted quickly by forming an alliance with black leader William Yardley. Later, a campaign worker reported to Houk, "Yardley and Sam Anderson got all the colored people together at night and with locked doors, they passed resolutions endorsing you."[49] The response of the Rule forces was that "Yardley . . . is a notoriously cheap piece of marketable material in every election."[50] The bitterness of the last remark clearly indicated that Rule had not been able to win the black vote and would be easily defeated by Houk. The significant point is that blacks were acting independently of white control in the mountain Republican party in east Tennessee.

West Virginia Republicans also encountered much hostility among black voters. Many black supporters seemed willing to leave the party in 1888 because they did not feel they were receiving fair treatment. The Colored Independent party made its appearance in July of that year. At that time one spokesman observed that there was increasing dissatisfaction with the Republican party among blacks.[51] Republican papers demonstrated a close connection between the new party and the Democrats and thus negated most of its appeal.[52] Nevertheless, blacks had once more shown themselves willing to break from a mountain Republican organization, thereby forcing the mountaineers to make adjustments.

The growing black demands were being made on a group of men who still retained strong racial feelings. The editor of a West Virginia

Republican paper probably expressed most mountain Republican feelings in the assertion, "They are just emerging from a purely animal existence and have their future to make out of very indifferent raw material."[53] Mountaineers also expressed their prejudice in more than words. Throughout the late nineteenth century, mountain men—like other southern whites—felt that lynching was a suitable means of social control. One eastern Tennessee Republican even justified the practice:

> However deplorable lynch law may be I say that negroes lynched in the South for assaulting white women are not *lynched because they are negroes but because of the crime they have committed*. . . . I say it is the *unwritten* law of the South to lynch a brute who assaults a woman without regard to his race or color. If more negroes are lynched for this crime than white men it is not because they are negroes but because in the South more negroes commit the crime than whites in the North.[54]

Such strong prejudice would seem to raise the question of how the mountain whites could work with the more aggressive black politicians. One answer appears to be demographic. Few blacks lived in the mountain counties; their small numbers apparently freed the mountain whites of the fear of "Negro domination." The percentage of blacks in 1870 in the mountain regions ranged from a high of 14 percent in southwestern Virginia and western North Carolina to a low of less than 3 percent in northwestern West Virginia.[55] The average for the mountain counties in all five states was less than 9 percent. The more detailed statistical study in the Appendix shows that the relationship between white Republican voting in 1876 and the proportion of blacks in the population produced a correlation coefficient of $-.68$,[56] which indicates an inverse relationship between the variables. As the percentage of blacks in the population rises, the percentage of whites voting Republican decreases; as the proportion of blacks in the population drops, the Republican share of the white vote increases. Thus, the small black population in the mountain counties made it easier for mountain Republicans to overlook their prejudice and work with blacks politically.

Despite the rapid growth in mining in the Appalachians of the upper South after 1880 and the increased presence of black miners, Republicans not only retained but even increased their support among mountain whites. Table 12 offers data to reconcile this statement with the previous analysis. Although the number of blacks living in the mountain counties was increasing rapidly during this period, blacks actually were declining in proportion to the rest of the population. In only 33 of the 147 mountain counties did the percentage of blacks rise faster than that of the total population. Even this figure is misleading because the number of blacks involved was so small; for example, the percentage

TABLE 12. Negro Population and Total Population
of Mountain Counties, 1870 and 1900

	1870		1900	
	Negro Population	Total Population	Negro Population	Total Population
Kentucky	8,621	211,232	11,178	449,975
West Virginia	7,715	234,440	16,154	695,363
Tennessee	36,238	327,035	65,387	625,971
North Carolina	29,673	207,318	53,145	424,579
Virginia	25,938	182,068	42,469	360,233
Total	108,185	1,252,093	188,333	2,556,121
Negro Population as Percentage of Total		8.64%		7.37%

SOURCES: *Ninth Census of the United States, 1870, Population and Social Statistics*, pt. 1, pp. 146–54, 220–26, 261–69, 278–83, 284–87. *Twelfth Census of the United States, 1900, Population*, pt. 1, pp. 540–41, 550–51, 556–57, 561–63.

increase in Clay County, West Virginia, between 1870 and 1900 was 450 percent, but in actual numbers the change was from 4 blacks in 1870 to a total of 18 in a population of 8,248 in 1900. In those few counties where there was a substantial increase in both percentage and numbers, such as Hamilton County (Chattanooga), Tennessee, Republican voting among whites decreased noticeably.[57] Thus, this demographic variable was constant throughout this period.

Equally important was the fact that black voters were the bulwark of an increasingly successful Republican party. Even in West Virginia, where blacks were a minority in the party, their votes were critical for Republican success. Nathan Goff would never have been elected governor or to Congress three times without the aid of black votes. The same situation obtained in the other four states where blacks were in the majority in the party. The victories achieved by Republicans in 1886 and 1888 only strengthened the bonds between black and white Republicans. These successes encouraged mountain Republicans to look for ways to win even greater ones.

Since a major barrier to Republican success had been Democratic control of the election machinery, most mountain Republicans eagerly supported the idea of a federal election law and led the way in trying to secure such legislation. Most mountain Republicans were positive that a federal election law would insure party success in their states, since it would guarantee black voting as well as accuracy in the counting of votes. Veteran mountain Republican congressman Leonidas Houk of Tennessee was the chief spokesman for the region in favor of the measure. During his first month in Congress in 1879, Houk endorsed the idea of federal control of elections, introducing such a piece of legislation in November 1889.[58] Although his own bill was dropped in favor of one proposed by Henry Cabot Lodge, Houk continued to support the idea. His position was stated clearly in a speech delivered in 1890: "In conclusion he urged that the colored people of the South should be given a fair chance. If the white people of the South would not take their hand off the Government must take it off. Let no man hold a seat on this floor who was returned by means of Winchester rifles, clubs and fraudulent ballot boxes."[59] In the floor debate on the Lodge bill, Houk continued his enthusiastic support of the concept of federal intervention.[60]

Although Houk was probably the leading spokesman for a federal election law, many other mountain Republicans supported Lodge's ideas. George W. Atkinson, congressman from West Virginia, proposed that criminal penalties be enforced if anyone interfered with federal elections.[61] Along the same lines, east Tennessee Republican congressman Alfred Taylor thought that the final version of Lodge's bill should be strengthened to insure compliance with the law.[62] Kentucky mountain Republican congressman H. Franklin Finley was quite satisfied, saying, "I most cheerfully endorse the bill as the best election bill that has ever been offered to any Congress in this country."[63] Republican voters in the mountain regions also seemed to accept the measure, according to Republican newspapers and meetings endorsing the Lodge proposal.[64] When the vote was taken in the House, seven of the eight mountain Republicans supported it, thereby allowing the measure to pass by a narrow margin.[65]

Some mountain Republicans, however, held another opinion of the legislation; the leader of this point of view was Congressman Hamilton G. Ewart of North Carolina. Ewart maintained that "this election bill is as damnable, illogical, inequitable, and vicious a piece of legislation as ever attempted to be placed upon the statute-books of this Republic."[66] He went on to explain his stand in the following terms: "Every year the Republican party in the States of Tennessee, North Carolina, and the two Virginias is becoming stronger and more aggressive. It is not acquiring this strength by making morbid appeals to the negro and by exciting their passions and prejudices, but by appealing to the sober judgement of the white voters of the South on the great issue of protection."[67] Nor was Ewart alone in this feeling. The Republican gubernatorial candidate in Tennessee opposed the bill, and Republican congressional candidates in North Carolina, Tennessee, and Virginia also attacked the Lodge proposal.[68]

When the Lodge bill did not pass in the United States Senate, mountain Republicans found themselves in a difficult position. The legislation had alienated many white voters in their districts; yet, since it had failed, blacks had no more protection than before. Consequently, the congressional elections of 1890 were a real setback for mountain Republicans, who lost five seats of the eight they had held.[69] It is difficult to assess exactly the significance of the election-law issue in defeating the party. The Republicans lost badly everywhere in 1890, and it seems clear that mountain voters (like other voters across the nation) reacted to issues other than the Lodge bill. The election in the First Congressional District of Tennessee offers the best illustration of mountain Republicans' reactions to the bill. There Alfred Taylor, a strong backer of the bill, was opposed by former congressman Random R. Butler for the Republican nomination. After a hotly contested primary campaign, both men claimed to be the regular party nominee.[70] The Democrats in this strongly Republican district decided not to run a candidate but to allow the two men to split their own party. In September Butler, in an obvious political maneuver, attacked the Lodge bill and federal control of elections.[71] Thus, the Republican voters of the district had a choice of candidates from their own party who took opposite positions on the issue. The election returns gave Taylor a narrow victory and indicated that he had won about 80 percent of the Republican vote.[72] It would be safe to conclude then, that though there was substantial opposition to the Lodge bill among the mountaineers, the legislation was backed by a majority of mountain Republicans.

The failures of the 1890 campaign and further defeats in the 1892 election prompted a serious reevaluation of the party's position. The Lodge bill became a serious political liability, and more and more mountain Republicans began to reject federal intervention in southern elections as a viable means of adding voters to the party.[73] The disenchantment with this approach to winning voters coincided with dissatisfaction with the bosses who had directed the party in the mountains during the 1880s. Between 1890 and 1894 all the old politicians were replaced by men who brought a new perspective to the party.

The new leaders shared a common goal of bringing more white voters into the Republican party. They believed that the strategy of relying exclusively on blacks and former Unionists, as the bosses had done, could never transform their party into the major party in the upper South. The emphasis now was exclusively on economic issues.[74] The advent of the "Democratic" depression of the 1890s made this decision a most fortuitous one. In both 1894 and 1896 the Republicans elected most of the congressmen from the mountain districts; they elected governors in four of the five upper South states during the same time; and, for the first time since the Readjuster period in Virginia, Republican senators represented the upper South in Washington.

This successful new mountain Republican leadership tended to ignore the older groups in the party, particularly the blacks. Another significant factor was pushing the Republican leadership in the same direction: the rise of southern Negrophobia as a conscious intellectual and social movement.[75] Lynchings continued at an ever-increasing rate, and rigid segregation became the goal of many white southerners. Ominously for the Republican party, the program of the southern racial purists demanded an end to Negro suffrage. The mountain Republican politicians thus were caught between their need to retain black votes and the need to appeal to white racist Democrats. Since the Democratic party offered blacks so little, Republican politicians for the most part believed it safe to ignore the blacks.

Mountain Republican leaders now thought they had to convince whites that "the Republican party is not the negro party."[76] Consequently, they tried to construct a "lily-white" movement. Mountain politicians tended to avoid blacks in their campaign appearances and to deny them federal patronage, but their statements and campaign strategies contradict the idea that they wanted to end Negro suffrage. Black voters, despite their occasional challenges to the party leadership, were too valuable as allies. The new mountain leaders tried to insure that black Republican voters had only a minimal voice in the party organization while they also sought to preserve the black right to vote. All white mountain Republicans seemed to agree that federal patronage should be distributed to whites only. One North Carolina black politician accurately observed that "the Republicans themselves don't think it wise for colored citizens to . . . fill state or federal positions."[77] Still, the appointment of blacks or the promise of appointment was made by mountain politicians when it was deemed necessary. The Stephen B. Elkins machine in West Virginia in some cases delayed giving patronage to black applicants in order to test their loyalty to the organization. These tactics were quite successful in ending a revolt against Elkins by blacks in West Virginia in 1900.[78] Even if a black did manage to secure a political job from mountain Republicans, he still had to contend with Republicans who thought he should not have the position. In March 1892 many white Republican Internal Revenue Service employees in the mountain counties in North Carolina refused to work with a recently appointed black worker and seriously disrupted the agency's operations.[79] A black deputy marshal in eastern Kentucky had great difficulty performing his duties because of the hostility of the mountaineers.[80] The dilemma faced by black appointees is well explained in the following letter from Charles M. Cansler, future educator and civil rights leader in eastern Tennessee: "I have recently been appointed to a position as substitute in the Railroad Mail Service for the line centering at Chattanooga, Tenn., from the Civil Service examination of last August. Because of the existing prejudice on part of the white clerks on these lines I have been unable to get such work as will enable me to secure a livelihood from this position."[81] For some mountain Republicans, it appears, the assignment of even one office to a black Republican was one too many.

Blacks were increasingly passed over as potential candidates for public office and were even discouraged from attending party conventions. The Kentucky Republican gubernatorial candidate in 1895, William Bradley, was apparently willing to make patronage commitments to blacks before he was nominated in order to insure that blacks would not demand a spot on the state ticket.[82] Blacks were excluded from Republican state conventions as early as 1888, and by 1900 North Carolina Republicans could boast that their state meeting "was a convention not only dominated by white men, but composed of white men."[83] Moving ever closer to segregation within the party, mountain Republicans became enthusiastic supporters of social segregation in churches, in schools, in public facilities, and in public transportation.[84]

Mountain Republicans used other means to give the illusion of eliminating the black man from politics while still striving to preserve his right to vote. One of their more effective tactics was to gerrymander black voters to prevent their candidates from winning in local elections. Table 13, showing the ward populations of the mountain city of Knoxville, Tennessee, provides a good illustration of this method. While black voters made up 35 percent of the electorate, they were in the majority in only one of the city's nine wards. The contrast between the Fourth and the Seventh wards is particularly instructive. In the former, only 165 white voters formed a majority, while in the latter 678 blacks were in the minority.

Another trick used by mountain Republicans to minimize black participation in campaigns was to run candidates who seemed hostile to black interests. Southwestern Virginia mountain Republicans ran James A. Walker for Congress four times in the 1890s, although his record as a Confederate general and former Democrat made him distinctly unappealing to blacks.[85] North Carolina mountain Republicans, reacting to the increasing racism of the opposition, supported Daniel L. Russell for governor in 1896, who was quoted as saying, "The negroes of the South

TABLE 13. Voter Registration by Race in Knoxville, Tennessee, 1894

Ward	White	Colored	Total
1	454	39	498
2	192	84	276
3	212	141	353
4	165	35	200
5	224	419	643
6	407	95	502
7	756	678	1,434
8	385	270	655
9	836	252	1,088
Total	3,631	2,013	5,644

SOURCE: *Clinton Gazette*, 17 Oct. 1894.

are largely savages."[86] The strategy behind Russell's nomination was explained by the candidate himself:

The Democrats will try the old dodge of trying the "Color line" but it worries them to discover just how to do it. They have been preaching . . . that Russell is dead against the negroes, that he favors white supremacy and that he is opposed to even the mildest form of negro government. Now they will proceed to prove that he is in favor of compelling every white woman to marry a negro, and that he, himself is a mulatto. This is a rather heavy job for them, but not too big for them to attempt.[87]

North Carolina black Republicans were so outraged by Russell's nomination that they called a convention to protest and demanded a new candidate.[88]

Two other techniques were used to deemphasize the presence of blacks in the Republican party. Kentucky Republicans in the gubernatorial and state campaign of 1895 simply refused to acknowledge the existence of black Republicans. The party's campaign committee would not work with blacks and forbade candidates to mention racial matters.[89] Their advice seems to have been generally followed. Harvey Samuel Irwin, a candidate for state railroad commissioner, was asked in an open letter if he would vote to repeal the separate-but-equal railway coach law. Irwin refused to answer and continued his campaign as if the question had never been asked.[90] Gubernatorial candidate William Bradley withdrew from a series of joint debates with his Democratic opponent when racial issues began to dominate the discussions.[91] Negroes, angered by these snubs, formed the Kentucky Colored Democrat Club to force a change in the Republican campaign. In Tennessee, mountain Republicans developed the novel idea of voluntary black disfranchisement. In 1894 Henry Clay Evans, the gubernatorial candidate, and his campaign manager, Newell Sanders, persuaded many blacks not to vote, in the expectation that their absence would reduce the racial excitement and fraud perpetrated by the Democrats.[92] All these elaborate strategies were aimed at convincing white voters that the Republican party was a white man's party while at the same time preserving the Negro's right to vote.

The Republican racial strategies convinced very few white voters. The controversy surrounding the Lodge bill provided the Democrats with the opportunity to revive the hostilities generated by Reconstruction. The active interference of the federal government in racial matters undermined the tenuous hold that the party-army had over many of its supporters. The bosses had succeeded in maintaining their power by anticipating the feelings and needs of their constituents. On the issue of race relations, few of them recognized that southern whites were becoming even more reactionary than they had been in the past. This failure to perceive the deepening concern of mountain whites further eroded the bases of support for the party-army and its leaders.

CHAPTER 8

DESTRUCTION OF THE BOSSES AND NEW REPUBLICAN LEADERSHIP

The radical changes taking place in mountain society were reflected in the region's politics. The men who directed the mountain Republican party-armies found that their support was declining and that they were being challenged by men who were part of the developing professional middle class. The new type of Republican politician often reflected the growing interest in industrialization among mountain people. Unlike the old leaders, the businessmen and lawyers that contested for control of the Republican organization did not avoid taking public stands on issues. They often proclaimed their adherence to the protective tariff, efficient government, and public subsidies for the exploitation of natural resources. These proposals seemed to promise the rapid economic development of the Applachian highlands and became quite popular with the electorate.

Outside events conspired to make the pledges of the challenging mountain politicians even more appealing. Starting in the spring of 1893, the United States experienced a severe economic collapse. Mountain workers and farmers shared in the unemployment and low prices suffered by other Americans. Just as the rest of their countrymen did, the mountain men turned to politics to find a solution to their distress. The conservative and deflationary policies pursued by President Grover Cleveland were intensely unpopular in the highlands, and so there was no movement of mountain voters into the Democratic party. In fact, the reverse was true. Mountain whites voted Republican in large numbers throughout the 1894–96 period. Many of the new Republicans were concerned primarily about economic issues and were repelled by the lack of substance in the platforms of the party-armies. The result was that this group of voters consistently supported the new leadership.

Another significant factor in the battle to control the Applachian Republican organizations was the ability of the middle-class professionals to raise large amounts of money to finance their campaigns. The old bosses had depended upon an exchange of services to maintain their power. They secured federal patronage jobs for their campaign workers who used their positions to work for the party during elections. The reform of the civil service system in 1883 made these arrangements increasingly difficult to continue. Since many mountain Republicans were illiterate, they could not pass the newly required examinations and could no longer be placed on the government payroll. The new leaders adopted a more direct and appealing system of reward—payment to their campaign workers immediately after the task was completed. Many men who had been ruined by the depression could not resist accepting the assured reward rather than the uncertain job. Thus, the old bosses soon lost their superiority in the organization that had sustained their machines for more than a decade.

With all of the difficulties facing them, the party-army bosses did not give up their power easily. They controlled the party structure, and they still spoke for many of the mountain people who resented the changes coming to mountain society. As the riot in Roanoke indicated, the transition from old to new in Appalachia was accompanied by considerable bitterness. Although the Republicans continued to win elections during this transition period the transfer of power generated considerable controversy and factionalism. By 1896 the issue had been settled, however, and the party-army and the mountain Republican party's commitment to local interests had disappeared.

One of the best examples of such changes in mountain politics can be found in the decline of the fortunes of the Houk machine in the Second Congressional District of Tennessee. Leonidas Houk had reached the height of his power in 1888, when he was unopposed for renomination and in the general election won the biggest majority in the district's history.[1] In January 1889 he was the Republican nominee for the United States Senate from Tennessee, indicating that he was considered the leading Republican in the state.[2] John C. Houk, the congressman's son, through his organizing skills, had been partially responsible for the machine's success. Although only in his twenties in the 1880s, John Houk commanded the respect of older and more experienced politicians. Apparently very shy and introverted, he kept in constant touch with local political leaders through a voluminous and frank correspondence. Letters and reports that have survived indicate that he could control county conventions and run general election campaigns with equal facility. By 1892 the machine was running so smoothly that Houk claimed he could have two thousand workers in the field—one for every fifteen voters in the district—within a day.[3]

Houk maintained his position by incorporating new issues into his veteran-oriented platform. During the 1887 campaign for statewide prohibition in Tennessee, refusing to be embarrassed by his hard-drinking reputation, he supported the drys.[4] A second major adjustment that Houk made in his platform required far less hypocrisy on his part than the liquor question. On 9 May 1888 the congressman made a major address in Congress in support of the principle of tariff protection.[5] Since eastern Tennessee was rapidly becoming industrialized, Houk's advocacy was undoubtedly a reaction to this new interest group; and his conversion to protection was matched by that of many other mountain Republicans. By embracing these and other popular issues, Houk made attack by his enemies difficult.

Despite his careful work, the election of 1888 was not only Houk's greatest triumph, but the start of the career of the man who eventually helped to destroy the Houk machine. Henry Clay Evans, an economic carpetbagger from Pennsylvania, won election as the first Republican congressman since Reconstruction from Tennessee's Third Congressional District. Evans was general manager of the Roane Iron Works and, after more than twenty years in eastern Tennessee, had amassed a considerable fortune. Together with fellow industrialist Newell Sanders, Evans had seized control of the Republican organization in the Third District in 1884.[6] Four years later, Evans campaigned strenuously, emphasizing his support of the protective tariff, and defeated the Democratic candidate, Creed Bates, by the small margin of 288 votes.[7]

Evans's victory greatly complicated the distribution of federal patronage in Tennessee. In Chattanooga, the evening of 9 January 1889, Tennessee's three Republican congressmen—Evans, Houk, and Alfred A. Taylor of the First District—met and agreed on the distribution of federal offices in the area.[8] Each man agreed to name one of the three major federal officials in eastern Tennessee and then extracted agreements like the following from their subordinates: "I hereby agree that if appointed U.S. District Attorney for the Eastern District of Tennessee I will consult with and make all subordinate appointments which may be, or come under my control in the respective geographical Districts composing said Judicial District—satisfactory to the Republican Congressman now representing said three Districts respectively."[9] These elaborate precautions did not prevent trouble. Evans had very close ties with the Harrison administration and, despite his freshman status in Congress, shortly controlled federal patronage in Tennessee.[10] Houk was soon attacking local Evans appointees and badgering administration officials as he tried to defend himself.[11] The battle became so intense that one eastern Tennessee applicant was informed, "You have been recommended for appointment as Revenue Agent, but I am not sure that the appointment can be made. Your congressmen have not agreed upon the man they want, and if an appointment of this kind goes to your state it may be found better to put it in the other end of the state."[12] Throughout 1889 and 1890 the fighting continued, with Evans generally emerging the victor.

Houk's concern over Evans's growing power led him to attempt a very dangerous political maneuver. Starting in December 1888, Houk and several other southern Republicans attempted to form a bloc of votes among the nineteen southern Republican congressmen.[13] The idea was that these votes represented a balance of power in the House of Representatives between the two parties and by concerted action could force the administration to grant patronage favors. Houk started by trying to pressure President Benjamin Harrison into appointing William Mahone as postmaster general and Frank S. Blair, solicitor general.[14] Harrison refused to be coerced; not only did he not make the appointments, but he passed over a Houk candidate for United States marshal of middle Tennessee and named his own brother.[15] An exasperated Houk remarked, "If Harrison has resolved to ruin the Republican party in this state, it can't be helped."[16]

Apparently not chastened by this experience, Houk attempted to organize southern Republicans when Congress met in the fall. Houk and a number of other southern Republicans refused to support any of the Republican candidates for Speaker of the House unless their patronage demands were met and the person agreed to help repeal the tobacco tax.[17] This strategy backfired when Evans and several other southern Republicans refused to act with Houk.[18] Eventually, both Houk and Evans voted for William McKinley, who lost to Thomas B. Reed.[19] Evans was not punished for supporting McKinley and was rewarded with several good committee appointments for refusing to back Houk.[20] Because of his manipulations to improve his position by applying pressure to national Republican leaders, Houk greatly weakened his position. In less than a year Houk had managed to alienate both the president and the Republican leadership in Congress. Even after Evans was defeated for reelection in 1890, he dominated the dispersal of patronage in Tennessee from his position as the assistant postmaster general.[21]

The feud was interrupted by Leonidas Houk's death in May 1891. The Houk machine quickly regrouped, with most of the regulars backing John Houk for the vacant position.[22] Some opposition did develop, however, and machine leaders decided to hold a direct primary instead of using the traditional county convention system. The other candidate was W. W. Woodruff, a wealthy businessman from Knoxville. The primary campaign was short, but it offered a major departure from previous Second District elections. Woodruff was able to pay his workers and even went to the extreme of purchasing all the carriages in Knoxville so that Houk could not rent any transportation to take his supporters to the polls.[23] The machine was able to withstand this challenge easily, for Houk won more than 70 percent of the vote.[24]

While quite successful in his first campaign and in the subsequent general election, John Houk did not prove to be his father's equal as a popular politician. Although the primary and campaign against the Democratic candidate lasted for five months, Houk did not make a single speech. Instead he brought in prominent outside speakers, including West Virginia Republican leader Nathan Goff.[25] Rather than mixing with the voters, the younger Houk depended completely on his party organization to reach them. He also could not maintain a broad platform, as his father had done. Ignoring the tariff issue to a great extent, he concentrated instead on the veteran vote. Thus, three major elements in the success of the Houk machine had disappeared with the death of Leonidas Houk. The personality and the public-speaking ability of the candidate were assets that had been lost, and those Republicans who were primarily concerned about business and industry felt neglected.

After Houk's victory in the special election in November 1891, the patronage battle between the Houk machine and Evans resumed. Although Evans was not a native of eastern Tennessee and had not experienced personally the difficulties the Unionists of the area had suffered during the Civil War, he was able to work well with his army veteran constituents, which made it very difficult for Houk to attack him at the local level.[26] In February 1892 Evans demonstrated his continued dominance by naming the president of the state Republican League.[27] Houk gained a measure of revenge in June when he blocked Evans's nomination to the Republican National Committee.[28] Houk's desperation to end Evans's power led to one of the most bizarre conclusions to a political campaign in Tennessee history.

Houk and his ally, John W. Baker, the Republican state chairman, had reached a fusion agreement in 1892 with John McDowell, the leader of the Tennessee Populists. In July McDowell visited Republican officials in Washington and returned with a promise of fifteen thousand dollars to help Populist candidates.[29] In return for this aid, McDowell agreed to an extensive working arrangement with the Tennessee Republicans. Houk realized late in the campaign that the fusion arrangements in the Third District would allow Evans to be elected to Congress again. Houk, therefore, leaked information to the Democrats, who exposed the payoff to McDowell.[30] All Populist and Republican candidates were severely hurt by the revelations, and Evans was defeated.

Despite the loss suffered by Evans in 1892, the Houk machine remained weakened. With Grover Cleveland and the Democrats controlling federal patronage, Houk had no way to reward his loyal followers. Sensing the significance of these developments, Henry R. Gibson, a former confidant of Leonidas Houk, announced in the spring of 1893 that he would challenge John Houk for the Republican congressional nomination in 1894.[31] A native of Maryland, Gibson had lived in eastern Tennessee since 1867 and for nearly a decade had been judge of the Chancellors Court in the Second Congressional District. A widely respected jurist, he eventually compiled several volumes of Tennessee laws. Gibson had been Leonidas Houk's right-hand man for a number of years and apparently expected to succeed him. The suddenness of the congressman's death, however, had not allowed Gibson the time he needed to get organized in 1891. By 1893 he was ready.

Although the machine seemed as strong as ever, Gibson had several advantages that previous challengers had not had. He had been part of the machine himself for twenty-five years, and many members of the organization had a personal loyalty to him. By these means Gibson was able to control some parts of the party in the Second District, thereby weakening Houk. In addition, Gibson had an enthusiastic following among reform-minded Republicans. He had been a leader in the 1887 campaign for prohibition in Tennessee and was widely regarded as the leading reform Republican in the state.[32] Since a majority of the constituents—particularly Republicans—had voted for the Prohibition Amendment in the Second Congressional District, this approval was quite significant. Also, although Gibson did not enjoy the close relationship with the voters that Leonidas Houk had had, he contrasted very favorably with the inarticulate John Houk.

Gibson was also a threat to John Houk because he represented the new forces working within the Republican party. As a lawyer, Gibson was part of the middle class in mountain society. He eagerly supported efforts to industrialize the region, which were popular with Republican voters. As a corollary to his interest in economic expansion, Gibson was the chief defender of protective legislation in eastern Tennessee. He also expressed interest in the plight of the industrial workers in the mountain counties. Houk refused to abandon his father's veteran-oriented platform and was unable to appeal to the growing number of voters born during and after the Civil War. Gibson's appeal to business leaders had one further result. He received large campaign contributions and was able to purchase controlling interest in every newspaper in the district except one.[33]

The campaign for the nomination began in May 1893 and lasted until the 10 March 1894 direct primary. One Gibson paper unhappily observed, "Would that the party could be delivered from such a campaign as is coming. There have been filthy ones before, but they cannot compare with the one just before us."[34] Houk's entire platform centered around the question of Gibson's Civil War record. Gibson maintained that he had served in the Union army, but Houk claimed that Gibson had falsified his records. In January 1894 the National Committee of the Grand Army of the Republic issued a report declaring Gibson to be ineligible for membership because he had been a civilian employee of the army throughout the war.[35] Jubilant with the results, Houk demanded that Gibson withdraw from the race.

Gibson, however, remained in the contest, and his followers started to employ the same smear tactics that Houk had used. Houk was accused of being an absentee congressman and of not voting on an important veterans' pension bill and on the Wilson tariff bill then pending in Congress. As a result of Houk's failure to vote on these bills, he was charged with working against the old soldiers and businessmen of the Second District. The Gibson forces next charged that Houk was being supported by the Democrats and that the editor of his paper was a Democrat. Although both of these allegations were manifestly untrue, they probably hurt Houk in the strongly Republican Second District. Finally, Houk was asked to explain his connection with the leaking of the Republican-Populist fusion agreement two years before.[36]

Houk's advisers warned him that the voters were getting tired of the dirty campaign and that he must challenge Gibson to a series of debates or at least make some public addresses.[37] Instead, he once again sought outside help, including some from North Carolina congressman Thomas Settle.[38] Pessimistic reports continued to come into Houk headquarters, and so on 12 February 1894, Houk made the first campaign speech of his life. Apparently dependent upon notes—very unusual among eastern Tennessee political speakers—Houk primarily addressed veterans in the audience.[39] It was obvious from his remarks that Houk was not going to attempt to broaden his appeal to the voters.

The results of the primary vindicated Gibson's new approach to the voters. He carried seven of the eleven counties in the district and won the popular vote with a total of 14,067, compared to 13,119 for Houk.[40] Defections from the machine had occurred all over the district, indicating the breadth of Gibson's appeal. Houk cried fraud and demanded that the district Republican committee, which he controlled, investigate and throw out any illegal votes. Houk specifically charged Gibson with buying black votes in Knoxville, but the returns appeared to refute this accusation. Houk had carried the city by a vote of 2,303 to 836, and in the two wards that included black voters in large numbers Houk won 61 and 89 percent of the vote.[41] These figures did not deter Houk's friends on the committee, and less than two weeks later they had thrown out enough votes to declare Houk the winner.[42] Many Second District Republicans refused to accept this decision, however, and mass meetings were held in several counties asking Gibson to remain a candidate. Gibson readily agreed and continued to stress his concern with economic issues.

In the midst of this frantic maneuvering, Houk was faced with a challenge from his old adversary, H. Clay Evans, who was actively seeking the Republican gubernatorial nomination in 1894. This quest Houk recognized as a threat to his control of the state party organization, and in concert with another eastern Tennessee Republican politician, Walter P. Brownlow, he attempted to thwart Evans. Houk selected state Republican committee chairman John W. Baker as the opposition candidate to Evans. Baker's task was to secure delegates in middle and west Tennessee for the state convention to be held in August. Baker succeeded; at the convention he had a small majority of the votes from those two sections.[43]

Houk and Brownlow assigned themselves the task of stopping Evans in eastern Tennessee. They never really had a chance, for Evans and his campaign managers literally bought votes in some areas.[44] Once again the new political tactics brought by increasing business participation in eastern Tennessee Republican politics had carried the day. Evans swept mountain counties, winning more than 70 percent of the delegates from that region, and was nominated on the first ballot.[45] The extent of Houk's failure was obvious, especially since Evans had won a majority of the votes from Houk's own district.

Now more and more isolated, Houk still refused to make any major changes in his campaign. He continued to discuss Gibson's war record to the exclusion of all other topics. In September Houk's campaign suffered a devastating blow when Gibson and his backers purchased control of the *Knoxville Republican*.[46] Houk attempted unsuccessfully to halt the sale through court action, and as a result of Gibson's purchase of the paper he was deprived of any means of reaching the voters.[47] With no other alternative available, Houk asked for a series of joint debates with Gibson, but the offer was rejected. Thus the long and sordid campaign ended with the contestants repeating much that they had said numerous times during the eighteen months since May 1893.

The election returns confirmed the original results of the spring primary and signaled the end of the Houk dynasty. Both Gibson and Evans were elected, although a Democratic legislature eventually deprived Evans of the governorship. In the Houk-Gibson race, Gibson not only won, but increased his majority to three thousand votes. Most of the gain occurred in Knoxville, where Houk's margin over Gibson was reduced by a thousand votes from the March primary.[48] Existing evidence indicates that the Democrats—who did not run a candidate—split their ballots fairly evenly between the two candidates, so that Gibson was the clear choice of the Republican voters.[49]

H. Clay Evans's position as the leading Republican in the state was secure also. In 1891 Evans had campaigned in Ohio for William McKinley, and the two men had become warm personal and political friends.[50] Evans became the leader of the McKinley forces in Tennessee and, much to Marc Hanna's delight, was able to secure most of the Tennessee delegation for McKinley.[51] The candidate's trust in Evans is clearly outlined in the following letter: "It seems to me the best way to do in all matters relating to Tennessee, is to refer them directly to Hon. H. Clay Evans of Chattanooga. He is my friend and I believe will advise you prudently."[52] After McKinley's election, Evans was named commissioner of pensions and distributed most of the patronage in Tennessee. It was not until Walter Brownlow challenged him in 1900 that Evans faced any opposition to his supremacy.

The Houk machine, then, was dead, its demise traceable to several basic causes. John Houk, although a skilled political manipulator, was a poor candidate who was unable to arouse the voters the way his father had. The machine also found that the old system of an exchange of services between worker and party boss could not compete with candidates who could pay their workers. In the end, however, the crucial failure was that of the voters to respond to the issues that had maintained the Houks in power for a decade and a half. War records and pensions for veterans no longer meant more to the voters than the state of the national economy.

The end of the Goff machine in West Virginia came peacefully, but its disappearance still signified a major shift in the mountain Republican organization. Unlike John Houk, Nathan Goff made every effort to bridge the gap between the old-time Unionists and the new industrial interests coming to prominence in his state. Goff himself represented both groups in his personal life. Not only had he been a Union soldier, but also he was a fairly wealthy mine owner who had been a consistent supporter of the protective tariff.[53] In addition, Goff had been the most popular

Republican candidate for public office since the end of Reconstruction. All of these factors would seem to have made Goff virtually impregnable as leader of the party. In fact, the Goff machine was replaced three years before the Houk organization was finally defeated.

One reason for the machine's quick decline was the fact that Goff had a number of powerful enemies within the party. His trick of not announcing his candidacy, all the while having his followers work at securing it for him, alienated a number of men. William P. Hubbard refused to submit to this tactic at the congressional nominating convention in 1884 and nearly defeated Goff.[54] He supported Goff's candidacy reluctantly in the general election and never again considered himself part of the machine. Two years later B. B. Dovener was forced to withdraw from the fight for the Republican nomination by similar maneuvering on Goff's part.[55] Again in 1888, Goff received the gubernatorial nomination after several prominent party leaders were forced to step aside.[56] Goff had also offended Albert Blakeslee White, the editor of the widely read *Parkersburg State Journal*, in 1886 by not sending promised funds to help White's candidacy for the state legislature.[57] Furthermore, almost every patronage appointment left someone dissatisfied. As a result, a significant minority among West Virginia Republicans already opposed Goff's leadership.

The decision of Stephen Elkins to make his political home in West Virginia gave leadership to the anti-Goff elements in the party. Elkins, an extremely wealthy land speculator and industrialist, had had a distinguished career as a power in the national Republican party. He was largely responsible for Blaine's nomination in 1884 and directed the Republican national campaign that year.[58] It was at this point that he first had contact with West Virginia party leaders. He arranged to have Blaine visit the state and provided advice and money that strengthened the party there.[59] After Blaine's loss in November, Elkins began to look seriously for a state in which he could win a United States Senate seat. West Virginia offered several advantages to the wealthy political manipulator. Through his father-in-law, Democratic senator Henry Davis, Elkins was able to make a series of investments in West Virginia mineral lands. Operating through a railroad corporation, the West Virginia Central, Elkins came to be one of the dominant figures in the exploitation of West Virginia's vast coal reserves. These business activities not only endeared Elkins to capital-starved West Virginia businessmen, but gave him other, more directly political, advantages as well. He could give jobs to political workers as a form of private patronage that allowed him to build an organization to rival Goff's.[60]

Elkins became directly involved in the state's local politics in 1888.

He was introduced to the state at a bipartisan business development convention in Wheeling in late February; there he pledged to aid the state in exploiting its mineral wealth.[61] The leading Republican paper, the *Wheeling Intelligencer*, gave Elkins considerable publicity and eased his way into the party.[62] He encouraged a seemingly reluctant Goff to be a gubernatorial candidate and pledged to back Goff for the Senate if the Republicans won control of the legislature. Elkins, who desperately desired the Senate seat, undoubtedly felt that Goff would find it difficult to resign the governorship without losing the support of the many Republicans who would want state patronage positions.[63] It appears that Elkins made substantial contributions to the Republican campaign, because in September he had to deny that he was planning to transport five thousand black voters into the state.[64] More money was available to Republicans in 1888 than ever before, and elated workers reported that they could now secure the votes of mountaineers who needed "encoinagement."[65]

The election results forced an unexpected trial of political strength between Goff and Elkins. The Republican campaign came very close to complete success.[66] Republicans, with the help of an Independent, organized the state senate; and the Democrats and Independents had only a slight majority in the assembly.[67] The Democrats still had a shaky majority of one in balloting for United States senator, but their ranks were so divided that it seemed possible that a Republican would be able to make a deal. Goff was the Republican candidate, but his efforts were complicated by the gubernatorial situation. Goff had been elected governor by 110 votes, but the Democrats were contesting the election; and, if Goff went to the Senate, the Democrats would get the governorship by default. Goff, however, demanded that Elkins support him for the Senate, and Elkins reluctantly agreed.[68] Elkins then turned his attention to trying to secure a cabinet appointment in the Harrison administration. Since Elkins was responsible for leading many Blaine followers to support Harrison, he seemed a logical choice. Some of Goff's friends, who were pushing him for a cabinet position, however, weakened Elkins's position so seriously that he was not appointed.[69] Goff failed by one vote of being elected to the Senate, and by March it was clear that the Democrats were not going to allow him to be elected governor.[70] The outcome of this first confrontation was a draw. Goff managed to maintain himself at the top of the party organization and to prevent Elkins from securing a cabinet position, but he had failed to win the Senate seat or the governorship.

The next battle came over who would control federal patronage for West Virginia under the Harrison administration. As with Clay Evans in Tennessee, Elkins was extremely successful, despite the presence of an already-existing party organization. George C. Sturgiss, Elkins's candidate for United States district attorney, was appointed over Goff's man.[71] With Elkins's support John W. Mason was named commissioner of the Internal Revenue Service.[72] Although Goff backed Albert White for collector of Internal Revenue, White was at best neutral in the Goff-Elkins battle.[73] Goff enjoyed some successes as well. His candidate for postmaster of Wheeling was successful, and he secured a large number of minor appointments for his followers.[74] But the influence that Elkins wielded could not be discounted. John Mason told one applicant, "Messrs. Elkins and Davis are largely interested in your office. They, of course, will have much to say regarding the removal, and the appointment of a successor. It would be well for you to confer with them."[75] This latter advice was more and more often followed by West Virginia mountain Republicans.

The political campaign of 1890 further weakened Goff's position as leader of West Virginia Republicans. There was a demand among Republicans in the Second Congressional District that Elkins oppose free-trade Democrat William Wilson.[76] Some substantial opposition to Elkins developed, however, and Elkins was not interested in entering a contest he might well lose.[77] Instead he supported George Harmen, who defeated A. Gordon Dayton, the candidate of the old machine, for the nomination.[78] At the state convention Elkins added another victory to his collection. His candidate, Frank Reynolds, was nominated over two competitors for the state supreme court.[79]

In an effort to offset Elkins's successes, Goff campaigned vigorously in the fall of 1890. He retained a great deal of popularity among average Republicans and was a much-requested campaign speaker.[80] Appearing all over the state, he spoke to large crowds and became recognized as the party leader in this effort.[81] Elkins, on the other hand, seemed to withdraw and to take very little active part in the canvassing. Once again Elkins had made a shrewd political decision. West Virginia Republicans had firmly committed themselves to the concept of the Lodge bill.[82] The Democrats seized the issue and ran a heavily racist campaign.[83] The result was a series of disastrous defeats for the Republicans throughout the state of West Virginia. Soon after the election was over, Goff's efforts were being unfavorably contrasted with those of Elkins in 1888.[84] Although this comparison was no doubt unfair to Goff, it was certain that his competitor had recognized the dangers of the 1890 campaign much more clearly than he had.

Goff apparently sensed his growing weakness and sought an honorable way to give up his position as party leader. Although he personally was able to adapt to the changing political conditions, Goff knew that his followers could not. Since Elkins was already the acknowledged leader of the new middle class, his power would continue to grow. Thus, Goff felt that he could best serve himself and the party by accepting a position as a federal judge.[85] Elkins was now recognized as the leading Republican in West Virginia and was appointed secretary of war by President Benjamin Harrison in December 1891.[86] Although no longer an active politician, Goff did help Elkins in 1892 by refusing to support a revolt against the new boss's delegation to the national convention.[87]

Elkins moved quickly to consolidate his hold on the Republican organization. He was very careful to avoid any appearance that he was purging Goff's friends from positions of influence. His actions during the 1892 gubernatorial nominating convention were an excellent example of his technique. Elkins refused to accept the nomination himself and instead chose former state senator Thomas E. Davis as the candidate.[88] Davis was closely associated with Goff and yet posed no threat to Elkins because he had no power base of his own. Unfortunately for Elkins and the Republicans, Davis turned out to be a poor public speaker and an unpopular campaigner.[89] The Democrats resorted to a strong racist platform and were able to retain control of the state government.[90] Despite his hold on the party, Elkins knew he could not be elected to the Senate unless the Republicans found a way to end Democratic hegemony in West Virginia. The political off year of 1893 was a momentous one for the Republicans. There was a major financial crisis that the Republicans eagerly used to their advantage. Elkins watched with great anticipation as the Democratic party split into business and agrarian factions and as Republicans swept to victory in elections throughout the country. His observations led him to the conclusion that the "trouble is, that there has been too much money spent in elections. I am satisfied that where the people are thoroughly aroused, money is not required beyond ordinary expenses of printing tickets, securing speakers and distributing campaign literature."[91] Thus Elkins began putting even more emphasis than before on the issues of the canvass. The protective tariff became the Republican rallying cry for the 1894 campaign.

The focal point of the 1894 West Virginia campaign was the battle for Congress in the Second District between Democrat William L. Wilson and Republican A. Gordon Dayton. Dayton showed that he was a strong candidate against his nationally known opponent. Dayton had been associated with the Goff wing of the party in 1890, but found this alliance no real handicap. His forces were in the field early, and he had a majority of delegates to the district nominating convention committed to him before his opposition could organize.[92] Both George C. Sturgiss and John W. Mason, strong Elkins men, made brief attempts to stop Dayton, but his position was secure.[93] It is significant to note that Elkins made little attempt to interfere in the contest. Unlike Goff, Houk, or Mahone, Elkins and the new business leaders seemed less concerned about absolute loyalty to their leadership than about winning. Dayton was popular, and Elkins was willing to work with him.

Another reason for Republican unity was Dayton's opponent. As the secretary of the Republican Congressional Committee reported to Dayton, "This Committee is fully in earnest about the necessity of carrying your District. It is more than the importance of securing one vote for the Republican party. The defeat of your opponent means a great national reverse to the enemy."[94] Democrat William Wilson was the recognized leader of the tariff reform forces in the country. Although a skilled campaigner, Wilson did not enjoy the luxury of a united party behind him. Davis and many business Democrats actually preferred his defeat to party victory.[95] In addition, the Democrats of West Virginia were badly split on the question of silver-money policy and were literally killing each other in campaign confrontations.[96] Wilson's vote to repeal the Sherman Silver Purchase Act alienated many Democratic voters.[97] Probably few of the free-silver advocates deserted Wilson because of the Republican party's similar stand on the issue, but Wilson undoubtedly recognized that they would not work to get him elected.[98]

Dayton, on the other hand, had help from Republicans all over the country. One Ohio man noted that although he was "an entire stranger" to Dayton, he still wanted to contribute to the campaign.[99] Another gift came with no strings attached from New York and the American Protective Tariff League.[100] Further, the Republican Congressional Committee kept its promises to Dayton and sent timely aid.[101] The only outside help that Wilson received was of rather dubious value. Col. Angus McDonald of Virginia came to the mountains to preach the glories of the Confederacy and to try to win back Democrats deserting to the Populists.[102] Since the majority of West Virginians had served in the Union army, this strategy was risky at best. And, as John Houk discovered in eastern Tennessee in 1894, the old issues no longer had an impact in the depression.

Most important, however, the full power of the Elkins machine was thrust into Dayton's efforts. George Sturgiss, who had been Dayton's major opponent for the nomination, quickly made peace and offered to do all he could to help against Wilson.[103] Elkins also actively worked for Dayton. In a Wheeling speech in October, he tied Wilson politically to the unpopular president, Grover Cleveland. Elkins even traveled with Dayton and filled a number of campaign appearances with the young lawyer.[104] Finally, Elkins paid the bills for the Republican campaign in 1894 and arranged for Dayton to receive financial assistance.[105] Thus Elkins continued to show a political flexibility that earlier mountain Republican bosses probably would have rejected. Dayton was not his candidate, but the new man did agree with Elkins's view on the tariff; and that was enough.

The combination of economic depression, popular issues, and party unity gave the Republicans a landslide victory in West Virginia in 1894. They carried thirty-three of the fifty-four counties, winning by a majority of more than thirteen thousand votes. Of particular significance was the rise of the Republican proportion of the vote in the mountain counties of northwestern West Virginia from 48 percent in 1892 to 54 percent in 1894.[106] Of more immediate interest to the Republicans, all four of the party's congressional candidates—including Dayton—had won, and the party had secured enough legislative seats to assure the election of a Republican United States senator.[107]

As the leading Republican in the state, Elkins was the logical choice of the party. Only longtime Republican leader George Sturgiss openly challenged him for the nomination. Even Sturgiss was forced to withdraw before the balloting began because he was unable to secure the backing of the old machine.[108] Despite the absence of announced candidates, Elkins realized that many West Virginia mountain voters felt that Goff deserved the office. The new boss neutralized this opposition a month after the election. At a meeting with Goff, Elkins agreed to support the federal judge for vice-president in 1896 and Goff issued a public statement backing Elkins.[109] Several weeks later the state legislature elected Elkins to the Senate on the first ballot.

Elkins was busy at the same time strengthening the party organization that he now controlled. The 1896 campaign was begun in September 1895, as the Republicans attempted to cover the state in preparation for the battle over protective tariff that they felt sure would follow.[110] The victory of 1894 had left the Republicans enthusiastic, and by the middle of November 1895 one worker reported that there were eighteen hundred agents of the American Protective Tariff League in West Virginia.[111] Each of these men would be expected to extol the virtues of the tariff and the Republican party for the next twelve months. In addition, Elkins and his aides worked hard to make sure that black Republicans were protected against Democratic attempts to intimidate them.[112]

The selection of delegates to the Republican National Convention in 1896, however, emphasized that Elkins exercised a different kind of control than had the party-army bosses. Elkins and a number of party leaders of the organization wanted the West Virginia delegation to go to the convention uninstructed.[113] Elkins had had great power at the national meetings in 1884, 1888, and 1892 and hoped to continue his influence in 1896. There was, however, opposition to the Elkins strategy from loyal members of the machine. Albert White was in contact with the backers of William McKinley and began to work actively to have the West Virginia delegates publicly committed to McKinley.[114] Elkins threatened to put his own name before the state convention in order to forestall White's efforts.[115] When White chose to ignore Elkins, the powerful boss found himself in a dilemma. McKinley obviously commanded a great deal of grass-roots support, and if Elkins were to retain his traditional position as a national power, he would have to risk losing it at the local level.[116] This risk he was unwilling to take, and in early May Elkins acquiesced to White's campaign and did not even go to the convention.[117] Again Elkins agreed to a policy that he had at first opposed, instead of trying to maintain rigid discipline and absolute loyalty. Rather than being a sign of weakness, this course of action proved to be a source of power because dangerous antagonisms to Elkins's leadership were avoided.

The absence of bitterness in Republican ranks was important as the Democrats mounted a strong free-silver campaign in West Virignia in 1896. Gordon Dayton was warned, "The fact is the County people are out of money and they have nothing that will command money at present, and they do not know the cause. We must educate these people."[118] This was to be the Republican strategy for the campaign—educate the voters against free silver. Elkins became a leader in this effort and gave a gold speech at the state convention to set the tone for the party's campaign.[119] Then local Republicans began to circulate documents and make speeches to voters in order to counteract Democratic speakers and literature.[120] The Republican campaign was once again well financed, but there is little evidence to suggest that an unusual amount came from the Republican National Committee.[121] Apparently it was assumed that Elkins could provide all the money the Republican needed.

Unlike 1894, the Democrats as well as the Republicans now were united on local politics. Democratic leader Henry Davis, who had refused to support William Wilson in 1894, wrote to a Republican candidate who asked for his support, "You know that while I have kind feelings for you, and liberal views in politics, I am a Democrat."[122] William M. Stewart, senator from Nevada, spoke in West Virginia and made free silver his only topic of discussion.[123] The silver forces were further strengthened when the Populists withdrew their ticket and joined with the Democrats.[124] The Republicans replied with a well-organized campaign based on sound money and the tariff. The nomination of George W. Atkinson for governor insured the unity of the party. Atkinson had been a prominent member of the old Goff machine, and once more Elkins displayed his flexibility by not opposing a man who was potentially an enemy. Elkins was rewarded when Atkinson campaigned energetically in forty-eight of the state's fifty-five counties and successfully aroused Republican voters.[125]

The election results once again confirmed the appeal of the Republican platform and the organizational strength of Elkins's machine. For the first time since Reconstruction, the Republicans won the state's electoral vote and the governorship. The margin of victory was slightly reduced over that in 1894, but Atkinson still won more than 53 percent of the vote, and the Republicans swept the congressional seats again.[126] The Republican victories set off a mad scramble for patronage positions. As one applicant noted, the "loaves and fishes" were more frantically sought than ever before. One man even applied a month before the election.[127] Under the circumstances, Elkins was appalled when he learned that McKinley had offered Goff a cabinet position and a share of the patronage. But when the president refused to guarantee Goff a Supreme Court appointment, the former West Virginia boss decided to remain in his current judicial position.[128] Elkins then was left to distribute patronage with a relatively free hand.

Elkins's position finally seemed secure. Goff had not accepted an opportunity to challenge his leadership, either in the Senate race in 1894 or with the cabinet appointment in 1896. The Republicans had won two decisive victories and seemed to be in firm control of the state. The new policies that Elkins espoused were popular with the voters of West Virginia and promised to remain so for many years. Equally significant was the flexible discipline Elkins exercised over the party organization. Unlike the earlier mountain Republican bosses, Elkins tried to conciliate opposing factions rather than to crush them. His acceptance of Dayton's and Atkinson's nominations were examples of this strategy. He was even able to step aside when his own followers demanded that delegates instructed for McKinley be sent to the national convention. This flexibility meant that much potential opposition was dissipated before it could fester and become dangerous. Elkins was now the undisputed leader of the mountain Republicans in West Virginia.

North Carolina mountain Republicans faced the most complex political situation in the upper South in the 1890s. Within the party not only did a transfer of power between old and new leaders take place, but the mountain whites were able to seize control of the state party organization for the first time. Simultaneously, the Republicans were forced to adjust their electoral strategy to accommodate the presence of an active Populist party in the state. Dr. John Mott quickly lost his position as party leader in the midst of this chaos, and a lengthy struggle ensued to determine who would succeed him. Mott, unlike John Houk and Nathan Goff, refused to accept his defeat and attempted to regain his preeminent position. That action by the old boss only added another element of uncertainty to an already confused situation.

Ironically, Mott's failure was caused by electoral victory. Mott's hold on the Republican organization in the mountains and at the state level was his position as collector of internal revenue. That position had been weakened when the Democrats controlled the office between 1885 and 1889. When the Republicans won the presidency in the election of 1888, Mott expected to be reappointed. Three Republican congressmen were elected at that same time, however, and they refused to recommend Mott for the position. During the previous decade there had been no elected officials to challenge Mott, and he had been able to stay in power. Now mountain Republican congressman Hamilton Ewart induced President Harrison to appoint John B. Eaves to the collector's office.[129] Ewart further strengthened his position by forcing Eaves to accept his campaign manager Jeter C. Pritchard as his assistant collector. Since Eaves was already the chairman of the state committee, Ewart and his allies from western North Carolina dominated the party's machinery.

Mott refused to acquiesce in the new arrangement. Mott accused Eaves of paying five thousand dollars to Ewart for his appointment, which weakened the latter's attempt to be confirmed by the Senate.[130] At the same time many members of the old Mott machine wrote letters to senators protesting Eaves's appointment. Newly elected Republican congressman John M. Brower complained that Eaves and his men were "treating him unfairly, and are using their official positions—to prevent his reelection."[131] The campaign against Eaves was successful, and the Senate refused to confirm him. Ewart moved quickly to maintain himself in power. In late August 1890 Ewart was unanimously renominated for Congress, despite Mott's opposition.[132] About a week later at the Republican state convention, Eaves won reelection as state chairman, with more than 80 percent of the vote. Eaves was also unanimously endorsed as the party's candidate for the collectorship.[133] The Harrison administration then recognized Ewart's position by appointing William W. Rollins as collector. Rollins, an ally of Ewart's, reappointed most of the men placed in office by Eaves.[134]

A powerful and ultimately successful attack on Ewart's position came from an unexpected source. The instigator was Ewart's ally, Jeter Pritchard. Pritchard represented the new business-oriented wing of the Republican party. A native of east Tennessee and a member of a Unionist family, Pritchard had been a lifelong Republican. Surviving photographs indicate that Pritchard was a large man, whose compelling eyes were accented by bushy eyebrows. An extravagant mustache and prominent nose gave additional character to his round face. Looking much like a successful banker or lawyer, Pritchard apparently moved easily into the business and political world of western North Carolina. In 1890 Pritchard had been elected to the state senate from the district that included his home county of Mitchell. Since this victory was achieved in the midst of general Republican defeats, it marked Pritchard as a new power in the party. In January 1891 he challenged Brower and Eaves for the Republican nomination for the United States Senate. Pritchard emerged victorious from the brief, but bitter, battle and once again showed his growing strength.[135]

Pritchard continued his assault on the regular party organization with the formation of the Protective Tariff League several months later. Pritchard attacked the old leadership, saying, "The young Republicans of North Carolina are tired of so much contention, especially so, when they feel that it is prompted by a desire to control the Federal patronage of this State." He further asserted that the "tariff will be the leading issue in the next campaign" and that the party in North Carolina had better prepare itself for that eventuality.[136] Eaves and other old-line Republicans opposed the new organization because they were afraid that emphasis on national issues like the tariff would take attention away from successful local issues such as the undemocratic county government system.[137] One opponent also asserted that the movement was designed to diminish the influence of blacks in the party.[138] Pritchard denied these charges vehemently and maintained that he was simply trying to appeal to the business wing of the Democratic party.

The first convention of the North Carolina Protective Tariff League, held in the mountain city of Asheville on 21 July 1891, was a complete success. More than five hundred delegates attended from all over the state. A number of blacks and Democratic businessmen came, allowing the organizers to claim that all segments of the state's population were represented.[139] Pritchard was elected president of the North Carolina League so as to encourage Republicans to join the organization.[140] Pritchard continued to deny that the league was a "lily-white" group, but he was forced to admit that some local units did have strict segregation policies.[141] As with the Elkins machine in West Virginia, the older elements in the party, including blacks, were largely ignored by the middle-class Republicans. Pritchard's new prominence also made him the target of a small but vocal group of Republicans who were members of the Farmers' Alliance. His position as the attorney for several North Carolina railroads was particularly galling to this part of the party in western North Carolina.[142]

The unsettled condition of the party caused by Pritchard's increasing power was exploited by Mott, who, working in conjunction with white Republicans from the black-belt counties, opposed placing a Republican state ticket before the voters in 1892.[143] Mott and former congressman Daniel Russell were the chief spokesmen for this group, one that maintained it was impossible for the Republicans to win. They cited the Payne Election Law, passed in 1889 by the Democrats to discourage illiterates from voting, as disfranchising too many Republicans for the party to have a chance. In addition, this group wanted to eliminate black voters from the party.[144]

The first confrontation between the two factions of the party came at the state convention in April, called to select delegates to the national convention. Eaves and Pritchard were in complete control, and Pritchard was named as one of the at-large delegates to the national convention. In a surprise maneuver Eaves was reelected state chairman over Mott's candidate by a vote of 167 to 50. Mott's protest that the election of a state chairman had not been on the agenda found little sympathy among mountain Republicans.[145] Mott further weakened his position by cutting himself off from any help from the national administration. While Pritchard supported President Benjamin Harrison for renomination, Mott and his supporters backed James G. Blaine's abortive candidacy.[146] Mott and Russell had now alienated themselves from the blacks, the mountain Republicans, and the Harrison administration.

The success of the party leadership in maintaining itself in power allowed Pritchard to pursue his own personal plans. He was able to win the nomination for Congress in the Ninth District over his former patron, Hamilton Ewart. Ewart complained that Internal Revenue Service officials had dominated the convention and charged that Pritchard courted black votes by supporting the Lodge elections bill.[147] Pritchard, apparently feeling that it was not necessary to answer these charges, began his campaign on a positive tack. He maintained that the mountain counties had to industrialize in order for that section to advance economically. To accomplish that end, he said, the protective tariff would have to be supported by electing business Republicans like himself.[148] Attempting to retain the support of the mountain farming population, Pritchard also expressed his commitment to retaining silver currency and even expanding its use.[149] This stance would later become a major problem for Pritchard, but at that time there seemed to be nothing inconsistent with his platform.

Pritchard's rise to power coincided with the appearance of the Populist party in North Carolina. The reactionary and inflexible policies of the North Carolina Democrats drove the leader of the state's Farmers' Alliance, Marion Butler, to create the new party in the summer of 1892.[150] Although weak in the mountain counties, the Populists nominated a congressional candidate in Pritchard's district. They also nominated a state ticket. Efforts to join the two parties in an anti-Democratic coalition failed, although there was some cooperation at the local level.[151] The election returns, which produced a Democratic governor, also showed that by combining their votes the Republicans and Populists would have a majority.[152] Soon after the election Butler began to explore the possibility of the two parties' working together at the state level. He suggested that both parties agree on a platform to repeal the county government system and the state election laws.[153] Butler's efforts to fuse with the Republicans were aided by a bill passed by the Democratic-controlled legislature restricting the political activities of the alliance. By the later fall Butler had convinced the Populist leadership to work with the Republicans.

The Republicans were deeply split over the issue, however. The old boss, John Mott, was so enthusiastic that he worked openly for the Populists. Most mountain Republicans were more restrained but still interested. Newly elected lowland Republican congressman Thomas Settle owed his seat to the presence of a Populist candidate in his district. Despite the fact that Settle was very dependent on the wealthy industrialists connected with the Duke family, he was willing to work with the new party.[154] Pritchard's position was determined by an agreement he reached with another rising Republican politician in the mountain counties, Richmond Pearson. Pearson and Pritchard both wanted the Republican nomination in the Ninth Congressional District. Seeking to avoid an open confrontation, Pearson secured a statement from Butler recognizing Pritchard as the logical Republican candidate for the first available United States Senate seat. After this deal was arranged, Pritchard withdrew from the congressional contest and supported Pearson for Congress.[155] Then both Pearson and Pritchard began to work actively to promote fusion between the Republicans and Populists.

The Fusionists in the Republican party, however, were not in control of their organization; they were forced to challenge state chairman Eaves in a protracted struggle. Opposition to the proposed fusion of the two parties came primarily from those Republicans who were in control of the state committee. Chairman Eaves maintained that fusion would rob Republicans of an expected victory. At best it would force them to share the honors with the Populists and at worst would allow a Democratic victory. Eaves attempted to work within the party to block cooperation, but as the success of the Fusionists became evident, he risked splitting the party by publicly opposing an alliance with the Populists.[156] Eaves was joined in the fight for a straight Republican ticket by the party's gubernatorial nominee in 1892, David M. Furches.[157] The Republican National Committee attempted to mediate the dispute. In April 1894 Schuyler S. Olds of the committee sent letters to the leading Republicans in the state; sixty of the replies have been preserved.[158] Approximately one-third of those answering Olds's letter opposed any type of fusion arrangement, and many others were skeptical about it for statewide elections.[159]

The Fusion campaign in the mountain counties was directed by Pearson. A Republican-turned-Democrat-turned-Republican, Pearson was very sensitive to changes in public opinion. His appeal to the voters was based on his desire to reach as many as possible while alienating none. His platform was an amazing amalgam of conflicting programs: he favored the protective tariff, graduated income tax, and free silver.[160] He worked very closely with Butler and the Populists, and at one point he allowed the Populist leader to revise his statements so that they would be acceptable to third-party voters.[161] In the fall campaign Pearson did not attempt to defend his own record, but instead attacked his opponent and the Democrats for economic failures and undemocratic practices in state government.[162] Apparently, no Republicans were seriously opposed to Pearson, for the Pritchard organization swung its power behind him.

Pritchard was having a much more difficult time trying to oust Eaves from his position as chairman. Eaves could be replaced only by a state convention, and he was determined to delay the convention until after the Populist convention, thereby avoiding cooperation.[163] Pritchard countered this tactic by addressing an open letter to Eaves, demanding that the party's state executive committee be called together to discuss fusion.[164] Eaves refused to do so. Then the cooperation Republicans took matters into their own hands and scheduled a committee meeting just before the Populist convention on 1 August.[165] But at that meeting the members of the committee who did attend recommended that the party fuse with the Populists and that Marion Butler and Jeter Pritchard be elected to the Senate.

The actions of the Populist convention virtually assured that the Republicans would join them. The Populists nominated one member of their own party, one Pritchard Republican, one Eaves Republican, and two progressive Democrats as their ticket for the state judicial election.[166] Some Republicans who had had reservations about fusion now became supporters of the movement.[167] The Eaves faction continued to fight and offered a limited compromise: they were willing to accept cooperation in some local elections, but not for state offices. The attempt at reconciliation by Eaves was too late, however, for he was overwhelmed at the state convention that met at the end of August. Fusion was endorsed by a vote of 147 to 27; Eaves was replaced as state chairman by Alfred E. Holton, a Pritchard supporter.[168] The final arrangements were left to the state executive committee, but the alliance had been forged.

The mountain voters experienced a rather unusual campaign in 1894, as did the rest of the state. The Republicans and Populists were on opposite ends of the political spectrum on national issues, but they worked well together in the fall campaign. Concentrating on discriminatory local government structures and election laws, the Fusionists blamed the Democrats for all local and national problems. In their zeal to be elected, both parties accepted part of the doctrine of the other in larger issues. The Populists ignored the racial question and in some cases even voted for black candidates. Many Republicans, including Pearson and Pritchard and the state convention, called for the free coinage of silver. The Democrats were not flexible enough to meet the threat posed by the Fusionists and had little to offer the voters in rebuttal.

The result was a sweeping Republican and Populist victory at all levels. The two parties gained control of many offices and now had a majority on the state supreme court. Their combined strength allowed them to organize both houses of the state legislature and to elect two United States senators.[169] No one challenged Marion Butler's claim to one Senate seat, but many Republicans felt that they were more deserving than Pritchard. Mott and Ewart attempted to secure the support of the Republican caucus but deferred to party chairman Eugene Holton. Pritchard easily defeated Holton in the contest before Republican legislators and then was elected to a short term created by the death of Senator Zebulon Vance.[170] Now Pritchard and the mountain Republicans were in complete control of the state party and sought to consolidate their position.

Pritchard attempted to make safe his patronage position within the Republican party by backing the winning Republican presidential nominee in 1896. By August 1895 Pritchard was the chief spokesman for the candidacy of William McKinley of Ohio.[171] Pritchard and Pearson, in fact, asked McKinley to intervene in the North Carolina situation, but the careful candidate declined.[172] Anti-Pritchard forces led by Thomas Settle backed Speaker of the House Thomas B. Reed.[173] Although the evidence is not completely clear, it appears that the Reed campaign in North Carolina was funded in part by money from the Dukes.[174] Despite this fact, the McKinley campaign was better financed and organized, and throughout the spring of 1896 more and more North Carolina Republicans backed the man from Ohio.[175] The Republican convention was a great triumph for the Pritchard forces. There was no opposition to instructing the state's delegation to vote for McKinley, and the convention also unanimously voted to support Pritchard's bid for reelection to the Senate.[176]

At the same time, Pritchard had to deal with one further source of possible trouble for his candidacy, the gubernatorial nomination. Pritchard had allied himself in this contest with racist former congressman Daniel Russell. Russell's opponent was Oliver H. Dockery, a longtime party stalwart who was backed by blacks and the Reed forces. The Pritchard-Russell forces attempted to limit the convention power of the chairman, Holton, two months before the meeting and were partially successful. The battle for delegates was sharply contested throughout the state, and a number of counties sent competing delegations.[177] As Russell and Pritchard had feared, Holton and the credentials committee rejected many of their contesting delegations, and it appeared that Dockery would win. This prospect also concerned minor candidates, who combined with Russell forces to override the credentials committee and accept a minority report that gave most of the contested delegates to Russell.[178] Apparently, Pritchard and James E. Boyd, a minor candidate who had worked for McKinley with Pritchard, reached an agreement whereby most of Boyd's votes went to Russell; Russell was nominated.[179] Following the convention many black Republicans staged a revolt against Russell, but it was quickly put down.[180]

Pritchard and the Republicans recognized that they still had to rely on the Populists for their continued success, and this dependence was to be the major problem for the party in 1896. Butler demanded that the two parties campaign on the basis of free silver and that the Populists be allowed to name the gubernatorial candidate on the Fusion state ticket. The Republicans rejected these proposals, whereupon the Populists rejected the Republican offer that said nothing about the national ticket and reserved the governorship and Senate seat for the Republicans.[181] Butler felt that "the very existence of the People's Party is at stake" and refused all compromises on his position.[182] At the Republican state convention in May, the party left several offices vacant to encourage possible future fusion. Then Butler and the Democrats reached an agreement to fuse on the national election.[183] When the Republican National Convention adopted a platform supporting gold currency, Pritchard was extremely concerned that it would weaken the chances for fusion.[184] At a conference in July Butler demanded that the Republicans abandon McKinley and Russell as the price of Populist cooperation; since compliance would have greatly weakened Pritchard within the party, he quickly rejected the demand.

The threat of local and state defeats eventually drove the Republicans and Populists together again. In early September arrangements were made with respect to legislative and congressional races in particular, and on some state offices as well. Despite the bitter defection of Populist gubernatorial candidate William A. Guthrie, the two fusion parties swept to victory again.[185] Republican Daniel Russell was elected governor—the only Republican elected governor of North Carolina between 1872 and 1972. The two parties again had complete control of the state legislature and elected most of the congressmen. Most encouraging for the Republicans was the fact that the party's voting strength had returned to and surpassed the levels achieved in the late 1880s.[186]

Pritchard and the young Republicans who came to power with him in 1896 had good reason to be optimistic. A combination of good fortune and careful planning had made them masters of their party and, in conjunction with the Populists, their state. McKinley's victory in the presidential election of 1896 further insured that the new leadership of the North Carolina Republican party could expect federal patronage to strengthen their organization. They were also aware that this success was secured by a fragile alliance of mountain whites, Populists, and black Republicans. The question that remained to be answered was whether the new middle-class politicians could keep these antagonistic elements working together.

The Republicans of Kentucky in the early 1890s seemed to enjoy the luxury of stable leadership within the party, in contrast to those in the other states. William Bradley retained his position as the acknowledged boss of Kentucky Republicans and in 1895 was elected governor. The state patronage that Bradley controlled further strengthened his hold on the organization and prompted him to run for president in 1896. This picture of surface unity masked some serious divisions within the party, however, and obscured the fact that a significant change in leadership had taken place in the mountain counties. In the highlands the business and professional wing of the party asserted itself, and in 1894 a new leader, David G. Colson, captured control of the organization. As in the other three states, the issues generated by the conflicts surrounding the Civil War had lost their impact, and the party turned increasingly to economic appeals to attract mountain voters.

The Kentucky mountain Republicans suffered from a confused

leadership situation as early as 1889. John D. White's unexpected withdrawal from mountain politics in 1884 had left H. Franklin Finley as the most powerful Republican in the mountain counties. Finley, however, could not be regarded as a party boss. The limited nature of his power was demonstrated by the battle to control federal patronage in 1889. Finley was working to secure control of the two major patronage positions. It soon became apparent that his influence was negligible, as unsuccessful Ninth District congressional candidate Drury J. Burchett was named United States marshal without Finley's backing.[187] In June, Bluegrass politician William Cassisus Goodloe was named collector of internal revenue for eastern Kentucky despite Finley's open opposition.[188] Unable to control matters in the mountain counties, Finley found that newly elected mountain Republican congressman John H. Wilson did have considerable influence with the Harrison administration. In one instance Wilson was able to dictate the appointment of an ally to an important position in Collector Goodloe's office, even over Finley's protest.[189]

A wealthy young mountain banker, David Colson saw the confused leadership situation among mountain Republicans as offering a chance for him to establish himself as the new boss of the organization. Colson, intensely ambitious, was looking for a chance to advertise himself politically when in 1889 an unexpected series of events presented an opportunity. When the Republican state convention met in May 1889 the party nominated John Z. Bartlett as its candidate for state treasurer.[190] Despite the fact that the Democratic treasurer had just defrauded the state, Bartlett recognized that he had little opportunity to win and declined to run.[191] Embarrassed that they might be left without a candidate in the major statewide race, the Republicans called a second convention and searched for someone who would make the race. Colson, a state legislator representing Bell County, was nominated without serious opposition.[192] Colson apparently was willing to run a losing campaign and, more important, was probably willing to absorb the cost himself. Colson ran a strong campaign, attacking Democratic corruption and stumping most mountain counties as he introduced himself to the voters. He was so successful that the Democrats had to make a major effort in the last two weeks before the voting to secure the victory.[193]

Developments in the spring of 1890 presaged a major power struggle among Republicans in eastern Kentucky. Wilson continued to pressure Finley on mountain patronage matters. First, he introduced a bill to divide Kentucky into two judicial districts, a maneuver that would have produced more patronage for mountain Republicans. This bill was particularly popular since there was a great demand for offices, and one administration official was forced to remark that it was not their policy to "multiply places" for solely political purposes.[194] At the end of May, Wilson was named to the Republican Congressional Committee that directed election strategy for the 1890 campaign. His selection would serve not only to strengthen him in the mountains, but the position could be used as an independent source of power. Two weeks later the Democratic legislature carefully gerrymandered Kentucky's congressional districts.[195] Conceding the mountain counties to the Republicans, the Democrats created an oversized Eleventh District, with a large Republican majority. Finley's position seemed to be strengthened until observers recognized that Wilson's home county had now been included in Finley's district. The two incumbent Republican congressmen were forced into a direct confrontation.

Despite the fact that Finley had not been able to establish himself as undisputed leader of mountain Republicans, he still appeared to have an important advantage over Wilson. Approximately two-thirds of the counties in the Eleventh District were part of Finley's old district, which meant that all he had to do to defeat Wilson was to hold his organization intact. He was unable to do so, however, and four weeks before the congressional nominating convention there were at least seven active candidates in the field. The results of the county conventions held ten days before the district meeting were not conclusive. Wilson was generally successful in retaining control over the counties in his former district and secured fifty-seven delegates. Finley, through various means—including running candidates who agreed to deliver their delegates to him—secured eighty delegates. The remaining sixty-four delegates were split among four other candidates, including Civil War veteran Silas Adams. Significantly, seventy-two of the delegates had been challenged, including Finley's own delegation from Whitley County.[196]

All observers expected a major power struggle at the nominating convention, and they were not disappointed. In the center of the controversy was David Colson, who as chairman of the Republican district committee could determine how the convention would be organized. Colson was regarded as an ally of Wilson, but he did not use his powers to aid Wilson as Houk and Mahone would have demanded. Finley's only hope was to make an alliance with one of the other candidates. It proved to be impossible to do so, as the hostile credentials committee decided four contested cases against Finley, an action that denied him nearly forty delegates. Greatly angered, Finley refused to concede defeat, and the convention was deadlocked for one hundred ballots and four days. After this exercise in futility, Finley requested permission to address the convention. Thundering denunciations like the Old Testament prophet he physically resembled, Finley accused the delegates of cheating his backers of their votes; then he walked out. The stunned delegates nominated Wilson without further controversy.[197] Colson was reelected chairman of the district committee, and the crucial meeting ended.

Wilson now faced the same problem that Finley had had: consolidation of his position in the party. Wilson apparently decided to challenge the Bradley machine at the state convention called to nominate the Republican candidate for governor in 1891.[198] Bradley was supporting Andrew T. Wood of Montgomery County for the nomination. Wood, a grizzly bear of a man, was a popular party leader "with a rugged, meat-ax style of oratory."[199] The opposition finally agreed to back mountain-county candidates George Denny and Silas Adams. Although Wilson was able to prevent Wood from sweeping all the county conventions in the mountains, the congressman could not match the opposition's thorough organization. Wood was nominated over Adams by a vote of 987 to 482 on the first ballot, and Bradley easily maintained his control of the state organization.[200]

As calamitous as this defeat was for Wilson's future, it was the contest between him and David Colson that truly revealed the congressman's weak position. Colson was the Bradley candidate for temporary chairman of the convention, and he easily defeated Wilson's candidate.[201] Colson's victory was clearly created by the machine, but later in the convention he was able to win a personal triumph as well. Chagrined by what he regarded as Colson's treachery, Wilson attempted to remove his young opponent as the Eleventh District representative to the state Republican committee. At a meeting of delegates to the convention from the Eleventh District, Wilson's efforts failed and Colson retained his position.[202] Wilson's attempt to shore up his own position failed; instead, Colson's convention victories indicated that Wilson now faced an ambitious opponent of demonstrated popularity who was allied to the powerful Bradley machine.[203] Wilson's position was further weakened when Wood proved to be a popular candidate in eastern Kentucky and thus made Wilson's convention activities appear even more self-serving.[204]

Wilson, in his search for votes, took an active part in the campaign to vote on a new state constitution for Kentucky in 1891. Although the Republican state convention had endorsed the new constitution, many mountain Republicans opposed it.[205] Their opposition centered on the fact that foreign capital was not allowed in Kentucky and that its lack would seriously delay economic development of the mountain region. Wilson became one of the leaders of the anticonstitution movement and spoke widely on the subject. When the vote was held in early August, the mountain counties cast a larger percentage of negative ballots than did the remainder of the state. Wilson could gain little comfort from this fact, however, since mountain voters did support the new document by a margin of 34,000 to 19,000 votes.[206] Wilson once again had failed to strengthen himself to any significant degree.

One remaining source of power available to Wilson was his relationship with the Harrison administration and his consequent ability to hand out patronage. Unfortunately for Wilson, Bradley had moved very close to the administration and was usually consulted on patronage matters.[207] In November 1891 Bradley announced his support for Harrison's renomination in 1892 and in turn was mentioned as a possible future cabinet member.[208] Clearly, then, the Harrison administration was going to provide little help for an acknowledged opponent of Bradley's. Ominously for Wilson, Bradley's eastern Kentucky ally, Colson, began an unofficial campaign to wrest the Eleventh District congressional nomination from Wilson in late 1891. Like Finley before him, Wilson had been unable to eliminate opposition to himself within the party and now faced a dangerous fight for renomination.

Colson organized his campaign quickly, and, like many other young Republicans, he emphasized economic issues. Colson announced that he supported the protective tariff in principle and the controversial McKinley Tariff as the best legislation passed on this question. He stated that he opposed inflating the money supply through the unlimited coinage of silver. Colson's hometown paper commented favorably on his business experience and concluded that he was the candidate who would be most likely to help eastern Kentucky to industrialize. Colson's supporters attacked Wilson for failing in this area. In particular, they attacked the congressman's failure to secure money to improve navigation on the Kentucky and Cumberland rivers.[209] Wilson was unprepared for an issue-oriented campaign and often refused to debate Colson, with the result that Colson's campaign gathered a great deal of momentum.

The more traditional political maneuvers were also part of Colson's campaign for the nomination. As the chairman of the district committee he was in a strategic position. Colson was able to persuade that committee, over Wilson's active opposition, that delegates from county conventions should be awarded on a proportional basis rather than by the winner-take-all arrangement that traditionally had been followed.[210] The result was that Wilson, who was strong in only one-third of the counties, was further weakened. After this victory Colson resigned his position as chairman to avoid the appearance of dictating the nomination. Later Colson demanded a direct popular primary and an end to the convention system of nomination.[211] Although this demand was not met, Colson had established himself as the candidate who was trying to elevate the party in eastern Kentucky above the problems of the past.

The fight for the nomination was further complicated when Silas Adams announced his candidacy in early May.[212] In July, Frank Finley announced that he, too, would be a candidate. The entry of these two men radically changed the situation.[213] Wilson was further weakened because many older Republicans, who were offended by the innovations introduced by Colson but who had stronger allegiances to Adams or Finley, deserted the struggling congressman. Wilson, now desperate, began a campaign of personal abuse of his opposition, which only undermined his position even more.[214] His situation became so hopeless that the other candidates began to ignore Wilson and concentrate on each other.

Adams's entrance into the race meant that new issues would be injected into the campaign. The former cavalry leader appealed directly to the Union army veterans, and he attacked Wilson for failing to help his constituents with their pension problems. This tactic further weakened Wilson, but it also put Colson at a disadvantage. He was too young to have fought in the war and found no way to counteract the Adams campaign. Adams was able to capitalize on the fact that many veterans in eastern Kentucky felt that they had been denied elective office by the older party leadership.[215] The result was that Adams gained rapidly on both Wilson and Colson.

Deeply concerned by Adams's success, Colson turned to a new strategy that would be the most notorious legacy of the new business Republican leadership. When the county conventions were held in early September, Colson and his workers purchased votes in large numbers. Two separate sources maintained that Colson may have spent as much as twenty thousand dollars in direct bribes and in providing drinks for voters.[216] Colson, who was a majority stockholder in a bank and the owner of valuable real estate, was unquestionably able to spend that amount of money. Considerable evidence suggests that the innovation that Colson introduced was not the buying of votes—this practice had certainly been used in earlier campaigns—but the systematic and widespread use of large amounts of money. This type of campaign alienated many older Republican leaders who could not hope to raise as much money as Colson.

Colson's efforts were partially successful. He emerged with the most delegates of any candidate so that, if the convention seated his delegations in three counties, Colson would be nominated on the first ballot.[217] His success, however, drove the rest of the party together in opposition to him. Colson's challenge to Frank Finley for control of

Finley's home county votes greatly angered the former congressman. Wilson and Adams recognized that if either of them were to have a chance they had to combine forces. They agreed that whoever obtained the most votes at the convention would also be supported by the other's delegates.[218] This combination of political enemies—Wilson, Adams, and Finley—demonstrated the threat that Colson posed to the traditional party leadership.

The district convention was a duplicate of the meeting two years earlier. The anti-Colson forces combined to organize the convention and to decide the disputed delegate cases against the leader. When the roll call for the first ballot was finished, Colson had 77 votes; Adams, 65; Wilson, 37; and Finley, 22.[219] For forty-five ballots the position of the candidates remained the same; then Wilson and Finley withdrew, and Adams was easily nominated. Colson retained his composure and assured the convention that he would work hard for Adams's election.[220] Colson kept his promise; as party treasurer for the state organization he directed ample resources into the Eleventh District to allow Adams to run an effective campaign.[221] The Democrats, hoping that they could take advantage of Republican dissatisfaction, ran an aggressive canvass. They attacked Republicans for the Lodge bill in a bitter campaign designed to play on the opposition's racial prejudice.[222] No part of this scheme worked, for Adams won a decisive victory.

Republican cooperation during the campaign masked persistent deep divisions in the party. Colson continued to work toward his objective of winning the Eleventh District congressional nomination. In 1893 he was elected mayor of his hometown of Middlesborough, winning nearly 80 percent of the votes.[223] Obviously the office was unimportant, but the victory did secure the county for Colson in 1894. Colson's overt ambitions created a situation in eastern Kentucky that resembled the events in the other mountain regions. Since the Republicans in the eastern counties were not dominated by a single boss, Colson had managed to split the Republican organization into two parts. One faction consisted of the traditional elements in the mountain Republican parties, including blacks and veterans. The other was the business wing of the party, which was led by young men like Colson and emphasized economic issues such as the tariff.

The confrontations that had taken place between these two groups in eastern Tennessee, northwestern West Virginia, and western North Carolina were repeated in 1894 in eastern Kentucky. The Colson faction began to agitate for a major change in the means of conducting the primaries, insisting on direct popular primaries. The implication was clear. It would be impossible for the trailing candidates to combine against the leader and deny him the nomination, as they had in 1890 and 1892. Colson's constant pressure was rewarded when the district committee agreed to submit the nomination to the Republican voters in a popular election.[224] The old party leaders resisted Colson's efforts, but found that the thirty-three-year-old banker had completely outmaneuvered them.

Opposition to Colson formed quickly as the old guard recognized that the critical test of strength was about to occur in a manner they could not regulate. Adams announced that he would be a candidate for reelection on the same platform as two years before.[225] In a surprise announcement, former congressman John D. White entered the campaign against Adams. From the very beginning, Adams and White worked in concert to defeat Colson. White in particular attacked the direct primary and announced that he would not enter it and instead would run as an Independent Republican candidate.[226] Colson countered, claiming that the popular primary would bring greater democracy into the party's decision-making process and would help keep the organization in eastern Kentucky from falling behind.[227]

As the day for the primary approached, a series of legal maneuvers by each candidate created one of the most confusing political campaigns in American history. White obtained an injunction to prevent the voting, but Colson was able to have his followers in ten counties hold the election anyway.[228] The results in this partial primary were Colson, 4,968; Adams, 1,316; White, 3.[229] The district committee met, despite a second restraining injunction obtained by White, and declared Colson to be the Republican nominee. The Adams and White backers left the committee and called a convention that nominated Adams.[230] Adams next secured an injunction to forbid Colson's being listed as the regular Republican candidate.[231] There were three Republican aspirants, each of whom realized that the person who was recognized as the legal Republican candidate would probably be elected. In the heavily Republican district in a Republican year, even a split in the party probably would not be fatal.

Unwilling to sacrifice the nomination he felt to be rightfully his, Colson struck back at his opponents. First, he went to court and was granted an injunction to stop any interference with his position as Republican candidate; shortly thereafter Adams's counterinjunction was dissolved.[232] Now that Colson had won that battle, White withdrew from the canvass so that the opposition vote would not be split. Sensing that victory was within his grasp, Colson appealed to party loyalty in his final campaign appearances and concentrated on economic issues.[233] The returns gave Colson 14,628 votes, Democrat George S. Stone 10,932, and Adams 4,975.[234] The presence of Stone insured that only Republicans voted for Colson and Adams. Thus, Colson won nearly three out of every four Republican votes and received more votes than Adams in fifteen of the district's seventeen counties. As in the other mountain regions, the professional middle class had established itself as the dominant faction in the party in eastern Kentucky. As one Republican newspaper observed, "The old politicians in the district were all against him, as in Colson's success they recognized the dissolution of their own fond aspirations."[235]

The political situation in Kentucky in 1895 and 1896 strengthened the hold on the mountain voters that the new leaders and platform had established, but it weakened Colson personally. In 1895 Bradley was the Republican gubernatorial nominee, and he campaigned on economic issues. Major party spokesmen, including White, Bradley, and Colson, appeared in every mountain county to urge their program on the mountain voters.[236] Bradley was elected and the mountain Republican voters endorsed the Republican platform, Bradley carrying the Eleventh District by 12,000 votes.[237] Success soon brought two fierce struggles within the party. First, Bradley intervened in the state legislature and prevented the election of a United States senator. The candidate chosen by the Republican caucus was not a member of the Bradley machine, and the governor preferred a possible party defeat to the elevation of a rival organization. At the same time, Bradley challenged William McKinley for control of the state's delegation to the national convention. The Kentucky governor was able to gain a majority of the state's delegates, but he split the party organization into two bitter factions. In the mountains one of the Bradley delegates was John White, a recent convert to the idea of the protective tariff.[238] McKinley forces were led by former congressmen Frank Finley and Silas Adams, and the campaign for delegates reopened many old political wounds.

The battles over the Senate seat and the presidential nomination weakened the entire Bradley organization. Colson was one of the victims of the disarray in Republican ranks. Trapped by his dependence on the Bradley machine at the state level and by his desire to support McKinley, Colson finally supported neither and thereby alienated many of his own former promoters.[239] White, with the backing of many Bradley leaders, challenged Colson and endorsed McKinley and the national platform.[240] The opposition to Colson had stolen his primary issue, and the contest would now be a matter of the personality of the two men and how well they were organized. In both instances White seemed to have the advantage. Colson was apparently egotistical and arrogant, while White was quite popular with the mountain voters. White was also backed by important elements of the Bradley machine and seemed to be better organized than Colson.

Despite these handicaps, Colson was able to win both the Republican nomination and reelection to Congress in 1896. He still controlled the district committee, which once again authorized a direct primary to select the Republican candidate.[241] In addition, Colson received some unexpected help when former congressman John H. Wilson announced that he was an independent silver Republican candidate and thereby weakened the anti-Colson coalition.[242] As in 1894, Colson turned to the widespread use of money to buy votes; White's efforts failed to counteract this strategy. Just before election day, Colson forces also circulated broadsides saying that White had withdrawn from the race and that White supported racially mixed schools.[243] The resort to dirty politics carried the election; Colson won 8,525 votes to 7,949 for White. Still, White won ten of the district's seventeen counties and felt, quite correctly, that only illegal activities on his opponent's part had defeated him.[244] As he had done two years before, White went to the courts for redress; but, also as had happened in 1894, Colson won the legal battle and was recognized as the regular Republican candidate.[245] Since McKinley forces were pushing furiously to carry Kentucky in the presidential voting, the party leaders put great pressure on mountain Republicans to support Colson in the general election. These efforts were quite successful, for Colson won a substantial majority over White and the Democratic candidate, and White won less than 15 percent of the Republican vote.[246]

Colson had survived, but he was not in a position of unquestioned power. Unlike Evans in east Tennessee, Elkins in northwestern West Virginia, and Pritchard in western North Carolina, Colson had been unable to consolidate his position. One major cause for his failure to construct a machine was the absence of a strong party-army organization in eastern Kentucky. The other business leaders were able to build on already existing organizations, whereas Colson was forced to use his financial resources to create a new party structure. Another factor that weakened Colson was eastern Kentucky's lack of industrialization. Unlike the other mountain regions, Kentucky's eastern counties had no railroad system, and the vast coal reserves were not being exploited as they would be in the twentieth century. Thus these counties lacked supporting institutions, like the large industrial and commercial concerns that undergirded the business wing of the party in other states. While he was a fairly wealthy man in eastern Kentucky, Colson was essentially a small-town banker; unlike Elkins, Evans, and the Dukes, he did not have unlimited resources at his disposal. Finally, the absence of a modern transportation system made it difficult for Colson, or for any politician, to coordinate political activities in the vast mountain district. The one great success of Colson's organization was its ability to replace Civil War issues with a platform centering on economic questions. Even Colson's political enemies were forced to acknowledge his success in this area and to adopt his platform. Thus, although Colson had been able to transform the perspective of mountain Republican voters, he was unable to establish himself securely as the political boss of eastern Kentucky.

Developments in the mountain Republican politics of southwestern Virginia, like those in eastern Kentucky, did not fit the precise pattern followed in the other three states in the upper South. As in Kentucky, no real change took place in the leadership of the party at the state level; and, just as in Kentucky, this seeming continuity masked some significant changes in the party in the mountain counties. As noted earlier, mountain Republican leaders worked well with state boss William Mahone. Mahone, as a Republican and former Confederate general, had spent most of his career trying to avoid Civil War issues, and so when mountain Republicans decided to emphasize the protective tariff Mahone enthusiastically agreed. As a former railroad president, Mahone himself embraced the business platform and swung the state organization in that direction.

Mountain Republicans did break away from Mahone's leadership, but the issue that caused the separation reflected conditions unique to Virginia among the states of the upper South. Fearing that the congressional elections of 1890 would be used to overthrow his influence in the party, Mahone moved to control them. He conferred with administration officials and received their assurance that they would not interfere with his plans.[247] Then he tried to force Republicans in Virginia not to make any congressional nominations at all.[248] Mahone claimed that this policy would encourage the Farmers' Alliance to split the Democratic party, but it is clear that the motivation of Mahone's policy was to prevent his opponents from exploiting his growing weakness within the party. When national party officials finally realized what Mahone's strategy was, they angrily opposed him and attempted to secure Republican candidates in each district.[249] Mahone continued to press his plans, however, and was able to prevent nominations in seven of Virginia's ten districts.

One of the districts that the Republicans contested was the Ninth District in the mountains of southwestern Virginia. When Mahone announced his plan, mountain leaders immediately protested. Campbell Slemp, future congressman from that district, explained their reasoning:

In regard to standing off and not participating in [the] election I hardly know what to say. I think it impossible to hold our organization together if we fail to enter the field with men. If we stand aloof and solicit an Independent Democrat I dont [sic] think we can concentrate our forces on him and many Republicans will vote the Regular Dem. rather than vote the indepen. and I am afraid that many good Republicans will believe we have given up the fight and fall back on the Dem. side as the permanent controlling party.[250]

Despite the presence of a leading spokesman of Alliance Democrats who wanted to run as an Independent, Ninth District Republicans met in convention and nominated George T. Mills as their candidate for Congress.[251] Realizing that he was unable to control the situation in the mountain counties, Mahone agreed to allow Mills to be recognized by the state Republican committee.[252]

Mills's candidacy represented the emergence of the business wing of the party in southwestern Virginia. Mills was a native of Pennsylvania and a mill owner in southwestern Virginia, and until 1890 he had been so concerned about the liberal economic policies of the Readjuster-Republican party that he had not voted.[253] Now he made the protective tariff the major plank in his platform and attempted to ignore all other issues.[254] There was another reason for Mills's narrow campaign. The Democrats were running exclusively on the Lodge Elections Bill, and the racial appeal was having a decided effect on the predominantly white electorate in the mountain counties.[255] Mills tried to counteract the Democratic canvass by announcing that he did not support the Lodge bill and then returned to talking about the tariff.[256] In late October the Republican campaign strategy paid an unexpected dividend. Former Confederate general and Democratic lieutenant governor of Virginia James A. Walker announced that he would vote for Mills and the principle of tariff protection.[257] Despite Walker's endorsement, Mills was easily defeated by his Democratic opponent. Still, the Republicans of the Ninth District had salvaged something from the wreckage, as Campbell Slemp had predicted. They had preserved their organization and had found an issue that would allow them to appeal to the increasing number of Democratic businessmen and industrial workers.

The election of minor state officials and members of the legislature in 1891 renewed the debate about political strategy. The Alliance Democrats were becoming more restive and were challenging the party's Bourbon leadership.[258] Once again, Mahone and the state committee called upon Republicans not to contest the elections, but to allow the

Democrats to fight among themselves.[259] The anti-Mahone men organized a state convention to nominate a state ticket. The meeting was held at Roanoke, but no prominent mountain Republicans attended, and none seems to have had any criticism of Mahone's policy. And yet mountain Republicans did run candidates for the state legislature.[260] The mountain Republican leadership and Mahone apparently had reached a tacit understanding. The mountain politicians would be allowed to run their own affairs, and in return for no interference from Mahone they would support him in his battle to control the state organization.

The same pattern was followed in 1892 as in 1890 and 1891, as Mahone once again tried to suppress Republican candidates. At the state convention in Roanoke in May, Mahone was again able to assert his dominant position. He was reelected state chairman and was able to prevent the delegates from supporting the renomination campaign of President Benjamin Harrison by the overwhelming vote of 392 to 174.[261] Although Harrison was nominated without Mahone's support, the Republican National Committee and the administration generally supported Mahone's campaign strategy. Apparently Mahone explained that he felt that the national ticket would fare better if the Republicans did not field congressional candidates, and the national leadership agreed. Once again the mountain Republicans of the Ninth District ignored Mahone's directives and nominated businessman Henry C. Wood to run against Democrat "Cyclone" Jim Marshall. The Republicans worked hard for Wood and were well organized, even in some areas of traditional Democratic strength.[262] Wood was no match for the colorful Marshall on the stump, however, and the Republicans once again suffered defeat.

The start of the "Democratic" depression in the spring of 1893 seemed to offer the Republicans an opportunity for substantial political gains in the gubernatorial elections of that year. One local leader reported to Mahone that the farmers "got comparitive nothing for their tobaco and they lay it to the change of the administration[.] they say under Harisons administration they got good prices and they say we are done with democracy."[263] Mahone, however, decided not to allow Republicans to offer candidates and further rejected any alliance with the Populists.[264] Once again many Republicans were dissatisfied with this decision. Blacks protested that the party was no longer attempting to win elections and was doing nothing to counter a call by the Populists to disfranchise the blacks.[265] Actually Mahone was seeking to arrange a working relationship with the Populists, and in the mountain counties the local Populist meetings were run by Republicans.

Mahone's efforts to fuse the two parties were unsuccessful, but mountain Republicans remained confident. When Mahone deferred to the Populists in the 1893 gubernatorial election, many Republicans refused to vote for the third-party candidate and thus insured his defeat. Mountain Republicans were not downcast, however, and one reported to Mahone that the party in that region was "thorougher" organized than at any time in the past. He continued, "We are anxious to make the next on the old lines."[266] Republicans in southwestern Virginia agreed with these sentiments and were determined to contest the 1894 congressional elections. By January, when all but four of the thirteen iron-producing companies in the mountain counties had closed, the Republican prospects looked excellent.[267] Determined to stay in power, Virginia Democrats passed a new franchise law directed at Republican voters. The Walton Election Law introduced the secret ballot into Virginia politics. The new ballot did not allow any party devices or straight-ticket voting, provisions that were designed to make it difficult for the illiterate voters—primarily blacks and mountain whites and often Republicans.[268] In the face of these new Democratic obstacles, Mahone once again tried to suppress Republican nominations; but, surprisingly, the state committee ruled that each district should decide this question for itself.[269] Thus the mountain Republicans were free to make their own decisions.

Despite the new Democratic election law, the Republicans in southwestern Virginia remained confident. In the local elections held in the spring and summer of 1894, the party won a series of impressive victories.[270] The new election law did not seem to be able to stop the Republican advance. Ninth District Democrats helped the Republican cause by bungling their nomination. Incumbent Jim Marshall was passed over, and a rather uninspiring individual, H. S. K. Morrison, was elected. When it was revealed that a fraudulent telegram had deprived Marshall of votes at the district convention, only with the greatest difficulty did the Democrats hold their party together.[271]

The Republicans, on the other hand, had found their candidate. At a county mass meeting in Pulaski County in July, James Walker announced that he would be willing to accept the Republican nomination. Walker's announcement was unexpected because he was regarded as the leading Democratic politician in the southwest. Walker, who had been wounded while serving under Stonewall Jackson, had been elected lieutenant governor in 1877 as a Democrat, despite his hostility to the Readjusters. He had actively opposed Mahone in several campaigns and was usually mentioned as a possible Democratic gubernatorial nominee. But he had been denied nomination to several offices, and by the mid-1880s he began to take an independent course in politics. As noted earlier, he endorsed the Republican congressional candidate in 1890. He also became a major spokesman for the protective tariff, perhaps reflecting his own substantial investments in mineral lands. Despite these developments, few Virginians expected the outspoken racist to become a Republican. Ironically, it was the silver question that precipitated the final decision. At this point, the Democratic leadership in Virginia opposed free silver, and Walker joined the Republicans as a high tariff, free-silver Republican—much like Jeter Pritchard and Richmond Pearson of North Carolina.[272]

The Republicans of southwestern Virginia were elated by Walker's decision, and he was unanimously nominated at the Republican district convention. Local Republican groups organized quickly, including many members of the party who had not campaigned in years.[273] Walker constantly stressed that only the Republicans could bring economic prosperity and industrial development to the mountain region. He also attacked the new Democratic election law as dishonest.[274] Walker's most significant contribution to the Republicans was his ability to appeal to Confederate veterans. Even the Democrats had to admit that he had been "a gallant soldier," and a useless arm was a constant reminder of his personal sacrifice. Late in the campaign Walker emphasized his relationship with the veterans by flying a Confederate flag from the pole in his yard.[275]

The stunned Democrats quickly recovered from the shock of Walker's announcement and conducted a bitter campaign against the man they now considered a traitor. First they accused him of being opportunistic and turning Republican to gain public office. Then the Democrats tried to destroy Walker's credibility among former Confederates by publishing his request for a pardon from President Andrew Johnson. Walker was quoted as writing that secession was wrong, and the Democrats held up this sentiment as an earlier example of his treason.[276] When these attacks had little impact, the Democrats were forced to resort to racist appeals. Although Walker was an acknowledged white supremacist and had spoken in favor of limiting black suffrage, one Democratic paper printed the following verse:

> Slowly and sadly we lay him down,
> For the field of his fames grows no bigger.
> We carve not a line, we raise not a stone
> But we leave him alone with his nigger.[277]

The racial attacks did not damage Walker either; on election day he won by a small but decisive majority.

Many Democrats hoped in vain that Walker would challenge Mahone's control of the party and that the Republicans would throw away their most recent victory. Rather, the two men worked together to try to capture the state legislative elections of 1895. In 1894 Mahone had made an exception to his policy of opposing the fielding of Republican candidates and had helped Walker secure valuable assistance from the Republican National Congressional Committee.[278] In the spring of 1895 Mahone, in partnership with Populist leader J. Haskins Hobson, created an Honest Elections League, modeled after the Fusion organization in North Carolina.[279] Mahone called an August convention of Gold Democrats, Republicans, Populists, and any other groups that wanted to come. Walker was at the convention, working effectively with Mahone to organize this new group.[280] Mountain politicians followed Walker's lead, and the legislative elections were closely contested in the southwest.[281] In early October Mahone died, and Walker had to try to hold the league together. When he was not able to do so, most Republicans were defeated in the mountain counties. Even in defeat the party was partially vindicated, since many winning Democratic candidates were forced to agree to vote against suffrage restrictions in the legislature.[282]

The prospect of almost certain victory in the 1896 presidential election encouraged Virginia Republicans to forget the failure of their fusion effort. The expected battle for control of the party organization after Mahone's death never fully developed. Walker sided with William Lamb, who succeeded Mahone as party chairman. Lamb, however, was unable to keep all the power the little boss had had, and at the state convention he was forced to compromise with the anti-Mahone forces. The compromise was facilitated by the fact that all of the factions supported the McKinley campaign, and outside pressure helped to force a peaceful settlement.[283] This unity was maintained throughout the canvass, and the McKinley managers directed some money into the state to encourage Republicans to mount a vigorous effort.[284] At no time was Mahone's strategy of not contesting offices suggested.

Party harmony was also the theme of the Republican campaign in the mountain counties. Walker was renominated without opposition, and there was little debate on the platform. The lack of discussion about the platform was the result of a decision that Walker had made to accept the national party plank on monetary policy. He reversed his previous stand and endorsed the gold standard.[285] The Democrats ridiculed Walker's inconsistency, but his strategic retreat avoided what would have been a very difficult situation in southwestern Virginia. The Republicans were well organized at all levels, and Walker's campaign aroused great enthusiasm. In addition, the Democrats of southwestern Virginia were split over economic issues and had a difficult time mounting a campaign.[286] Consequently, Walker was reelected to Congress by a small majority comparable to the one in 1894.

Walker moved to entrench himself as party leader in the mountain counties by trying to gain control of the state party organization. In late November Walker and James Brady, leader of the anti-Mahone forces, called a meeting of the state committee over the protests of the chairman, William Lamb. Lamb refused to attend the meeting, and Walker presided. A new state committee dominated by Brady and Walker was selected, and Lamb's influence was ended.[287] Now Walker, like Elkins, Evans, and Pritchard, dominated an organization of mountain Republicans that was committed to supporting business interests in the mountains. Although Walker was more dependent than the others on his Civil War record, he still represented the triumph of the new forces within the party.

The revolution in leadership, therefore, had taken place in all five mountain Republican parties of the upper South. The party-armies and their bosses had not been able to fight off their challengers. Party workers found the promise of patronage less enticing than an immediate cash reward. Voters demanded that their political leaders stand for more than defense of community values. The victories that the new middle-class leaders achieved in the early 1890s seemed only to confirm their greater political insight. Economic issues had proven to be very effective in creating strong Republican organizations in four of the five states—only in Virginia did the state party fail to make important gains. To many Republicans in the mountains, the future promised even greater success.

CHAPTER 9

REACTION, DEFEAT, AND DISFRANCHISEMENT

The promised Republican victories in the upper South after 1896 never materialized, partly because the new mountain Republican leaders were forced to expend much of their energy retaining their position within their own party. Moreover, the Democrats had reorganized and mounted a massive counterattack that limited suffrage and reduced Negro participation in politics in three states. The Republicans continued to pay the price of their attempt to achieve victories in the South with black voters. Ironically, it was the party's willingness to adapt and become a southern institution that led to its defeat. Republicans had simply refused to disappear after Reconstruction, and the economic crisis of the 1890s showed their ability to win southern elections. The Democrats responded by offering token reforms to poor whites in return for their support in the campaign to eliminate blacks from the electorate. This story is one of sordid opportunism, strident racism, and cruel violence that brought an end to political democracy in many parts of the upper South for more than half a century.

Republican resistance to these changes was seriously weakened by internal stresses within their own organizations. The mountain Republican business leadership was unable to maintain the tight discipline that the party-army bosses had had. Several interrelated factors may explain this failure. The rapid advance of civil service regulations effectively reduced the number of unskilled jobs available for party leaders to use as a reward to faithful workers. This problem became acute when the McKinley administration took office in 1897 and many mountain Republicans were left without the jobs they felt they deserved. A number of mountain political leaders demanded a modification of the regulations to help relieve the pressure on them.[1] At the same time, the business leaders were stressing a particular policy position and calling on Democrats who agreed with them to switch parties. By the same logic these leaders were saying to Republicans who opposed the Republican party's business orientation that they should consider voting with the Democrats. The new party leadership also found it difficult to impose discipline because they were so close to victory that they feared loss of any votes to the opposition. These factors, combined with the bitterness generated among the former leaders of the mountain Republicans by their loss of power, created a situation extremely conducive to major battles within the party.

The rise of Walter P. Brownlow to Republican leadership in eastern Tennessee is an excellent example of the internal strife. Brownlow had worked vigorously from 1886 through 1892 to secure the Republican congressional nomination in the First District. He found, however, that incumbent congressman Alfred Taylor was too strongly entrenched. But some forces undermined Taylor's position. Caught in the middle of the battle between H. Clay Evans and John C. Houk for control of the state organization, Taylor weakened his position considerably.[2] In addition, Taylor, like numbers of mountain Republicans, finding that many party members favored free silver, had to try to satisfy both sides of the increasingly controversial coinage issue.[3] Furthermore, Republicans were having doubts about Taylor's competence as a congressman. Although he was a very effective public speaker—he and his brother Robert Taylor were Republican and Democratic gubernatorial nominees in 1886 and provided Tennessee with its most entertaining statewide campaign— Taylor did not accomplish much in Washington. One observer characterized him as more of an "ignoramous" and more "lazy" than John Houk.[4] The depression of the 1890s made the voters less tolerant of men like Taylor and eager for a change.

Sensing the new situation, Brownlow mounted a major effort to unseat Taylor in 1894. As early as September 1893, Brownlow began to organize his workers and prepare for the coming campaign. A political manipulator in the John Houk tradition, Brownlow showed his determination to replace Taylor by making the first public addresses of his political career. Brownlow stressed that as a longtime civil servant in Washington he had done more for the people than Taylor had and should be rewarded for it. To attest to his influence, he even secured the backing of many prominent national Republican leaders.[5] Under this relentless pressure, Taylor gave up and announced that he would not seek nomination.[6] The path for Brownlow's election finally seemed clear. He had control of the district committee and induced its members to call an early convention. Brownlow's success turned old ally Augustus Pettibone against him, and Pettibone encouraged William C. Anderson and W. E. F. Milburn to challenge Brownlow. Anderson and Milburn combined forces at the convention; after 144 ballots Brownlow finally gave up and switched his support to Anderson, who was nominated.[7] Taylor had been beaten, and yet Brownlow had been unable to secure the nomination.

Like David Colson in eastern Kentucky when he found the old party leaders blocking his way, Brownlow resorted to the direct popular primary as a means to win the nomination. He still controlled the district committee despite Anderson's victory, and in the spring of 1896 Brownlow was able to persuade the members to call a direct primary to decide the nomination. Brownlow attempted to assure all members of the party a fair deal on patronage by vowing that all positions would be filled on the advice of local committees. Both Anderson and Milburn entered the race again, and the chief issue appears to have been which of the three men could do the most for the veteran. The vote was close, but Brownlow's gamble on the popular primary was rewarded. He carried seven of the twelve counties and won 8,832 votes, while Milburn received 6,591 and Anderson 5,379.[8] Although Brownlow's share of the vote was only 40 percent, he did have the nomination and he was easily elected to Congress in November.

Brownlow moved quickly to consolidate his position. He challenged H. Clay Evans for control of the state organization and of federal patronage. Evans seemed to have the upper hand as the most popular Republican in the state, an original McKinley man, and the recently appointed commissioner of pensions. As Robert Marcus has pointed out, however, this last fact actually became a great weakness.[9] When politicians moved from one level to another in the Gilded Age—in this case from state to national—they had to relinquish the power they had held in their former positions. With Evans away in Washington, Brownlow moved quickly to gain control of most of the federal patronage in the state.[10] He was able to win the post of state chairman of the party and to be named the Republican national committeeman from Tennessee. He further strengthened his position by winning the party's consent to allow him to appoint many members of the state committee, a factor that insured his continued control of that body.[11] In a very short period of time Brownlow had accumulated an amazing amount of political power.

Evans and the business wing of the Tennessee mountain Republican party were unwilling to concede control to Brownlow, however. Both Evans and Brownlow began working to secure delegates for the 1900 state convention as early as the summer of 1899.[12] Evans's campaign was slowed by charges that, as commissioner of pensions, he was being unfair to veterans. Although he was eventually cleared of any discrimination against the former soldiers, the controversy undoubtedly weakened his attractiveness among the old Unionists of eastern Tennessee.[13] Throughout the spring of 1900 the two factions fought each other at numerous county conventions; in many cases each side claimed victory, and competing delegations were sent to the state convention. The convention itself was a disaster for the party, for the assemblage split into two groups, each nominating delegates to the national convention, a state ticket, and a slate of presidential electors.[14] Brownlow, however, still controlled the nationally recognized state committee, and his delegates were seated at the national convention.[15] Much to the disgust of many mountain Republicans, Brownlow and Evans refused to compromise their differences after the national convention, and the two "peanut politicians" left the party convention with two state tickets and two sets of electors.[16] Finally the Republican National Committee intervened and forced an elaborate compromise that gave the Evans faction some power, but left Brownlow still in control.[17]

Not unexpectedly, the Republican party was seriously weakened in Tennessee by this episode. Even in the strongholds in eastern Tennessee, the open fight for the control of the party organization had alienated many voters. Significantly, the defeat of Evans and the business wing of the party had been accomplished in a practically issueless campaign. Brownlow, by returning to the methods of Leonidas Houk, had gained control of the party. His victory demonstrated that the continuing mastery of the businessmen depended on their paying attention to practical political details as well as having a popular platform.

David Colson's political career in eastern Kentucky was even less successful than Evans's in eastern Tennessee. Colson's control of the unwieldy Republican organization in Kentucky's Eleventh District was tenuous at best. His record in Congress was very undistinguished, and he made no attempt to secure any special interest legislation to encourage groups to support him. Colson was also severely criticized for his failure to have more mountain Republicans appointed to patronage positions under the new McKinley administration.[18] These signs of political weakness brought immediate challengers to Colson's position. When John White campaigned vigorously in the local elections of 1897, most observers felt that this was just a prelude to his running against Colson a year later. Even more menacing was the presence of Vincent Boreing as an active speaker in these same elections. Boreing, the head of the Grand Army of the Republic in the Eleventh District, was, like Colson, a wealthy businessman and could afford to spend as freely to secure votes as the congressman.[19] Colson reacted by becoming very aggressive about foreign policy. He was one of the earliest advocates of the American war against Spain. When the fighting came, Colson sought and received a commission as colonel and raised a regiment of mountain men for the war. Unlike Theodore Roosevelt, however, Colson did not profit politically from his martial efforts. His regiment never left Kentucky, and Colson became involved in an altercation with another soldier in which he was wounded and slightly paralyzed.[20] Instead of being a military hero with an assured political future, Colson was a wounded man who had to withdraw from the 1898 congressional race.

His withdrawal left White and Boreing to fight for the seat in Congress. In the spring of 1898 the Kentucky legislature, in an effort to gerrymander the rest of the state, had made the Eleventh District more definitely Republican than before. Thus the person who secured the Republican nomination would have a great advantage and an almost certain victory in November. White demanded that the nomination be decided by the old convention system. Instead, the district committee agreed to Boreing's request for a direct popular primary, and White announced that he would run as an Independent Republican candidate because direct primaries favored the wealthy.[21] This move seemed to be a strategic error on White's part since both the district and the state committees recognized Boreing as the party's candidate.[22] In addition, White espoused two issues that were quite unpopular among mountain Republican voters. First he supported the Goebel Election Bill recently passed by the Kentucky legislature, which was designed, in part, to reduce the Republican vote in the mountain counties. Most mountain men resented the implication that their elections were unusually corrupt. Then White further alienated mountain voters by opposing the Spanish-American War and the expansion of foreign holdings that followed the war.[23] All available evidence indicates that both the war and the new empire were popular among the mountain population. Consequently, Boreing captured an easy victory over White and a token Democrat. White appealed the verdict to the state election board created by the Goebel bill and to Congress, but was turned down in both cases.[24]

Boreing, like Brownlow in Tennessee, moved quickly to secure his position. He campaigned strenuously for the state ticket in the fall elections of 1899, making sure that he met as many mountain voters as possible. In Congress he introduced several pieces of legislation designed to impress voters in eastern Kentucky. One measure would have split the state into two federal judicial districts and would have insured more patronage positions for mountain Republicans. Boreing also introduced a bill that would have improved the mountain roads and greatly aided business. Like all mountain Republican politicians and as a leader of the GAR, Boreing was particularly concerned about veterans. He introduced legislation to erase early desertions and Confederate service from the records of soldiers who were subsequently honorably discharged from the Union army.[25] It did not matter that these ideas did not become law immediately because the new congressman had demonstrated that he cared.

At the same time that Boreing was building a record of positive achievement, the opposition was eliminating itself. In January 1900 Colson became involved in a violent confrontation in the Kentucky capital of Frankfort. The mountain soldier, Ethelbert D. Scott, who had wounded Colson in the army, publicly insulted the former congressman. Both men rushed together and began to assault each other. When bystanders tried to separate the men, Colson drew a revolver and killed Scott and another man. In the confusion Colson was again wounded seriously and confined for an extended period.[26] White avoided possible consideration by leaving the Republican party. Demonstrating a tendency unusual among mountain Republican politicians, he once again placed principle above partisan considerations. Following his long term commitment, White joined the Prohibition party and was their gubernatorial nominee in the special election of 1900. White further alienated Republicans by attending an antiimperialist convention in Indianapolis that endorsed Democratic candidate William Jennings Bryan for the presidency.[27] When no other competition presented itself, the district committee decided it was useless to hold a primary; so they simply nominated Boreing.[28] During the fall campaign vice-presidential candidate Theodore Roosevelt toured the mountains, helping Boreing to win an overwhelming victory.

The new mountain Republican leaders in southwest Virginia, western North Carolina, and West Virginia were able to retain control of the party organization. Congressman James Walker in the Ninth District of Virginia was easily able to stay in power. Opposition to Walker, in fact, was limited largely to Republicans who lived outside the highlands. The occasion was the state and legislative elections of 1897. The split in the state organization between the old Mahone machine headed by William Lamb and the anti-Mahone group led by James Brady finally had an impact on the Ninth District. The Brady faction seized control of the state committee in the summer of 1897 and ordered the Republicans throughout the state not to run candidates against the Democrats. The chairman of the Ninth District, H. E. McCoy, supported this strategy in an apparent effort to replace Walker as the leading Republican in the area.[29] The Lamb faction revolted and held a state convention in southwest Virginia to nominate a state ticket. Walker supported the Independent Republican candidates and encouraged mountain Republicans to run legislative candidates. Because the efforts were too late to allow for thorough organization, the Republicans suffered an overwhelming defeat in the mountain counties.[30] Despite the apparent success of the Brady strategy to prevent Republican victories, McCoy was unable to translate this success into a power base for himself. Walker was easily renominated as the Republican candidate for Congress in 1898 and 1900.[31]

Walker's ability to retain secure control of the Ninth District organization did not bring him victory, however. The Ninth District Democrats ended their internal disputes and selected popular state judge William F. Rhea to oppose Walker. The campaign conducted by Rhea was heavily racist and bitterly personal; Walker was again accused of being a traitor to the South because he had asked for a pardon after the Civil War. The two candidates had to be restrained from shooting each other on two separate occasions, and finally Walker refused to make joint appearances with Rhea. On election day the Democratic poll watchers used violence in some instances to reduce the Republican vote, and Rhea was declared the victor.[32] Walker immediately contested the result, demanding that the House of Representatives seat him rather than Rhea. While Walker was in the process of gathering evidence to support his case, he became involved in a western-style shooting in which he was wounded and he, in turn, wounded Rhea's lawyer.[33] Walker was tried for attempted murder by a Democratic district attorney, but was acquitted by a mountain jury.[34] The contest was ultimately unsuccessful, and Rhea retained his seat.

The campaigns of 1900 in Virginia's Ninth District were a repetition of the situation in 1898. In the spring a referendum required by the Democratic state legislature calling for a state constitutional convention was contested. Republicans, realizing that the objective was to deprive blacks of their right to vote, opposed the plan. Walker and southwestern Republicans worked hard; only one county in the Ninth District favored the convention.[35] Although the convention passed in the statewide voting, Ninth District Republicans were so encouraged by the vote in their region that they made a major attempt to elect Walker in 1900. Walker once again centered his campaign on economic matters, with both mountain Republicans and national Republicans offering support.[36] Rhea and the Democrats again resorted to racism and violence and by these means were able to defeat Walker. This last failure discouraged Walker so that he never sought the congressional nomination again. Walker's inability to win, it should be stressed, was not due to a lack of unity in the mountain Republican party in southwestern Virginia. Perhaps the formidable threat posed by the Virginia Democrats was responsible; but, unlike Republicans in eastern Tennessee, Virginia mountain Republicans did not contribute to their own defeat.

Western North Carolina Republican leaders Jeter Pritchard and Richmond Pearson faced a situation similar to Walker's and suffered the same fate. While they were able to retain control of the Republican organization in the mountain counties without difficulty, the two men were finally defeated by an aggressive state Democratic organization. The major problem of the business wing of the party was in their relationship with their partners in the Fusion government, the Populists. The first controversy between the two groups was the only one that threatened Pritchard's position. After the Fusion forces once again secured control of the state legislature in 1896, Populist leader Marion Butler announced that he opposed Pritchard's reelection. Citing Pritchard's support of McKinley as treason to the silver cause, Butler demanded that the Populists support someone else.[37] Old boss John Mott, Governor Daniel Russell, and the Populist candidate—and silver Republican leader—for lieutenant governor, Oliver Dockery, all volunteered to take Pritchard's place.[38] Pritchard moved quickly to quash the revolt against him. First he warned Republicans about splitting the party and pressured them into conformity. Then with the aid of Populist congressman Harry Skinner—a rival of Butler's for party leadership—he obtained the support of enough Populists to secure his election.[39] Pritchard had retained both his seat and his position of leadership, but the cost had been great. The Fusion government and the Populist party were now hopelessly split, and the future of the coalition was gloomy.

The congressional and legislative elections of 1898 and 1900 tested the Pritchard leadership group in the Republican party. The resurgent Democrats ran a heavily racist campaign, claiming that Fusion victories would mean black political domination.[40] In the face of this outside threat, the members of the coalition closed ranks. The Populists readily agreed to fusion and made a special arrangement in Pearson's district to help him.[41] Factionalism within the Republican party was kept to a minimum by the critical situation, and Pritchard directed a vigorous Republican campaign in the mountains.[42] Large Democratic gains in predominantly black counties and in counties near the South Carolina border ended Fusion rule in North Carolina. As in Virginia, factionalism among mountain Republicans played a minor role in the Democratic victories. The same could not be said of the Populists, however. A careful survey of election returns indicates that many Populists were drawn to the Democratic party by the racist appeals and that this defection was an important factor in the Democratic victory.

The triumphant North Carolina Democrats decided to make future

Republican challenges impossible. They introduced a suffrage amendment to the state constitution that was designed to remove blacks from the electorate. The measure easily passed the legislature, and the popular referendum was scheduled for the summer of 1900.[43] Pritchard faced a particularly difficult task in holding the Republican forces together in this situation. White Republicans, like other white southerners of the 1890s, shared a growing feeling of racial fear and hysteria. A number of defections took place, including that of former congressman Thomas Settle, but Pritchard was able to hold most Republicans in the mountain section in line by a shrewd choice of attacks on the amendment.[44] He charged that the suffrage provision would ultimately disfranchise many poor and illiterate whites as well as eliminating black voters. Since many mountain voters—Democrats as well as Republicans—fell into the categories that Pritchard had cited, the Republican campaign gained great strength in western North Carolina. That the Democrats were forced to call the legislature into special session to make changes in the amendment attests to the success of Pritchard's strategy.[45] This legislation blunted the Republican drive, and in the spring Republican governor Russell undercut Pritchard's efforts by saying the issue was not a party question. Still, when the vote on the amendment was held in August, virtually every mountain Republican and a significant number of mountain Democrats voted against it.[46] The amendment passed easily despite the vote in the mountain counties, and Republicans now faced political ruin. As in Virginia, the mountain Republicans had been remarkably loyal to the new business leadership of the party, even in the face of sickening racism and certain defeat.

Only in West Virginia did the new leaders keep control of the state organization and manage to keep the party in power as well. Special conditions in West Virginia were largely responsible for this success. Because the black population of the state was small, the typical Democratic racist appeals did not have the impact there that they did in other states. Further, the Democrats of West Virginia were badly split on the currency question, with most of the leaders supporting the gold standard. Since many West Virginia Democrats agreed with the free-silver plank in the party platform, the leaders of the party often found it difficult to arouse their followers. On the other hand, the West Virginia Republicans were virtually unanimously agreed on the business-oriented platform proposed by Senator Elkins.

Only the question of the distribution of patronage threatened to disrupt Republican harmony, but even in this potentially dangerous area the Elkins machine was fortunate. The national Republican victory of 1896 was matched by the election of a Republican governor of West

Virginia; consequently, many Republicans who were denied federal positions could be given places working for the state. The governor was George Atkinson, a leading member of the old Nathan Goff organization, and he carefully included many older Republicans that Elkins might have neglected. Despite these advantages, the party leadership split badly over the appointment of the collector of internal revenue for the state. Elkins's candidate was Albert White, a Parkersburg newspaper editor, who had been collector during Benjamin Harrison's administration. White apparently had attacked some anti-Elkins politicians and was not a popular individual. A number of prominent Republicans, including Governor Atkinson and Congressman Gordon Dayton, sponsored another candidate for the position.[47] While this movement was not a direct challenge to unseat Elkins, it was an attempt to reduce his authority in the party.

Elkins tried to give the appearance of not dictating the appointment in order to placate the opposition, but he was determined that White would be named collector. Dayton apparently discovered that Elkins had been secretly backing White and demanded that he and Elkins settle the situation in the presence of President McKinley.[48] Such a meeting was exactly what Elkins wanted to avoid. He told Dayton that actually it was the president who wanted White and that he, Elkins, had always been neutral in the matter. Dayton went to talk with McKinley and, as Elkins reported to White, "returned very buoyant, saying that the President was very pleasant and left the matter entirely with me."[49] This outcome gave the anti-White forces great hope and left Elkins no alternative. He met with the president two days later and requested that White receive the position; McKinley agreed. Elkins, in the same letter to White, explained the result: "You could have been nominated a month ago, but I felt that Davis and Dayton would feel that they had not been fairly treated. Giving them all the opportunity to be heard, however, has not served to satisfy them. They believe, and always will believe that I did not treat Davis justly." The White appointment was unpopular among many West Virginia Republicans, and opposition to it continued long after he was confirmed by the Senate.

The 1898 battle for a United State Senate seat once again threatened to undermine Elkins's position. John Mason, a former leader of the Goff machine, called for a convention to nominate Goff as the Republican candidate. Elkins and other members of the new leadership were not opposed to Goff's candidacy, since the former congressman was still very popular and his name would virtually insure Republican success.[50] In addition, Goff's election in 1898 would remove him as a rival for Elkins's seat in 1900. The only condition that Elkins required was that

Goff become an active candidate and campaign openly for the position. To do so would have meant that Goff had to give up his secure federal judgeship, and this he refused to do.[51] When Goff backed out, the Elkins machine had a candidate ready to campaign for the position. Wealthy industrialist Nathan B. Scott, a staunch ally of Elkins's, who had been appointed federal commissioner of internal revenue in 1897, immediately announced his availability. Scott, Elkins, and the Republican National Committee poured money into Scott's campaign so as to retain Republican control of the West Virginia legislature. Scott also needed to insure that the members elected by the party would be loyal to him and told Albert White to "take whatever *grease is necessary* with you, and call on me for it afterwards, to control that convention."[52] Despite Scott's efforts, opposition to him appeared within the party.

Governor Atkinson attempted to assume leadership of the old Goff faction. As he had in the dispute over the collector's job, Elkins feigned neutrality while he actually worked for one candidate. Elkins secretly encouraged Scott, but he did not want to alienate the popular governor or the still-potent Goff loyalists. In July Elkins called Scott and Atkinson together to resolve the conflict between the two men. Elkins said that Scott was willing to drop out if Atkinson was able to finance the remainder of the Republican canvass. Atkinson was caught in Elkins's clever trap; he could not provide the necessary money and he was forced to acknowledge that it would be not completely fair for Scott to spend the money and not be rewarded.[53] Atkinson refused to withdraw officially from the race, but he could not fault Elkins when the latter openly backed Scott. The governor continued to snipe at Scott, however, claiming that he was purchasing the Senate seat. This charge brought the following reply from Scott: "I don't want to buy it. I only want to use whatever funds are necessary in order to protect myself and my friends."[54] While Scott was able to make this rather subtle distinction, most observers at the time probably agreed with Atkinson's analysis. It did not weaken Scott's position, however, since most local politicians were delighted to have their campaigns paid for by outsiders.

The contest for the Republican gubernatorial nomination in 1900 offered one final opportunity for the old Goff machine to assert itself. Elkins selected Albert White as the machine's candidate and assured White that he and the national committee would take care of the expenses.[55] As in the fight over the collector's position in 1897, opposition to White surfaced quickly. Atkinson and other members of the machine supported Congressman Romeo Freer in their attempt to thwart White and Elkins.[56] The revolt spread beyond just a few politicians this time, and some important segments of the West Virginia Republican party threatened to rise up against the machine. Veterans and blacks were particularly dissatified and swung their support to Freer.[57] The situation was especially dangerous for Elkins, since these two groups represented a substantial proportion of the party membership in the state. Both had enjoyed much more prestige and power during the Goff years and were undoubtedly upset at their loss of status. In addition, White was accused of being opposed to labor unions because of an incident involving the International Typographical Union and a newspaper in which White had part ownership. Since organized labor was becoming a more important part of West Virginia politics all the time, White appeared to be in serious trouble. He was, however, able to persuade a number of labor leaders to justify his actions in the episode in question and did not suffer much damage.[58]

The other elements of the anti-White coalition were not as easily pacified. They tried to hide their attack on the machine by endorsing McKinley for president and Elkins for senator. Elkins once again wanted to avoid the appearance of dictating the nomination.[59] This position meant that White was the major target of the opposition attacks and at the same time could not openly call for Elkins's help. At the senator's suggestion, White made every effort to be fair at the primary conventions and absolutely refused to criticize the opposition. White maintained that Freer had every right to run for the nomination, and Freer's efforts were praised in White's own newspaper.[60] Unfortunately for White's opposition, they had picked a poor man as their candidate. Freer was a reformed alcoholic; and, as White began to win a series of early victories, Freer began to drink heavily again. After Freer missed an important convention in Preston County in late March, his state committee disowned him and Freer was forced to withdraw from the race. Freer, Atkinson, and the other antimachine leaders quickly made peace with Elkins and White, and the united Republican party of West Virginia overwhelmingly elected White as governor and Elkins as senator in 1900.[61] The success of the Elkins machine in maintaining control and unity of the West Virginia Republican organization was impressive. Its ample financial resources and Elkins's willingness to allow the opposition to have its say in public allowed the machine to survive all challenges without being weakened. The corresponding disunity of the Democrats in the state insured that the Republicans would retain control of West Virginia.

Despite the emphasis that the Democrats placed on racist appeals, they were unable to attract mountain Republican voters during the late 1890s. Democratic success during this period in reestablishing their predominant position in four of the five states in the upper South would seem to contradict this assertion. Mountain Republicans stayed loyal to their party, although their own racism appeared to be quite strong. Two elections in the upper South illustrate the mountain Republican's reluctance to desert his party under pressure. The battle for a state judicial post in Breathitt and surrounding counties in Kentucky in 1897 almost turned into a farce when the Democratic candidate, David B. Redwine, and the editor of the *Hazel Green Herald*, Spencer Cooper, decided to conduct a racially oriented cartoon campaign directed against Republican George W. Gourley. Cooper went further than Redwine had expected, running cartoons of the Republican ticket with caricatures of Gourley and "Sambo." Some other cartoons indicated that blacks could dominate the local court system if the Republicans won. On 21 October Redwin repudiated Cooper, and the enraged editor exposed the entire arrangement, claiming that Redwine was balking at paying the newspaper for its work. The *Herald* quickly changed its position and backed Gourley in the last weeks.[62] The somewhat confused situation ended on election day, when Redwine was elected in one of the few Democratic strongholds in the region. It seems clear that Redwine had commissioned the racist cartoons, but he found that they were having no impact on mountain Republican voters. Faced with the possibility of alienating some of his own supporters, Redwine had reversed his position and, public embarrassment not withstanding, was able to salvage a political victory.

The famous "Red Shirt" campaign of 1898 in North Carolina is another excellent example of the resistance of white mountain Republicans to antiblack propaganda. As Democratic leader Furnifold Simmons noted, "the keynote of the campaign was White Supremacy."[63] Simmons and other party leaders found mountain whites very resistant to their canvass and were forced to emulate Redwine and Cooper and conduct a crude cartoon campaign.[64] White government unions were started throughout the western part of the state, and an editorial flaunting the sexual attractiveness of black men to white women and written by a North Carolina black editor were spread throughout the mountains. Whole issues of newspapers that were widely read in the region were devoted to stories of supposed black domination of the eastern section of the state.[65] As noted earlier, the Republican response was not to defend the rights of blacks, but instead to reply with a series of racist attacks on the Democrats. The election returns revealed a slight decrease in Republican votes in the mountain counties, which allowed the Democrats to win several important legislative races in the area. The conclusion that the racist campaign could be judged a success cannot be supported, however, as table 14 shows. The Republican share of the vote in western North Carolina declined only 2.2 percent between 1896 and

TABLE 14. Percentage of Republican Vote in Mountain Counties, Upper South, 1896, 1898, and 1900

	1896	1898	1900
North Carolina	51.1%	49.3%	52.2%
Virginia	51.7	48.1	49.2
Tennessee	65.8	57.9	56.7
Kentucky	59.7	50.2	57.8
West Virginia	53.5	51.9	55.1

SOURCE: ICPR Election Data. The data for Kentucky in 1898 are somewhat misleading because of the presence of a large number of votes cast for an Independent Republican candidate who received support from both Republicans and Democrats.

1898. Only the West Virginia mountain Republicans showed a smaller loss than those in North Carolina, and the 1900 results indicate that North Carolina Republicans were simply following the same pattern as other mountain voters. In fact, the normal American voter reaction being to reduce support of the party that won the previous presidential election, the Republican loss of voters in 1898 was quite predictable. Certainly a few mountain Republicans were persuaded by the Democratic appeals, but most of them refused to be driven into the "white man's" party.

As noted in the developments in North Carolina, the Democrats then turned to a much more certain strategy to end the Republican threat—disfranchisement. Actually, Democrats in the upper South had already experimented with measures designed to limit the franchise long before the late 1890s. Virginia's Conservative party introduced a poll tax in 1876, and for a couple of years it aided in the further weakening of the state's moribund Republican party. Mahone and the Readjusters were able to neutralize the effect of the tax by paying it for their supporters in 1879 and 1881, and they swept to power.[66] Among the major reforms of the Readjuster-Republican coalition was one to repeal the poll tax, with the resultant appearance of political democracy in Virginia. One of the first concerns of the Democrats after they regained power in 1883 was to secure an election law that was more effective than the poll tax. The Anderson-McCormick law that was passed in 1884 gave local election officials great discretion and led to widespread fraud in many Virginia counties.[67]

The rise of the Populists in the early 1890s caused Democrats in Virginia to examine their election laws again. The Anderson-McCormick law had not been completely satisfactory; the Republicans had won six of ten congressional elections in 1886 and had come within fifteen hundred votes of carrying the state in 1888. Even the weak Virginia Populist party won about 40 percent of the vote in the gubernatorial election of 1893. As a result, the Democrats in 1894 passed the Walton law, which provided for the use of secret ballots, which one Republican complained "practically disfranchises the illiterate vote."[68] Although the Republicans were further diminished as many of their poor and uneducated followers lost their franchise, they were able to elect James Walker to Congress in 1894 and 1896 in the mountain district. In 1897 the Democrats attempted to call a state constitutional convention, but the referendum was voted down. A second referendum was held in 1900, passing in a close vote over determined Republican opposition.[69] The convention that produced the 1901 state constitution added a lengthy residence requirement and literacy test to the state's election laws. The result was proclaimed as state law because the Democrats refused to allow the people to vote on the document.[70] Blacks and poor whites were virtually eliminated from the electorate, and the Republican party disappeared everywhere in the state except in the mountain counties.

Tennessee Democrats also made early efforts to reduce the black vote. Facing an opponent that grew stronger with each election in the 1880s, the Tennessee Democrats passed four measures in 1889 and 1890 designed to reduce the number of black voters. The new laws were directed primarily at cities—where blacks formed a disproportionately large share of the population—and required registration of voters, separate ballot boxes for state and federal elections, a poll tax, and a secret ballot law.[71] Knoxville and Chattanooga were the cities in eastern Tennessee most affected by the new legislation, and the mountain Republicans worked to counter it. A Republican judge issued an injunction to prevent the use of these laws in the Chattanooga city elections of 1889.[72] When the injunction was dissolved, the Republicans responded by placing "education rooms" near the polling places to instruct the illiterate voters. The result was the election of a Republican mayor and of twelve Republicans to the sixteen-man city council.[73]

The new laws had a cumulative effect, however, and every year after 1890, when the poll tax was first required, more and more city voters were disfranchised. For example, the total vote in Knoxville in 1888 was 3,983; but in 1900, after the city had greatly increased its population through the annexation of suburbs, the total vote was 3,609.[74] Still, the Republicans elected William Rule mayor of Knoxville in 1897, which suggested that with the proper organization the party could negate the effect of the legislation. In 1897 there was a movement by some

Tennessee Democrats to call a constitutional convention to institute more radical measures, but a coalition of Republicans and conservative Democrats defeated the referendum.[75] Thus, Tennessee Democrats had not passed legislation that eliminated the black and illiterate white votes completely, but they settled for laws that did insure Democratic success except in extraordinary circumstances.

Democrats in West Virginia and Kentucky were not as successful in their attempts to gain control of the electoral machinery as were those in the other three states. Since the Republicans retained control of the West Virginia state government throughout this period, no disfranchising legislation at all was passed in that state. Kentucky Republicans had elected their first governor in 1895 and their first senator in 1897; and, when the Democrats won control of the legislature in the fall elections of 1897, they passed a state election law.

The 1899 gubernatorial election was to be the first real test of the law. William Goebel, the reluctant sponsor of the elections bill, secured the Democratic nomination at a chaotic convention and was immediately faced with a revolt against his candidacy. Conservative Democrats, who opposed Goebel, were determined to put an end to Republican victories, if possible. They passed the Goebel bill, which created a state election commission selected by the—Democratic—legislature.[76] Republican governor William Bradley vetoed the bill, but, despite some Democratic opposition to the measure, the legislature repassed it. When Republicans challenged the law in the federal courts, the Supreme Court upheld the statute.[77] The congressional elections of 1898 offered the first test of the new law, and local Democratic officials used it in the mountain counties of the Ninth District to throw out enough ballots to defeat Republican incumbent Samuel Pugh. The members of the state election commission, perhaps not wanting to give the Republicans a campaign issue, reversed the decision and gave Pugh the election certificate.[78]

In 1899 Goebel's antirailroad opposition met and nominated former governor John Young Brown.[79] The Republicans nominated state attorney general William Taylor and immediately made the Goebel bill the major issue in the campaign. The Republicans claimed that Goebel had sponsored the legislation to count himself in, although the bill specifically excluded the office of governor from the jurisdiction of the board. Many Democrats agreed with this analysis, and one paper asserted that the only way to prevent Goebel's assuming the governor's chair was "by killing him."[80] Goebel himself conducted a vigorous campaign against the influence of the Louisville and Nashville Railroad on the state government and the Republican party.[81] The election was very close, the Democratic split allowing Taylor to win by a plurality of two thousand votes out of a total of nearly four hundred thousand. The Goebel board met in early December and, to everyone's surprise, certified Republicans as victors in all state contests under its jurisdiction.[82] Goebel and the Democratic nominees appealed their case to the state legislature, which, with its Democratic majority, was expected to seat Goebel.

Mountain Republicans began to form private militia companies in an effort to protect Taylor's title to the office. Several thousand of these marksmen were transported to the state capital by the Louisville and Nashville Railroad. The city of Frankfort looked like an armed camp when, in early February 1900, an assassin firing from one of the state office windows shot and wounded Goebel. The Democratic legislature immediately convened and named Goebel the officially elected governor; and, as he lay dying, Goebel took the oath of office.[83] The confused situation that followed was not a credit to either party. Suffice it to say that the Goebel bill was repealed as a result of a political understanding reached between Republicans and Democrats in the summer of 1900.[84] The state of Kentucky held a special election in 1900 to settle the disputed governor's race, and the Democrat won. Although they controlled the state government again, the Democrats did not seek to change the election laws. The attempt to seize control of Kentucky's elections had failed, and the state's Democrats were forced to battle on equal terms with their Republican opponents.

The significance of the disfranchisement movement can be seen in the pattern of partisan politics in each state after 1900. In Virginia and North Carolina, where the election laws were the most discriminatory, the Republican party ceased to be a threat in state elections. Virginia Republicans often did not run gubernatorial candidates after 1900 and, when they did, had no illusions about winning. Instead, the power in the party shifted to the remarkably successful Slemp family of southwestern Virginia. Campbell Slemp and his son C. Bascom Slemp constructed a Republican machine in Virginia's Ninth District that returned the Slemps to Congress in every election between 1902 and 1920. The machine insured that Republican voters were properly registered, paid their poll tax, and were properly instructed on how to vote. Since many mountain Republicans could not or would not pay their own poll tax, the Slemp organization spent tens of thousands of dollars every two years paying taxes and buying votes. In 1904, with the aid of President Theodore Roosevelt, the Slemps seized control of the state Republican organization and retained it until 1929. After his father's death in 1907, Bascom succeeded him in Congress and moved quickly to purge the blacks from Virginia's lily-white Republican party. Unwilling to spend his money or risk his position to build up the state party, Slemp concentrated on retaining his seat in Congress and controlling Virginia's Republican delegates to the national conventions.[85] With both the Democrats and the leading Republican in Virginia committed to a weak state Republican party, it is no surprise that the party failed.

North Carolina Republicans made a much more aggressive fight than their counterparts in Virginia, but they enjoyed no greater success. From 1900 until 1909 Jeter C. Pritchard and his followers continued to dominate the party, and in each election the now all-white Republicans gradually increased their votes. Factional battles within the dominant Democratic party and the presence of William Jennings Bryan as leader of that party drove many Democrats into the Republican party. One of the recent converts, John Motley Morehead, was one of three Republicans to be elected to Congress in 1908, as the Republicans won more than 45 percent of the presidential vote. Republican growth was halted the next year when party factionalism boiled over and Morehead was named party chairman. The badly divided party lost all of its congressional seats in 1910, and the Taft-Roosevelt battle in 1912 shattered the party completely. As in Virginia, Republicans would still win occasional congressional elections in the mountain region, but the party was dead in the remainder of the state.[86] Once again the combination of Republican internal weakness and powerful election laws had destroyed the party organization.

The Republican party in Tennessee, Kentucky, and West Virginia did not face the same obstacles and was able to retain its position as a major factor in the political life of each state. Although many blacks were not allowed to vote in Tennessee, the party there did not end its alliance with blacks. This arrangement was particularly true in eastern Tennessee, where local Republican officials allowed blacks to continue to vote. The result was that Republicans continued to dominate the First and Second congressional districts and to elect the governor three times between 1900 and 1922.[87] Kentucky Republicans also worked with blacks in their state and dominated the congressional districts in the mountains. Despite the absence of major restrictive legislation, Kentucky Republicans remained a minority after 1900. When the Democrats were not united, however, the party had enough strength to elect governors and senators.[88] West Virginia Republicans, under the leadership of Elkins and other businessmen, dominated the state until the 1930s. Differing from Republicans in the other states, the leadership of the West Virginia party became increasingly inflexible—perhaps because of their majority status—and the party offered little to its constituents after the Progressive era.[89] The party in these three states remained a viable and active organization capable of winning state elections because of the absence or weakness of Democratic disfranchisement efforts.

The one thing that did remain constant about the Republican party in the upper South in the two decades after 1900 was the continued strength of the mountain Republican organizations. Even clever Democratic gerrymanders and a selective application of the election laws could not prevent James Jefferson Britt from winning election to Congress in western North Carolina in 1914 and 1916. Bascom Slemp retained his seat in 1910 despite Democratic efforts to reduce registration, a future Democratic governor for an opponent, and an estimated fifty-thousand-dollar Democratic fraud fund. In the other three states, securing the Republican nomination in the mountain districts was usually sufficient to win the election. The coalition of Unionists, dissatisfied Democrats, and middle-class professionals had been welded together by the party-army and the trials of the 1890s. The mountain Republicans were the only element of the original Republican party of the South to survive the racist onslaught that swept the region in this period. Internal dissensions and the aggressive and unscrupulous opposition had ended any hope that the Republicans would control the upper South, but the loyalty of the mountain voters remained unshaken.

The general failure of the Republican party in the South after Reconstruction has made the success of the mountain Republicans seem to be an historical accident. That assessment both is unfair to the people involved and hides the complexity of the developments in that region. Mountain republicanism was not an automatic and unthinking response to the Civil War crisis. The party adapted itself to the local conditions in the highlands better than did the Democrats, and it acted as the spokesman for the mountain people. When an economic crisis struck the upper South in the early 1890s, it was the mountain Republicans and their allies who adjusted most rapidly to the changing demands of the electorate. Only when racial issues were dominant was the party on the defensive in the mountains.

During the decade of Reconstruction, Republican political leaders found it difficult to appeal to mountain voters. Mountain whites resented federal intervention into their lives on behalf of blacks. Congressional Reconstruction policies were supported reluctantly. At the same time, congressional policies had helped to create the Republican parties in these five states and could not be disowned by Republicans who had gained power under them. Quickly the conflict between national and southern interests undermined the mountain Republican parties and forced them out of positions of power. At one time during the 1870s it appeared that the Republican party in the mountains would suffer the fate of the other groups of white opposition in the South.

It was at this critical point that the party adopted the demands of the local electorate. Sensing the desire of the mountain people to withdraw from the conflicts generated by national developments, a new group of Republican leaders promised to alleviate problems and act as a buffer against the rest of the world. These men and the organizations they created stressed the Republican party's concern for their constituents' immediate needs. At the same time the new leaders glorified the Civil War role played by the mountain people and took advantage of the people's pride in their own heritage. Finally, the racial issues raised by Reconstruction were ignored by the local Republican politicians. This strategy was quite successful, and the Party gained adherents steadily between 1876 and 1888.

The reintroduction of national issues into mountain politics in the 1890s changed the nature of mountain Republican parties. The Lodge Elections Bill of 1890 weakened the Republicans throughout the upper South by threatening to allow federal intervention in racial matters again. The electoral defeats that followed critically weakened the locally oriented politicians. Rapid industrialization in some parts of the mountain region had created a new middle class of business and professional people who immediately challenged the old bosses for control of the Republican organizations. Aided by the onset of the 1890s economic collapse, the middle-class leaders gained control of the mountain Republican parties and also nearly succeeded in creating state coalitions to defeat the Democrats. Only by blatantly resorting to racism and fraud did the Democrats maintain their power.

A final assessment of the mountain parties during the last third of the nineteenth century must take into account all of these developments. It is true that the leaders and the party organization had no special claim to greatness. While the machines created by men like Houk, Mahone, and Elkins were very effective, they differed little from others found throughout the country. No mountain political leader introduced a new idea or program during this entire period, and the legislative records of mountain congressmen are barren of achievement. The exception to this rule was the mountain Republican relationship with Mahone and the Readjusters in Virginia. Mahone was undoubtedly the most creative southern politician in this era, but once again the mountain Republican contribution was the largely passive one of following the little boss's lead. The most damning indictment, however, is that the middle-class and business leadership of the party did not object to the rape of the land and the people of Appalachia in the twentieth century. The Republicans were so anxious to share in American prosperity themselves that they ignored the growing evidence of outside economic domination of the region.

Despite these obvious and serious failures, the mountain Republican parties were a valuable and positive part of the political life of the upper South during the last third of the nineteenth century. Southern Democrats during the Gilded Age were determined to reduce the level of government to its lowest possible point so as to decrease taxes. As a result, they did not provide the people with services adequate for their needs. Republicans were also committed to a laissez-faire philosophy of government, but they labored to expand educational programs, to end the practice of employing convict labor, and to increase the number of institutions for the insane, the blind, and other groups of handicapped persons. An even more important part of the Republican party's appeal—in the eyes of mountain voters, at least—was its call for government assistance in opening up and developing the mountain region.

Although the mountain Republicans provided flawed answers to problems that confronted them, they did ask some crucial questions about conditions that were changing mountain society and they did make an effort to find practical and popular answers. The absence of any program presented by the opposition ended the political dialogue and left the Republicans with unchallenged and unexamined policies. Whenever a difficult political decision had to be made, southern Democrats retreated behind their breastworks of racism and ran up the flag of white supremacy. If that failed, they cynically abandoned any pretense of observing democratic principles and resorted to fraud and violence. This failure of the southern political system to solve the problems must be borne primarily by those who refused to allow the voters an opportunity to participate in the process of governing. The mountain Republicans represented a minority view, the smaller segment in the white population of the South, and their position threatened many powerful political interests in the lowland South. These interests used all means necessary to suppress their highland opposition.

The mountain Republican voters, however, proved to be resistant to the opposition appeals based on fear and hate. They refused to panic, despite the fact that the people of Appalachia faced a difficult problem of adjusting to outside pressure during this period. First the Civil War and then industrialization threatened mountain society. Some of the people lashed out violently as their world changed. The disruption of Reconstruction and the 1890s framed a period when the mountain Republicans successfully created a highland identity to encourage mountain whites to distinguish themselves from other white southerners. It was in this central period from approximately 1876 to 1890 that the Republican party earned the loyalty of the Appalachian voters, a voting pattern that remained consistent until the depression of the 1930s. It was a constant reminder of both the independence and the limitations of a people and a political party in a region facing the forces that created modern America.

APPENDIX

A STATISTICAL PROFILE OF THE MOUNTAIN REPUBLICANS

The superficial characteristics of mountain Republicans are well known. They were poor, rural, farmers or miners, relatively nonracist, native born, Protestant, poorly educated, and devoted to the preservation of the Union. With slight variations these same descriptions could be applied to most southerners. The problem, then, that confronts the investigator is to determine what factors can explain the phenomenon of white southerners voting Republican after the Reconstruction period. This analysis will be divided into two distinct parts that will examine the two crucial questions raised by Republican voting in the mountain counties. The first question of who were the original mountain Republicans will be answered by examining the returns from the presidential election of 1876. After that section, the reasons for Republican growth and success between 1876 and 1896 will be discussed.

One major problem faces anyone who tries to analyze the mountain people in detail: they form a remarkably homogenous group in the period between 1865 and 1900. With the exception of the small groups of blacks and immigrants, the mountain people shared the same demographic characteristics. The result is that many of the types of tests and comparisons that can be applied to other regions are not fruitful when studying the mountain people. Thus, the most effective techniques for explaining historical developments are statistically unsophisticated. More exact tests were run, but the results of these analyses added little new information. Therefore, this material will be presented in as traditional a format as possible in an effort to make the information available to those who consciously avoid social science methodology.

The conclusions drawn from the census data seem to confirm the mountaineer stereotype. In 1870 the highland region was predominantly rural, with only 76,196 people living in urban areas out of a total population of 1,684,192.[1] Only two mountain cities—Wheeling, West Virginia, and Chattanooga, Tennessee—had a population of 10,000 as late as 1880. The following request, written by an eastern Kentucky newspaper editor in 1896, shows the extent to which rural traditions persisted in the mountain counties: "We have over SIX HUNDRED DOLLARS due us on subscriptions, job work and advertising. We need the money, and must have a settlement. If you haven't the money to pay up, bring us hams, chickens, corn, oats, wood, hay, or almost anything a family can use to advantage, and we will make arrangements for settling."[2] While many mountaineers maintained a more sophisticated lifestyle, it is accurate to say that most highlanders were part of rural America.

Another factor that was frequently cited as a unique characteristic of the mountaineers was cultural isolation. Some analysts have even concluded that this circumstance was partly responsible for the appearance and success of the Republican party in the region. In fact, inadequate transportation facilities and the desire of Democratic state governments to retain low taxes did limit formal educational opportunities in the mountain counties. One reflection of this fact was the inadequate educational facilities and consequent illiteracy in the mountain counties. As table 1 indicates, the mountain counties recorded a higher level of illiteracy than in all counties of the area.

Testing these figures with a more refined technique reveals some interesting information. The correlation coefficient range runs from +1.0, a perfect positive correlation, to −1.0, a perfect inverse relationship, with 0.0 indicating no correlation. The scores of +.30 or higher and −.30 or lower are accepted by many data analysts as showing a significant relationship.[3] As table 1 suggests, the correlation between mountain counties and illiteracy is +.42, which is a fairly weak positive relation-

TABLE 1. Illiteracy in the Upper South, 1870

Percentage of Illiterate White Males over 21	35+	25–34	15–14	5–14	0–4
Mountain Counties	32	49	43	19	4
All Counties	59	112	151	111	18

ship. One might conclude from this evidence that illiteracy could be regarded as a variable that explains mountain republicanism.

That is not the case, however. Table 2 shows the relationship between illiteracy and republicanism among mountain whites eligible to vote. This table is not as clear as the previous ones, and the correlation coefficient of +.05 explains why.

TABLE 2. Illiteracy and White Republican Voting, Presidential Election, 1876

Percentage of Illiterate White Males over 21		60+	50–59	40–49	40–39	20–29	10–19	0–9	—
35+	(32)	8	7	6	4	5	1	—	1
25–34	(49)	3	3	14	9	10	5	4	1
15–24	(43)	—	5	10	9	7	2	9	1
5–14	(19)	1	2	7	1	3	—	4	1
0–4	(4)	1	—	—	—	2	—	1	—

White Republican Vote as Percentage of Total Vote

There is a slight positive relationship between the two variables, but that relationship is not statistically significant. Illiteracy, therefore, may explain something important about the mountaineer existence, but it fails to explain much about mountain politics.

The relationship between politics and religion in the mountain counties must also be explored. However, before too many conclusions are drawn from these data, one example will demonstrate the need for caution on this point. As discussed earlier, the Methodist Episcopal church, led by William G. Brownlow, invaded east Tennessee after the Civil War and became deeply involved in politics. The Methodist Episcopal church became identified with unionism and the Republican party in this region, and it appears that people joined it to express a political preference. Table 3 shows the high correlation between Republican voting and membership in the Methodist Episcopal church.

The same results could be obtained in most of the mountain counties of West Virginia as well. It seems in this case that, rather than church affiliation explaining something about political preference, the reverse is true. A study of the Disciples of Christ in this period discloses many of the same factors at work in the factionalism in that denomination.[4] Although there are some statistically significant correlations

TABLE 3. Church Membership, 1890, and Party Vote, Presidential Election, 1876 (in percentages)

	Rep.	M.E.	Dem.	M.E.South
Anderson	54.9	67.8	45.1	32.2
Bledsoe	44.5	66.4	55.5	33.6
Blount	59.0	57.0	41.0	43.0
Bradley	54.3	63.4	45.7	36.6
Campbell	65.2	74.8	34.8	25.2
Carter	76.8	72.7	23.2	27.3
Claiborne	55.4	41.0	44.6	59.0
Cocke	59.0	49.2	41.0	50.8
Cumberland	49.4	35.1	50.6	68.9
Grainger	57.2	58.3	42.8	41.7
Greene	50.4	65.4	49.6	34.6
Hamblen	54.1	50.1	45.9	49.9
Hamilton	53.9	53.4	46.1	46.6
Hancock	62.2	71.5	37.8	28.5
Hawkins	52.6	31.3	47.4	68.7
James	55.6	38.5	44.4	61.5
Jefferson	68.6	58.6	31.4	41.4
Johnson	77.8	85.8	22.2	14.2
Knox	55.6	56.8	44.4	43.2
Loudon	62.5	52.3	37.5	47.7
McMinn	53.6	48.3	46.4	51.7
Marion	55.4	48.3	44.6	51.7
Meigs	65.2	57.8	34.8	42.2
Monroe	36.1	46.2	63.9	53.8
Morgan	62.8	33.3	37.7	66.7
Polk	38.3	31.9	61.7	68.1
Rhea	31.3	45.8	68.7	54.2
Roane	66.8	62.7	33.2	37.3
Scott	81.7	100.0	18.2	0.0
Sequatchie	30.8	16.6	69.2	83.4
Sevier	81.9	81.9	18.1	18.1
Sullivan	34.0	28.1	66.0	71.9
Union	61.9	56.4	38.1	43.6
Washington	55.0	51.0	45.0	49.0

between church membership and politics in the mountain regions, conclusions drawn from these relationships must be tentative at best.

Another variable often used to differentiate mountain counties from the remainder of the South is the ethnic composition of the region's population. Traditional explanations for mountain republicanism have usually stressed the relative absence of blacks and the relatively large immigrant population, particularly in mining areas. Table 4 confirms the expected inverse relationship between white Republican voting and concentration of black population.

TABLE 4. White Republican Vote and Negro Population in Five States, 1876

Percentage of Negroes in Population	\multicolumn{8}{c}{Percentage of White Republican Vote}
	60+	50–59	40–49	30–39	20–29	10–19	0–9	—
0–10	13	19	34	29	30	14	16	4
11–20	—	2	8	13	12	15	18	10
21–30	—	—	—	1	5	14	18	11
31+	—	—	—	—	3	11	56	80

A correlation coefficient of −.68 simply supports the obvious conclusion that southern whites voted Republican only when there were relatively few blacks to threaten white political dominance. Table 5 shows that mountain whites reacted to this pattern exactly as did their lowland counterparts.

TABLE 5. White Republican Vote and Negro Population in Mountain Counties, 1876

Percentage of Negroes in Population	\multicolumn{8}{c}{Percentage of White Republican Vote}
	60+	50–59	40–49	30–39	20–29	10–19	0–9	—
0–10	13	15	31	18	24	5	4	2
11–20	—	2	6	4	2	1	8	1
21–30	—	—	—	1	1	2	4	1
31+	—	—	—	—	—	—	2	—

APPENDIX

A significant factor in determining the Republican vote in the mountains is the relative absence of blacks. The persuasive evidence on this point is the most decisive of all the indicators evaluated.

The second part of the ethnic explanation offers a somewhat more difficult analytical situation. As the overwhelming proportion of traditional Protestants in the mountain population would suggest, few immigrants or children of immigrants lived in the region. Geographical isolation was at least part of the explanation, but another reason, to be explored later, was the absence of industry to attract the Europeans. Table 6 demonstrates the predominance of the native-born population in the upper South. Besides the counties in northwestern West Virginia, only one county had as much as one-tenth of its population in the immigrant category. The result is that analysis is virtually impossible, but because of the small number of people involved this factor is not really significant.

The conditions in northwestern West Virginia were somewhat different, however. There the immigrant population was large enough to measure. Unfortunately, analysis of these data was not very fruitful. No direct correlation was demonstrated between white Republican voting and the presence of nonnative population. Further inspection of the census reports of 1870 shows that most immigrants were either Irish or German and that the Irish were found in the predominantly Republican counties and the Germans in Democratic areas. The exact impact of this variable on mountain republicanism is difficult to assess. The correspondence of mountain Republican leaders in West Virginia rarely mentions any ethnic group in particular, indicating perhaps that they played little part in the politics of the period.

Surprisingly, economic factors seemed to have as little influence on mountain partisan alignments as the immigrant population. For example, historians have cited the fact that mountain farms were smaller and less productive as a contributing cause to the highlanders' hostility toward the Confederacy. The census of 1870 reveals that the same

TABLE 6. Population Having at Least One Foreign-born Parent, 1870 (in percentages)

	0–5	6–10	11–20	20+
All Counties	375	33	23	4
Mountain Counties	126	11	11	1
NW West Virginia	20	5	10	1

conditions prevailed after the war. The clarity of this analysis disappears when one restricts the data to the mountain counties alone. Republican counties and Democratic counties display no significant statistical variation in farm size or in the value of production. Just as do the data on illiteracy, the census data on farm size reveal that the mountaineers as a whole did suffer deprivation, but the presence of large numbers of poor farmers explains little about why mountain men supported the Republican party.

Industrialization also played a very small role in the creation of the mountain Republican parties, despite the fact that mountain Republicans favored industrial development of the region. Outside northwestern West Virginia, however, there was little per capita investment in manufacturing and when this variable was tested with Republican voting in 1876 the result was a +.02 correlation coefficient. A further investigation of the data does reveal that the mountain counties were the home of heavy industry in the five states. Half of all manufactured products produced in the mountain counties came from heavy industry. The lowland counties were much more widely diversified industrially, with such light manufacturing as textiles and tobacco products playing a major role in their economies. Thus it would seem possible that the geographical split in the type of industry found in the upper South would have had political consequences. Yet election returns from the thirteen mountain counties with concentrations of heavy industry would seem to show that such was not the case. In 1876 the Republicans won seven counties and 51 percent of the vote; the Democrats won six counties and 49 percent of the vote. While these percentages were higher than the Republican share of the vote in the mountains as a whole, it would be difficult on the basis of these figures to assign more than a minor role to the development of heavy industry in producing mountain Republicans in 1876.

All of the above results seem only to emphasize the importance of Unionist experience in explaining the early history of mountain republicanism. The rating in table 7 of eastern Tennessee counties by their support of the Union in 1861 and the Republican party in 1876 adds credence to that conclusion. Since all of the counties recorded much higher percentages for the Union in the February 1861 balloting than they did for the Republicans in 1876, all eastern Tennessee Republicans could have had a Unionist background. But it is also clear that not all Unionists became Republicans.

Many of the former Unionists apparently became Democrats. Anderson County, Tennessee, offers an excellent example. In that eastern Tennessee county the Unionist vote was 92.8 percent in June 1861,

TABLE 7. Antisecession Vote, 1861, and Republican Vote, 1876, Eastern Tennessee

1861	1876
1. Scott	1. Sevier
2. Sevier	2. Scott
3. Campbell	3. Johnson
4. Carter	4. Carter
5. Anderson	5. Jefferson
6. Morgan	6. Roane
7. Johnson	7. Campbell
8. Hawkins	8. Morgan
9. Claiborne	9. Hancock
10. Blount	10. Blount-Cocke

TABLE 8. Antisecession Vote, 1861, and Democratic Vote, 1876, Selected Northwestern West Virginia Counties (in percentages)

	Antisecession 1861	White Republican 1876	Black Population 1870	Possible Democrat 1876
Brooke	86.87	41.73	1.78	43.36
Cabell	77.27	33.41	1.91	41.95
Doddridge	93.45	45.51	0.49	47.45
Kanawha	78.57	29.97	10.01	39.59
Ohio	95.42	44.28	1.54	49.60
Putnam	78.60	32.13	3.34	43.13
Wayne	74.61	26.14	1.95	46.52
Webster	32.73	11.72	0.00	21.01
Wetzel	81.44	28.59	0.13	52.72
Wirt	84.36	41.03	0.60	42.73

but the Republican vote was only 54.9 percent in 1876. Although circumstances like war-related deaths and population increase would explain part of the change, a large number of Unionists in 1861 did vote Democratic in 1876. This same trend was especially strong in the mountain counties in northwestern West Virginia. Table 8 indicates that in as many as ten counties in that region a majority of former Unionists may have voted against the Republicans. While population changes explain some of these data, there is little question that many 1861 Union supporters did not become Republicans.

One could nevertheless argue that being a Unionist was still a precondition for being a Republican, even if not all Unionists joined the party. However, some evidence shows that even this assumption is not entirely accurate. In six West Virginia mountain counties the Republican share of the vote was higher in 1876 than the Unionist vote in 1861. The best example of this situation is Pocahontas County, West Virginia, where less than 4 percent of the voters supported the Union and yet the white Republican proportion of the vote in 1876 was slightly more than 20 percent. In addition, in another state the vast majority of western North Carolina men served in the Confederate army, and yet there was a significant white Republican minority in that region. Therefore, the statement that all mountain Republicans were former Unionists must be altered. While most of them probably were, it seems obvious that the party had a number of men in it who overcame their hostility to the Union war effort in order to be members of the party.

The relationship between unionism and the Republican party is best illustrated by a series of elections in Kentucky in the 1860s. Using the percentage of the male population that volunteered for the federal army as the variable for Unionist support, several pro-Union candidates were tested for their level of Unionist strength.[5] In the 1860 presidential election, John Bell, Stephen Douglas, and Abraham Lincoln split the vote of the supporters of the Union. Four years later, Lincoln and the Republicans still were not able to claim the distinction of being the party of Kentucky's Unionists. The correlation coefficient of the relationship between Lincoln's vote and Union volunteering was +.22—not statistically significant. After the Civil War ended, most of the returning Confederate veterans joined the Democratic party. Despite this fact, many Unionists refused to become Republicans. In the gubernatorial election of 1867, the Unionist Democrats ran a candidate against the regular Democrats and Republicans. While the correlation coefficient of the relationship between Union Democratic voting and Union volunteering (+.34) was lower than the Republican results (+.59), the Republicans could not claim to be the sole Unionist spokesman.[6] Finally in the presidential election of 1868, the Republicans were the recognized leaders of the Unionist forces, although the relatively low correlation coefficient of +.64 indicates that many Unionists became Democrats.[7] Thus, it is obvious that the relationship between unionism and republicanism was a complex and fluid arrangement during this early period.

Several conclusions that can be drawn from these data tell something about the origins of the Republican party in the mountain areas of the upper South. For the most part, the mountain Republicans had opposed secession and the Confederacy, but this factor was obviously not conclusive. Many Unionists did not become Republicans, while a few mountaineers who had rejected the Union did become Republicans. Undoubtedly the strongest variable modifying their behavior was the presence of blacks in their communities. A clear and decisive relationship is demonstrated between black population and white mountain republicanism, and it appears obvious that the absence of blacks and a Unionist background were both necessary to sustain republicanism. Other variables did not have the same high level of impact. The results show that the inhabitants of the mountain counties were indeed rural, impoverished, and uneducated, but no significant correlation seems evident between these conditions and republicanism. It seems probable that some mountain voters were affected by religious affiliation, ethnic background, and the level of industrialization, but the highly homogeneous mountain population and still largely undeveloped commercial life meant that the number was small.

The Republican proportion of the vote in the mountain counties grew dramatically between 1876 and 1896. In the former year the Republicans won only 43.9 percent of votes in the highlands. Two decades later the party's share of the ballots increased 13 percent to 56.8 percent. These figures are even more startling when one realizes that the Republican percentage in national elections during that same period increased less than 2 percent. Even in the traditionally Republican states, the party's proportion of the vote grew by only 4 percent.[8] The achievement of the mountain Republicans was clearly a significant one.

Further investigation of the increase of the Republican vote in the mountain counties is quite illuminating. Table 9 shows that the new Republican voters were not evenly distributed among counties and states. Nearly one-third of the mountain counties showed a greater-than-average increase in Republican vote. Particularly interesting is the contrast between Virginia and Tennessee. In heavily Unionist eastern Tennessee, only five of the thirty-four counties showed a gain of 15 percent or more, while twenty of the twenty-one counties in southwestern Virginia reached the same level. This general pattern seemed to hold in the other states as well. Both eastern Kentucky Republicans and those in northwestern West Virginia showed smaller growth, despite their

TABLE 9. Republican Vote from 1876 to 1896 in the Mountain Counties (in percentages)

	Less than 5.0	5.0–9.9	10.0–14.9	15.0–19.9	More than 20.0
Kentucky	5	7	16	4	2
North Carolina	2	9	3	7	5
Tennessee	4	15	10	4	1
Virginia	—	1	—	1	19
West Virginia	6	15	8	5	2
Total	17	47	37	21	29

largely Unionist population, and heavily Confederate western North Carolina counties had a high level of Republican gains.

Some additional observations can be made when the data are rearranged. The statistics below indicate that a distinct time factor was involved in the Republican growth pattern. Table 10 shows that the party-army was primarily responsible for the improvement in party fortunes.

TABLE 10. Increase of Republican Vote in the Mountain Counties (in percentages)

	Less than 5	5.0–9.9	10.0–14.9	15.0–19.9	More than 20
1876–88	34	47	38	12	20
1888–96	125	25	5	—	—

The Republican share of the vote rose by at least 10 percent in seventy mountain counties between 1876 and 1888, but only five counties attained the same increase for the 1888 to 1896 period. These figures are confirmed by regional totals, which show that the Republican proportion of the vote increased 10.08 percent between 1876 and 1888 and only 2.83 percent in the following eight years. These statistics once again emphasize the tremendous contribution that the post-Reconstruction bosses made to the mountain Republican parties.

An inspection of the census returns offers some insight into the increase in Republican vote. As noted in the previous chapters, the change in party leadership was facilitated by the presence in the region of a rapidly growing urban population that demanded a more sophisticated style of politics. Between 1880 and 1900 the population of cities of 2,500 people or more increased from 76,196 to 279,680. The proportion of mountain people living in urban areas in relation to the total population rose from about 5 percent to slightly more than 11 percent during this period. In 1880 only ten counties contained urban areas, but by 1900 thirty-one counties did. Table 11 indicates, however, that these significant developments had only a slight effect on voting patterns.

TABLE 11. Republican Vote in Thirty-one Mountain Counties with Urban Populations, 1900 (in percentages)

	Less than 5	5.0–9.9	10.0–14.9	15.0–19.9	More than 20
1876–96	6	13	3	4	5
1876–88	10	12	4	1	4
1888–96	23	7	1	—	—

In comparison with the figures in tables 9 and 10, these counties actually show less growth in the 1876 to 1888 and 1876 to 1896 periods. The 1876 to 1888 comparison particularly confirms the experience of the Houk machine in Knoxville, where the party-army could not appeal to urban voters. The results of the returns from 1888 to 1896 show that the voters in urban areas were slightly more likely to have switched to the Republican party than the average rural voter. Thus the increase in urbanization in the mountain region and the shift of Republican policy to appeal to these voters are factors that undoubtedly help explain a small part of the Republican gains.

Urbanization was usually prompted by industrialization, and most mountain Republican politicians felt that as this process continued it would strengthen the party. The business wing of the party in the early 1890s was particularly convinced of this fact. Elkins, the Dukes, Evans, Pritchard, Walker, and Colson all supported the protective tariff because they felt it was a popular political issue as well as enlightened financial policy. By 1894 each mountain Republican party was firmly committed to emphasizing economic issues and basing its campaign on them.

The wisdom of this policy is further confirmed by the statistics concerning the growth of capital invested in manufacturing in the mountain counties. By 1900 twenty-eight counties in the region had a total capitalization of at least one million dollars. An inspection of voting returns in these industrialized counties shows a stronger-than-average increase in the Republican vote. Table 12 demonstrates the impact of industrialization on voting patterns.

The results are approximately the same as those reflected in table 11. As with the urban counties, these industrialized areas reveal a striking improvement over the rest of the mountain counties in the 1888–96 period. In the years between 1876 and 1888, 46 percent of all mountain counties registered gains of at least 10 percent in the Republican vote, while only 39 percent of these selected counties did so. From 1888 to 1896, however, 19 percent of all mountain counties showed Republican gains of 5 percent, while 39 percent of the industrialized counties showed similar gains. Clearly, the Republicans' support of the protective tariff was an effective political strategy in the later period.

Results in selected counties emphasize the point even more effectively. The individual counties cited below indicate that large-scale industrialization could and did radically change the politics of the area involved. For example, the two southwest Virginia counties with the greatest capitalization in 1900 were Alleghany and Smyth. In Alleghany in 1876 the Republican share of the vote was 23 percent; in 1896 it was 68 percent. Smyth recorded the Republican proportion of the vote in 1876 as 17 percent; in 1896 it had reached 52 percent. Although other highly capitalized areas did not have as dramatic increases as these two counties, they did reflect some significant gains. Buncombe County, North Carolina, which included the rapidly growing city of Asheville, a center of manufacturing in the region, gave the Republicans 37 percent of the vote in 1876 and 53 percent in 1896. A similar increase from 45 to 61 percent in the Republican share of the vote from 1876 to 1896 was recorded in Boyd County, the most heavily capitalized county in southeastern Kentucky.

TABLE 12. Increase of Republican Vote in Twenty-eight Mountain Counties with One Million Dollars of Manufacturing Capital, 1900 (in percentages)

	Less than 5	*5.0–9.9*	*10.0–14.9*	*15.0–19.9*	*More than 20*
1876–96	6	10	2	4	6
1876–88	11	6	5	3	3
1888–96	17	9	2	—	—

One possible explanation for the change of voting patterns in the urban and industrialized counties was that immigrants and blacks were attracted there and supplemented mountain voters who continued to vote in their traditional manner. As pointed out in chapter 7, this explanation will not hold up with regard to blacks. Between 1870 and 1900 the proportion of blacks in the mountain population was actually declining rather than expanding. In addition, in the few counties where the black population did experience a large increase, white voters rejected the party in large numbers; and in nine counties where the black proportion of the population increased, the Republican percentage of the vote actually declined between 1888 and 1896. Thus it seems obvious that the growth of the Republican party in the mountains of the upper South during this period did not come about because of an increase in black voters.

Apparently, the immigrant vote may well have had a more important impact on the increase of Republican voting. While most mountain inhabitants were native-born, in twenty-one mountain counties, at least 5 percent of the population in 1900 had at least one foreign-born parent. Many of the outsiders were imported into the mining areas by the mine owners in an effort to prevent the growth of strong labor organizations.[9] Political developments in these twenty-one counties parallel the pattern observed in urban and industrialized counties. During 1876 to 1888, when 46 percent of the mountain counties had Republican gains of 10 percent or more, only 15 percent of the immigrant counties showed a growth of 5 percent in Republican vote, 29 percent of the selected counties showed a similar increase.

The possible benefit flowing from the immigrant vote was negated in part by hostility from the native white population. During the 1890s there was evidence that the American Protective Association played a small role in mountain Republican politics. The APA, the strongest nativist organization active in the Gilded Age, attempted to prevent immigrants, particularly Catholics, from being elected to public office. A general anti-Catholic feeling prevailed among many of the Protestants in the highlands, but the political effects were slight in most areas.[10] Only in urban areas with substantial immigrant populations, such as Knoxville and Chattanooga, Tennessee, and Ashland, Kentucky, was the APA able to influence Republican policies.[11] Governor William Bradley of Kentucky was the only prominent Republican politician to be identified publicly with the APA.[12] Bradley embraced the APA because of the order's power in the city of Louisville, not because of pressure from southeastern Kentucky. Thus, the small increase in immigrant population in the mountain counties explains only a small part of the Republican majority, particularly before 1896.

The religious variable appears to have had an equally minor impact on Republican growth in this period. The pietistic swing from the Republicans to the Democrats in 1896 traced by Jensen and Kleppner in the Midwest does not occur in the mountain counties.[13] Southern Baptists, traditionally strong supporters of the Republican cause in the highlands, showed no slackening of enthusiasm. In fact, in both of the periods under discussion, the Republican vote increased slightly more rapidly in Baptist counties than in the average counties; neither is there a radical departure from the average counties in the counties where the Methodists were dominant. One is forced to conclude that religious affiliation had little, if any, impact on the pattern of Republican growth between 1876 and 1896.

These traditional demographic variables do not really illuminate a great deal about Republican growth in the mountain counties. In some obvious cases, large-scale industrialization encouraged rapid Republican growth between 1888 and 1896, but the relative rarity of industrial development eliminates this factor as the major reason for the party's success. An inspection of the tables in this section reveals that most of the Republican growth had taken place by 1888. Only twenty-two mountain counties had larger gains after 1888 than in the years before, and nearly half of that number showed substantial industrial development. Therefore, an analysis of Republican growth in the vast majority of mountain counties must first account for the success of the party-armies.

A close look at the advances made by Republicans in southwestern Virginia and western North Carolina reveals a significant trend. In both regions there was little unionism with which to build a powerful Republican party after the Civil War. There was little attraction to the black man's party, and despite conflicts within the Democratic ranks the mountain voters stayed with that party. The Democratic leadership, however, abused its position in both states and drove from the party large numbers of men who considered themselves Democrats. The state debt controversy that led to an inequitable tax system in Virginia and the grossly undemocratic local government laws in North Carolina were other relevant factors. The Democratic party leadership in both states first ignored and then attempted to suppress dissent within their own party. The result was that the rebels, like the Readjusters and Mahone in Virginia and the Independents and Pearson in North Carolina, eventually were out of the party.

While this process was taking place at the state level, much the same was going on at the local level. A Kentucky mountain newspaper reported, "Thos. W. Rose . . . is a candidate for the Republican nomination for congress in this district. A few years [ago] he was an ardent democrat, and being defeated for the nomination for State Senator, he deserted that party and went over to the radicals."[14] A Virginia newspaper sadly commented when a prominent mountain Democrat became a Republican, "The truth of the matter is that his services were never properly appreciated by the Democratic party."[15] Two years later the same paper observed that virtually all Republicans in southwestern Virginia had been Democrats at some time in their lives.[16] This state of affairs was true as well for many other Republicans throughout the other four mountain regions. The Republican party always made free and honest elections a major plank in its platform and as a consequence attracted many dissatisfied Democrats who found neither within their own party.

Table 13 gives statistical support for this line of analysis. The level of the Democratic vote in 1876 is correlated with the growth of the Republican vote. Thirty-one of the ninety-seven counties that the Democrats carried showed Republican gains of at least 15 percent over the twelve years. In contrast, only one of the fifty-four counties controlled by Republicans showed a similar increase. A closer inspection of the figures reveals another significant observation. Republican success was particularly consistent in those counties where the Democrats won at least 60 percent of the vote in 1876. Republicans increased their proportion of the vote by at least 10 percent in forty-seven out of the sixty-five

TABLE 13. Democratic Percentage for Presidential Election, 1876, and Increase of Republican Percentage, 1876–1888, All Mountain Counties

Democratic Percentage	\multicolumn{5}{c}{Percentage Increase of Republican Vote}
	0–4.9	5–9.9	10–14.9	15–19.9	20+
90+	—	—	—	—	3
80–89.9	—	1	3	1	8
70–79.9	1	4	6	3	6
60–69.9	3	9	9	6	2
50–59.9	19	15	5	1	1
Less than 50.0	20	18	15	1	—

strongly Democratic counties. In these areas, winning the Democratic nomination meant automatic election; therefore, the fight to control the local Democratic organization was often bitterly contested. The losers frequently turned to the Republicans, it appears, in an effort to secure a power base that was unavailable in their old party.

The failure of the Democrats to allow state governments to fund projects in the mountain counties alienated many voters. One eastern Tennessean was driven to conclude, "The more I see of the diabolical doings of those divisions the more convinced I am that it would be in the interest of all East Tennessee to be severed from them."[17] Not many voters were willing to take the extreme step of secession from the rest of the state, but most of them did resent what appeared to be overt discrimination. In contrast, Republican mountain politicians like Houk, Goff, and White secured grants from the Congress for federal buildings and improvement of river navigation for the region. There seems to be little doubt that a small, but significant, number of Democrats left their party in protest over its failure to meet the needs of the mountain area.

A consistent pattern of Republican growth in the years between 1876 and 1896 now seems clear. A base level of support in 1876 had been created by the unionism of many mountain men and by the relative absence of blacks in the region. Although the Republicans were a distinct minority in the area at the time, careful organization preserved this base intact. Throughout the 1880s, groups of dissatisfied Democrats, including the Readjusters in Virginia, rejected the undemocratic features of their party, and by 1888 the Republicans were in power in the mountain counties. This work was nearly undone by the debate over the Lodge Elections Bill, which reawakened many of the racial fears of mountain whites that had been quiet since Reconstruction. The depression of the 1890s prompted almost all of the deserters to return to Republican ranks. A significant change of emphasis in the party platform during this period allowed the party to take maximum advantage of the economic situation. The protective tariff became the party's major issue, vigorously promoted by a new group of party leaders who were closely connected with the business community. Their appeal was particularly successful among voters in urban and industrialized counties in the mountain region. By 1896 the combination of all of these elements had given the party a commanding position in the mountain counties.

NOTES

CHAPTER 1
1. Two unpublished studies trace the development of the mountaineer stereotype: Henry D. Shapiro, "A Strange Land and Peculiar People" and Cratis D. Williams, "The Southern Mountaineer in Fact and Fiction."
2. A good example of this point of view is Harry M. Caudill, *Night Comes to the Cumberlands*.
3. See Hugh T. Lefler and Albert R. Newsome, *North Carolina*; William C. Pendleton, *Political History of Appalachian Virginia, 1776–1927*; Thomas D. Clark, "The People, William Goebel, and the Kentucky Railroads," pp. 34–48; and Verton M. Queener, "A History of the Republican Party in East Tennessee."
4. Some observers feel that this was a static situation. See V. O. Key, *Southern Politics in State and Nation*, pp. 280–84.
5. Robert H. Wiebe, *The Segmented Society*.
6. William H. Riker, *Federalism*, pp. 111–36. Riker compares the United States with Canada, Australia, India, Argentina, Brazil, West Germany, and the Soviet Union. He investigates popular loyalty to federalism, institutions of federalism, and centralization. The United States clearly has one of the most complex systems.
7. For a British historian's perceptive insights into that process, see W. R. Brock, *An American Crisis*.
8. Henry Adams, *Democracy*, p. 90.
9. Robert D. Marcus, *Grand Old Party*, p. viii.
10. Examples include Richard Jensen, *The Winning of the Midwest*; Paul Kleppner, *The Cross of Culture*; Samuel T. McSeveney, *The Politics of Depression*; and J. Morgan Kousser, *The Shaping of Southern Politics*.
11. W. Dean Burnham, "The Changing Shape of the American Political Universe," pp. 10, 22.
12. Robert H. Wiebe, *The Search for Order, 1877–1920*, pp. 44–75.
13. Ibid., pp. 111–32.
14. The most complete discussion of this point is found in Samuel P. Hays, "Political Parties and the Community-Society Continuum," pp. 152–81.
15. Frederick L. Olmsted, *The Slave States before the Civil War*, pp. 207–32.
16. Henry D. Shapiro, "A Preface to Prejudice," p. 38.
17. George M. Frederickson, *The Black Image in the White Mind*, pp. 256–82.

CHAPTER 2
1. *New York Times*, 22 Mar. 1875.
2. Cassius M. Clay, *The Life of Cassius Marcellus Clay*, p. 234.
3. Frank Aglionby to _____ Aglionby, 30 Oct. 1859, Aglionby Papers; *Buckhannon Delta*, 17 Mar. 1874.

4. *Knoxville Whig*, 18 May 1861.
5. J. Carlyle Sitterson, "Economic Sectionalism in Ante-Bellum North Carolina," pp. 143–44.
6. Ibid., p. 145.
7. Guion G. Johnson, "Social Characteristics of Ante-Bellum North Carolina," pp. 149–50.
8. *New York Times*, 22 Mar. 1875.
9. Cratis D. Williams, "The Southern Mountaineer in Fact and Fiction," p. 9.
10. Richard P. McCormick, *The Second American Party System*, pp. 227–30, 338–41.
11. E. Merton Coulter, *William G. Brownlow*, pp. 123–25.
12. Richard G. Lowe, "The Republican Party in Antebellum Virginia, 1856–1860," p. 264.
13. Ibid., p. 265n.
14. Ibid., p. 277.
15. E. Merton Coulter, *The Civil War and Readjustment in Kentucky*, pp. 54–55.
16. "Proceedings of the East Tennessee Convention, held at Greenville on the 17th day of June, 1861," *War of the Rebellion*, ser. 1, vol. 52, pt. 1, p. 178.
17. Richard O. Curry, *A House Divided*, pp. 141–52.
18. W. Dean Burnham, *Presidential Ballots, 1836–1892*, pp. 852–64.
19. Eric R. Lacy, *Vanquished Volunteers*, p. 217.
20. T. H. Reeves to [William Rule], 5 Feb. 1887, Rule Papers.
21. Lacy, *Vanquished Volunteers*, p. 217.
22. Oliver P. Temple, *East Tennessee and the Civil War*, p. 177.
23. Lewis Collins and Richard H. Collins, *History of Kentucky*, 1:89.
24. Ibid., p. 93.
25. William D. Cotton, "Appalachian North Carolina," pp. 84–85.
26. Lewis P. Summers, *History of Southwest Virginia, 1746–1786*, p. 512.
27. Mrs. Rufus Lenoir to Sarah Joyce Lenoir, 27 May 1861, Lenoir Papers.
28. *War of the Rebellion*, ser. 1, vol. 2, pp. 955–56.
29. Cotton, "Appalachian North Carolina," p. 88; John G. Barrett, *The Civil War in North Carolina*, pp. 181–82.
30. Collins and Collins, *History of Kentucky*, p. 91; Thomas Speed, *The Union Cause in Kentucky, 1860–1865*, p. 33.
31. Gary L. Williams, "Lincoln's Neutral Allies," pp. 73–75.
32. Coulter, *Readjustment in Kentucky*, p. 102; Ray P. Basler, *The Collected Works of Abraham Lincoln*, vol. 4:497.
33. Francis N. Boney, *John Letcher of Virginia*, p. 116.
34. *War of the Rebellion*, ser. 1, vol. 2, p. 630.
35. Curry, *House Divided*, p. 86.
36. Thomas E. Posey, *The Negro Citizen of West Virginia*, p. 11.
37. Ibid., p. 16; J. N. Panton to Waitman T. Willey, 23 Jan. 1863, Willey Papers.
38. Arthur I. Boreman to Francis H. Pierpont, 27 Feb. 1863, Pierpont Papers (WVUL).
39. *War of the Rebellion*, ser. 1, vol. 52, pt. 1, p. 176.
40. "A Card," Leonidas C. Houk, 10 July 1861, Houk Papers.
41. James W. McKee, Jr., "Felix K. Zollicoffer," p. 45.
42. T. H. Reeves to [William Rule], 5 Feb. 1887, Rule Papers.
43. *War of the Rebellion*, ser. 1, vol. 4, p. 231.
44. Ibid., p. 250; T. H. Reeves to [William Rule], 5 Feb. 1887, Rule Papers.
45. William G. Brownlow, *Sketches of the Rise, Progress, and Decline of Secession*, pp. 305–6.
46. *War of the Rebellion*, ser. 1, vol. 31, pt. 1, p. 269; John C. West, *A Texan in Search of a Fight*, p. 130.
47. *War of the Rebellion*, ser. 1, vol. 31, pt. 3, pp. 382, 392, 394, 817–18.
48. Ibid., pt. 1, p. 349.
49. West, *Texan*, p. 136; *Southern Advocate*, 9 Oct. 1862.

50. *War of the Rebellion*, ser. 1, vol. 31, pt. 3, p. 871.
51. Ibid., p. 446.
52. Ibid., p. 849.
53. Ibid., p. 508.
54. Thomas W. Humes, *Report to the East Tennessee Relief Association*, p. 3.
55. *Knoxville Whig*, 13 Feb. 1864.
56. Humes, *Report*, pp. 5–7; *Knoxville Whig*, 16 Apr. 1864.
57. Humes, *Report*, p. 17.
58. *War of the Rebellion*, ser. 1, vol. 7, p. 119; ibid., vol. 10, pt. 1, p. 50.
59. Ibid., vol. 39, pt. 1, p. 234; *Knoxville Whig*, 31 Aug. 1864.
60. Sarah E. Thompson, Statement, 3 Sept. 1864, Thompson Papers.
61. *Knoxville Whig*, 23 Apr. 1864.
62. *War of the Rebellion*, ser. 1, vol. 16, pt. 1, p. 1146.
63. Collins and Collins, *History of Kentucky*, pp. 105, 124, 143.
64. Ibid., pp. 115, 128.
65. Ibid., p. 127.
66. Boney, *John Letcher*, pp. 158–59.
67. Norris M. Snider to Francis H. Pierpont, 3 June 1862, Pierpont Papers (WVUL).
68. *War of the Rebellion*, ser. 1, vol. 25, pt. 1, pp. 11–12; ibid., vol. 37, pt. 1, p. 92.
69. Arthur I. Boreman to Francis H. Pierpont, 27 Feb. 1863, Pierpont Papers.
70. *War of the Rebellion*, ser. 1, vol. 25, pt. 1, pp. 92, 97.
71. Rufus Lenoir to Walter W. Lenoir, 21 Apr. 1862, Lenoir Papers.
72. Horace W. Raper, "William W. Holden and the Peace Movement in North Carolina," p. 497.
73. Lizzie Pickens to Rufus Lenoir, 21 Sept. 1862, Lenoir Papers.
74. Harold D. Moser, "Reaction in North Carolina to the Emancipation Proclamation," p. 61.
75. Barrett, *Civil War North Carolina*, p. 198.
76. Cotton, "Appalachian North Carolina," p. 126.
77. Barrett, *Civil War North Carolina*, pp. 185–86.
78. Georgia L. Tatum, *Disloyalty in the Confederacy*, p. 120.
79. Richard E. Yates, "Governor Vance and the Peace Movement," p. 102.
80. *War of the Rebellion*, ser. 1, vol. 39, pt. 1, pp. 234, 237; ibid, Vol. 53, p. 326.
81. Barrett, *Civil War North Carolina*, p. 242.
82. *War of the Rebellion*, ser. 1, vol. 53, p. 326.
83. Henry T. Shanks, "Disloyalty to the Confederacy in Southwestern Virginia, 1861–1865," pp. 125–26; Boney, *John Letcher*, p. 163; *Southern Advocate*, 7, 14 July 1862.
84. Boney, *John Letcher*, p. 192.
85. Shanks, "Disloyalty," p. 127.
86. *War of the Rebellion*, ser. 4, vol. 3, pp. 803, 814.
87. Ross A. Webb, *Benjamin Helm Bristow*, pp. 40–41.
88. Collins and Collins, *History of Kentucky*, pp. 137–38.
89. Palmer H. Boeger, "The Great Kentucky Hog Swindle of 1864," p. 64.
90. *Louisville Journal*, 30 Aug. 1867.
91. James R. Bentley, "The Civil War Memoirs of Captain Thomas Speed," p. 256.
92. Collins and Collins, *History of Kentucky*, p. 15.
93. Robert W. Bayless, "The Attitude of West Virginia Senators and Congressmen toward Reconstruction, 1863–1871," p. 4.
94. E. C. Bunker to Waitman T. Willey, 4 Aug. 1863, Willey Papers.
95. Peter C. Van Winkle to Willey, 13 Sept. 1864; H. Dering to Willey, 31 May 1864, ibid.
96. *Tribune Almanac and Political Register, 1869*, p. 68.
97. *Knoxville Whig*, 14 Sept. 1864.
98. Ibid., 1 Mar. 1865.

99. Moser, "Reaction to Emancipation Proclamation," p. 58; Bryan Tyson, Circular Letter, 24 Sept. 1862, Tyson Papers.
100. *War of the Rebellion*, ser. 4, vol. 3, p. 815.

CHAPTER 3

1. U.S. Bureau of the Census, *Ninth Census of the United States, 1870, Population and Social Statistics*, pt. 1, pp. 146–54, 220–26, 261–69, 278–83, 284–87.
2. Kenneth M. Stampp, *The Era of Reconstruction, 1865–1877*, pp. 122, 144–45.
3. James A. Padgett, "Reconstruction Letters from North Carolina," pp. 70–86.
4. E. Merton Coulter, *William G. Brownlow*, pp. 122–25.
5. William G. Brownlow, *Sketches of the Rise, Progress, and Decline of Secession*, pp. 307–29.
6. Thomas B. Alexander, *Political Reconstruction in Tennessee*, pp. 60–61.
7. James W. Patton, *Unionism and Reconstruction in Tennessee, 1860–1869*, pp. 101–2.
8. Ibid., p. 110n; Alexander, *Reconstruction in Tennessee*, p. 93.
9. *Knoxville Whig*, 14 Mar., 11 Apr., 9 May 1866.
10. Patton, *Unionism in Tennessee*, p. 118.
11. *Knoxville Whig*, 2 Jan. 1867.
12. Patton, *Unionism in Tennessee*, pp. 126–28; Alrutheus A. Taylor, *The Negro in Tennessee, 1865–1880*, p. 16.
13. Walter F. Fleming, *Documentary History of Reconstruction*, p. 311.
14. James B. Campbell, "Some Social and Economic Phases of Reconstruction in East Tennessee, 1864–1869," p. 94; *Knoxville Whig*, 27 Feb. 1867.
15. *Knoxville Whig*, 4 Apr. 1866; *Athens Republican*, 9 July 1868; Alexander, *Reconstruction in Tennessee*, p. 144; Susie L. Owens, "The Union League of America," pp. 57–58.
16. *Knoxville Whig*, 8 May 1867.
17. Alexander, *Reconstruction in Tennessee*, p. 153.
18. Patton, *Unionism in Tennessee*, p. 140.
19. *Knoxville Whig*, 30 May 1866.
20. Isaac P. Martin, *History of Methodism in the Holston Conference*, pp. 74–76; William B. Hesseltine, "Methodism and Reconstruction in East Tennessee," pp. 46–48.
21. *Knoxville Whig*, 30 Jan. 1864.
22. Ibid., 23 Jan. 1864.
23. Ibid., 4 June 1864.
24. Campbell, "Social Reconstruction," pp. 27–28; Martin, *Methodism*, pp. 81–85.
25. Patton, *Unionism in Tennessee*, pp. 92–93.
26. "Methodist Churches, North and South, " pp. 633, 635.
27. Hesseltine, "Methodism," p. 57.
28. *Knoxville Whig*, 30 May, 26 Dec. 1866.
29. Ibid., 6 Nov. 1867.
30. Ibid., 23 Jan. 1867.
31. *Athens Republican*, 27 Feb. 1868.
32. In 1866 the average age of southern M.E. ministers was 41, for the Union clergy the average was 46. Martin, *Methodism*, pp. 300–308; *Bristol News*, 24 Mar. 1871.
33. *Clinton Gazette*, 16, 23 Mar. 1888.
34. Campbell, "Social Reconstruction," p. 103; Thomas B. Alexander, "Ku Kluxism in Tennessee, 1865–1869," p. 203.
35. James C. Parker, "Tennessee Gubernatorial Elections," p. 36.
36. *Knoxville Whig*, 30 Oct. 1867.
37. Senter to Leonidas C. Houk, 15 Apr. 1869, Houk Papers; *Knoxville Whig*, 28 Apr. 1869.
38. *Athens Republican*, 10 June 1869; *Louisville Courier-Journal*, 9 June 1869.
39. *Knoxville Whig*, 26 May 1869; *Athens Republican*, 27 May 1869.
40. *Louisville Courier-Journal*, 12 June 1869.

41. Alexander, *Reconstruction in Tennessee*, pp. 212–13.
42. *Knoxville Whig*, 23 June 1869; *Athens Republican*, 17 June 1869.
43. *Knoxville Whig*, 30 June 1869.
44. *Athens Republican*, 29 July 1869.
45. Ibid., 11 Sept. 1869.
46. *Louisville Courier-Journal*, 7 Oct. 1869.
47. *Congressional Globe*, 15 Dec. 1869, 41st Cong., 2nd sess., 15 December 1869, p. 138.
48. *Bristol News*, 21 Jan. 1870.
49. Alexander, *Reconstruction in Tennessee*, p. 275n.
50. State of Tennessee, *Journal of the Convention of Delegates to Make a New Constitution*, pp. 173, 179–80, 253.
51. *Bristol Courier*, 13 Oct. 1870.
52. Freeman to Leonidas C. Houk, 27 Dec. 1871, Houk Papers.
53. *Tribune Almanac and Political Register, 1876*, p. 74.
54. *Mountain Echo*, 2 Jan. 1874.
55. *Bristol News*, 3 Feb., 16 June, 4 Aug. 1874.
56. *Knoxville Chronicle*, 8 Aug. 1874.
57. *Bristol News*, 11 Aug. 1874.
58. Verton M. Queener, "A Decade of East Tennessee Republicanism, 1867–1876," p. 83.
59. *Bristol News*, 22 Sept. 1874.
60. *Louisville Courier-Journal*, 17 Sept. 1874.
61. *Bristol News*, 3 Nov. 1874.
62. *Tribune Almanac, 1876*, p. 74.
63. *Memphis Weekly Appeal*, 26 Jan. 1876.
64. A. J. Ricks to William Rule, 1 May 1876, Rule Papers.
65. *Knoxville Chronicle*, 26 Aug. 1876; *Memphis Weekly Appeal*, 22 Nov. 1876.
66. *Memphis Weekly Appeal*, 30 Aug. 1876.
67. Ibid., 27 Sept., 11 Oct. 1876; *Bristol News*, 8 Nov. 1876.
68. *Knoxville Chronicle*, 12 Oct. 1876.
69. Taylor, *Negro in Tennessee*, p. 258.
70. Richard O. Curry, "Crisis Politics in West Virginia, 1861–1870," p. 92.
71. Peter G. Van Winkle to Waitman T. Willey, 8 May, 9 June 1865, Willey Papers.
72. Curry, "Crisis Politics," p. 93.
73. *Tribune Almanac, 1869*, p. 68.
74. G. M. Humphreys to Waitman T. Willey, 7 Mar. 1867, Willey Papers; Arthur I. Boreman to James W. Miller, 26 Jan. 1867, Mason Papers; Arthur I. Boreman to William H. H. Flick, 24 Sept. 1868, Flick Papers.
75. Forest Talbott, "Some Legislative and Legal Aspects of the Negro Question in West Virginia during the Civil War and Reconstruction," p. 121.
76. William E. Stevenson to Arthur I. Boreman, 8 Mar. 1869, Stevenson Papers.
77. *Wheeling Intelligencer*, 1 Sept. 1869.
78. Harvey M. Rice, "The Conservative Re-action in West Virginia, 1865–1871," p. 63.
79. William P. Hubbard to Flick, 19 Apr. 1871, Flick Papers.
80. John M. Leutz to William E. Stevenson, 3 Mar. 1870, Stevenson Papers; Booker T. Washington, *Up from Slavery*, pp. 53–54.
81. T. M. Harris, Circular Letter, 9 May 1870, Mason Papers.
82. T. R. Carskadon to William H. H. Flick, 22 Aug. 1870; F. M. Reynolds to Flick, 6 Sept. 1870, Flick Papers.
83. Curry, "Crisis Politics," p. 100.
84. William E. Stevenson to Nathan Goff, 13 Nov. 1870; A. T. Sherman to Goff, 4 Feb. 1871, Goff Papers.
85. Talbott, "Negro Question," p. 223.
86. J. J. Barrick to William H. H. Flick, 30 May 1872, Flick Papers.

87. *Tribune Almanac, 1873*, p. 83.
88. *Buckhannon Delta*, 26 Jan. 1874.
89. George C. Sturgiss, Notes of the Secretary of the Republican State Convention, 12 Aug. 1874, Mason Papers.
90. *Buckhannon Delta*, 24 Sept., 8 Oct. 1874.
91. *Tribune Almanac, 1876*, p. 56.
92. John A. Hedrick to Benjamin S. Hedrick, 5 June 1865, Hedrick Papers.
93. J. G. de Roulhac Hamilton, *Reconstruction in North Carolina*, p. 133.
94. William D. Cotton, "Appalachian North Carolina," p. 171.
95. Marion Roberts to Thaddeus Stevens, 15 May 1866, in Padgett, "Reconstruction Letters," pp. 187–90. William W. Holden to Andrew Johnson, 11 July 1866, Holden Papers; J. L. Johnson to Benjamin S. Hedrick, 16 July 1866, Lenoir Papers; W. T. Caldwell to Jonathan Worth, 31 July 1866, in J. G. de Roulhac Hamilton, ed., *The Correspondence of Jonathan Worth*, 2:710–11.
96. Jonathan Worth to Benjamin S. Hedrick, 21 June 1866, in Hamilton, *Correspondence*, 2:641–42; Alfred Dockery to Thomas Settle, 29 Sept. 1866, Settle Papers.
97. Holden to David M. Carter, 27 Nov. 1866, Carter Papers.
98. Jonathan Worth to Andrew Johnson, 29 Mar. 1867, in Hamilton, *Correspondence*, 2:925; Thomas Settle, speech, Mar. 1867, Settle Papers.
99. W. C. Ken to Benjamin S. Hedrick, 22 Mar. 1867, Hedrick Papers.
100. Hamilton, *Reconstruction*, p. 337.
101. *Raleigh Standard*, 18 July 1867; Owens, "Union League," p. 212.
102. Horace W. Raper, "William Woods Holden," pp. 214–15.
103. Owens, "Union League," pp. 222–23.
104. John Pool to David M. Carter, 31 Sept. 1867, Carter Papers.
105. *Asheville Pioneer*, 14 May 1868.
106. C. C. Jones to Caldwell, 27 Feb. 1868, Caldwell Papers.
107. Pearson to William L. Scott, 16 July 1868, Scott Papers; Thomas Settle to Pearson, 8 Aug. 1868, Settle Papers.
108. *Tribune Almanac, 1869*, pp. 76–77.
109. Ibid., *1872*, p. 69; *Asheville Pioneer*, 7 Nov. 1867.
110. *Tribune Almanac, 1869*, p. 76.
111. *Louisville Courier-Journal*, 26 Nov. 1868.
112. *Statesville American*, 23 Aug. 1869.
113. Richard L. Hoffman, "The Republican Party in North Carolina, 1867–1871," pp. 81–82.
114. William K. Boyd, ed., *Memoirs of W. W. Holden*, pp. 188–92, 199.
115. William L. Scott to Payne, 18 July 1870, Scott Papers.
116. Hamilton, *Reconstruction*, p. 501.
117. *Tribune Almanac, 1872*, p. 69.
118. *Asheville Pioneer*, 20 July 1871; J. W. Berry to Tod R. Caldwell, 25 Feb. 1871, Caldwell Papers.
119. *Asheville Pioneer*, 31 Aug. 1871.
120. Allen W. Trelease, *White Terror*, p. 340.
121. *Asheville Pioneer*, 22 June, 6 July 1871.
122. Ibid., 9, 30 Nov. 1871.
123. Douglas C. Dailey, "The Elections of 1872 in North Carolina," p. 342.
124. M. A. Smith to Tod R. Caldwell, 22 Mar. 1872, Caldwell Papers.
125. *Asheville Pioneer*, 11, 24 Apr. 1872.
126. Ibid., 25 Apr., 30 May 1872.
127. Caldwell to Henry Wilson, 12 June 1872, in Padgett, "Reconstruction Letters", pp. 70–71.

128. *Tribune Almanac, 1873*, p. 74.
129. *Asheville Citizen*, 8 May 1873.
130. Ibid., 18, 25 Sept. 1872, 12 Nov. 1874.
131. A. C. Bryan to Thomas Settle, 1 Jan. 1873, Mott to Settle, 27 Apr. 1874, George H. Brown to Settle, 18 Nov. 1874, Settle Papers; Mott to Ramsay, 9 Apr. 1874, S. A. Caldwell to Ramsay, 18 May 1874, Ramsay to Samuel F. Phillips, 17 Aug. 1874, Ramsay to U. S. Grant, 8 Jan. 1875, Ramsay to G. H. Raum, 12 Mar. 1877, Ramsay Papers; *Statesville Landmark*, 21 Nov. 1874.
132. *Asheville Citizen*, 4 June 1874.
133. *Asheville Pioneer*, 6 June 1874; O. H. Dockery to Daniel L. Russell, 7 June 1874, Russell Papers.
134. *Asheville Pioneer*, 13 June 1874.
135. *Statesville Landmark*, 28 Nov. 1874.
136. *Asheville Western Expositor*, 7 Jan. 1875; *Asheville Citizen*, 5 Aug. 1875.
137. *Asheville Citizen*, 15 Apr. 1875.
138. Ibid., 17 June 1875.
139. *Asheville Citizen*, 12 Aug. 1875.
140. George T. Palmer, *A Conscientious Turncoat*, p. 181.
141. Edward I. Malberg, "The Republican Party in Kentucky, 1856–1867," p. 92.
142. Collins and Collins, *History of Kentucky*, 1:163; E. Merton Coulter, *The Civil War and Readjustment in Kentucky*, p. 276.
143. Ross A. Webb, "Kentucky," pp. 119–20.
144. E. Merton Coulter, *The Civil War and Readjustment in Kentucky*, p. 306.
145. Jacqueline Balk and Ari Hoogenboom, "The Origins of Border State Liberal Republicanism," p. 236.
146. Webb, "Kentucky," p. 123.
147. *Louisville Journal*, 30 Aug. 1867.
148. Ibid., p. 326.
149. Collins and Collins, *History of Kentucky*, 1:185.
150. Coulter, *Readjustment Kentucky*, p. 412.
151. Ibid., p. 361.
152. *Louisville Courier-Journal*, 4, 5 Apr. 1869.
153. Ibid., 3 July 1869.
154. Ibid., 3 Aug. 1869.
155. *Tribune Almanac, 1871*, p. 65.
156. Webb, "Kentucky," pp. 128–29.
157. *Louisville Courier-Journal*, 29 July 1870.
158. *Tribune Almanac, 1871*, p. 65.
159. One party worker remarked, "I think our party would be gainers by a general amnesty and let bye gones be bye gones"; William H. Grainger to Benjamin H. Bristow, 26 Oct. 1870, Bristow Papers (LC); William Brown to Bristow, 20 Apr. 1871, Harlan Papers (UL).
160. Trelease, *White Terror*, p. 316.
161. *Louisville Commercial*, 18 May 1871.
162. *New York Times*, 20 May 1871.
163. *Louisville Courier-Journal*, 19 May 1871.
164. Ibid., 31 May, 14 June 1871; *Louisville Commercial*, 4 July 1871.
165. John D. White to John M. Harlan, 2 June 1875, Harlan Papers (UL).
166. *Tribune Almanac, 1876*, p. 8.
167. Ross A. Webb, *Benjamin Helm Bristow*, pp. 103–7.
168. W. J. Landrum to Bristow, 16 Sept. 1871, Bristow to E. B. French, 8 Sept. 1871, Walter Evans to Bristow, 21 Sept. 1871, Bristow Papers (LC).

169. Webb, *Bristow*, p. 106.
170. Bland to Bristow, 23 Feb. 1872, Bristow Papers (LC); Edwin B. Thompson, "Benjamin Helm Bristow," p. 64.
171. Edgar Needham to Benjamin H. Bristow, 14 Feb. 1872, Bristow Papers (LC).
172. *Louisville Courier-Journal*, 13, 14 Mar. 1872.
173. Ibid., 1, 31 Oct. 1872; Hambleton Tapp, "Three Decades of Kentucky Politics, 1870–1900," p. 100.
174. *Barboursville Mountain Echo*, 19 June 1874.
175. *Louisville Courier-Journal*, 11 Aug. 1874.
176. *Tribune Almanac, 1876*, p. 82.
177. *Barboursville Mountain Echo*, 25 Sept. 1874.
178. Ibid., 2, 30 Oct. 1874.
179. Ibid., 9, 16 Oct. 1874.
180. Trelease, *White Terror*, p. 316; *Mountain Echo*, 9 Oct. 1874.
181. *Barboursville Mountain Echo*, 23, 30 Oct. 1874.
182. *Louisville Courier-Journal*, 9 June 1875.
183. White to Harlan, 2 June 1875, Harlan Papers (UL).
184. *Louisville Courier-Journal*, 9 June 1875.
185. Webb, "Kentucky," p. 143; *Louisville Courier-Journal*, 29 July 1875.
186. W. C. Goodloe to Bristow, 8 July 1875, Bristow Papers (UKL).
187. *Louisville Courier-Journal*, 5 July 1875.
188. Harlan to _____, 21 July 1875, Harlan Papers (UL).
189. *Tribune Almanac, 1876*, p. 81.
190. A. W. Campbell to Pierpont, 16 June 1865, Pierpont Papers (WVUL).
191. James D. Smith, "Virginia during Reconstruction, 1865–1870," p. 245.
192. Fleming, *History of Reconstruction*, 1:230–31; Jack P. Maddex, Jr., *The Virginia Conservatives, 1867–1879*, p. 41.
193. Richard G. Lowe, "Republicans, Rebellion, and Reconstruction," p. 245.
194. Maddex, *Virginia Conservatives*, pp. 49–50.
195. Owens, "Union League," p. 290.
196. Ibid., pp. 294–95.
197. James L. McDonough, "John Schofield as Military Director of Reconstruction in Virginia," p. 248.
198. Hamilton J. Eckenrode, *The Political History of Virginia during the Reconstruction*, pp. 94–103.
199. I. Parker Jordan to Pierpont, 24 Apr. 1868, Pierpont Papers (WVUL); R. F. Walker to William Mahone, 23 Mar. 1868, McGill-Mahone Papers.
200. Smith, "Virginia Reconstruction," p. 127.
201. Mahone to William Lamb, 17 May 1868, Letterbook, vol. 10, pp. 327–28, A. B. Garland to Mahone, 18 Aug. 1868, Mahone Papers.
202. *Louisville Courier-Journal*, 4 Jan. 1869.
203. R. F. Walker to William Mahone, 16 Mar. 1869, Mahone Papers.
204. *Abingdon Virginian*, 7, 28 May 1869; F. B. Hurt to William Mahone, 22 Apr. 1869, McGill-Mahone Papers.
205. Richard G. Lowe, "The Republican Party in Antebellum Virginia, 1856–1860," pp. 357–58; Charles E. Wynes, *Race Relations in Virginia, 1870–1902*, p. 6.
206. *Cincinnati Enquirer Manual 1870*, p. 109.
207. *Louisville Courier-Journal*, 2 Dec. 1869.
208. *Bristol News*, 28 Oct. 1870.
209. William C. Pendleton, *Political History of Appalachian Virginia, 1776–1927*, p. 315.
210. *Bristol News*, 2, 23 Dec. 1870, 20 Jan. 1871.
211. Charles C. Pearson, *The Readjuster Movement in Virginia*, p. 40.
212. *Bristol News*, 29 Oct. 1872; *Tribune Almanac, 1876*, pp. 55–56.

213. *Abingdon Virginian*, 1 Aug. 1873; *Louisville Courier-Journal*, 1 Aug. 1873; *Bristol News*, 22 Apr. 1873.
214. *Bristol Republican*, 9 Sept. 1873; Pearson, *Readjuster Movement*, pp. 47–48; Maddex, *Virginia Conservatives*, pp. 109–10; *Bristol News*, 11 Nov. 1873.
215. *Tribune Almanac, 1874*, pp. 64–65.
216. *Abingdon Virginian*, 9 Oct. 1874.
217. Ibid., 18 Sept. 1874; *Bristol News*, 8, 29 Sept. 1874; *Tribune Almanac, 1876*, pp. 55–56.
218. *New York Times*, 26 May 1876; James D. Brady, Circular Letter, 26 July 1876, Scrapbook, vol. 1, Brady Papers.

CHAPTER 4

1. *Asheville Pioneer*, 7 Nov. 1874.
2. Ibid.
3. *Louisville Courier-Journal*, 10 Sept. 1869.
4. James R. Parton, *Life of Andrew Jackson*, vol. 3, quoted in Matthew Josephson, *The Politicos, 1865–1896*, p. 67.
5. John W. Mason, draft of address delivered at West Virginia College, Flemington, West Virginia, 11 July 1877, Mason Papers.
6. James W. Couch to William Mahone, 27 May 1880, Mahone Papers.
7. *Knoxville Whig*, 17 May 1875; *London Mountain Echo*, 20 June 1879.
8. James J. McDonald to William Mahone, 24 Apr. 1890, T. S. Curlett to Mahone, 7 Nov. 1891, Mahone Papers.
9. M. N. Corbett to Thomas Settle, III, Jan. 1896, Settle Papers.
10. Clipping, 1884, Scrapbook, Houk Papers.
11. W. E. Sims to William Mahone, 18 Oct. 1883, Mahone Papers.
12. Hugh Sterling to Nathan Goff, Jr., 31 Aug. 1882, Goff Papers.
13. Clipping, 27 Oct. 1890, Scrapbook, Houk Papers.
14. Robinson to William Mahone, 13 Nov. 1880, Mahone Papers.
15. Clipping, 4 May 1883, Scrapbook, Bradley Papers.
16. Claude J. Archer, "The Life of John Chiles Houk," pp. 23–24; John C. Houk to Oliver P. Temple, 26 Oct. 1884, Leonidas C. Houk to Temple, 13 Jan. 1885, Temple Papers.
17. William Lamb to William Mahone, 26 Aug. 1889, Mahone Papers.
18. Alex R. Campbell to Albert B. White, 14 Oct. 1898, White Papers. An outstanding example of consultation with local leaders is found in a separate folder in the Elkins Papers. Elkins wrote, "Preliminary to the campaign in 1900 and with a view to obtaining accurate information as to the political situation in your county I write to ask you your views on the subject." Stephen B. Elkins to A. Howard Fleming, 12 Mar. 1899, Elkins Papers. All the replies of the county chairmen have been preserved and demonstrate how valuable they were as sources of information.
19. C. W. Murdaugh to William Mahone, 1 May 1882, Mahone Papers.
20. Albert B. White to Stephen B. Elkins, 4 Mar. 1900, Elkins Papers.
21. W. S. Newton to Thomas Settle, II, 5 Sept. 1874, Settle Papers.
22. J. L. Hamilton to William Mahone, 2 Jan. 1888, Mahone Papers.
23. *Athens Republican*, 29 Oct. 1868.
24. W. F. Mercier to William Mahone, 4 Aug. 1881, Mahone Papers.
25. J. W. Wall to William Mahone, 7 Nov. 1882, ibid.
26. Samuel B. Rose to Leonidas C. Houk, 19 July 1888, Houk Papers.
27. *Abingdon Virginian*, 22 Oct. 1885.
28. John C. Houk to H. Clay Evans, 28 Mar. 1892, Houk Papers.
29. William Mahone, Circular Letter, 3 Nov. 1885, Scrapbook, vol. 34, Mahone Papers.
30. Virgil C. Jones, *The Hatfields and the McCoys*, p. 200.
31. Ibid., p. 34.
32. R. F. Walker to Asa Rogers, 3 Nov. 1889, Mahone Papers.

33. *Winston Union Republican*, 21 Sept. 1876.
34. Lincoln C. Houk to Leonidas C. Houk, 24 Oct. 1880, Houk Papers.
35. J. P. Kavanaugh to William Mahone, 15 Jan. 1881, Mahone Papers.
36. N. A. Chapline to Alston G. Dayton, 26 Sept. 1894, Dayton Papers.
37. John P. Stagg to William Mahone, 19 Oct. 1883, Mahone Papers.
38. M. M. Shoffner to Thomas Settle, III, 20 Oct. 1894, Settle Papers.
39. *Parkersburg Daily State Journal*, 30 Sept. 1896, as quoted in Barbara A. Ferrell, "West Virginia and the Election of 1896," p. 29.
40. J. A. Byerly to Thomas Settle, III, 7 Nov. 1892, Settle Papers.
41. *Maryville Republican*, 22 Sept. 1874, Scrapbook, Houk Papers.
42. W. E. Clarke to Thomas Settle, III, 14 June 1892, Settle Papers.
43. James D. Brady to William Mahone, 11 Aug. 1881, Mahone Papers.
44. P. H. McCaull to William Mahone, 10 Nov. 1887, ibid.
45. *Middlesboro News*, 12 Nov. 1892.
46. D. R. Nelson to Oliver P. Temple, 22 Oct. 1881, Temple Papers.
47. W. H. Ash to William Mahone, 4 Aug. 1888, Mahone Papers.
48. *London Mountain Echo*, 17 Feb. 1882.
49. *Knoxville Republican*, 11 Nov. 1892.
50. John M. Bishop to Will A. McTeer, 24 Nov. 1887, McTeer Papers.
51. R. S. Daniels to the editor of the *New York Times*, 20 July 1872, in James A. Padgett, "Reconstruction Letters from North Carolina," *North Carolina Historical Review* 19 (Jan. 1942): 75–76.
52. William Allen to Leonidas C. Houk, 5 Sept. 1883, Houk Papers.
53. Augustus E. Willson to Benjamin Harrison, 5 May 1890, Willson Papers.
54. Isaac N. Link to Thomas Settle, III, 21 Dec. 1894, Settle Papers.
55. N. V. Wesson to William Mahone, 22 Nov. 1880, Mahone Papers.
56. William C. Mackey to William Mahone, 15 May 1891, ibid.
57. Daniel L. Russell to Benjamin N. Duke, 2 Dec. 1898, Duke Papers.
58. J. W. Stewart to Leonidas C. Houk, 18 Jan. 1886, Houk Papers.
59. John S. Wise to the Republican voters of Virginia, 15 Mar. 1888, Scrapbook, vol. 36, Mahone Papers.
60. February 1886, Mahone Papers.
61. Gerald W. Smith, "Nathan Goff, Jr.," p. 57.
62. *New York Times*, 28 Feb. 1876.
63. John C. Houk to D. M. Coffman, 22 Aug. 1893, Houk Papers.
64. *Richmond Whig*, 13 Oct. 1882.
65. William Mahone, Circular Letter, 3 Nov. 1885, Scrapbook, vol. 34, Mahone Papers.
66. William Mahone to J. B. Raulston, 23 Oct. 1883, Letterbook, vol. 15, ibid.
67. George R. Underwood to John C. Houk, 12 Nov. 1891, Houk Papers.
68. *London Mountain Echo*, 14 Feb. 1896.
69. Alfred Dockery to Thomas Settle, II, 29 Sept. 1886, Settle Papers.
70. Republican Plan of Organization, 23 May 1888, Settle Papers.
71. Plan of Organization of the Republican Party of Virginia, 4 Sept. 1889, McGill-Mahone Papers.
72. William Mahone, Circular Letter, 3 Nov. 1885, Scrapbook, vol. 34, Mahone Papers.
73. *London Mountain Echo*, 18 June 1880.

CHAPTER 5
1. Vincent P. DeSantis, *Republicans Face the Southern Question*, pp. 66–103.
2. Ibid., pp. 133–81.
3. *Clinton Gazette*, 30 May 1889.
4. J. A. Hamby to Houk, 12 Oct. 1869, Houk Papers; *Knoxville Chronicle*, 23 Aug. 1882.
5. *Knoxville Whig*, 9 Nov. 1864, 14 Nov. 1866, 9 Jan. 1867.

6. Ibid., 25 July 1866.
7. William Rule, ed., *Standard History of Knoxville, Tennessee*, pp. 485–86.
8. *War of the Rebellion*, ser. 1, vol. 2, pt. 1, pp. 151, 168.
9. F. C. Ainsworth to John C. Houk, 19 Jan. 1895, Houk Papers.
10. Ibid.
11. *War of the Rebellion*, ser. 1, vol. 52, pt. 1, pp. 44–46.
12. Ibid.
13. Amos L. Gentry, "Public Career of Leonidas Campbell Houk," p. 6.
14. Rule, *History of Knoxville*, p. 486.
15. "Proceedings of the Republican Convention of the Second District of Tennessee," 24 Aug. 1882, Rule Papers.
16. John B. Brownlow comment written on the margin of *Knoxville Whig*, 8 May 1867.
17. Political broadside, 1 Aug. 1865, Houk Papers.
18. Compiled from *Knoxville Whig*, 16 Aug. 1865, and Scrapbook, Houk Papers.
19. *Knoxville Whig*, 21 Feb., 7 Mar. 1866.
20. Ibid., 17 June 1868.
21. Ibid.
22. Ibid., 29 July 1868; *Maryville Republican*, 27 June 1868.
23. Gentry, "Houk," pp. 17–19.
24. *Knoxville Whig*, 2 Sept. 1868. The third and fourth candidates were Joseph A. Cooper and John Williams.
25. Ibid. John B. Brownlow wrote in the margin of the *Knoxville Whig*, 2 Sept. 1868, that only the personal intervention of his father prevented Maynard's defeat.
26. *Knoxville Press and Herald*, 14 Sept. 1868.
27. *Tribune Almanac and Political Register, 1869*, p. 81. The total vote was Maynard, 10,403, Houk, 2,681.
28. DeWitt C. Senter to Leonidas C. Houk, 23 Aug. 1869, Houk to A. A. Freeman, 6 Jan. 1871, Houk Papers.
29. Verton M. Queener, "A Decade of East Tennessee Republicanism, 1867–1876," pp. 83–84.
30. Leonidas C. Houk, Circular Letter, Jan. 1874, G. A. Guenther to Houk, 14 Jan. 1874, Allen Garner, Jr., to Houk, 18 February 1874, D. P. Gass to Houk, 23 Feb. 1874, Houk Papers.
31. Gentry, "Houk," pp. 42–43.
32. *Louisville Courier-Journal*, 5 Oct. 1874.
33. Gentry, "Houk," pp. 43–44.
34. Thornburgh to William Rule, 9, 16 Apr., 4 Aug. 1876, J. Nat Lyle to Rule, 19 Apr. 1876, Rule Papers.
35. J. R. Robinson to Oliver P. Temple, 14 Feb. 1876, W. R. Murphy to Temple, 24 Apr. 1876, Abijah Fowler to Temple, 27 June 1876, Temple Papers.
36. G. W. Graham et al. to Rutherford B. Hayes, 5 Mar. 1877, D. G. Thornburgh to Houk, 6 Mar. 1877, Houk to Hayes, 19 Mar. 1877, R. N. Hood to David M. Key, 22 May 1877, D. K. Young to Key, 4 June 1877, G. G. Dibrell to Charles Devens, 5 June 1877, James P. Brownlow to Devens, 7 June 1877, Houk Papers.
37. *Knoxville Chronicle*, 8 Aug. 1878.
38. Gentry, "Houk," pp. 47–48.
39. Houk, 9,548; Watkins, 7,167; ICPR Election Data.
40. Memorandum (June 1886), Houk Papers.
41. Ari Hoogenboom, *Outlawing the Spoils*, p. 251; *Congressional Record*, 47th Cong., 2nd Sess., 16 January 1883, p. 867.
42. Leonidas C. Houk to Oliver P. Temple, 30 June 1882, Temple Papers.
43. Richard W. Austin to Leonidas C. Houk, 11 May 1880, Houk Papers, John C. Dougherty to Stephen B. Elkins, 28 May 1888, Elkins Papers.

44. E. A. Cannon to Leonidas C. Houk, 13 Feb. 1882, Houk Papers.
45. Verton M. Queener, "A History of the Republican Party in East Tennessee," p. 55n.
46. Frank W. Klingberg, "The Southern Claims Commission," map opposite p. 256.
47. *Knoxville Chronicle*, 20 Apr. 1881. Also, R. C. Swan to Leonidas C. Houk, 8 Jan. 1880, James K. Martin to Houk, 19 Jan. 1880, Samuel D. Bronson to Houk, 1 May 1880, C. Austin to Houk, 24 Dec. 1880 and 21 Feb. 1881, J. E. Klepper to Houk, 3 Dec. 1881, Thomas W. Humes to Houk, 31 Jan. 1882, Houk Papers. This is only a representative sample of many letters.
48. *Congressional Record*, 47th Cong., 2nd Sess., 16 February 1883, pp. 2829–34.
49. Memorandum, July 1888, Houk Papers.
50. F. A. Chapman to Leonidas C. Houk, 9 Dec. 1878, Hugh Dowling to Houk, 17 Jan. 1880, William P. Hoskins to Houk, 10 Mar. 1880, A. J. Campbell to Houk, 10 June 1880, ibid.
51. Emanuel Griffitts and Jerome Griffitts to Leonidas C. Houk, 13 Mar. 1882, M. J. Condon and S. P. Condon to Houk, 19 Apr. 1882, ibid.
52. H. Clay Evans to Leonidas C. Houk, 22 May 1882, ibid.
53. E. B. Stahlman to Leonidas C. Houk, 17 Jan. 1888, ibid.
54. Oliver P. Temple to Leonidas C. Houk, 28 Apr. 1883, ibid.; Houk to Temple, 30 Apr. 1883, Temple Papers.
55. Leonidas C. Houk to Rufus Ingalls, 22 May 1888, Ekin Papers.
56. J. Nat. Lyle, Circular Letter, 6 Mar. 1880, Houk Papers; *Memphis Weekly Appeal*, 21 Apr. 1880. Lyle's connection with the anti-Houk forces began before 1880. Lyle to William Rule, 19 Apr. 1876, Rule Papers.
57. H. Reid to Leonidas Houk, 3 Apr. 1880, J. E. Campbell to Houk, 6 Apr. 1880, Houk Papers.
58. *Knoxville Chronicle*, 3 Nov. 1880.
59. Joseph A. Cooper to Rutherford B. Hayes, 19 Apr. 1879, Houk Papers.
60. "Official Brief Against William Rule," 11 Apr. 1881, ibid.
61. Scrapbook, ibid.
62. D. R. Nelson to Temple, 22 Oct. 1881, Temple Papers.
63. John A. Silsby to Will A. McTeer, 27 May 1882, McTeer Papers; Felix A. Reeve to Rule, 20 June 1882, H. C. Whitaker to Rule, 22 June 1882, G. W. Shipman to Rule, 23 July 1882, John B. Brownlow to Rule, 3 Aug. 1882, Rule Papers.
64. *Memphis Weekly Appeal*, 3 May 1882.
65. J. L. Randee (?) to Leonidas C. Houk, 29 June 1882, Oliver P. Temple to Houk, 12 July 1882, Houk Papers.
66. National Republican Congressional Committee to John M. Cordell, September 1882, ibid. Houk's success in convincing local Republicans of his party regularity was demonstrated in a poll of Republicans that his workers took just before the election. The results were Houk, 9,341; Rule, 1,408; doubtful, 1,294. Memorandum, October 1882, ibid.
67. ICPR Election Data.
68. Scrapbook, Houk Papers.
69. John M. Bishop to Will A. McTeer, 24 Nov. 1887, McTeer Papers.
70. G. Wayne Smith, "Nathan Goff, Jr., and the Solid South," p. 7.
71. Leonard M. Davis, "The Speeches and Speaking of Nathan Goff, Jr.," pp. 24–25.
72. Ibid., pp. 31–33.
73. Leonard M. Davis and James H. Henning, "Nathan Goff," pp. 305–6.
74. Gerald W. Smith, "Nathan Goff, Jr.," p. 80.
75. George C. Sturgiss to Waitman T. Willey, 22 June 1870, Willey Papers.
76. Smith, "Nathan Goff, Jr.," p. 114.
77. Richard Burke to Goff, 21 Apr. 1873, Goff Papers.
78. *Buckhannon Delta*, 8 Oct. 1874.
79. Davis, "Speeches of Goff," p. 49.

80. Goff to John W. Mason, 26, 27 July 1876, Mason Papers.
81. *Wheeling Intelligencer*, 4 Oct. 1876; Goff to John W. Mason, 14 Aug. 1876, Mason Papers.
82. George F. Evans to Goff, 5 Aug. 1876, Goff Papers.
83. *Wheeling Intelligencer*, 4 Oct. 1876; Goff to John W. Mason, 14 Aug. 1876, Mason Papers.
84. George W. Patton to William H. H. Flick, 11 June 1877, Flick Papers.
85. George W. Atkinson to William H. H. Flick, 19 Jan., 2 Apr. 1877, ibid.
86. Stephen B. Elkins to John W. Mason, 21 May 1880, Mason Papers; Paul D. Casdorph, "West Virginia and the 1880 Republican National Convention," p. 147.
87. George W. Atkinson to William H. H. Flick, 18 Apr. 1880, George C. Sturgiss to Flick, 21 Apr. 1880, A. G. Tibbitts to Flick, 1 May 1880, Flick Papers.
88. Alf. W. Burnett to Goff, 1 July 1880, Goff Papers.
89. George C. Sturgiss to William H. H. Flick, 19 July 1880, Flick Papers.
90. S. P. McCormick to William H. H. Flick, 19 July, 22 Aug. 1880, ibid.; McCormick to Waitman T. Willey, 30 July 1880, Willey Papers.
91. *Weston Republican*, 4 Sept. 1880.
92. ICPR Election Data.
93. John T. Siler to William H. H. Flick, 15 Feb. 1881, T. R. Carskadon to James A. Garfield, 17 Jan. 1881, George F. Evans to Garfield, 19 Feb. 1881, Flick Papers.
94. *Weston Republican*, 29 Jan. 1881; C. F. Scott to Waitman T. Willey, 26 Mar. 1881, Willey Papers.
95. S. H. Yocum to Goff, 9 Mar. 1881, James B. Belford to Goff, 10 Mar. 1881, Goff Papers.
96. G. C. Landerett to Nathan Goff, 29 Apr. 1881, John Buckland to Goff, 4 May 1881, ibid.
97. *Weston Republican*, 1 July 1882.
98. William E. Chandler to John W. Mason, 20 July 1882, Goff to Mason, 22 July 1882, "Abstract of Recommendations Favoring the Appointment of W. H. H. Flick," July 1882, Mason Papers.
99. G. W. Feidt to Mason, 25 Aug. 1882, Mason Papers; *Weston Republican*, 2 Sept. 1882.
100. John Jameson to Mason, 13 Sept. 1882, Mason Papers.
101. *Wheeling Intelligencer*, 6 Oct. 1882; Davis, "Speeches of Goff," pp. 66–67.
102. *Wheeling Intelligencer*, 14 Feb. 1884; Davis, "Speeches of Goff," pp. 73–74.
103. S. P. McCormick to William H. H. Flick, 24 May 1883, Flick Papers.
104. McCormick to Flick, 18 Apr. 1884, ibid.
105. Thomas H. B. Staggers to A. Gordon Dayton, 14 Mar. [1884], Dayton Papers.
106. *Buckhannon Delta*, 20 Mar. 1884; *Weston Republican*, 26 Apr. 1884; *Wheeling Intelligencer*, 1 May 1884.
107. *Buckhannon Delta*, 22 May 1884; *Wheeling Intelligencer*, 22 May 1884.
108. *Wheeling Intelligencer*, 31 July 1884.
109. Ibid., 28, 29 Aug. 1884.
110. Ibid., 11 Aug. 1884; W. J. W. Conden and O. G. Schofield, Circular Letter, 9 Aug. 1884, Willey Papers.
111. J. H. Barrett to Elkins, 4 Sept. 1884, Mason Papers.
112. *Wheeling Intelligencer*, 7 Oct. 1884.
113. W. J. W. Conden to John W. Mason, 6 Oct. 1884, Mason Papers.
114. *London Mountain Echo*, 14 Apr. 1876.
115. White to John M. Harlan, 2 June 1875, Harlan Papers (UL).
116. *London Mountain Echo*, 14 Jan., 9 June 1876.
117. Ibid., 28 Apr. 1876.
118. Ibid., 16 June 1876.
119. Ibid., 2 July 1875; *Louisville Courier-Journal*, 2 Aug. 1876.

120. *London Mountain Echo*, 12 May 1876.
121. Ibid., 21 Jan., 16 June 1876.
122. Ibid., 30 Apr., 7, 14 May 1875.
123. White to Harlan, 2 June 1875, Harlan Papers (UL).
124. *Louisville Courier-Journal*, 29 July 1875.
125. *London Mountain Echo*, 25 Feb. 1876.
126. Ibid., 5 Oct. 1876.
127. Ross A. Webb, *Benjamin Helm Bristow*, pp. 236–37; Augustus E. Willson to [John M. Harlan], 10 May 1876, Willson Papers; *Louisville Courier-Journal*, 14 May 1875, 19 May 1876.
128. Bristow to Willson, [May 1876], 19 June 1876, Willson to [John M. Harlan], 10 May 1876, Willson Papers.
129. *Louisville Courier-Journal*, 4 July, 14 Aug. 1876; *New York Times*, 14 Nov. 1876; Bristow to Carl Schurz, 14 Apr. 1877, in Frederic Bancroft, ed., *The Writings of Carl Schurz*, 3:411.
130. *Wheeling Intelligencer*, 10 Apr. 1877.
131. David G. Farrelly, "John M. Harlan's One-Day Diary, August 21, 1877," pp. 159–60.
132. Webb, *Bristow*, pp. 270–71.
133. Farrelly, "Harlan's Diary," pp. 165–67.
134. Harlan to Beck, 31 Oct. 1877, Harlan Papers (UL); Harlan to William Lindsay, 8 Sept. 1877, Lindsay Family Papers.
135. Bristow to Carl Schurz, 24 Sept. 1878, in Bancroft, *Schurz*, 3:422.
136. John W. Finnell to John M. Harlan, 17 Apr. 1879, Augustus E. Willson to Harlan, 19 Apr. 1879, Harlan Papers (UL); Tapp, "Kentucky Politics," pp. 167–68.
137. *London Mountain Echo*, 18 Apr. 1879.
138. Ibid., 4, 11 July, 8 Aug. 1879; Tapp, "Kentucky Politics," pp. 175–76.
139. *London Mountain Echo*, 23 Jan. 1880.
140. Ibid., 6, 27 Feb., 12 Mar. 1880.
141. Clipping, 24 Mar. 1880, Scrapbook, Willson Papers; *New York Times*, 15 Apr. 1880.
142. *London Mountain Echo*, 23 Apr. 1880.
143. Ibid., 12 Mar. 1880.
144. Ibid., 19 Mar. 1880.
145. Ibid., 2 Sept. 1880.
146. Ibid., 8 Oct. 1880.
147. Augustus E. Willson to John M. Harlan, 24 Sept. 1880, Harlan Papers (UL).
148. ICPR Election Data.
149. *London Mountain Echo*, 6 Jan., 24 Feb., 5 May 1882.
150. Ibid., 19 May 1882.
151. Ibid., 23 Dec. 1881.
152. Ibid., 8 Sept. 1882.
153. Ibid., 6 Jan. 1882.
154. Ibid., 27 May 1881; Clipping, 16 Mar. 1881, Scrapbook, Willson Papers; Thomas to John M. Harlan, 23 Dec. 1880, Harlan Papers (UL).
155. *London Mountain Echo*, 1 July 1881.
156. Ibid., 5 Aug. 1881.
157. R. C. Burns to John M. Harlan, 7 Oct. 1881, Harlan Papers; White to Harry I. Todd, 7 Jan. 1881, Todd Papers (FCL); Daniel W. Lindsey to Chester A. Arthur, 7 Apr. 1882, Lindsey Papers.
158. *London Mountain Echo*, 9 Dec. 1881.
159. Ibid., 8 Sept. 1882.
160. Ibid., 13 Oct. 1882.
161. Ibid., 6 Oct. 1882.
162. Ibid., 18 Aug., 20 Oct. 1882.
163. ICPR Election Data.

164. Mott to Ramsay, 9 Apr. 1874, S. A. Caldwell to Ramsay, 18 May 1874, Ramsay to Samuel F. Phillips, 17 Aug. 1874, Ramsay Papers; *Asheville Pioneer*, 14 Feb. 1874.
165. Mott to Thomas Settle, 27 Apr. 1874, George H. Brown to Settle, 18 Nov. 1874, Settle Papers.
166. *Statesville Landmark*, 21 Nov. 1874.
167. Ramsay to J. W. Douglas, 4 Dec. 1874, Samuel F. Phillips to Ramsay, 17 Dec. 1874, Ramsay to Grant, 8 Jan. 1875, Ramsay Papers.
168. *Asheville Citizen*, 15 July 1875; *Statesville American*, 15 Apr. 1876; Robert P. Dick to Thomas Settle, 7 Sept. 1876, Settle Papers; James G. Ramsay to G. H. Raum, 12 Mar. 1877, Ramsay Papers.
169. O. H. Dockery to Carl Schurz, 22 July 1877, in James A. Padgett, "Reconstruction Letters from North Carolina," *North Carolina Historical Review* 19 (July 1942): 299.
170. William D. Cotton, "Appalachian North Carolina," p. 333.
171. *Asheville Citizen*, 18 July 1878, 6 Nov. 1879.
172. *Appleton's Annual Cyclopedia, 1878*, p. 630.
173. *Winston Union Republican*, 19 Sept. 1878.
174. William J. Clark to Thomas Settle, 20 Jan. 1880, Settle Papers; *Memphis Weekly Appeal*, 4 Feb. 1880; *Statesville Landmark*, 6 Feb. 1880.
175. *Statesville Landmark*, 9 Apr. 1880.
176. John B. Gretter to Thomas Settle, 31 Mar. 1880, Settle Papers; *Winston Union Republican*, 27 May 1880.
177. *Winston Union Republican*, 2 June 1881.
178. Ibid., 9 June 1881.
179. *Statesville Landmark*, 17 June 1881.
180. Ibid., 24 June 1881; *Winston Union Republican*, 16 June 1881.
181. *Statesville American*, 2 July 1881.
182. Ibid., 16 July 1881.
183. *Statesville Landmark*, 19 Aug., 2 Sept. 1881.
184. *Winston Union Republican*, 3 Nov. 1881.
185. O. J. Surry to _____, 11 Nov. 1881, Russell Papers; D. C. Pearson to William Mahone, 8 Dec. 1881, Mahone Papers; *Statesville Landmark*, 20 Jan. 1882.
186. Keogh to Daniel L. Russell, 29 Dec. 1881, Russell Papers; *Statesville Landmark*, 10, 24 Feb. 1882.
187. Clipping, 17 Apr. 1882, Scrapbook, vol. 34, p. 52. Mahone Papers; *Winston Union Republican*, 30 Mar. 1882.
188. *Statesville Landmark*, 28 Apr. 1882.
189. Ibid., 9 June 1882.
190. Ibid., 16 June, 7 July 1882.
191. *Winston Union Republican*, 13 July 1882; *Asheville News*, 18 July 1882.
192. *Winston Union Republican*, 7 Sept. 1882.
193. Ibid., 14 Sept. 1882, supplement; *Statesville Landmark*, 8 Sept. 1882.
194. *Statesville Landmark*, 6 Oct. 1882.
195. Mott to Talton L. L. Cox, 29 Aug. 1882, Cox Papers.
196. ICPR Election Data.
197. *Bristol News*, 3, 10 Oct. 1876.
198. ICPR Election Data.
199. *Bristol News*, 2 Nov. 1875; *New York Times*, 14 Nov. 1875.
200. Carl N. Degler, *The Other South*, p. 271.
201. Mahone to Riddleberger, 31 Aug. 1877, Letterbook No. 27, p. 303, Mahone Papers.
202. *Bristol News*, 13 Nov. 1877.
203. ICPR Election Data.
204. Elizabeth A. Hancock, ed., *Autobiography of John E. Massey*, p. 147.

205. William C. Pendleton, *Political History of Appalachian Virginia, 1776–1927*, pp. 334–35; *Bristol News*, 15, 22 Apr. 1879.
206. Jack P. Maddex, Jr., *The Virginia Conservatives, 1867–1879*, p. 273; Charles E. Wynes, *Race Relations in Virginia, 1870–1902*, p. 19.
207. Pendleton, *Political History of Appalachian Virginia*, p. 336.
208. R. T. Thorp to William Mahone, 6 Nov. 1879, Mahone Papers; *Abingdon Standard*, 20 Nov. 1879.
209. ICPR Election Data.
210. T. J. Kilpatrick to Mahone, 29 Oct. 1881, Mahone Papers; *Woodstock Virginian*, 19 May 1882.
211. *Woodstock Virginian*, 3 December 1880.
212. Lewis to James A. Garfield, 21 Jan. 1881, Scrapbook, vol. 18, pp. 24–26, Joseph B. Strayer to William Mahone, 11 Feb. 1881, Mahone Papers.
213. William E. Cameron to Mahone, 14 Mar. 1881, V. D. Groner and Stith Bolling to Mahone, 14 Mar. 1881, "Resolutions of the Convention of the Colored People of Virignia," 14 Mar. 1881, Joseph T. Wilson et al., "An Address," Mar. 1881, Mahone Papers.
214. Massey to William Mahone, 13 Apr. 1881, Mahone to Massey, [Apr. 1881], Harrison H. Riddleberger to Mahone, 7 June 1881, ibid.; Hancock, *Autobiography of Massey*, pp. 193–96; *Bristol News*, 7 June 1881.
215. J. H. Rives, "History of the Lynchburg Convention," Scrapbook, vol. 22, p. 22, Mahone Papers.
216. Ibid.
217. V. D. Groner to William Mahone, 10 Aug. 1881, C. C. Clarke to Mahone, 10 Aug. 1881, ibid.
218. James D. Brady to William Mahone, 11 Aug. 1881, C. C. Clarke to Mahone, 11 Aug. 1881, ibid.
219. *Bristol News*, 16 Aug. 1880; *Woodstock Virginian*, 2 Sept. 1881; William C. Wickham to editor of *Richmond Debt Payer*, 24 Aug. 1881, Scrapbook, vol. 32, p. 36, Mahone Papers.
220. William C. Pendleton to William Mahone, 16 Nov. 1880, John Tyler, Jr., to Mahone, 16 Jan. 1881, "Resolutions of Readjusters of Wythe County," 11 Apr. 1881, Scrapbook, vol. 19, p. 119, Mahone Papers; *Bristol News*, 8 Feb., 22 Mar., 12, 26 Apr. 1881.
221. Mahone, Circular Letter, 24 Sept. 1881, Mahone Papers.
222. *Memphis Weekly Appeal*, 6 Sept. 1882.
223. ICPR Election Data; William Jennings Dickerson to Mahone, 14 Nov. 1881, Mahone Papers.
224. Hancock, *Autobiography of Massey*, p. 200.
225. Frank P. Ruffin, "Mahoneism Unveiled," 28 Nov. 1881, Mahone Papers.
226. Frank H. Alfriend to Riddleberger, 17 Nov. 1881, Wise to Riddleberger, 2 Dec. 1881, Riddleberger Papers; H. W. Blair to Mahone, 7 Dec. 1881, Lewis to Mahone, 9 Dec. 1881, Mahone Papers; *Memphis Weekly Appeal*, 30 Nov. 1881.
227. *Bristol News*, 31 Jan. 1882; Leonidas Baughan to William Mahone, 11 Feb. 1882, Mahone Papers.
228. James T. Quinn, "John S. Barbour, Jr. and the Restoration of the Virginia Democracy, 1883–1892," pp. 32–33.
229. Degler, *Other South*, pp. 282–85.
230. James T. Moore, "Black Militancy in Readjuster Virginia, 1879–1883," pp. 177–82.
231. *Richmond Whig*, 21 Sept. 1882.
232. ICPR Election Data.
233. *Woodstock Virginian*, 2 Feb. 1883.
234. Ibid., 1 June 1883; *Bristol News*, 29 May 1883.
235. William Townes to William Mahone, 30 Aug. 1883, William E. Cameron to Mahone, 13 Sept. 1883, Robert T. Thorp to Mahone, 18 Sept. 1883, Mahone Papers.
236. A. K. Grim to William Mahone, 22 Oct. 1883, ibid.

237. *Woodstock Virginian*, 2 Nov. 1883; W. E. Craig to William Mahone, 1 Nov. 1883, C. S. Wingfield to Mahone, 2 Nov. 1883, Mahone Papers.
238. "Coalition Rule in Danville," Scrapbook, vol. 31, p. 25, Mahone Papers.
239. Ibid.
240. K. M. McLaughlin to William Mahone, 4 Nov. 1883, C. C. Clarke to Mahone, 4 Nov. 1883, Miner F. Chamberlain to Mahone, 5 Nov. 1883, Mahone Papers.
241. Wynes, *Race Relations*, p. 31.
242. John T. S. Melzer, "The Danville Riot, November 3, 1883," pp. 92–93.
243. A. A. McDonald to Mahone, 10 Nov. 1883, Mahone Papers.
244. J. H. Ballard to Mahone, 8 Nov. 1883, ibid.
245. ICPR Election Data for 1882 returns; the 1883 election data are in Scrapbook, vol. 2, p. 7, Mahone Papers.
246. Angus Campbell, Philip E. Converse, Warren E. Miller, and Donald E. Stokes, *Elections and the Political Order*, pp. 42–43.
247. *Memphis Weekly Appeal*, 20 Feb. 1884.
248. Raymond H. Pulley, *Old Virginia Restored*, pp. 45–46.
249. Clipping, Scrapbook, vol. 2, p. 10, Mahone Papers.
250. G. E. Bowden to William Mahone, 29 Apr. 1884, T. S. Curlett to Mahone, 29 Apr. 1884, C. C. Clarke to Mahone, 3 May 1884, Clipping, Scrapbook, vol. 32, p. 14, ibid.; *Wytheville Dispatch*, 24 Apr., 8 May 1884.
251. James D. Brady, "Statement on Behalf of the William Mahone Delegation," Mahone Papers.
252. *Wytheville Dispatch*, 28 Aug. 1884.
253. Ibid., 4 Sept. 1884.
254. Ibid., 18 Sept. 1884; *Abingdon Virginian*, 4 Sept. 1884.

CHAPTER 6
1. Houk to Oliver P. Temple, 3 Aug. 1884, Temple Papers.
2. Houk to Oliver P. Temple, 4 Dec. 1884, 6 June 1886, ibid.; Henry R. Gibson to Houk, 5 Dec. 1884, Richard W. Austin to creditors of the *Knoxville Chronicle*, 5 June 1886, Houk Papers; *Maryville Times*, 1 Sept. 1886.
3. *Johnson City Comet*, 4 Feb., 25 Mar., 29 Apr. 1886, 19 Apr., 3 May, 1888; *Maryville Times*, 12 May 1886.
4. I. A. Dail to Lincoln C. Houk, 25 June 1887, Houk Papers; *Johnson City Comet*, 11 Feb. 1886.
5. Houk to S. W. Hawkins, 2 July 1887, Houk Papers.
6. Gibson to Will A. McTeer, 9 July 1887, McTeer to Joe H. Fussell, 12 Aug. 1887, Letterbook, McTeer Papers.
7. *Athens Athenian*, 21 Oct. 1887.
8. *Maryville Times*, 9 Nov. 1887.
9. J. H. Griffiths to [Houk], 13 Jan. 1887, Houk Papers.
10. F. H. Dunning to Houk, 13 Feb. 1888, Lincoln C. Houk to Houk, 14 Feb. 1888, Shelley to Houk, 3 Apr. 1888, ibid.; *Clinton Gazette*, 5 Apr. 1888.
11. Rule to Houk, 2 July 1888, Houk Papers.
12. John C. Houk to John Reeder, 14 Nov. 1888, ibid.
13. *Big Sandy News*, 24 Dec. 1885.
14. *Weston Republican*, 18 Sept. 1886.
15. *Wheeling Intelligencer*, 22, 25 Aug. 1888.
16. An excellent description of Elkins's earlier career can be found in Robert D. Marcus, *Grand Old Party*, pp. 64–67, 84–89, 104–15.
17. *Wheeling Intelligencer*, 2 Feb. 1888; John A. Williams, "New York's First Senator from West Virginia," p. 79.
18. Williams, "First Senator," pp. 80–81; *Wheeling Intelligencer*, 6 Mar. 1888.

19. *Wheeling Intelligencer*, 19, 20 Oct. 1888.
20. Ibid., 16 Nov. 1888.
21. Elkins to John W. Mason, 7 Dec. 1888, Mason Papers.
22. *Statesville Landmark*, 12 Aug. 1886.
23. Ibid., 16 Sept. 1886.
24. *Winston Union Republican*, 19 Aug. 1886.
25. Ibid., 30 Sept. 1886.
26. *Statesville Landmark*, 21 Oct. 1886.
27. *Winston Union Republican*, 1 Dec. 1887.
28. William D. Cotton, "Appalachian North Carolina," pp. 523–24.
29. Entries 6, 7 Aug. 1888, Journal, Leach Papers; E. O. Martin to Thomas Settle, 25 Sept. 1888, Settle Papers.
30. Cotton, "Appalachian North Carolina," pp. 548–49.
31. *Wytheville Dispatch*, 1 Jan. 1885; Mahone to Brady, 13 Feb. 1885, Mahone Papers.
32. R. F. Walker to Mahone, 19 Mar. 1885, H. J. Williamson to Mahone, 16 May 1885, W. S. Oakey to Mahone, 18 May 1885, Mahone to J. B. Raulston, 12 June 1885, Letterbook, vol. 27, p. 3, Mahone Papers.
33. Allen W. Moger, *Virginia*, p. 59.
34. *Wytheville Dispatch*, 8 Oct. 1885; *Abingdon Virginian*, 22 Oct. 1885; Mahone to John S. Wise, 28 Sept. 1885, S. W. Aston to Mahone, 16 Oct. 1885, Mahone Papers.
35. H. C. Parsons to Mahone, 17 Oct. 1885, Mahone Papers.
36. Brady to _____, 9 Sept. 1886, Brady, Circular Letter, 16 Sept. 1886, Brady Papers; Mahone to Brady, 16 Aug., 24 Sept. 1886, Letterbook, vol. 38, pp. 3–4, 439–43, Mahone Papers.
37. *Wytheville Dispatch*, 7 Oct. 1886.
38. ICPR Election Data.
39. W. E. Craig to Mahone, 7 Sept. 1887, McGill-Mahone Papers.
40. Howson W. Cole, "Harrison Holt Riddleberger, Readjuster," pp. 125–26.
41. Green B. Raum to Mahone, 8 Apr. 1887, B. F. Jones to J. D. Cameron, 23 May 1887, James M. Swank to Mahone, 5 July 1887, Leland Stanford to Mahone, 3 Oct. 1887, Mahone Papers.
42. *Tribune Almanac and Political Register, 1888*, p. 80.
43. "Call for the Republican National Convention of 1888," 9 Dec. 1887, Mahone Papers.
44. B. F. Jones to Mahone, 17 Jan. 1888, ibid.
45. Sherman to Mahone, 10 Jan., 1 Apr. 1888, ibid.
46. *Richmond Dispatch*, 16 Mar. 1888.
47. J. L. Hamilton to Mahone, 9 Feb. 1888, I. C. Fowler to Mahone, 23 Apr. 1888, Mahone Papers.
48. Mahone, "Windy Wise Woefully Worsted," [May 1887], Mahone and W. C. Elam, "The Virginia Delegation, 1888" (June 1888), ibid.; *Danville Register*, 7 June 1888; Curtis C. Davis, "Very Well-Rounded Republican," p. 479.
49. Clipping, 21 July 1888, Scrapbook, vol. 37, p. 10, I. C. Fowler to Mahone, 29 June 1888, Mahone Papers.
50. W. H. Strothen to Mahone, 13 Aug. 1888, M. S. Quay to Mahone, 18 Aug. 1888, ibid.; James D. Brady et al. to Republican Voters of Virginia, 17 Aug. 1888, Brady Papers.
51. Leonidas C. Houk to Mahone, 14 Oct. 1888, Mahone Papers.
52. Clipping, 18 Jan. 1889, Scrapbook, vol. 39, p. 18, ibid.; John M. Langston, *From the Virginia Plantation to the National Capitol*, pp. 444–45.
53. Langston, *Plantation to Capitol*, pp. 446–47; Frederick Douglass to George Fayerman et al., 15 Aug. 1888, Scrapbook, vol. 38, p. 28, R. H. Hampton and William T. Crowder, Circular Letter, 2 Aug. 1888, Scrapbook, vol. 37, p. 39, Mahone Papers.
54. O. L. Hardy to Mahone, 1 Aug. 1888, W. H. Ash to Mahone, 4 Aug. 1888, "The

Fraud, Outrages, and Trickery of the 'Mahone Machine' Exposed," Scrapbook, vol. 38, p. 36, Mahone Papers; Langston, *Plantation to Capitol*, p. 447.

55. W. A. Jamieson to Mahone, 15 Oct. 1888, T. S. Curlett to Mahone, 15 Oct. 1888, Mahone Papers.

56. Langston, *Plantation to Capitol*, pp. 479–81.

57. Cole, "Riddleberger," pp. 145–47; V. D. Groner to Stephen B. Elkins, 19 Mar. 1889, Elkins Papers.

58. Clipping, 20 July 1889, Scrapbook, Brady Papers; William Lamb to Mahone, 31 July 1889, Mahone Papers.

59. B. W. Perkins to Mahone, 24 July 1889, A. M. Lybrook to Mahone, 24 July 1889, John S. Clarkson to Mahone, 30 July 1889, Mahone Papers.

60. Stanley P. Hirshson, *Farewell to the Bloody Shirt*, pp. 185–86; "Protest of Virginia Republicans Against William Mahone," Sept. 1889, Mahone Papers.

61. J. W. Conrad to M. S. Quay, 24 Aug. 1889, John S. Clarkson to Mahone, 2 Nov. 1889, Mahone Papers; *Wheeling Intelligencer*, 3 Oct. 1889.

62. J. L. Hamilton to Mahone, 19 Aug. 1889, Mahone Papers.

63. ICPR Election Data.

64. *London Mountain Echo*, 27 Apr. 1883.

65. *Louisville Courier-Journal*, 19 Apr., 1, 3 Mar. 1884.

66. Clipping, 11 May 1883, Scrapbook, Bradley Papers.

67. *London Mountain Echo*, 28 Mar. 1884; *Louisville Commercial*, 26 Mar. 1884.

68. William C. Goodloe to Benjamin H. Bristow, 19 Apr. 1884, Bristow Papers (UKL).

69. *Louisville Commercial*, 2 May 1884.

70. Ibid.

71. Ibid., 3 May 1884.

72. *London Mountain Echo*, 5 June 1885, 4 June 1886.

73. Ibid., 17 July 1885.

75. Ibid., 4 June, 6 Aug. 1886.

75. Clipping, Mar. 1887, Scrapbook, Willson Papers.

76. *London Mountain Echo*, 30 Aug. 1878.

77. Ibid., 30 July 1880.

78. *Hazel Green Herald*, 1 July 1885.

79. Ibid., 12 Aug. 1885.

80. *London Mountain Echo*, 10 Sept. 1886, 5 Oct. 1888.

81. The most complete discussion of southern Democrats in this period is C. Vann Woodward, *Origins of the New South, 1877–1913*.

82. *Asheville Advance*, 14 June 1885.

83. Ibid., 19 Sept. 1886.

84. *Statesville Landmark*, 23 Sept. 1886; *Asheville Skyland Herald*, 6 Oct. 1886.

85. *Asheville Advance*, 19 Oct. 1886.

86. Ibid., 30 Oct., 4 Nov. 1886; *Winston Union Republican*, 18 Nov. 1886.

87. *Statesville Landmark*, 3, 17 Feb. 1887; *Winston Union Republican*, 3 Feb. 1887.

88. Josephus Daniels, *Tar Heel Editor*, pp. 361–62; *Winston Union Republican*, 4 Oct. 1888.

89. Richmond Pearson et al., Circular Letter, 21 July 1888, Pearson Papers; *Winston Union Republican*, 13 Sept. 1888.

90. *Wheeling Intelligencer*, 23 Aug. 1888.

91. W. J. J. Cowden to T. S. Riley, 12 Sept. 1888, Riley to Cowden, 13 Sept. 1888, Goff Papers.

92. Cowden to Riley, 13 Sept. 1888, ibid.; *Wheeling Intelligencer*, 1 Oct. 1888.

93. S. P. McCormick to William H. H. Flick, 16 Sept. 1888, Flick Papers.

94. T. H. B. Dawson to William H. H. Flick, 24 Sept. 1888, A. C. Scherr to Flick, 25 Sept. 1888, ibid.; *Wheeling Intelligencer*, 13 Sept. 1888.

95. The most complete discussion of this complex situation is James H. Jacobs, "The West Virginia Gubernatorial Election Contest, 1888–1890," pp. 159–220, 263–311.
96. *Wheeling Intelligencer*, 19 Mar. 1889.
97. S. W. Kendig to A. Gordon Dayton, 28 Mar. 1889, Dayton Papers.
98. *Wheeling Intelligencer*, 28 Mar. 1889.
99. Ibid., 29 June 1889.
100. John W. Mason to H. C. Showalter, 3 Apr. 1889, Letterbook, Mason Papers.
101. Mason to S. A. Scott, 13 Aug. 1889, Mason to Vickery, 28 Aug. 1889, Letterbook, ibid.
102. Leonidas C. Houk to William Windom, 8 July 1889, Houk Papers; Mason to H. Clay Evans, 15 Aug. 1889, Letterbook, Mason to John J. Mott, 5 Aug. 1889, Letterbook, Mason to J. M. Brower, 28 Aug. 1889, Letterbook, Mason Papers.

CHAPTER 7

1. U. S. Bureau of the Census, *Eleventh Census of the United States, 1890, Manufactures*, pt. 2, p. 626; U. S. Bureau of the Census, *Twelfth Census of the United States, 1900, Manufactures*, pt. 2, p. 944.
2. U. S. Bureau of the Census, *Ninth Census of the United States, 1870, Wealth and Industry*, p. 578; *Twelfth Census, 1900, Manufactures*, pt. 2, p. 850.
3. U. S. Bureau of the Census, *Tenth Census of the United States, 1880, Statistics of Manufactures* p. 318; *Twelfth Census, 1900, Manufactures*, pt. 2, p. 664.
4. *Tenth Census, 1880, Statistics of Manufactures*, p. 368; *Eleventh Census, 1890, Manufactures*, pt. 2, p. 618.
5. *Clinton Gazette*, 16 July, 5 Nov. 1891.
6. A. C. Hutson, "The Coal Miners' Insurrections of 1891 in Anderson County, Tennessee," pp. 103–21; A. C. Hutson, "The Overthrow of the Convict Lease System in Tennessee," pp. 82–103.
7. *Wheeling Intelligencer*, 4 Mar., 26 Apr., 10 June 1894.
8. J. S. Ragsdale to Thomas Settle, 26 Jan. 1895, Settle Papers.
9. *Twelfth Census, 1900, Population*, pt. 1, pp. 175–85, 286–95, 365–76, 396–402, 408–12.
10. Ibid.
11. *Chattanooga Times*, 1 Apr. 1894; Clipping, 27 Aug. 1895, Scrapbook, Willson Papers; Clipping, 4 Apr. 1896, Scrapbook, Bradley Papers; James Boyle to H. Clay Evans, 21 Apr. 1896, Evans Papers; John E. Wiltz, "APA-ism in Kentucky and Elsewhere," pp. 150–52.
12. *Maryville Times*, 8 Apr. 1891; *Weston Republican* 9 May 1891; *Wheeling Intelligencer*, 19 Apr. 1892; *Clinton Gazette*, 22 June 1893.
13. *Middlesboro News*, 30 June 1900.
14. John Fox, Jr., "The Southern Mountaineer," pp. 562–63.
15. The most complete account of this famous feud is Virgil C. Jones, *The Hatfields and the McCoys*.
16. Harry M. Caudill, *Night Comes to the Cumberlands*, p. 48.
17. R. L. McClure, "Mazes of a Kentucky Feud," pp. 2217–18; "Hanging of Bad Tom Smith," p. 748.
18. Ferdinand Tonnies, *Community & Society*, pp. 42–44, 64–67, 76–78.
19. Robert H. Wiebe, *The Search for Order*, pp. 11–75, 133–63.
20. Eric J. Hobsbawm, *Primitive Rebels*, p. 23.
21. Ibid., p. 24.
22. William J. Crotty, James F. Kirkham, and Sheldon G. Levy, *Assassination and Political Violence*, p. 24.
23. In February 1890 newspaperman Charles E. Kincaide shot former Kentucky Democratic congressman William P. Taulbee. Kincaide had exposed Taulbee's adulterous relationship with a government clerk and ended Taulbee's political career. The shooting was the climax of a continuing personal and political battle between the two men. *Wheeling*

Intelligencer, 1 Mar. 1890; *London Mountain Echo*, 7 Mar. 1890. Former Virginia Republican congressman James A. Walker was seriously wounded in March 1899, while collecting evidence to challenge the election of the Democratic candidate. After a heated verbal exchange, Walker wounded W. S. Hamilton, the lawyer for the opposition. Walker was in turn shot by G. D. Davis, a secretary recording the testimony for the Democrats. *Clinton Gazette*, 15 Mar. 1899; *Big Stone Gap Post*, 16 Mar. 1899. Republican congressman David G. Colson was wounded twice in two separate incidents involving the same individual. The first confrontation between Colson and Ethelbert D. Scott took place after both joined the army to fight in the Spanish-American War. The second shooting took place in January 1900, just before the assassination of Democratic gubernatorial contestant William Goebel. Scott, apparently drunk, verbally abused Colson. In the confusion that followed, Colson shot and killed Scott and in turn was severely wounded. *Middlesboro Record*, 19 Jan. 1900; *Hazel Green Herald*, 18 Jan. 1900.

24. Thomas D. Clark, "The People, William Goebel, and the Kentucky Railroads," pp. 34-48.

25. See chap. 8.

26. See Wiebe, *Search for Order*, pp. 133-63.

27. Caudill, *Night Comes to the Cumberlands*, p. 49.

28. *Louisville Courier-Journal*, 13 June 1898.

29. *Wytheville Dispatch*, 3 Sept. 1897.

30. A typical incident was reported as follows: "While he was doing this [destroying the still], a man came into the distillery who appeared to be the owner, and Mr. Bouldin attempted to place him under arrest, but he escaped from the premises, returning in a few minutes with a double-barreled shot gun, and fired the contents of both barrels into the body of Mr. Bouldin, inflicting very severe wounds in his left arm and his side in the region of the heart." John W. Mason to B. H. Bunn, 4 Mar. 1892, Letterbook, Mason Papers.

31. *Maryville Times*, 28 Sept. 1892.

32. John A. Waits, "Roanoke's Tragedy," pp. 22-23.

33. *Roanoke Times*, 21 Sept. 1893.

34. Ibid., 23 Sept. 1893.

35. Ibid., 22 Sept. 1893.

36. Ibid.

37. Ibid., 26 Nov. 1893.

38. H. Wayne Morgan, *From Hayes to McKinley*, p. 339.

39. "Several gentlemen have said to me—'rather than permit free negroes to vote and hold office, we are ready for another war' I tell them, 'no'. Let us have peace. The last war nearly ruined us—another will finish the job." R. M. Pearson to William L. Scott, 16 July 1868, Scott Papers.

40. Alexander Gates et al. to William L. Scott, 31 May 1871. Scott Papers.

41. Houk to Oliver P. Temple, 30 Apr. 1883, Temple Papers.

42. Vincent P. DeSantis, *Republicans Face the Southern Question*, pp. 66-103, 133-81.

43. *Memphis Weekly Appeal*, 23 Aug. 1882.

44. Ibid., 11 Oct. 1876.

45. *Appleton's Annual Cyclopedia, 1883*, p. 461; *Memphis Weekly Appeal*, 22 Aug. 1883.

46. *Knoxville Tribune*, 5 Sept. 1876; *Big Sandy News*, 19 May 1887; *London Mountain Echo*, 19 May 1882; *Memphis Weekly Appeal*, 30 Mar. 1881; *Nashville American*, 9 Mar. 1884; *Statesville Landmark*, 27 May 1881, 17 Mar., 26 May 1882; J. D. Alton et al., Minutes of Meeting, 2 Apr. 1881, Holden Papers.

47. *Memphis Weekly Appeal*, 30 Mar. 1881.

48. J. L. Randle to Houk, 29 June 1882, W. H. Dietz to Houk, 20 July 1882, Houk Papers.

49. Oliver P. Temple to Houk, 12 July 1882, ibid.

50. Clipping, 1882, Rule Papers.

51. *Wheeling Intelligencer*, 13 Sept. 1888.

52. *Weston Republican*, 12 Oct. 1888.
53. *Wheeling Intelligencer*, 28 Mar. 1876.
54. John B. Brownlow to Oliver P. Temple, 1 Jan. 1894, Temple Papers.
55. *Ninth Census, 1870, Population and Social Statistics*, pt. 1, pp. 146–54, 220–26, 261–69, 278–83, 284–387.
56. ICPR Election and Census Data.
57. The white Republican share of the vote declined in Hamilton County from 35 percent in 1880 to 21 percent in 1900. These figures were computed using a method popularized by Allen W. Trelease in "Who Were the Scalawags?" (pp. 445–68). Another reason for the decline in the Republican vote in Hamilton County was the passage of discriminatory election laws in Tennessee in the late 1880s. See Joseph H. Cartwright, *The Triumph of Jim Crow*, pp. 223–54.
58. Houk, *Freedom of Election in the South*, 3 Apr. 1879, Houk Papers; *Wheeling Intelligencer*, 7 Nov. 1889.
59. *Wheeling Intelligencer*, 6 Mar. 1890.
60. *Congressional Record*, 51st Cong., 1st Sess., 30 June 1890, pp. 6769–71.
61. *Wheeling Intelligencer*, 24 May 1890.
62. *Congressional Record*, 51st Cong., 1st Sess., 2 July 1890, p. 6929.   63. Ibid., 30 June 1890, p. 6774.
64. *Weston Republican*, 7 June, 2 Aug. 1890; *Johnson City Comet*, 7 Aug. 1890; *Wheeling Intelligencer*, 21 Aug. 1890; *Winston Union Republican*, 4 Sept. 1890.
65. *Congressional Record*, 51st Cong., 1st Sess., 2 July 1890, pp. 6940–41.
66. Ibid., 28 June 1890, p. 6688.
67. Ibid., p. 6689.
68. D. C. Kelley to Will A. McTeer, 29 Sept. 1890, McTeer Papers; John C. Houk to Leonidas C. Houk, 4 Aug. 1890, Houk Papers; *Winston Union Republican*, 16 Jan., 2 Oct. 1890; *Statesville Landmark*, 10 July, 9 Oct. 1890; *Big Stone Gap Post*, 22 Aug., 26 Sept. 1890; *Wheeling Intelligencer*, 15 Sept. 1890; *Johnson City Comet*, 25 Sept. 1890.
69. Outspoken supporters of the Lodge bill, Taylor and Houk were reelected despite racist opposition. *Clinton Gazette*, 30 Oct. 1890; *Chattanooga Times*, 1 Nov. 1890.
70. *Johnson City Comet*, 17 Apr. 1890.
71. Ibid., 25 Sept. 1890.
72. ICPR Election Data. Using Lewis Baxter's vote as the Republican gubernatorial candidate and assuming that no Democrats would vote for the advocate of the Lodge bill, the Republicans divided approximately as follows: Taylor, 11,500; Butler, 2,200.
73. Augustus E. Willson, Circular Letter, 4 Nov. 1892, Willson Papers; D. M. Furches to Thomas Settle, III, 29 July 1892, Settle Papers; *Weston Republican*, 24 Jan. 1891; *Winston Union Republican*, 11 June 1891; *Big Sandy News*, 21 Oct. 1892.
74. John W. Mason to Thomas E. Davis, 6 Aug. 1892, Letterbook, Mason Papers; Charles F. Ballard to Augustus E. Willson, 29 Feb. 1892, Willson, Circular Letter, 4 Nov. 1892, Willson Papers; *Wheeling Intelligencer*, 4 June 1891; *Winston Union Republican*, 11 June 1891; *Clinton Gazette*, 1 Dec. 1892; *Big Sandy News*, 23 Feb. 1894; *Big Stone Gap Post*, 13 Aug. 1896.
75. George M. Frederickson, *The Black Image in the White Mind*, pp. 256–82.
76. Clipping, 1879, Scrapbook, Willson Papers.
77. M. N. Corbitt to Thomas Settle, III, 26 July 1892, Settle Papers.
78. H. F. Camble to Albert B. White, 7 Feb. 1900; Daniel W. Shaw, *The Second Emancipation of the Negro*, 16 Aug. 1900, White Papers; H. C. Duncan to A. Brooks Fleming, 10 Mar. 1900, Fleming Papers; H. M. Adams to Stephen B. Elkins, 20 Mar. 1900, I. R. LeSage to Elkins, 20 Mar. 1900, Phil Waters to Elkins, 22 Mar. 1900, Elkins Papers.
79. John W. Mason to W. W. Rollins, 20 Mar. 1892, Letterbook, Mason Papers.
80. *Mt. Vernon Signal*, 16 July 1897.
81. Cansler to Leonidas C. Houk, 2 Jan. 1891, Houk Papers.
82. *Big Sandy News*, 2 Aug. 1895.

83. *Asheville Citizen*, 29 July 1888; *Winston Union Republican*, 10 May 1900.
84. Clipping, 27 Aug. 1895, Scrapbook, Bradley Papers; *Wheeling Intelligencer*, 20 Feb. 1892; *Big Stone Gap Post*, 18 Oct. 1894; *Big Sandy News*, 30 Aug. 1895.
85. *Big Stone Gap Post*, 6 Sept. 1894.
86. *Winston Union Republican*, 26 July 1888.
87. Russell to J. H. Ramsay, 27 May 1896, RamsayPapers.
88. James E. Shepard to Thomas Settle, III, 19 May 1896, M. N. Corbitt to Settle, 27 May 1896, *To the People of North Carolina*, 6 June 1896, Settle Papers.
89. "Republican Campaign of Kentucky, 1895," Todd Papers.
90. Clipping, 30 June 1895, Scrapbook, Bradley Papers.
91. "Republican Campaign of Kentucky, 1895," Todd Papers.
92. Rufus Terral, *Newell Sanders*, pp. 81–82; Ben W. Hooper, *The Unwanted Boy*, p. 28.

CHAPTER 8
1. ICPR Election Data.
2. J. W. Andes to Leonidas C. Houk, 15 Jan. 1889, Houk Papers.
3. Houk to H. Clay Evans, 28 Mar. 1892, ibid.; Houk to Oliver P. Temple, 6 June 1892, Temple Papers, John C. Houk to Wolf and Cohen, attorneys, 17 Mar. 1892, Houk Papers.
4. Houk to S. W. Hawkins, 2 July 1887, Houk Papers.
5. Houk, "Let Us Have an American Tariff," ibid.
6. Ironically, Houk had helped Evans capture the Republican organization in the Third District. R. W. Austin to Houk, 11 Aug. 1884, ibid.
7. ICPR Election Data.
8. *Clinton Gazette*, 10 Jan. 1889; A. M. Felknor to Houk, 10 Jan. 1889, Houk Papers.
9. H. B. Lindsay, Memorandum, 5 Apr. 1889, Houk Papers.
10. Shelby M. Cullom to Evans, 30 May 1889, Scrapbook, vol. 48, John Wanamaker to Evans, 20 Apr. 1890, Scrapbook vol. 49, Evans Papers.
11. Houk to William Windom, 8 July 1889, Houk Papers; John W. Mason to J. A. Greer, 29 July 1889, Mason Papers.
12. John W. Mason to B. Thornburgh, 29 July 1889, Mason Papers.
13. Leonidas C. Houk et al., Circular Letter, 4 Dec. 1889, Houk Papers.
14. John C. Houk to Oliver P. Temple, 13 Jan. 1889, Temple Papers; *Clinton Gazette*, 17 Jan. 1889; Leonidas C. Houk et al., to Harrison, 31 Jan. 1889, F. H. Dunning to John C. Houk, 11 Feb. 1889, E. B. Morton to John C. Houk, 15 Feb. 1889, J. C. Napier to John C. Houk, 26 Feb. 1889, Houk Papers.
15. *Chattanooga Republican*, 5 May 1889.
16. Houk to John C. Houk, 30 Apr. 1889, Houk Papers.
17. *Maryville Times*, 11 Sept. 1889; *Clinton Gazette*, 19 Sept. 1889.
18. *Maryville Times*, 11 Sept. 1889; *Chattanooga Republican*, 1 Dec. 1889.
19. *Chattanooga Republican*, 1 Dec. 1889.
20. Ibid., 29 Dec. 1889.
21. Rufus Terral, *Newell Sanders*, pp. 79–80.
22. J. E. Cassady to Houk, 30 May 1891, Houk Papers.
23. *Clinton Gazette*, 30 July 1891.
24. *Knoxville Republican*, 14 Aug. 1894.
25. Houk to Goff, 12 Oct. 1891, Houk Papers.
26. Evans to N. B. Gahagan, 12 Jan. 1891, Gahagan Papers.
27. D. C. Hill to Houk, 12 Feb. 1892, Houk Papers.
28. Houk to Benjamin Harrison, 26 June 1892, ibid.
29. John W. Baker to Houk, 25 July 1892, Houk to Anthony Higgins, 23 Sept. 1892, ibid.
30. *Chattanooga Times*, 23–26 Oct., 6 Nov. 1892.
31. *Knoxville Republican*, 12 May 1893.
32. Will A. McTeer to Joe H. Fussell, 12 Aug. 1887, McTeer Papers.

33. *Clinton Gazette*, 25 Apr. 1894.
34. *Maryville Times*, 17 Jan. 1894.
35. John G. B. Adams, Circular Letter, 20 Jan. 1894, Houk Papers.
36. *Maryville Times*, 7 Feb., 7 Mar. 1894.
37. Richard W. Austin to Houk, 19 Sept. 1893, J. P. Edmundson to Houk, 20 Oct. 1892, Houk Papers.
38. Houk to Settle, 29 Jan. 1894, Richard W. Austin to Settle, 4 Oct. 1894, Settle Papers.
39. "A Surprise," 12 Feb. 1894, Houk Papers.
40. *Knoxville Republican*, 13 Sept. 1894.
41. Ibid.; *Clinton Gazette*, 17 Oct. 1894.
42. *Maryville Times*, 21 Mar. 1894.
43. *Chattanooga Times*, 23 Aug. 1894.
44. Terral, *Sanders*, p. 80.
45. *Chattanooga Times*, 23 Aug. 1894.
46. *Knoxville Republican*, 6 Sept. 1894.
47. *Chattanooga Times*, 19 Aug. 1894.
48. *Knoxville Republican*, 8 Nov. 1894.
49. John F. Powers to Houk, 21 Nov. 1894, J. J. Duff to Houk, 22 Nov. 1894, Allen G. Mathews to Houk, [November 1894], D. B. Simpson to Houk, 24 Nov. 1894, Houk Papers.
50. William M. Hahn to Evans, 29 Apr. 1891, Scrapbook, vol. 50, Evans Papers; *Chattanooga Republican*, 18 Oct. 1891.
51. McKinley to Evans, 26 Feb. 1896, Scrapbook, vol. 51, Hanna to Evans, 29 Apr. 1896, Scrapbook, vol. 49, Evans Papers; J. H. Neil to Newell Sanders, 12 Mar. 1896, Sanders Papers.
52. McKinley to J. J. Schmidlapp, 29 Jan. 1896, Scrapbook, vol. 51, Evans Papers.
53. *Wheeling Intelligencer*, 19 Sept. 1884, 23 Aug., 1 Oct. 1888; *Weston Republican*, 25 Sept. 1886; Goff, "American Markets for American Labor," 27 Apr. 1888, Goff Papers.
54. *Wheeling Intelligencer*, 28, 29 Aug. 1884.
55. *Weston Republican*, 18 Sept. 1886; *Wheeling Register*, 28 Oct. 1886.
56. *Wheeling Intelligencer*, 21–23 Aug. 1888.
57. Gerald W. Smith, *Nathan Goff, Jr.*, pp. 145–46.
58. Robert D. Marcus, *Grand Old Party*, pp. 64–67, 84–85.
59. J. H. Barrett to Elkins, 4 Sept. 1884, W. J. W. Cowden to John W. Mason, 6 Oct. 1884, Mason Papers; Elkins to William H. H. Flick, 25 Sept. 1884, Flick Papers; *Wheeling Intelligencer*, 7 Oct. 1884; *Buckhannon Delta*, 14 Oct. 1884.
60. John A. Williams, "Davis and Elkins of West Virginia," pp. 27, 54.
61. *Wheeling Intelligencer*, 29 Feb., 1 Mar. 1888.
62. Ibid., 6 Mar. 1888.
63. John A. Williams, "New York's First Senator from West Virginia," p. 82.
64. *Wheeling Intelligencer*, 8 Sept. 1888.
65. For contrast see Diary, Aug.–Nov. 1884, Mason Papers; Nathan B. Scott to William H. H. Flick, 25 Sept. 1888, H. R. Riddle to Flick, 16 Aug. 1888, Flick Papers.
66. *Wheeling Intelligencer*, 29 Sept., 19, 20 Oct. 1888.
67. Ibid., 16 Nov. 1888.
68. Elkins to John W. Mason, 7 Dec. 1888, Mason Papers.
69. George C. Sturgiss to John W. Mason, 24 Dec. 1888 and 9 Feb. 1889, Elkins to Mason, 3 Jan., and 2 Feb. 1889, ibid.; William P. Hubbard to Elkins, 31 Dec. 1888, Elkins Papers; *Wheeling Intelligencer*, 25 Feb. 1889; Gerald W. Smith, "Nathan Goff, Jr.," p. 232; Leonard M. Davis and James H. Henning, "Nathan Goff," p. 334.
70. *Wheeling Intelligencer*, 14, 16, 22 Feb., 5, 13 Mar. 1889.
71. Williams, "Davis and Elkins," pp. 149–50.
72. Elkins to Benjamin Harrison, 4 Mar. 1889, Mason Papers.
73. John W. Mason to Eugene Brown, 22 May 1889, Letterbook, ibid.

74. John W. Mason to Samuel R. Steele, 11 July 1889, Letterbook, Mason to Granville W. Kern, 5 Apr. 1889, Letterbook, Mason to E. W. Walters, 18 Apr. 1889, Letterbook, Mason to Frank H. Smith, 23 Apr. 1889, Letterbook, ibid.; *Wheeling Intelligencer*, 6, 9 Apr., 15 May 1889.

75. Mason to W. H. Gilbert, 29 Mar. 1889, Letterbook, Mason Papers.

76. *Weston Republican*, 26 Apr., 7 June 1890; George A. Dunnington to Elkins, 2 June 1890, Elkins Papers.

77. John W. Mason to E. I. Allen, Letterbook, 24 June 1890, Mason to John P. Jones, 16 July 1890, Mason Papers; Francis Heermans to A. Gordon Dayton, 16 July 1890, Dayton Papers; *Wheeling Intelligencer*, 28 June 1890.

78. George C. Sturgiss to Dayton, 1 Aug. 1890, E. I. Allen to Dayton, 16 Aug. 1890, Dayton Papers; John W. Mason to Harmen, 3 Sept. 1890, Letterbook, Mason Papers; *Weston Republican*, 12 Sept. 1890.

79. *Wheeling Intelligencer*, 20 Aug. 1890.

80. Ibid., 7 Oct. 1890; G. W. B. Black to Goff, 29 Sept. [1894], Goff Papers.

81. *Wheeling Intelligencer*, 13, 18 Oct., 1 Nov. 1890.

82. Ibid., 31 Dec. 1889, 24 May, 21 Aug. 1890; *Weston Republican*, 7 June, 2 Aug. 1890.

83. *Wheeling Intelligencer*, 25 Oct. 1890.

84. Ibid., 6 Nov. 1890; C. C. Church to Elkins, 15 Nov. 1890, Elkins Papers.

85. John W. Mason to William P. Hubbard, 6 Mar. 1891, Letterbook, Mason to Goff, 21 Mar. 1891, Letterbook, Mason Papers.

86. Smith, "Nathan Goff, Jr.," p. 323.

87. *Wheeling Intelligencer*, 26 Mar. 1892.

88. Williams, "Davis and Elkins," pp. 162–63.

89. John W. Mason to Davis, 6 Aug. 1892, Letterbook, Mason Papers.

90. *Weston Republican*, 2 Apr. 1892.

91. Elkins to Albert B. White, 29 Nov. 1893, White Papers.

92. Jeff Lipscomb to Dayton, 23 July 1894, J. L. Rumbarger to Dayton, 26 July 1894, J. W. White to Dayton, 27 July 1894, J. Forsythe Harrison to Dayton, 30 July 1894, Dayton Papers.

93. F. Heermans to Dayton, 10 Aug. 1894, C. B. Kefauver to Dayton, 14 Aug. 1894, Joseph M. Shaw to Dayton, 18 Aug. 1894, William G. Conley to Dayton, 21 Aug. 1894, Jeff Lipscomb to Dayton, 22 Aug. 1894, ibid.; Sturgiss to Mason, 31 Aug. 1894, Mason Papers.

94. Thomas H. McKee to Dayton, 10 Sept. 1894, Dayton Papers.

95. Williams, "Davis and Elkins," pp. 200–202.

96. Ibid., pp. 197–98.

97. Festus P. Summers, *William L. Wilson and Tariff Reform*, p. 217.

98. Stephen B. Elkins to William E. Chandler, 25 June 1894, Chandler Papers.

99. L. K. Anderson to Dayton, 3 Oct. 1894, Dayton Papers.

100. Wilbur F. Wakeman to Dayton, 25 Oct. 1894, ibid.

101. Lewis D. Apsley to Dayton, 30 Oct. 1894, ibid.

102. I. G. Pownall to Dayton, 16 Oct. 1894, ibid.

103. Sturgiss to Dayton, 15 Sept. 1894, ibid.

104. Oscar D. Lambert, *Stephen Benton Elkins*, p. 176.

105. Elkins to John W. Mason, 27 Oct. 1894, Mason Papers; Elkins to Albert B. White, 13 Nov. 1894, White Papers; James M. Swank to Dayton, 23 Nov. 1894, Dayton Papers.

106. ICPR Election Data.

107. Lambert, *Elkins*, p. 177.

108. Elkins to Albert B. White, 1, 17 Dec. 1894, White Papers.

109. Elkins to Albert B. White, 17 Dec. 1894, ibid.; Elkins to John W. Mason, 18 Dec. 1894, Mason Papers.

110. C. D. Elliott to A. Gordon Dayton, 5 Sept. 1895, Dayton Papers.

111. E. I. Allen to A. Gordon Dayton, 14 Nov. 1895, ibid.

112. Grant Pitzer to A. Gordon Dayton, 23 Oct. 1895, ibid.
113. Elkins to Albert B. White, 10 Apr. 1896, Warren Miller to White, 22 Jan. 1896, C. D. Elliott to White, 3 Mar. 1896, White Papers.
114. Joseph P. Smith to White, 15, 25 Feb. 1896, Ibid.; White to John W. Mason, 28 Apr. 1896, Mason Papers.
115. Elkins to White, 15 Apr. 1896, White Papers.
116. Marcus, *Grand Old Party*, pp. 206–7.
117. Elkins to White, 5 May 1896, White Papers.
118. J. Matlick to Dayton, 5 June 1896, Dayton Papers.
119. Elkins to Albert B. White, 3 Aug. 1896, White Papers.
120. A. M. Babb to A. Gordon Dayton, 25 Aug. 1896, Dayton Papers.
121. A. B. Smith to A. Gordon Dayton, 27 Aug. 1896, William M. O. Dawson to Dayton, 28 Aug. 1896, ibid.
122. Davis to A. Gordon Dayton, 11 Sept. 1896, ibid.
123. William M. O. Dawson to Stephen B. Elkins, 31 July 1896, Elkins Papers.
124. Barbara A. Ferrell, "West Virginia and the Election of 1896," p. 56.
125. Ibid., p. 29.
126. ICPR Election Data.
127. J. A. Fickinger to A. Gordon Dayton, 20 Nov. 1896, Robert W. Cassady to Dayton, 5 Oct. 1896, Dayton Papers.
128. Williams, "Davis and Elkins," pp. 229–30.
129. *Winston Union Republican*, 13 June 1889.
130. *Statesville Landmark*, 20 Feb. 1890.
131. John W. Mason to A. H. Brooks, 29 Nov. 1889, Letterbook, Mason Papers.
132. *Winston Union Republican*, 28 Aug. 1890.
133. Ibid., 11 Sept. 1890.
134. *Asheville Citizen*, 24 Oct. 1890.
135. *Winston Union Republican*, 8 Jan. 1891; *Statesville Landmark*, 12 Feb. 1891; *Asheville Citizen*, 29 Jan. 1891.
136. *Winston Union Republican*, 4, 11 June 1891.
137. *Asheville Citizen*, 11 June 1891; M. D. Kimbrough to Thomas Settle, III, 8 June 1891, Settle Papers.
138. *Winston Union Republican*, 11 June 1891.
139. *Statesville Landmark*, 30 July 1891.
140. Pritchard and F. T. Walser to Thomas Settle, III, 18 Aug. 1891, Settle Papers; *Winston Union Republican*, 30 July 1891.
141. *Winston Union Republican*, 17 Sept. 1891.
142. Ibid., 3 Dec. 1891.
143. *Statesville Landmark*, 28 July 1892; Joseph F. Steelman, "Vicissitudes of Republican Party Politics," p. 432.
144. *Statesville Landmark*, 11 Aug. 1892; S. A. White to Thomas Settle, III, 13 Aug. 1892, Settle Papers.
145. *Winston Union Republican*, 21, 28 Apr. 1892.
146. Steelman, "Vicissitudes," p. 434.
147. *Asheville Citizen*, 11 Aug. 1892.
148. Ibid., 15 Sept., 13 Oct. 1892.
149. Ibid., 20 Oct. 1892.
150. Helen G. Edmonds, *The Negro and Fusion Politics in North Carolina*, p. 26.
151. C. C. Cheek to Thomas Settle, III, 27 Oct. 1892, Settle Papers; *Statesville Landmark*, 3 Nov. 1892.
152. ICPR Election Data.
153. Butler to Thomas Settle, III, 24 Apr. 1893, Settle Papers.

154. Philip Walter to Settle, 8 Sept., 4 Nov. 1892, W. A. Albright to Settle, 27 July 1892, Archibald Brady to Settle, 16 July 1892, ibid.; B. N. Duke to Settle, 13 Sept. 1892, Letterbook No. 5023, p. 304, Settle to Duke, 27 Oct. 1893, Duke Papers.
155. Butler to Pearson, 19 Feb. 1894, Pearson Papers; *Asheville Citizen*, 22 Mar. 1894.
156. Eaves to Richmond Pearson, 3 Mar., 10 Apr. 1894, Pearson Papers; *Statesville Landmark*, 21 June 1894.
157. *Winston Union Republican*, 7 Apr. 1894.
158. Olds, Circular Letter, [Apr. 1894], Settle Papers.
159. All the surviving letters are found in the April, May, and June 1894 folders in the Settle Papers.
160. Pearson to A. D. K. Wallace, 1 June 1894, Pearson Papers.
161. Butler to Pearson, 12 June 1894, ibid.
162. *Asheville Citizen*, 6, 13 Sept., 11 Oct. 1894.
163. Marion Butler to Richmond Pearson, 26 June 1894, Pearson Papers.
164. Hiram L. Grant, Circular Letter, 12 July 1894, Settle Papers.
165. *Winston Union Republican*, 2 Aug. 1894.
166. Edmonds, *Fusion Politics*, p. 35.
167. W. A. Albright to Thomas Settle, III, 2 Aug. 1894, Settle Papers.
168. Joseph F. Steelman, "Republican Party Strategists and the Issue of Fusion with Populists in North Carolina, 1893-1894" pp. 263-64; *Winston Union Republican*, 6 Sept. 1894.
169. Edmonds, *Fusion Politics*, p. 37.
170. *Winston Union Republican*, 17 Jan. 1895.
171. Ibid., 22 Aug. 1895.
172. McKinley to Pearson, 12 Sept. 1895, Pearson Papers.
173. Settle to James S. Clarkson, 16 Apr. 1896, Clarkson to Settle, 18 Apr. 1896, Settle Papers.
174. Thomas Settle, III, to Benjamin N. Duke, 12 Jan. 1896, Duke Papers.
175. Frank W. Leach to Thomas Settle, III, 1 Feb. 1896, Archibald Brady to Settle, 7 Apr. 1896, Settle Papers; Jeter C. Pritchard to James H. Ramsay, 27 Feb. 1896, Ramsay Papers; *Statesville Landmark*, 17 Mar. 1896; *Winston Union Republican*, 9 Apr. 1896.
176. *Statesville Landmark*, 19 May 1896.
177. W. F. Everett to Thomas Settle, III, 24 Apr. 1896, Settle Papers; J. T. Sharp to Daniel L. Russell, 9 May 1896, Russell Papers.
178. *Winston Union Republican*, 21 May 1896.
179. Convention tally sheet, 14 May 1892, Settle Papers; *Statesville Landmark*, 19 June 1896.
180. M. N. Corbett to Thomas Settle, III, 27 May 1896, "To the People of North Carolina," 6 June 1896, J. W. Hardin to Settle, 8 July 1896, Settle Papers.
181. *Winston Union Republican*, 13 Feb., 9, 21 Apr. 1896.
182. Butler to J. A. Sims, 17 Feb. 1896, Butler Papers.
183. W. H. Kitchin to Butler, 5 June 1896, ibid.
184. Pritchard to William E. Chandler, 9, 22 July 1896, Chandler Papers.
185. Guthrie to Marion Butler, 16 Oct. 1896, Butler Papers; *Winston Union Republican*, 29 Oct. 1896.
186. ICPR Election Data. In 1888 the Republican share of the congressional vote was 46.6% and in 1896 it was 47.7%.
187. *London Mountain Echo*, 5 Apr. 1889.
188. *Big Sandy News*, 27 June 1889; Clipping, 9 May 1889, Scrapbook, Willson Papers.
189. John W. Mason to Goodloe, 7 Oct. 1889, Letterbook, Mason Papers.
190. Hambleton Tapp, "Three Decades of Kentucky Politics, 1870-1900," p. 289.
191. *Big Sandy News*, 6 June 1889.

192. Ibid., 11 July 1889.
193. *London Mountain Echo*, 8 Aug. 1889.
194. John W. Mason to A. L. Burnham, 6 June 1890, Letterbook, Mason Papers.
195. *London Mountain Echo*, 30 May, 13 June 1890.
196. *Louisville Courier-Journal*, 2, 21, 25 Sept. 1890.
197. Ibid., 1, 4 Oct. 1890.
198. *London Mountain Echo*, 22 May 1891.
199. *Louisville Courier-Journal*, 8 May 1891.
200. Ibid., 11, 15, 21 May 1891.
201. *London Mountain Echo*, 22 May 1891.
202. Clipping, 21 May 1891, Scrapbook, Colson Papers.
203. *Louisville Courier-Journal*, 23 May 1891.
204. *Hazel Green Herald*, 5 June 1891; *Williamsburgh Times*, 19 June, 31 July 1891.
205. *London Mountain Echo*, 29 May 1891; *Hazel Green Herald*, 19 June 1891.
206. *Hazel Green Herald*, 18 Sept. 1891; Rhea A. Taylor, "Conflicts in Kentucky as Shown by the Constitutional Convention of 1890–91," p. 276.
207. John W. Mason to Bradley, 4 Mar. 1891, Mason Papers.
208. *Hazel Green Herald*, 27 Nov. 1891; *Mountain Echo*, 17 Nov. 1891.
209. *Middlesboro News*, 20 Feb., 2 Apr., 11 June, 30 July 1892.
210. Ibid., 2 Apr. 1892.
211. Ibid., 4 June 1892.
212. Ibid., 7 May 1892.
213. *Williamsburgh Times*, 13 July 1892.
214. *Middlesboro News*, 25 July, 30 July 1892.
215. Ibid., 20 Aug. 1892; *London Mountain Echo*, 19, 25 Aug. 1892.
216. *Williamsburgh Times*, 21 Sept. 1892; *Louisville Courier-Journal*, 2 Sept. 1892.
217. *Louisville Courier-Journal*, 10 Sept. 1892.
218. *Middlesboro News*, 3 Sept. 1892; *Louisville Courier-Journal*, 6 Sept. 1892.
219. *London Mountain Echo*, 16 Sept. 1892.
220. *Louisville Courier-Journal*, 16 Sept. 1892.
221. *Williamsburgh Times*, 5 Oct. 1892.
222. *Big Sandy News*, 21 Oct. 1892; *Hazel Green Herald*, 28 Oct. 1892.
223. *Middlesboro News*, 4 Aug. 1894.
224. Ibid., 10, 31 Mar., 11 Aug. 1894; *Louisville Commercial*, 17 Aug. 1894.
225. *Middlesboro News*, 4 Aug. 1894.
226. Ibid., 7 July 1894; *Hazel Green Herald*, 30 Aug. 1894.
227. Colson, Circular Letter, 12 Sept. 1894, Scrapbook, Colson Papers.
228. *Louisville Commercial*, 28 Sept. 1894.
229. *Middlesboro News*, 6 Oct. 1894.
230. Ibid., 6, 13 Oct. 1894; *Louisville Courier-Journal*, 5 Oct. 1894.
231. A. R. Dyche et al., Circular Letter, [Oct. 1894], Scrapbook, Colson Papers.
232. *Louisville Courier-Journal*, 17, 20 Oct. 1894.
233. "Stand By Your Ticket," [Oct. 1894], Scrapbook, Colson Papers.
234. ICPR Election Data.
235. *Louisville Commercial*, 8 Nov. 1894.
236. *Big Stone Gap Post*, 12 Sept. 1894; *Middlesboro News*, 21 Sept., 12 Oct., 2 Nov. 1895; *London Mountain Echo*, 4 Oct. 1895; Clipping, 3 Oct. 1895, Scrapbook, Bradley Papers.
237. *London Mountain Echo*, 22 Nov. 1895.
238. Ibid., 17 Apr. 1896.
239. *Louisville Courier-Journal*, 15 Apr. 1896.
240. *London Mountain Echo*, 12 July 1896.
241. Ibid., 3 July 1896.
242. *Hazel Green Herald*, 30 July 1896.

243. *London Mountain Echo*, 14, 21 Aug. 1896.
244. Ibid., 28 Aug. 1896.
245. Ibid., 9, 23 Oct. 1896.
246. Full returns are not available; these statistics were determined from the votes of eleven of the district's seventeen counties. *Louisville Courier-Journal*, 4, 5 Nov. 1896.
247. *Wytheville Dispatch*, 9 May 1890.
248. *Roanoke Times*, 17 July 1890.
249. Robert H. Walker to Mahone, 12, 27 Sept., 30 Oct., 2 Nov. 1890, Mahone Papers.
250. Slemp to Mahone, 14 July 1890, ibid.
251. *Big Stone Gap Post*, 22 Aug., 19 Sept. 1890.
252. "To the Rep. of the First, Second and Ninth Congressional Districts," 20 Oct. 1890, Mahone Papers.
253. *Wytheville Dispatch*, 26 Sept., 3 Oct. 1890.
254. Ibid., 10 Oct. 1890.
255. *Abingdon Virginian*, 4 Sept. 1890; *Roanoke Times*, 16 Sept. 1890.
256. *Big Stone Gap Post*, 26 Sept. 1890.
257. *Roanoke Times*, 25 Oct. 1890.
258. R. O. Halsey to C. H. Pierson, 17 Apr. 1891, "Minutes of the Old Hickory Alliance," 17 Aug. 1891, Pierson Papers.
259. *Wytheville Dispatch*, 14 Aug. 1891.
260. Ibid., 9 Oct. 1891; G. M. Zirkle to Mahone, 1 Oct. 1891, Mahone papers; *Big Stone Gap Post*, 23 Oct. 1891.
261. *Roanoke Times*, 6 May 1892; Donald M. Dozer, "Benjamin Harrison and the Presidential Campaign in 1892," p. 55.
262. William E. Craig to Mahone, 1 Nov. 1892, Mahone Papers.
263. H. J. Wale to Mahone, 27 June 1893, ibid.
264. *Wytheville Dispatch*, 18 Aug. 1893.
265. *Roanoke Times*, 14 Sept. 1893.
266. W. A. Jamieson to Mahone, 16 Dec. 1893, Mahone Papers.
267. *Wytheville Dispatch*, 19 Jan. 1894.
268. William C. Pendleton, *Political History of Appalachian Virginia, 1776–1927*, p. 375.
269. *Wytheville Dispatch*, 15 June 1894.
270. *Big Stone Gap Post*, 31 May 1894; *Roanoke Times*, 11 Aug. 1894.
271. *Wytheville Dispatch*, 10, 17, 24 Aug. 1894.
272. *Roanoke Times*, 25 Oct. 1890, 11 Aug. 1893; *Big Stone Gap Post*, 10 Oct. 1895.
273. *Big Stone Gap Post*, 6 Sept. 1894.
274. *Wytheville Dispatch*, 21 Sept. 1894; *Abingdon Virginian*, 5 Oct. 1894.
275. *Big Stone Gap Post*, 6 Sept. 1894; *Wytheville Dispatch*, 19 Oct. 1894.
276. *Big Stone Gap Post*, 27 Sept., 18 Oct. 1894.
277. *Wytheville Dispatch*, 26 Oct. 1894.
278. Ibid., 7 Sept. 1894.
279. Hobson to Mahone, 3 Jan., 3 June 1895, Mahone Papers.
280. Mahone, Circular Letter, 15 June 1895, Hobson to Mahone, 26 June 1895, ibid.; William D. Sheldon, *Populism in the Old Dominion*, p. 111.
281. J. Hampton Hoge to Mahone, 16 July 1895, R. T. Thorp to Mahone, 22 Aug. 1895, Mahone Papers; *Big Stone Gap Post*, 3 Oct. 1895.
282. *Big Stone Gap Post*, 24 Oct., 26 Dec. 1895.
283. Clipping, 29 Oct. [1895], Scrapbook, Brady Papers; *Big Stone Gap Post*, 30 Apr. 1896.
284. Sheldon, *Populism*, pp. 135–36.
285. *Abingdon Virginian*, 3 July 1896; *Big Stone Gap Post*, 23 July, 6 Aug. 1896; Pendleton, *Political History of Appalachian Virginia*, p. 392.
286. *Big Stone Gap Post*, 1, 15 Oct., 5 Nov. 1896.
287. Clipping, 26 Nov. 1896, Scrapbook, Brady Papers; *Abingdon Virginian*, 4, 11 Dec. 1896.

CHAPTER 9

1. For examples, see *Maryville Times*, 16 Jan. 1897; *Statesville Landmark*, 14 Dec. 1897; *Clinton Gazette*, 22 Dec. 1897; *Jonesboro Herald and Tribune*, 15 Jan. 1898; *Big Stone Gap Post*, 18 Aug. 1898; John D. Fulton to Albert B. White, 7 Feb. 1900, White Papers.

2. Elijah W. Halford to Evans, 4 July 1892, Scrapbook, vol. 48, Evans Papers; Houk to George W. Winstead, 8 July 1892, Houk Papers.

3. Walter P. Brownlow to Cal Reeves, Aug. 1893, Brownlow Papers.

4. John B. Brownlow to Oliver P. Temple, 13 Nov. 1892, Temple Papers.

5. Brownlow to U. S. Gray, 11 Sept. 1893, Brownlow Papers; *Jonesboro Herald and Tribune*, 13 Dec. 1893, 31 Jan. 1894.

6. *Johnson City Comet*, 18 Jan. 1894.

7. Ibid., 8 Feb., 15 Mar. 1894; *Chattanooga Times*, 10 Mar. 1894; *Jonesboro Herald and Tribune*, 14 Mar. 1894.

8. *Jonesboro Herald and Tribune*, 12 Feb., 4 Mar., 1, 29 Apr. 1896.

9. Robert D. Marcus, *Grand Old Party*, pp. 202–28.

10. *Maryville Times*, 24 July 1897; *Rockwood Times-Republican*, 4 Nov. 1897; John C. Houk to the editor of the Washington *American*, [1897], Houk Papers; *Johnson City Comet*, 14 Apr. 1898.

11. Rufus Terral, *Newall Sanders*, pp. 79–81.

12. *Rockwood Times-Republican*, 1 June 1899; *Maryville Times*, 22 July 1899; T. H. Baker to Evans, 1 Nov. 1899, Sanders Papers.

13. D. E. Sickles to Evans, 17 June 1899, Scrapbook, vol. 51, Evans Papers; *Clinton Gazette*, 9, 23 Aug. 1899.

14. Russell A. Alger to Evans, 26 Apr. 1900, Scrapbook, vol. 48, Evans Papers; *Maryville Times*, 28 Apr. 1900; *Clinton Gazette*, 28 Apr. 1900; Verton M. Queener, "The Origin of the Republican Party in East Tennessee," pp. 237–40.

15. *Maryville Times*, 28 Apr., 23 June 1900.

16. Ibid., 25 Aug. 1900; *Rockwood Times-Republican*, 4 July 1900.

17. *Clinton Gazette*, 8 Sept. 1900.

18. *Hazel Green Herald*, 11 Mar. 1897; *Pineville Bell County Citizen*, 7 Oct. 1897.

19. *Big Stone Gap Post*, 9 Sept. 1898, 3 Mar. 1898; *Middlesboro Weekly Herald*, 15 Oct. 1897.

20. *Big Sandy News*, 1 Apr. 1898; *London Mountain Echo*, 10 June 1898; *Middlesboro Record*, 29 Jan., 24 June 1898; *Louisville Courier-Journal*, 9 Aug. 1898.

21. *London Mountain Echo*, 3, 23 June 1898; *Louisville Courier-Journal*, 23 July 1898.

22. *London Mountain Echo*, 30 Sept., 4 Nov. 1898.

23. Ibid., 3 May, 4 Nov. 1898.

24. Ibid., 9 Dec. 1898; *Louisville Courier-Journal*, 3 Nov. 1898; *Hazel Green Herald*, 8 Dec. 1898; *Middlesboro News*, 10 Feb. 1900.

25. *London Mountain Echo*, 20 Oct. 1899; *Middlesboro News*, 10 Feb., 24 Mar. 1900.

26. *Hazel Green Herald*, 18 Jan. 1900; *Middlesboro Record*, 19 Jan. 1900.

27. *London Mountain Echo*, 31 Aug. 1900.

28. *Middlesboro News*, 28 July 1900.

29. *Abingdon Virginian*, 8 July 1897; *Wytheville Dispatch*, 24 Sept. 1897; William C. Pendleton, *Political History of Appalachian Virginia, 1776–1927*, pp. 398–400.

30. *Big Stone Gap Post*, 9 Sept., 14 Oct. 1897; *Wytheville Dispatch*, 1, 8, 15 Oct., 10 Dec., 1897; Pendleton, *Political History of Appalachian Virginia*, p. 399.

31. *Big Stone Gap Post*, 4 Aug. 1898, 16 Aug. 1900.

32. Ibid., 18 Aug., 1, 22 Sept., 6 Oct. 1898; *Wytheville Dispatch*, 2 Sept., 6 Oct. 1898; Pendleton, *Political History of Appalachian Virginia*, pp. 407, 425.

33. Laura Keene Gleaves to Mrs. Willie Caldwell, [Mar. 1899], S. E. Goodell to editor of *Washington Post*, 10 June 1899, Mrs. Willie Caldwell, "Biography of James A. Walker" (unpublished manuscript), pp. 355–64, Walker Papers.

34. *Big Stone Gap Post*, 17 Nov. 1898, 16 Feb., 16 Mar. 1899; *Clinton Gazette*, 15 Mar. 1899;

Abingdon Virginian, 20 July 1899; Pendleton, *Political History of Appalachian Virginia*, pp. 409–10.

35. *Big Stone Gap Post*, 19 Apr. 1900; Pendleton, *Political History of Appalachian Virginia*, pp. 440, 443; Raymond H. Pulley, *Old Virginia Restored*, pp. 74–75.

36. Clipping, 1 Aug. 1900, Hubard Papers; Walker to H. Clay Evans, 28 Sept. 1900, Scrapbook, vol. 51, Evans Papers; *Big Stone Gap Post*, 11 Oct. 1900; *Bristol News*, 16 Oct. 1900; Pendleton, *Political History of Appalachian Virginia*, p. 424.

37. *Statesville Landmark*, 4 Dec. 1896.

38. Mott to Butler, 10, 24 Nov. 1896, Dockery to Butler, 26 Nov. 1896, Butler Papers; A. H. Paddason to Russell, 30 Nov. 1896, Russell Papers.

39. Richmond Pearson to William E. Chandler, 9 Nov. 1896, Chandler Papers; Pritchard to G. Z. French, 28 Nov. 1896, Russell Papers; *Winston Union Republican*, 21 Jan. 1897; Rosalie F. McNeill, "The First Fifteen Months of Governor Daniel Lindsay Russell's Administration," p. 31.

40. *Asheville Citizen*, 20 Sept., 3 Nov. 1898; *Statesville Landmark*, 14, 28 Oct. 1898.

41. *Asheville Citizen*, 20 May 1898; Cyrus Thompson to Pearson, A. E. Holton to Pearson, 9 Sept. 1898, Pearson Papers.

42. *Asheville Citizen*, 8, 11 Feb., 4 Aug. 1898; *Winston Union Republican*, 13, 20, 27 Oct. 1898.

43. *Statesville Landmark*, 21 Feb. 1899.

44. Ibid., 9 June 1899; *Asheville Register*, 11 Aug., 8 Sept. 1899.

45. *Statesville Landmark*, 23 Jan. 1900; Helen G. Edmonds, *The Negro and Fusion Politics in North Carolina*, p. 204.

46. *Statesville Landmark*, 9 Mar. 1900.

47. Atkinson to White, 19 Nov. 1896, White to Warren Miller, 21 Dec. 1896, Nathan B. Scott to White, 26 Feb. 1897, White Papers.

48. Elkins to White, 10 June 1897, ibid.

49. Elkins to White, 20 June 1897, ibid.

50. Albert B. White to Mason, 14, 20 Jan. 1898, Elkins to Mason, 15 Feb. 1898, Mason Papers; Mason to White, 15 Jan. 1898, Elkins to White, 26 Feb. 1898, White Papers.

51. Goff to Albert B. White, 4 June 1898, White Papers.

52. Scott to White, 4, 7 June, 29 July, 8 Aug., 31 Oct. 1898, Elkins to White, 5 Oct. 1898, ibid.; Marcus A. Hanna to Elkins, 21 Oct. 1898, Elkins Papers.

53. Scott to White, 8 July 1898, Elkins to White, 14, 18 July 1898, White Papers; John A. Williams, "Davis and Elkins of West Virginia," pp. 234–35.

54. Scott to White, 8 Aug. 1898, White Papers.

55. Elkins to White, 3 July 1899, ibid.

56. Atkinson to John W. Mason, 30 Oct., 6 Dec. 1899, Mason Papers; *Wheeling Intelligencer*, 6 Dec. 1899, 16 Jan. 1900.

57. White to Elkins, 2 May 1898, C. C. Payne to Elkins, 10 Mar. 1900, T. F. Latham to Elkins, 19 Mar. 1900, Elkins Papers.

58. James J. Peterson, Statement, 9 Dec. 1899, L. A. Fraser, Statement, 9 Dec. 1899, Fraser to White, 8 Jan. 1900, S. C. Harless to White, 1 Jan. 1900, White Papers; *Wheeling Intelligencer*, 25 Dec. 1899.

59. *Wheeling Intelligencer*, 23 Jan., 9, 27 Feb. 1900.

60. White to Elkins, 5 Feb., 4 Mar. 1900, C. D. Elliott to Elkins, 12 Mar. 1900, Elkins Papers.

61. Freer to John W. Mason, 25 Mar. 1900, Mason Papers; Harry H. McIntire to White, 26 Mar. 1900, Elkins to White, 27 Mar. 1900, White Papers; Atkinson to Elkins, 28 Mar. 1900, Elkins Papers; *Wheeling Intelligencer*, 20 Feb., 6, 8, 23, 24, 26 Mar. 1900.

62. *Hazel Green Herald*, 2, 16, 23 Sept, 7, 21, 28 Oct. 1897.

63. J. Fred Rippy, ed., *F. M. Simmons, Statesman of the New South*, p. 26.

64. Ibid., pp. 24–25; *Asheville Citizen*, 26 Aug. 1898.

65. *Asheville Citizen*, 20 Sept. 1898; *Statesville Landmark*, 4 Oct. 1898.

66. This is particularly well documented for 1881 in the Mahone Papers. C. G. Hedwison to Mahone, 10 Oct. 1881, Frank L. Slade to Mahone, 19 Oct. 1881, James D. Brady to Mahone, 19 Oct. 1881, Mahone Papers.

67. J. Morgan Kousser, *The Shaping of Southern Politics*, p. 172.

68. C. M. Gibbens to William Mahone, 14 Mar. 1894, Mahone Papers.

69. Charles E. Wynes, *Race Relations in Virginia, 1870–1902*, pp. 55, 58; Kousser, *Southern Politics*, pp. 174–78.

70. Kousser, *Southern Politics*, pp. 78–79.

71. Ibid., pp. 109–19.

72. *Clinton Gazette*, 3, 10 Oct. 1889.

73. *Chattanooga Republican*, 13 Oct. 1889.

74. Kousser feels that the secret ballot provision was the most decisive part of the Tennessee legislation; however, the Republican success in 1889 with secret ballots and no poll tax and Republican defeats in Chattanooga in 1890 and after with secret ballots and a poll tax argues against his conclusion. For Knoxville vote totals, see the *Knoxville Journal*, 9 Nov. 1888, 8 Nov. 1900.

75. "Read and Sound the Alarm," 5 Aug. 1897, Houk Papers; *Maryville Times*, 10, 17 July 1897; *Clinton Gazette*, 22 July, 5, 12 Aug. 1897.

76. Nicholas C. Burckel, "William Goebel and the Campaign for Railroad Regulation in Kentucky, 1888–1900," pp. 48–49.

77. *Hazel Green Herald*, 24 Feb. 1898; *London Mountain Echo*, 5 May 1900.

78. *Hazel Green Herald*, 1, 8 Dec. 1898.

79. *Louisville Courier-Journal*, 23–30 June, 3, 17 Aug. 1899.

80. Burckel, "Goebel and Railroad Regulation," p. 49; *Hazel Green Herald*, 14 Sept. 1899.

81. *Louisville Courier-Journal*, 2 Sept., 28 Oct. 1899.

82. W. T. Ellis to John M. Harlan, 14 Dec. 1899, Harlan Papers (UL).

83. Thomas D. Clark, "The People, William Goebel, and the Kentucky Railroads," pp. 45–46.

84. *Hazel Green Herald*, 16 Aug. 1900.

85. For details, see Pendleton, *Political History of Appalachian Virginia*; Guy B. Hathorn, "The Political Career of C. Bascom Slemp."

86. Joseph F. Steelman, "The Progressive Era in North Carolina, 1884–1917"; David C. Roller, "The Republican Party of North Carolina."

87. Ben W. Hooper, *The Unwanted Boy*, pp. 33–49.

88. Glenn Finch, "The Election of United States Senators in Kentucky," pp. 38–50; Thomas D. Clark, *Kentucky*.

89. John A. Williams, *West Virginia*.

APPENDIX

1. All statistics are from the data bank at the Inter-University Consortium for Political Research (ICPR) unless otherwise noted.

2. *Hazel Green Herald*, 25 June 1896.

3. Hubert M. Blalock, *Social Statistics*, pp. 273–325.

4. David E. Harrell, "The Disciples of Christ and Social Forces in Tennessee, 1865–1900," pp. 30–47.

5. The statistics concerning Union volunteering were computed from State of Kentucky, General Assembly, "Legislative Document No. 26," and ICPR 1860 population data.

6. The voting returns for 1860, 1864, and 1867 are found in *Louisville Journal*, 30 Aug. 1867.

7. The voting returns for 1868 are found in Ruth McQuown and Jasper B. Shannon, *Presidential Politics in Kentucky, 1824–1948*, pp. 42–44.

8. Paul T. David, *Party Strength in the United States, 1872–1970*, pp. 30, 44, 296.

9. Kenneth R. Bailey, "A Judicious Mixture," pp. 142–47; *Roanoke Times*, 8 July 1890; *Wytheville Dispatch*, 3 Oct. 1890; *Middlesboro News*, 9 Apr. 1892.

10. Fred B. Lee to John C. Houk, 21 Jan. 1892, Houk Papers; *Wheeling Intelligencer*, 19 Apr. 1892; *Clinton Gazette*, 22 June 1893.

11. *Chattanooga Times*, 1 Apr. 1894; *Louisville Courier-Journal*, 2 Oct. 1894; James Boyle to H. Clay Evans, 21 Apr. 1896, Evans Papers.

12. "The Republican Campaign of Kentucky, 1895," Todd Papers; *Louisville Courier-Journal*, 5 Apr. 1896.

13. Paul Kleppner, *The Cross of Culture*, pp. 338–68; Richard Jensen, *The Winning of the Midwest*, pp. 269–87.

14. *Hazel Green Herald*, 23 Sept. 1885.

15. *Big Stone Gap Post*, 27 Sept. 1894.

16. Ibid., 23 Apr. 1896.

17. Joe Foute to John C. Houk, 7 Nov. 1896, Houk Papers.

SELECTED BIBLIOGRAPHY

I. MANUSCRIPTS

Frances Yates Aglionby Papers, Duke University Library.
American Political Broadsides Collection, Duke University Library.
James Denis Brady Papers, University of Virginia Library.
William O'Connell Bradley Papers, University of Kentucky Library.
Benjamin Helm Bristow Papers, Library of Congress.
Benjamin Helm Bristow Papers, University of Kentucky Library.
Walter Preston Brownlow Papers, Lawson McGhee Library, Knoxville, Tennessee.
Marion Butler Papers, Southern Historical Collection, University of North Carolina Library.
Tod Robinson Caldwell Papers, Southern Historical Collection, University of North Carolina Library.
David Miller Carter Papers, Southern Historical Collection, University of North Carolina Library.
William Eaton Chandler Papers, New Hampshire Historical Society, Concord, N.H.
David Grant Colson Papers, Southern Historical Collection, University of North Carolina Library.
Talton L. L. Cox Papers, Duke University Library.
Alston Gordon Dayton Papers, West Virginia University Library.
Benjamin Newton Duke Papers, Duke University Library.
James Adams Ekin Papers, Duke University Library.
Stephen Benton Elkins Papers, West Virginia University Library.
Henry Clay Evans Papers, Chattanooga Public Library.
Aretas Brooks Fleming Papers, West Virginia University Library.
William Henry Harrison Flick Papers, West Virginia University Library.
George Nathaniel Folk Papers, Southern Historical Collection, University of North Carolina Library.
Andrew Jackson Gahagan and Jesse Dugger Gahagan Papers, Chattanooga Public Library.
Nathan Goff, Jr., Papers, University of West Virginia Library.
John Marshall Harlan Papers, Filson Club Library, Louisville, Kentucky.

John Marshall Harlan Papers, Law Library, University of Louisville.
Benjamin Sherwood Hedrick Papers, Duke University Library.
William Woods Holden Papers, Duke University Library.
Leonidas Campbell Houk and John Chiles Houk Papers, Lawson McGhee Library, Knoxville, Tennessee.
Robert Thruston Hubard Papers, University of Virginia Library.
J. Granville Leach Papers, North Carolina Department of Art, Culture, and History, Raleigh, North Carolina.
Thomas Lenoir Papers, Duke University Library.
Lindsay Family Papers, University of Kentucky Library.
Daniel Weisiger Lindsey Papers, Filson Club Library, Louisville, Kentucky.
Virgil S. Lusk Papers, North Carolina Department of Art, Culture, and History, Raleigh, North Carolina.
McGill-Mahone Papers, University of Virginia Library.
Will A. McTeer Papers, Lawson McGhee Library, Knoxville, Tennessee.
William Mahone Papers, Duke University Library.
John W. Mason Papers, West Virginia University Library.
Thomas Amos Rogers Nelson Papers, Lawson McGhee Library, Knoxville, Tennessee.
Richmond Pearson Papers, Southern Historical Collection, University of North Carolina Library.
Francis Harrison Pierpont Papers, Duke University Library.
Francis Harrison Pierpont Papers, West Virginia University Library.
Charles Herbert Pierson Papers, University of Virginia Library.
James Graham Ramsay Papers, Southern Historical Collection, University of North Carolina Library.
Harrison Holt Riddleberger Papers, College of William and Mary Library.
William Rule Papers, Lawson McGhee Library, Knoxville, Tennessee.
Daniel Lindsay Russell Papers, Southern Historical Collection, University of North Carolina Library.
Newell Sanders Papers, Chattanooga Public Library.
William Lafayette Scott Papers, Duke University Library.
Thomas Settle, Jr., and Thomas Settle, III, Papers, Southern Historical Collection, University of North Carolina Library.
William E. Stevenson Papers, West Virginia State Department of Archives and History, Charleston, West Virginia.
Oliver Perry Temple Papers, University of Tennessee Library.
Sarah E. Thompson Papers, Duke University Library.
George Davidson Todd Papers, Filson Club Library, Louisville, Kentucky.
Harry Inness Todd Papers, Filson Club Library, Louisville, Kentucky.
Harry Inness Todd Papers, Kentucky Historical Society, Frankfurt, Kentucky.
Bryan Tyson Papers, Duke University Library.
James Alexander Walker Papers, Southern Historical Collection, University of North Carolina Library.
Albert Blakeslee White Papers, West Virginia University Library.

Waitman Thomas Willey Papers, West Virginia University Library.
Augustus Everett Willson Papers, Filson Club Library, Louisville, Kentucky.

II. GOVERNMENT DOCUMENTS AND STATISTICAL SOURCES

Appleton's Annual Cyclopedia, 1876–1901.
Cincinnati Enquirer Manual and Political Register for 1870.
Congressional Globe, 1861–1872.
Congressional Record, 1873–1900.

Inter-University Consortium for Political Research, Ann Arbor, Michigan.
  Election Data
  Presidential Elections: 1876, 1880, 1884, 1888, 1892, 1896, 1900
    Kentucky
    North Carolina
    Tennessee
    Virginia
    West Virginia
  Congressional Elections: 1876, 1878, 1880, 1882, 1884, 1886, 1888, 1890, 1892, 1894, 1896, 1898, 1900
    Kentucky
    North Carolina
    Tennessee
    Virginia
    West Virginia
  Gubernatorial Elections
    Kentucky—1879, 1883, 1887, 1891, 1895, 1899, 1900
    North Carolina—1876, 1880, 1884, 1888, 1892, 1896, 1900
    Tennessee—1876, 1878, 1880, 1882, 1884, 1886, 1888, 1890, 1892, 1894, 1896, 1898, 1900
    Virginia—1877, 1881, 1885, 1889, 1893, 1897
    West Virginia—1876, 1880, 1884, 1388, 1892, 1896, 1900
  Census Data
    Population—1860, 1870, 1880, 1890, 1900
    Agriculture—1870, 1880, 1890, 1900
    Manufacturing—1870, 1880, 1890, 1900
    Religion—1890

(New York) *Tribune Almanac and Political Register*, 1869–1876.
State of Kentucky. General Assembly. "Legislative Document No. 26: Annual Report of the Adjutant General," *Kentucky Documents, 1863–1864*. Frankfort, 1864.
State of Tennessee. General Assembly. Minority Report of General Committee of Investigation, Contest for Governor, Peter Turney, Contestant vs. H. Clay Evans, Contestee.
———. *Journal of the Convention of Delegates to Make a New Constitution*. Nashville: Jones, Purvis and Co., 1870.

U.S., Bureau of the Census. *Ninth Census of the United States, 1870*. Washington, D.C.: Government Printing Office, 1872.

_____. *Tenth Census of the United States, 1880*. Washington, D.C.: Government Printing Office, 1881.

_____. *Eleventh Census of the United States, 1890*. Washington, D.C.: Government Printing Office, 1894.

_____. *Twelfth Census of the United States, 1900*. Washington, D.C.: Government Printing Office, 1901.

War of the Rebellion: A Compilation of the Offical Records of the Union and Confederate Armies. 128 vols. Washington, D.C.: Government Printing Office, 1880–1901.

III. NEWSPAPERS

Abingdon Standard
Abingdon Virginian
Asheville Advance
Asheville Citizen
Asheville News
Asheville Pioneer
Asheville Register
Asheville Skyland Herald
Asheville Western Expositor
Athens Athenian
Athens Republican
Barboursville Mountain Echo
Big Sandy News
Big Stone Gap Post
Bristol Courier
Bristol News
Bristol Republican
Buckhannon Delta
Chattanooga Republican
Chattanooga Times
Clifton Forge Review
Clinton Gazette
Danville Register
Hazel Green Herald
Johnson City Comet
Jonesboro Herald and Tribune
Knoxville Chronicle
Knoxville Chronicle
Knoxville Journal
Knoxville Press and Herald
Knoxville Republican
Knoxville Tribune
Knoxville Whig
London Mountain Echo
Louisville Commercial
Louisville Courier-Journal
Louisville Journal
Maryville Republican
Maryville Times
Memphis Weekly Appeal
Middlesboro News
Middlesboro Record
Middlesboro Weekly Herald
Mt. Vernon Signal
Nashville Amerian
New York Times
Pineville Bell County Citizen
Raleigh Standard
Richmond Dispatch
Richmond Whig
Roanoke Times
Rockwood Roane County Republican
Rockwood Times-Republican
Southern Advocate (Bristol)
Statesville American
Statesville Landmark
Weston Republican
Wheeling Intelligencer
Williamsburgh Times
Winston Union Republican
Woodstock Virginian
Wytheville Dispatch

IV. BOOKS, ARTICLES, AND UNPUBLISHED WORKS

Adams, Henry. *Democracy: An American Novel.* New York: New American Library, 1961.

Alexander, Thomas B. "Ku Kluxism in Tennessee, 1865–1869." *Tennessee Historical Quarterly* 8 (September 1949): 195–219.

———. "Persistent Whiggery in the Confederate South, 1860–1877." *Journal of Southern History* 27 (August 1961): 305–29.

———. *Political Reconstruction in Tennessee.* Nashville: Vanderbilt University Press, 1950.

———. "Political Reconstruction in Tennessee, 1865–1870." In *Radicalism, Racism, and Party Alignment: The Border States during Reconstruction,* edited by Richard O. Curry, pp. 37–79. Baltimore: Johns Hopkins University Press, 1969.

Archer, Claude J. "The Life of John Chiles Houk." Master's thesis, University of Tennessee, 1941.

Bailey, Kenneth R. "A Judicious Mixture: Negroes and Immigrants in the West Virginia Mines, 1880–1917." *West Virginia History* 34 (January 1973): 141–61.

Balk, Jacqueline, and Hoogenboom, Ari. "The Origins of Border State Liberal Republicanism." In *Radicalism, Racism, and Party Alignment: The Border States during Reconstruction,* edited by Richard O. Curry, pp. 220–44. Baltimore: Johns Hopkins University Press, 1969.

Bancroft, Frederic, ed. *The Writings of Carl Schurz.* 6 vols. New York: G. P. Putnam's Sons, 1913.

Bardolph, Richard. "Inconstant Rebels: Desertion of North Carolina Troops in the Civil War." *North Carolina Historical Review* 41 (Spring 1964): 163–89.

Barker, Adelaide A. "William O'Connell Bradley." Master's thesis, University of Kentucky, 1927.

Barrett, John G. *The Civil War in North Carolina.* Chapel Hill: University of North Carolina Press, 1963.

Basler, Roy P., ed. *The Collected Works of Abraham Lincoln.* 8 vols. New Brunswick, N.J.: Rutgers University Press, 1953.

Bayless, Robert W. "The Attitude of West Virginia Senators and Congressmen toward Reconstruction, 1863–1871." Master's thesis, West Virginia University, 1947.

Bentley, James R. "The Civil War Memories of Captain Thomas Speed." *Filson Club History Quarterly* 44 (July 1970): 235–72.

Blake, Nelson M. *William Mahone of Virginia, Soldier and Political Insurgent.* Richmond: Garrett & Massie, Publishers, 1935.

Blalock, Hubert M. *Social Statistics.* New York: McGraw-Hill Book Co., 1960.

Boeger, Palmer H. "The Great Kentucky Hog Swindle of 1864." *Journal of Southern History* 28 (February 1962): 59–70.

Boney, Francis N. *John Letcher of Virginia: The Story of Virginia's Civil War Governor.* Tuscaloosa: University of Alabama Press, 1966.

Boyd, William K., ed. *Memoirs of W. W. Holden.* Durham, N.C.: Trinity College Historical Society, 1911.

Bradley, William O. *Stories and Speeches of William O. Bradley*. Compiled by M. H. Thatcher. Lexington, Ky.: Transylvania Printing Co., 1916.

Brock, W. R. *An American Crisis: Congress and Reconstruction, 1865–1867*. New York: Harper & Row, Publishers, 1963.

Brownlow, William G. *Sketches of the Rise, Progress, and Decline of Secession*. New York: Decapo Press, 1968.

Burckel, Nicholas C. "William Goebel and the Campaign for Railroad Regulation in Kentucky, 1888–1900." *Filson Club History Quarterly* 48 (January 1974): 43–61.

Burnham, W. Dean. "The Changing Shape of the American Political Universe." In *Voters, Parties, and Elections: Quantitative Essays in the History of American Popular Voting Behavior*, edited by Joel H. Silbey and Samuel T. McSeveney. Lexington, Mass.: Xerox College Publishing, 1972.

──────. *Presidential Ballots, 1836–1892*. Baltimore: Johns Hopkins University Press, 1955.

Campbell, Angus; Converse, Philip E.; Miller, Warren E.; and Stokes, Donald E. *Elections and the Political Order*. New York: John Wiley & Sons, 1966.

Campbell, Angus, and Miller, Warren E. "The Motivational Basis of Straight and Split Ticket Voting." *American Political Science Review* 51 (June 1957): 293–312.

Campbell, Edward C. "James Alexander Walker: A Biography." Master's thesis, Virginia Polytechnical Institute and State University, 1972.

Campbell, James B. "East Tennessee during the Federal Occupation, 1863–1865." East Tennessee Historical Society's *Publications* 19 (1947): 64–80.

──────. "East Tennessee during the Radical Regime, 1865–1869." East Tennessee Historical Society's *Publications* 20 (1948): 84–102.

──────. "The Significance of the Unionist Victory of February 9, 1861, in Tennessee." East Tennessee Historical Society's *Publications* 14 (1942): 11–30.

──────. "Some Social and Economic Phases of Reconstruction in East Tennessee, 1864–1869." Master's thesis, University of Tennessee, 1946.

Cartwright, Joseph H. *The Triumph of Jim Crow: Tennessee Race Relations in the 1880s*. Knoxville: University of Tennessee Press, 1976.

Casdorph, Paul D. "West Virginia and the 1880 Republican National Convention." *West Virginia History* 24 (January 1963): 147–55.

Caudill, Harry M. *Night Comes to the Cumberlands: A Biography of a Depressed Area*. Boston: Little, Brown & Co., 1962.

Cheek, William F. "A Negro Runs for Congress: John Mercer Langston and the Virginia Campaign of 1888." *Journal of Negro History* 52 (January 1967): 14–34.

Clark, Thomas D. *Kentucky: Land of Contrast*. New York: Harper & Row, Publishers, 1968.

──────. "The People, William Goebel, and the Kentucky Railroads." *Journal of Southern History* 5 (February 1939): 34–48.

Clay, Cassius M. *The Life of Cassius Marcellus Clay*. Cincinnati: J. Fletcher Brennan & Co., 1886.

Cole, Howson W. "Harrison Holt Riddleberger, Readjuster." Master's thesis, University of Virginia, 1952.

Collins, Lewis, and Collins, Richard H. *History of Kentucky*. 2 vols. Covington, Ky.: Collins & Co., 1874.

Cotton, William D. "Appalachian North Carolina: A Political Study, 1860–1889." Ph.D. dissertation, University of North Carolina, 1954.
Coulter, E. Merton. *The Civil War and Readjustment in Kentucky*. Gloucester, Mass.: Peter Smith, 1966.
―――. *William G. Brownlow: Fighting Parson of the Southern Highlands*. Chapel Hill: University of North Carolina Press, 1937.
Crotty, William J.; Kirkham, James F.; and Levy, Sheldon G. *Assassination and Political Violence: A Report to the National Commission on the Causes and Prevention of Violence*. New York: Bantam Books, 1970.
Curry, Richard O. "Crisis Politics in West Virginia, 1861–1870." In *Radicalism, Racism, and Party Alignment: The Border States during Reconstruction*, edited by Richard O. Curry, pp. 80–104. Baltimore: Johns Hopkins University Press, 1969.
―――. *A House Divided: A Study of Statehood Politics and the Copperhead Movement in West Virginia*. Pittsburgh: University of Pittsburgh Press, 1964.
Dailey, Douglas C. "The Elections of 1872 in North Carolina." *North Carolina Historical Review* 40 (Summer 1963): 338–60.
Daniels, Josephus. *Tar Heel Editor*. Chapel Hill: University of North Carolina Press, 1939.
David, Paul T. *Party Strength in the United States, 1872–1970*. Charlottesville: University Press of Virginia, 1972.
Davis, Curtis C. "Very Well-Rounded Republican: The Several Lives of John S. Wise." *Virginia Magazine of History and Biography* 71 (October 1963): 461–87.
Davis, Leonard M. "The Speeches and Speaking of Nathan Goff, Jr." Ph.D. dissertation, Northwestern University, 1958.
Davis, Leonard M., and Henning, James H. "Nathan Goff—West Virginia Orator and Statesman." *West Virginia History* 12 (July 1951): 299–337.
Degler, Carl N. "Black and White Together: Bi-racial Politics in the South." *Virginia Quarterly Review* 67 (Summer 1971): 421–44.
―――. *The Other South: Southern Dissenters in the Nineteenth Century*. New York: Harper & Row, Publishers, 1974.
DeSantis, Vincent P. *Republicans Face the Southern Question–The New Departure Years, 1877–1897*. Baltimore: Johns Hopkins University Press, 1959.
Dozer, Donald M. "Benjamin Harrison and the Presidential Campaign in 1892." *American Historical Review* 54 (October 1948): 49–77.
Durden, Robert F. *The Climax of Populism: The Election of 1896*. Lexington: University Press of Kentucky, 1965.
Eckenrode, Hamilton J. *The Political History of Virginia during the Reconstruction*. Baltimore: Johns Hopkins University Press, 1904.
Edmonds, Helen G. *The Negro and Fusion Politics in North Carolina: 1894–1901*. Chapel Hill: University of North Carolina Press, 1951.
Farrelly, David G. "John M. Harlan's One-Day Diary, August 21, 1877: An Interpretation of the Harlan-Bristow Controversy." *Filson Club Historical Quarterly* 24 (April 1950): 158–68.
Ferrell, Barbara A. "West Virginia and the Election of 1896." Master's thesis, West Virginia University, 1967.

Finch, Glenn. "The Election of United States Senators in Kentucky: The Beckman Period." *Filson Club History Quarterly* 44 (January 1970): 38–50.

Finnie, Gordon E. "The Antislavery Movement in the Upper South before 1840." *Journal of Southern History* 35 (August 1969): 319–42.

Fleming, Walter F. *Documentary History of Reconstruction: Political, Military, Social, Religious, Educational & Industrial 1865 to the Present Time*. Vol. 1. Gloucester, Mass.: Peter Smith, 1960.

Fox, John, Jr. "The Southern Mountaineer." *Scribner's Magazine* 29 (April, May 1901): 387–99, 556–70.

Frederickson, George M. *The Black Image in the White Mind: The Debate on Afro-American Character and Destiny, 1817–1914*. New York: Harper & Row, Publishers, 1971.

Frost, William G. "Our Contemporary Ancestors in the Southern Mountains." *Atlantic Monthly* 83 (March 1899): 311–19.

———. "The Southern Mountaineer." *Review of Reviews* 21 (March 1900): 303–31.

Gentry, Amos L. "Public Career of Leonidas Campbell Houk." Master's thesis, University of Tennessee, 1939.

Goodman, Leo A. "Some Alternatives to Ecological Correlation." *American Journal of Sociology* 64 (May 1959): 610–25.

Gray, Myra G. "A. W. Campbell—Party Builder." *West Virginia History* 7 (April 1946): 221–37.

Hamilton, J. G. de Roulhac. *Benjamin Sherwood Hedrick*. Chapel Hill: University of North Carolina Press, 1910.

———. *Reconstruction in North Carolina*. New York: Columbia University Press, 1914.

———, ed. *The Correspondence of Jonathan Worth*. 2 vols. Raleigh: North Carolina Historical Commission, 1909.

Hancock, Elizabeth A., ed. *Autobiography of John E. Massey*. New York: Neale Publishing Co., 1909.

"Hanging of Bad Tom Smith." *Harper's Weekly* 39 (10 August 1895): 748.

Harrell, David E. "The Disciples of Christ and Social Forces in Tennessee, 1865–1900." East Tennessee Historical Society's *Publications* 37 (1966): 30–47.

Hartz, Louis. "John M. Harlan in Kentucky, 1855–1877: The Story of His Pre-Court Political Career." *Filson Club History Quarterly* 14 (January 1940): 17–40.

Hathorn, Guy B. "The Political Career of C. Bascom Slemp." Ph.D. dissertation, Duke University, 1950.

Hays, Samuel P. "Political Parties and the Community-Society Continuum." In *The American Party Systems: Stages of Political Development*, edited by William N. Chambers and W. Dean Burnham, pp. 152–81. New York: Oxford University Press, 1967.

Hesseltine, William B. "Methodism and Reconstruction in East Tennessee." East Tennessee Historical Society's *Publications* 3 (1931): 42–61.

Hirshson, Stanley P. *Farewell to the Bloody Shirt: Northern Republicans and the Southern Negro, 1877–1893*. Bloomington: Indiana University Press, 1962.

Hobsbawn, Eric J. *Primitive Rebels: Studies in Archaic Forms of Social Movement in the 19th and 20th Centuries*. New York: W. W. Norton & Co., 1965.

Hoffman, Richard L. "The Republican Party in North Carolina, 1867–1871." Master's thesis, University of North Carolina, 1960.
Hoogenboom, Ari. *Outlawing the Spoils: A History of the Civil Service Reform Movement, 1865–1883*. Urbana: University of Illinois Press, 1968.
Hooper, Ben W. *The Unwanted Boy: The Autobiography of Governor Ben W. Hooper*. Edited by Everett R. Boyce. Knoxville: University of Tennessee Press, 1963.
Howard, Victor B. "The Kentucky Press and the Black Suffrage Controversy, 1865–1872." *Filson Club History Quarterly* 47 (July 1973): 215–37.
―――. "The Kentucky Press and the Negro Testimony Controversy, 1866–1872." *Register* of the Kentucky Historical Society 71 (January 1973): 29–50.
Humes, Thomas W. *The Loyal Mountaineers of East Tennessee*. Knoxville: Ogeden Bros. & Co., 1888.
―――. *Report to the East Tennessee Relief Association*. Knoxville: East Tennessee Relief Association, 1865.
Hutson, A. C. "The Coal Miners' Insurrections of 1891 in Anderson County, Tennessee." East Tennessee Historical Society's *Publications* 7 (1935): 103–21.
―――. "The Overthrow of the Convict Lease System in Tennessee." East Tennessee Historical Society's *Publications* 7 (1936): 82–103.
Isaac, Paul E. *Prohibition and Politics: Turbulent Decades in Tennessee, 1885–1920*. Knoxville: University of Tennesse Press, 1965.
Jacobs, James H. "The West Virginia Gubernatorial Election Contest, 1888–1890." *West Virginia History* 7 (April, July 1946): 159–220, 263–311.
Jensen, Richard. *The Winning of the Midwest: Social and Political Conflict, 1888–1896*. Chicago: University of Chicago Press, 1971.
Johnson, Guion G. "Social Characteristics of Ante-Bellum North Carolina." *North Carolina Historical Review* 6 (April 1929): 140–57.
Jones, Virgil C. *The Hatfields and the McCoys*. Chapel Hill: University of North Carolina Press, 1948.
Josephson, Matthew. *The Politicos, 1865–1896*. New York: Harcourt, Brace & World, 1938.
Key, V. O. *Southern Politics in State and Nation*. New York: Random House, 1949.
Kirby, Jack T. *Darkness at the Dawning: Race and Reform in the Progressive South*. Philadelphia: J. B. Lippincott Co., 1972.
Kleppner, Paul. *The Cross of Culture: A Social Analysis of Midwestern Politics, 1859–1900*. New York: Free Press, 1970.
Klingberg, Frank W. "The Southern Claims Commission: A Study in Unionism." Ph.D. dissertation, University of California at Los Angeles, 1948.
Kousser, J. Morgan. "Ecological Regression and the Analysis of Past Politics." *Journal of Interdisciplinary History* 4 (Autumn 1973): 237–62.
―――. *The Shaping of Southern Politics: Suffrage Restriction and the Establishment of the One-Party South, 1880–1910*. New Haven: Yale University Press, 1974.
Lacy, Eric R. *Vanquished Volunteers: East Tennessee Sectionalism from Statehood to Secession*. Johnson City, Tenn.: East Tennessee State University Press, 1965.
Lambert, Oscar D. *Stephen Benton Elkins*. Pittsburgh: University of Pittsburgh Press, 1955.

Langston, John M. *From the Virginia Plantation to the National Capitol*. New York: Arno Press, 1969.

Lefler, Hugh T., and Newsome, Albert R. *North Carolina: The History of a Southern State*. Chapel Hill: University of North Carolina Press, 1954.

Lewis, J. Eugene. "The Tennessee Gubernatorial Campaign and Election of 1894." *Tennessee Historical Quarterly* 13 (June, September, December 1954): 99–126, 224–43, 301–28.

Logan, Rayford W. *The Betrayal of the Negro: From Rutherford B. Hayes to Woodrow Wilson*. London: Collier-MacMillan, 1965.

Lonn, Ella. *Desertion during the Civil War*. Gloucester, Mass.: Peter Smith, 1966.

Lowe, Richard G. "The Republican Party in Antebellum Virginia, 1856–1860." *Virginia Magazine of History and Biography* 81 (July 1973): 259–79.

———. "Republicans, Rebellion, and Reconstruction: The Republican Party in Virginia, 1856–1870." Ph.D. dissertation, University of Virginia, 1968.

McClure, R. L. "Mazes of a Kentucky Feud." *Independent* 55 (17 September 1903): 2216–24.

McCormick, Richard P. *The Second American Party System: Party Formation in the Jacksonian Era*. Chapel Hill: University of North Carolina Press, 1966.

McDonough, James L. "John Schofield as Military Director of Reconstruction in Virginia." *Civil War History* 15 (September 1969): 237–56.

McKee, James W. "Felix K. Zollicoffer: Confederate Defender of East Tennessee." East Tennessee Historical Society's *Publications*, 44 (1971): 34–58; 45 (1972): 17–40.

McNeill, Rosalie F. "The First Fifteen Months of Governor Daniel Lindsay Russell's Administration." Master's thesis, University of North Carolina, 1939.

McQuown, Ruth, and Shannon, Jasper B. *Presidential Politics in Kentucky, 1824–1948*. Lexington: University of Kentucky Press, 1950.

McSeveney, Samuel T. *The Politics of Depression: Political Behavior in the Northeast, 1892–1896*. New York: Oxford University Press, 1972.

Maddex, Jack P., Jr. *The Virginia Conservatives, 1867–1879: A Study in Reconstruction Politics*. Chapel Hill: University of North Carolina Press, 1970.

Malberg, Edward I. "The Republican Party in Kentucky, 1856–1867." Master's thesis, University of Kentucky, 1967.

Marcus, Robert D. *Grand Old Party: Political Structure in the Gilded Age, 1880–1896*. New York: Oxford University Press, 1971.

Martin, Isaac P. *History of Methodism in the Holston Conference*. Nashville: Parthenon Press, [1945].

Melzer, John T. S. "The Danville Riot, November 3, 1883." Master's thesis, University of Virginia, 1963.

"Methodist Churches, North and South." *Methodist Quarterly* 17 (October 1865): 629–36.

Moger, Allen W. *Virginia: Bourbonism to Byrd, 1870–1925*. Charlottesville: University Press of Virginia, 1968.

Moore, James T. "Black Militancy in Readjuster Virginia, 1879–1883." *Journal of Southern History* 41 (May 1975): 167–86.

_____. *Two Paths to the New South: The Virginia Debt Controversy, 1870–1883*. Lexington: University Press of Kentucky. 1974.

Morgan, H. Wayne. *From Hayes to McKinley: National Party Politics, 1877–1896*. Syracuse: Syracuse University Press, 1969.

Moser, Harold D. "Reaction in North Carolina to the Emancipation Proclamation." *North Carolina Historical Review* 44 (Winter 1967): 53–71.

Olmsted, Frederick L. *The Slave States before the Civil War*. Edited by Harvey Wish. New York: Capricorn Books, 1959.

Owens, Susie L. "The Union League of America: Political Activities in Tennessee, the Carolinas, and Virginia, 1865–1870." Ph.D. dissertation, New York University, 1943.

Owsley, Frank L., and Owsley, Harriet C. "The Economic Structure of Rural Tennessee, 1850–1860." *Journal of Southern History* 8 (May 1942): 161–82.

Padgett, James A. "Reconstruction Letters from North Carolina." *North Carolina Historical Review* 18 (April, July, October 1941): 171–95, 278–300, 373–97; 19 (January, April, July, October 1942): 59–94, 187–208, 280–302, 381–404; 20 (January, April, July, October 1943): 54–82, 157–80, 259–82, 341–70; 21 (January, April, July 1944): 46–71, 139–57, 232–47.

Palmer, George T. *A Conscientious Turncoat: The Story of John M. Palmer, 1817–1900*. New Haven: Yale University Press, 1941.

Parker, James C. "Tennessee Gubernatorial Elections: 1869—The Victory of the Conservatives." *Tennessee Historical Quarterly* 33 (Spring 1974): 34–48.

Patton, James W. *Unionism and Reconstruction in Tennessee, 1860–1869*. Chapel Hill: University of North Carolina Press, 1934.

Pearson, Charles C. *The Readjuster Movement in Virginia*. New Haven: Yale University Press, 1917.

Pendleton, William C. *Political History of Appalachian Virginia, 1776–1927*. Dayton, Va.: Shenandoah Press, 1927.

Polakoff, Keith I. *The Politics of Inertia: The Election of 1876 and the End of Reconstruction*. Baton Rouge: Louisiana State University Press, 1973.

Posey, Thomas E. *The Negro Citizen of West Virginia*. Institute, W.Va.: Press of West Virginia State College, 1934.

Pulley, Raymond H. *Old Virginia Restored: An Interpretation of the Progressive Impulse, 1870–1930*. Charlottesville: University Press of Virginia, 1968.

Queener, Verton M. "A Decade of East Tennessee Republicanism, 1867–1876." East Tennessee Historical Society's *Publications* 14 (1942): 59–85.

_____. "The East Tennessee Republicans as a Minority Party, 1870–1896." East Tennessee Historical Society's *Publications* 15 (1943): 49–73.

_____. "The East Tennessee Republicans in State and Nation, 1870–1900." *Tennessee Historical Quarterly* 2 (June 1943): 99–128.

_____. "A History of the Republican Party in East Tennessee." Ph.D. dissertation, Indiana University, 1940.

_____. "The Origin of the Republican Party in East Tennessee." East Tennessee Historical Society's *Publications* 13 (1941): 66–90.

Quinn, James T. "John S. Barbour, Jr. and the Restoration of the Virginia Democracy, 1883–1892." Master's thesis, University of Virginia, 1966.

Raper, Horace W. "William W. Holden and the Peace Movement in North Carolina." *North Carolina Historical Review* 31 (October 1954): 493–516.

———. "William Woods Holden: A Political Biography." Ph.D. dissertation, University of North Carolina, 1951.

Reichard, Gary W. "The Aberration of 1920: An Analysis of Harding's Victory in Tennessee." *Journal of Southern History* 36 (February 1970): 33–49.

Rice, Harvey M. "The Conservative Re-action in West Virginia 1865–1871." Master's thesis, West Virginia University, 1933.

Riker, William H. *Federalism: Origin, Operation, Significance*. Boston: Little, Brown & Co., 1964.

Rippy, J. Fred, ed. *F. M. Simmons, Statesman of the New South: Memoirs and Addresses*. Durham, N. C.: Duke University Press, 1936.

Robison, Daniel M. "The Political Background of Tennessee's War of the Roses." East Tennessee Historical Society's *Publications* 5 (1933): 125–41.

Roller, David C. "The Republican Party of North Carolina: 1900–1916." Ph.D. dissertation, Duke University, 1965.

Rule, William, ed. *Standard History of Knoxville, Tennessee*. Chicago: Lewis Publishing Co., 1900.

Russ, William A. "Radical Disfranchisement in North Carolina, 1867–1868." *North Carolina Historical Review* 11 (October 1934): 271–83.

Shanks, Henry T. "Disloyalty to the Confederacy in Southwestern Virginia, 1861–1865." *North Carolina Historical Review* 21 (April 1944): 118–35.

Shapiro, Henry D. "A Preface to Prejudice: Local Color Writers and the Discovery of Appalachia." *Mountain Review* 3 (October 1976): 38–41.

———. "A Strange Land and Peculiar People: The Discovery of Appalachia, 1870–1920." Ph.D. dissertation, Rutgers University, 1966.

Sheldon, William D. *Populism in the Old Dominion: Virginia Farm Politics, 1885–1900*. Princeton: Princeton University Press, 1935.

Sitterson, J. Carlyle. "Economic Sectionalism in Ante-Bellum North Carolina." *North Carolina Historical Review* 16 (April 1939): 134–46.

Smith, Gerald W. "Nathan Goff, Jr.: A Biography." Ph.D. dissertation, West Virginia University, 1954.

———. *Nathan Goff, Jr.: A Biography*. Charleston, W.Va.: Educational Foundation, Inc., 1959.

———. "Nathan Goff, Jr., and the Solid South." *West Virginia History* 16 (October 1955): 5–21.

Smith, James D. "Virginia during Reconstruction, 1865–1870—a Political, Economic and Social Study." Ph.D. dissertation, University of Virginia, 1960.

Speed, Thomas. *The Union Cause in Kentucky, 1860–1865*. New York: G. P. Putnam's Sons, 1907.

Stampp, Kenneth M. *The Era of Reconstruction, 1865–1877*. New York: Random House, 1967.

Steelman, Joseph F. "The Progressive Era in North Carolina, 1884–1917." Ph.D. dissertation, University of North Carolina, 1955.

———. "Republican Party Strategists and the Issue of Fusion with Populists in

North Carolina, 1893-1894." *North Carolina Historical Review* 47 (July 1970): 244-69.

———. "Vicissitudes of Republican Party Politics: The Campaign of 1892 in North Carolina." *North Carolina Historical Review* 43 (October 1966): 430-42.

Summers, Festus P. *William L. Wilson and Tariff Reform*. New Brunswick, N.J.: Rutgers University Press, 1953.

Summers, Lewis P. *History of Southwest Virginia, 1746-1786: Washington County, 1777-1870*. Baltimore: Genealogical Publishing Co., 1966.

Talbott, Forest. "Some Legislative and Legal Aspects of the Negro Question in West Virginia during the Civil War and Reconstruction." *West Virginia History* 24 (January, April 1963): 110-33, 211-47.

Tapp, Hambleton. "Three Decades of Kentucky Politics, 1870-1900." Ph.D. dissertation, University of Kentucky, 1950.

Tatum, Georgia L. *Disloyalty in the Confederacy*. Chapel Hill: University of North Carolina Press, 1934.

Taylor, Alrutheus A. *The Negro in Tennessee, 1865-1880*. Washington, D.C.: The Associated Publishers, 1941.

Taylor, Rhea A. "Conflicts in Kentucky as Shown by the Constitutional Convention of 1890-91." Ph.D. dissertation, University of Chicago, 1948.

Taylor, Robert L. "Apprenticeship in the First District: Bob and Alf Taylor's Early Congressional Races." *Tennessee Historical Quarterly* 28 (Spring 1969): 24-41.

Temple, Oliver P. *East Tennessee and the Civil War*. Cincinnati: Robert Clarke Co., 1889.

Terral, Rufus. *Newell Sanders: A Biography*. Kingsport, Tenn.: n.p., 1935.

Thompson, Edwin B. "Benjamin Helm Bristow: Symbol of Reform." Ph.D. dissertation, University of Wisconsin, 1940.

Tonnes, Ferdinand. *Community & Society*. Translated and edited by Charles P. Loomis. New York: Harper & Row, Publishers, 1957.

Trelease, Allen W. *White Terror: The Ku Klux Klan Conspiracy and Southern Reconstruction*. New York: Harper & Row, Publishers, 1971.

———. "Who Were the Scalawags?" *Journal of Southern History* 29 (November 1963): 445-68.

Waits, John A. "Roanoke's Tragedy: The Lynch Riot of 1893." Master's thesis, University of Virginia, 1972.

Washington, Booker T. *Up from Slavery: An Autobiography*. New York: Bantam Books, 1956.

Webb, Ross A. "Benjamin H. Bristow: Civil Rights Champion, 1866-1872." *Civil War History* 15 (March 1969): 39-53.

———. *Benjamin Helm Bristow: Border State Politician*. Lexington: University Press of Kentucky, 1969.

———. "Kentucky: 'Pariah among the Elect.'" In *Radicalism, Racism, and Party Alignment: The Border States during Reconstruction*, edited by Richard O. Curry, pp. 105-45. Baltimore: Johns Hopkins University Press, 1969.

West, John C. *A Texan in Search of a Fight*. Waco, Texas: Texian Press, 1969.

Wiebe, Robert H. *The Search for Order: 1877-1920*. New York: Hill & Wang, 1967.

---. *The Segmented Society: An Historical Preface to the Meaning of America*. New York: Oxford University Press, 1975.
Williams, Cratis D. "The Southern Mountaineer in Fact and Fiction." Ph.D. dissertation, New York University, 1961.
---. "The Southern Mountaineer in Fact and Fiction." *Appalachian Journal* 3 (Autumn 1975): 8–61.
Williams, Gary L. "Lincoln's Neutral Allies: The Case of the Kentucky Unionists." *South Atlantic Quarterly* 73 (Winter 1974): 70–84.
Williams, John A. "Davis and Elkins of West Virginia: Businessmen in Politics." Ph.D. dissertation, Yale University, 1967.
---. "New York's First Senator from West Virginia: How Stephen B. Elkins Found a New Political Home." *West Virginia History* 31 (January 1970): 73–87.
---. *West Virginia: A Bicentennial History*. New York: W. W. Norton & Co., 1976.
Wiltz, John E. "APA-ism in Kentucky and Elsewhere." *Register* of the Kentucky Historical Society 56 (April 1958): 143–55.
---. "The 1895 Election: A Watershed in Kentucky Politics." *Filson Club History Quarterly* 37 (April 1963): 117–36.
Woodward, C. Vann. *Origins of the New South, 1877–1913*. Baton Rouge: Louisiana State University Press, 1951.
Wynes, Charles E. *Race Relations in Virginia, 1870–1902*. Charlottesville: University Press of Virginia, 1961.
Yates, Richard E. "Governor Vance and the Peace Movement." *North Carolina Historical Review* 17 (January, April 1940): 1–25, 89–113.

INDEX

A
Abingdon, 20
Abolitionists, 12
Adams, Henry, 6
Adams, Silas, 168–69, 171–74
Alleghany County, 217
Amnesty, 53
American Medical Association, 8, 127
American Protective Association, 125, 218
American Protective Tariff League, 155–56
Amherst College, 79
Anderson, Sam, 133
Anderson, William C., 78, 184–85
Anderson County, 73, 78–80, 84, 125, 211–12
Anderson-McCormick Act, 68, 107, 194
Appalachia, 11, 13, 76, 108, 128, 143, 202. *See also* Appalachian society
Appalachian mountains, 15, 60, 134, 142
Appalachian society, 3–4, 12, 31, 124, 127, 129, 204. *See also* Appalachia; Mountain population
Arthur, Chester, 63, 77, 89–90, 98–99, 102, 107, 118, 132
Asbury, J. W., 133
Asheville, 46, 160, 217
Ashland, 218
Atkinson, George W., 89–90, 136, 158, 192–94

B
Bailey, David, 107
Baker, John W., 146, 149
Baltimore and Ohio Railroad, 58
Barbour, James, 105–6
Barboursville, 78
Bartlett, John Z., 167
Bates, Creed, 144
Baxter, Lewis, 244 (n. 72)
Beales, James F., 85
Bell, John, 15–16, 18, 213
Bell County, 167

Bishop, John M., 86
Blacks: 36, 53–54, 61, 90, 102, 114, 129, 165, 178, 194, 218; suffrage, 5, 9–10, 31–35, 42, 45, 52, 57, 60, 183, 196–97; and mountain Republicans, 77, 84, 123, 132–41, 160, 172, 209, 214. *See also* Lily white Republicans; Lynching
Blaine, James G.: 68–69, 83, 93, 95, 161; supported by Goff machine, 89–91; opposes Readjusters, 105, 107; visits W. Va., 151
Blair, Frank S., 145
Blair, Henry W., 95
Blair Education Bill, 82–83
Bland, M. H., 53
Blount County, 37
Border State convention, 18
Boreing, Vincent, 186–88
Boreman, Arthur I., 28, 41
Botts, John M., 57
Bowen, Henry, 107
Boyd, James E., 165
Boyd County, 217
Bradley, William O.: 54, 94, 119, 139–40, 169–70, 174–75, 218; gubernatorial administration of, 129, 166, 198
Brady, James, 71–72, 115–16, 182, 188–89
Breathitt County, 195
Breckinridge, John C., 16
Breckinridge, Robert J., 26
Bristow, Benjamin H., 26, 53–55, 71, 93–94
Britt, James J., 201
Brown, John: raid of, 12
Brown, John Y., 198
Brownlow, John B., 233 (n. 25)
Brownlow, William G.: 13, 15, 28, 33, 41, 75, 79, 207; as governor, 34–37; as U.S. Senator, 38–40, 81–82
Brower, John M., 159–60
Bryan, William J., 188, 200
Buchanan County, 100
Buckner, Simon B., 20

271

Buncombe County, 217
Burchette, Drury, 167
Burnside, Ambrose E., 22–23
Burr, Aaron, 62
Butler, Marion, 162–66, 190. *See also* Populist party
Butler, Random R., 38, 40, 86, 111–12, 244 (n. 72)

C
Caldwell, Tod R., 46–49, 75
Cameron, William, 70, 102–7, 114
Campbell, Archibald W., 27–28
Campbell, John A., 20
Campbell County, 83
Cansler, Charles M., 139
Carpetbaggers, 48, 57–58
Carter County, 39
Casper, Henry, 132
Catholic church, 33, 218
Chattanooga, 22, 84, 124, 135, 139, 144, 150, 206, 218, 254 (n. 74)
Cherokee County, 25
Civil Rights Act: 1866, 30–31; 1875, 32, 39–41, 43–44, 54–56, 60, 76, 81, 88
Civil Service system, 143, 183
Civil War: 8, 33, 36, 41, 50, 64, 75, 78, 80, 108, 120, 122, 126, 128, 146–47, 166, 176, 189, 201, 203, 207, 213; in the mountains, 12–26; impact of, on mountain Republicans, 5, 9, 11, 62–74, 76, 83, 148, 182. *See also* Guerrilla war
Clay County: Ky., 54, 95, 129; W. Va., 134–35
Cleveland, Grover, 77, 110, 142, 147, 156
Cochrane, John B., 54
Cockrill, Harrison, 55
Colored Independent party, 133
Colson, David G., 166–76, 185–88, 216, 243 (n. 23)
Committee on Organization of the Soldiers' and Sailors' State League, 87
Community: geographically based, 4–11, 76
Confederacy, 3, 5, 19, 24, 29, 36, 210, 214
Confederate army, 18, 20, 22, 78, 87, 99. *See also* Desertion; Veterans, in the Confederate army
Confiscation: of Confederate property, 45–46
Conscription: Confederate, 24–25
Conservative party: Virginia, 56–60, 64, 100–101, 196
Conservative Union Democrats: Kentucky, 50–51. *See also* Union Democrats

Constitutional Convention: Tenn., 1865, 28, 79; Tenn., 1871, 38–39; W. Va., 1871, 43; Va., 1901, 197
Constitutional Union party, 16, 45
Convict lease system, 125
Cooke, C. L., 99
Cooper, John A., 85
Cooper, Peter A., 80
Cooper, Spencer, 195
Cooper, Tom N., 97–98
Covington, 53
Custom House Ring, 80, 82, 85

D
Dandridge, 85
Daniel, John, 103
Danville, 106
Danville Circular, 66, 106
Davis, G. D., 243 (n. 23)
Davis, Henry G., 113, 151, 153, 155, 157
Davis, Jefferson, 24
Davis, Thomas E., 154, 192
Dawson, John, 105
Dayton, A. Gordon, 153–58, 192
Democratic party: 6, 15–16, 26, 66–68, 74, 81, 87, 89, 94, 96, 98–99, 105–7, 110, 119–20, 122, 135, 141, 147, 150, 152, 154–55, 157, 159, 162, 165, 168, 172, 177–78, 179–81, 190, 198–201, 203, 206, 213, 219; Independent, 40, 49, 77, 82; mountain, 100, 137, 177, 180, 189; racism of, 9, 10, 115, 121, 140, 183, 189, 191, 194–95; during Reconstruction, 34, 37–40, 42–44, 47–49, 51–53, 55–56, 60
Denny, George, 169
Department of Agriculture, 76, 83
Desertion, 24, 69
Disciples of Christ, 207
Dockery, Oliver H., 98–99, 165, 190
Douglas, Stephen A., 16, 213
Douglass, Frederick, 116
Dovener, B. B., 113, 151
Duke family, 162, 165, 175, 216
Duval, Isaac H., 87, 90

E
East Tennessee. *See* Eastern Tennessee
East Tennessee Relief Association, 23
East Tennessee University, 79
Eastern Kentucky: 14, 125, 136, 139, 167, 169–76, 185–86, 214, 217–18, 220; secession in, 15, 17–18; Civil War in, 23–24, 26, 29; Reconstruction in, 50, 52–55; party-army in, 74, 91–92, 95, 117, 119. *See also* Kentucky

Eastern Tennessee: 13–14, 125, 132–36, 139, 143–49, 155, 160, 172, 175, 184, 186, 190, 197, 200, 207, 211–12, 214, 221; secession in, 15, 17–18, 20–21; Civil War in, 22, 26, 29; Reconstruction in, 33–41; party-army in, 64, 67, 71, 73–74, 77–78, 80–86, 89–90, 111–12. *See also* Tennessee
Eaves, John B., 159–64
Egbert, George T., 100
Elkins, Stephen B., 91, 113, 121, 138, 160, 175, 182, 200, 202, 216, 231 (n. 18); becomes leader of W. Va. Republicans, 151–58; as U.S. Senator, 191–94
Emancipation of slaves, 29, 78
Estill County, 52, 55
Etheridge, Emerson, 35
Evans, H. Clay: 141, 153, 175, 182, 216; and the Houk machine, 144–50, 245 (n. 67); and Walter P. Brownlow, 184–86
Evans, Walter P., 94–95, 118
Ewart, Hamilton G., 114, 121, 136, 159–61, 164

F
Farmers' Alliance, 120, 161–62, 176–77
Federal army, 22–23, 25–26, 28, 68, 87. *See also* Civil War
Feuds, 10, 126–27, 129
Fifteenth Amendment, 31, 41–43, 52, 60, 87. *See also* Blacks, suffrage
Finley, H. Franklin, 118–19, 167–72, 174
Flick, William H. H., 42, 90
Flick Amendment, 43
Folk, G. N., 98–99
Fourteenth Amendment, 31, 38, 41, 52
Fox, Fountain, 118
Free silver, 155, 157, 163–65, 180, 184, 190–91
Freeman, A. A., 39
Freer, Romeo, 91, 193–94
Fulkerson, Abram, 102
Funder party, 100–107. *See also* Readjuster party
Furches, David M., 163
Fusion, 99, 162–66, 190. *See also* Populist party

G
Garfield, James, 69, 77, 85, 89, 102
Garrard County, 54, 94
Gaston County, 124
Germans, 84, 210
Gibson, Henry R., 112, 147–50
Goebel, William, 128, 198–9
Goebel Election Bill, 187, 198–99
Goff, Nathan: 96, 108–9, 112–14, 119, 121–22, 135, 146, 192–94, 221; in Reconstruction, 44, 63–65, 69–71; creates party-army, 86–91; and Stephen B. Elkins, 150–59
Goodloe, David R., 45
Goodloe, William C., 167
Gourley, George W., 195
Grand Army of the Republic, 69, 148, 186–87
Grant, Jesse R., 53
Grant, Ulysses S., 38, 43, 48, 53–54, 58, 68–69, 83, 93–94, 97
Greeley, Horace, 43, 48, 86
Greenback party, 89–91, 97
Groner, V. D., 116–17
Greene County, 17
Greeneville Union convention, 21, 78
Guerrilla war, 22–26, 63
Guthrie, William A., 166

H
Hamilton, W. S., 243 (n. 23)
Hamilton County, 124, 135, 244 (n. 57)
Hancock, Winfield, 101
Hanna, Marcus, 150
Harlan, John M., 51–55, 92–94
Harlan County, 52
Harmen, George, 153
Harris, J. C. L., 114
Harris, Thomas M., 87
Harrison, Benjamin, 116–17, 122, 131, 145, 152–54, 159, 161, 167, 170, 178, 192
Harrison, William H., 15
Hatfield-McCoy feud, 126
Hayes, Rutherford B., 40, 76, 85, 88, 93–94, 132
Haywood County, 25
Hazel Green Herald, 195
Heroes of America, 25–26, 29, 45
Hobsbawm, Eric J., 127–28
Hobson, Edward H., 51
Hobson, J. Haskins, 181
Holden, William W., 25–26, 44–47
Holton, Alfred E., 164–65
Holston Conference: Methodist Episcopal Church, 36
Honest Election League, 181
Houk, John C., 67, 143–50, 155, 159, 184
Houk, Leonidas C., 96, 108–9, 111–12, 122, 132–33, 136, 143–45, 147, 155, 168, 186, 216, 221, 245 (n. 6); creates a party-army, 64–69, 72, 77–91, 234 (n. 66)
Hubbard, William P., 151
Hughes, Robert W., 59–60
Hunnicutt, James W., 57

INDEX 273

I

Illiteracy, 206–7
Imboden, John, 24
Immigrants, 125, 209–10, 218
Industrialization, 7, 10, 76, 124–29, 150, 161, 203, 211, 216–19, 221
Internal Revenue Service, 48–49, 59, 96–97, 99, 117–18, 122, 129, 138, 161
International Typographical Union, 194
Iredell County, 96
Irish, 84, 210
Irwin, Harvey S., 140

J

Jackson, E. Polk, 95
Jackson, John J., 43
Jackson, Stonewall, 179
Jackson County, 27
Jacob, John J., 43
Jefferson County, 79
Jensen, Richard, 219
Johnson, Andrew: 18, 28, 75, 87, 178; as President, 30–34, 37, 44, 50, 56
Joint Committee on Reconstruction, 31
Jones, William, 24

K

Kenton County, 53
Kentucky: 16, 22, 78, 125–26, 128–29, 133, 136, 139–41, 166–69, 174, 187, 195, 198–200, 213, 218, 220; Civil War in, 25, 27, 29; Reconstruction in, 31, 50–54, 56; party-army in, 63, 68–69, 71, 73, 91–94, 119. *See also* Eastern Kentucky
Kentucky Colored Democrat Club, 141
Keogh, Thomas, 98, 114
Kincaide, Charles E., 242 (n. 23)
Kirk, George, 25
Kitchen, Buck, 121
Kleppner, Paul, 219
Knott County, 126
Know-Nothing party, 15
Knox County, 79–82
Knoxville: 34, 36, 40, 66, 79, 82, 84–86, 132–33, 139, 146, 149–50, 197, 216, 218; siege of, 22
Knoxville Daily Chronicle, 85–86
Knoxville Republican, 68, 149
Knoxville Union convention, 78
Knoxville Whig, 15, 78
Kousser, J. Morgan, 254 (n. 74)
Ku Klux Klan, 32, 42, 47–49, 52, 55, 63

L

Lamb, William, 181–82, 188
Langston, John M., 116
Lee, Fitzhugh, 67, 115
Lee, Robert E., 24, 29
Letcher, John, 24
Lewis, John F., 58, 102
Lexington, 27
Liberal party: North Carolina, 98–99
Liberal Republicans, 32, 39, 42. *See also* Republican party
Lily white Republicans, 138, 160, 199–200
Lincoln, Abraham, 17, 21, 26–28, 36, 68, 78–79, 213
Lodge, Henry C., 132, 136
Lodge Elections Bill, 10, 132, 137, 141, 153, 161, 172, 177, 202, 221
Longstreet, James, 22
London, 78
Loudon County, 83, 112
Louisiana Commission, 93
Louisville, 26, 53–54, 94, 117–18, 218
Louisville and Nashville Railroad, 84, 198–99
Lyle, J. Nat., 85
Lynching, 39, 126, 130, 134, 138

M

McClellan, George B., 20, 27
McCormick, Richard P., 15
McCoy, H. E., 188–89
McDonald, Angus, 155
McDowell, John, 146–47
McKinley, William, 145, 150, 157–58, 164–66, 174–75, 181, 183, 186, 190, 192, 194
McKinney, Phillip, 117
Madison County, 25
Magoffin, Beriah, 20
Mahone, William: 58, 145, 155, 168, 196, 219; and the Readjuster party, 99–109, 114–17, 122; and the party-army, 64, 67, 69–72, 176–81. *See also* Readjuster party
Maney, George, 40–41
Marcus, Robert D., 6, 185
Marshall, Jim, 178–79
Mason, John W., 65, 90, 122, 153, 155, 192
Massey, John, 102, 104–5
Maxwell, Edwin, 91
Maynard, Horace, 21, 38–40, 79–82, 85
Merrimon, A. S., 48
Methodist Episcopal church, 35–37, 207–8, 219, 226 (n. 32)
Middle class: professional and business, 8–10, 128–29, 142–43, 154, 174, 182, 185, 202
Middlesborough, 170
Milburn, W. E. F., 184–85
Militia: state, 35, 38, 47, 50, 106, 129–30
Mills, George T., 177
Mitchell County, 129, 160

Montgomery County, 95, 169
Morehead, John M., 200
Morgan, John H., 23
Morgan County, 80
Morrison, H. S. K., 179
Mott, John J., 49, 159, 161–62, 164, 190; creates a party-army, 63–64, 72, 96–100, 109, 114
Mountain population, 3–5, 8, 19–20, 42, 61, 75, 126, 128, 202, 205–6, 209, 216. *See also* Appalachian society
Mountain Republicans: 3–4, 9–10, 19, 29, 186–88, 197, 201–3, 205, 210–11, 214, 216; and Reconstruction, 30–31, 33, 35, 37–42, 44, 46–50, 53, 56–57, 59, 61; and the party-army, 62–65, 67–74, 76–77, 87, 93–94, 96, 99–101, 108, 110, 114–16, 122; and business leadership, 143, 153, 156, 158–59, 161–62, 164, 166–67, 169, 172, 174, 176, 178–79, 182–83; and blacks, 131–41, 190–91, 194–96, 209. *See also* Republican party

N
Nashville, 37
Neutrality, 20
North Carolina: 13, 25, 124, 148, 180–81, 217, 219; and Reconstruction, 31, 44, 46, 48–49; and the party-army, 62–63, 65, 67, 69–71, 84, 96, 108, 114, 119–20, 122; and new Republican leaders, 158–62, 164–66, 190; Republicans and race relations, 133, 136–40, 195–96, 199–200. *See also* Western North Carolina
North Carolina Protective Tariff League, 160
Northwestern Virginia, 13–14, 16–18, 20. *See also* West Virginia
Northwestern West Virginia: 89, 134, 156, 172, 175, 210–11, 213–14; and the Civil War, 23, 26–27, 29; and Reconstruction, 41–43. *See also* West Virginia

O
Ohio County, 17
Olds, Schuyler S., 163
Olmsted, Frederick L., 8

P
Parton, James, 62
Patronage: the political use of, 49, 52, 54, 59, 69–70, 77, 79, 81–82, 88–90, 92, 96, 102, 104, 109–10, 118, 122, 138–39, 144–45, 152–53, 158, 164, 166–67, 182, 185–86, 191
Parkersburg, 190

Parkersburg State Journal, 151
Party-army: mountain Republican, 62–76, 110, 123–24, 128, 131–32, 141, 215, 219; creation of, 85–86, 90–91, 95, 108; decline of, 142–43, 157, 175, 182
Patton, George L., 89
Paul, John, 102
Payne Election Law, 161
Pearne, Thomas H., 36
Pearson, Richmond M.: (1805–1878), 46; (1852–1923), 120–21, 162–64, 180, 190, 219
Pendleton Civil Service Act, 82–83. *See also* Civil Service system
Pensions, 69–70, 76, 84, 90
Petersburg, 100, 102, 116
Pettibone, Augustus E., 112, 184
Pierpont, Francis H., 20, 56–57
Pocahontas County, 213
Polk, James K., 14
Poll tax, 103–4, 196–97
Populist party: in N.C., 159, 162–66, 190; in Tenn., 146–48; in Va., 178–79, 196–97; in W. Va., 155, 157
Preston County, 194
Pritchard, Jeter C., 159–66, 175, 180, 182, 190–91, 200, 216
Prohibition, 91–92, 95, 97–98, 112, 117–18, 144, 147
Prohibition party, 118, 188
Pugh, Samuel, 198
Pulaski County: Ky., 129; Va., 179

R
Raleigh Standard, 25
Ramsay, James G., 49, 97
Randall, W. H., 54
Rangers, 24
Ray, Montreval, 25
Readjuster party, 64, 101–8, 115, 138, 177, 179, 196, 202, 219, 221
Reconstruction: impact of, 5, 9, 11, 29, 62–63, 74–76, 79, 87, 93, 96–97, 100, 111, 114, 120, 122, 124, 132, 141, 151, 158, 183, 201–3, 205, 221; Presidential, 30, 33–34, 44–45, 56; in Tenn., 33–41; in W. Va., 41–44; in N.C., 44–50; in Ky., 50–56; in Va., 56–60. *See also* Ku Klux Klan
Red Shirts: North Carolina, 195
Redwine, David R., 195
Reed, Thomas B., 145, 164–65
Reorganized Government of Virginia, 20, 56
Republican Congressional Committee, 86, 168, 181
Republican League, 146

INDEX 275

Republican National Committee, 89, 91, 114, 117, 146, 155, 157, 163, 178, 186, 193
Republican party: 3, 5–6, 9–17, 21, 128, 133–39, 141, 184–86, 189–90, 193, 197–200, 204, 206, 213, 216–17, 219–21; in the Civil War, 26–29; in Reconstruction, 30–32, 34, 36–47, 49–61; party-army in, 63–64, 70, 76–77, 81, 86–91, 94–99, 101–3, 105, 107, 109–14, 116–22; new leadership in, 142–47, 149, 151–52, 154–61, 163–67, 169–83. *See also* Liberal Republicans; Mountain Republicans
Reynolds, Frank, 153
Rhea, William F., 189
Richmond, 56, 67, 101
Riddleberger, Harrison H., 104, 114–15
Riddleberger Debt Bill, 104
Rives, J. B., 59
Roane Iron Works, 144
Roanoke, 129–31, 178
Roanoke County, 124
Roanoke Iron Works, 131
Rockcastle County, 12
Rollins, William W., 159
Roosevelt, Theodore, 187–88, 199–200
Rose, Thomas W., 220
Royall, William, 105
Rucker, I. R., 129
Rule, William, 79, 82, 85–86, 112, 133, 197, 234 (n. 66)
Russell, Daniel L., 70, 139–40, 161, 165–66, 190–91
Rutherford County, 48

S
Salyersville, 119
Sands, Joseph H., 130–31
Sanders, Newell, 141, 144
Scott, Ethelbert D., 188, 243 (n. 23)
Scott, Nathan B., 193
Secession, 3, 8–9, 16–17, 33, 36, 75, 180, 214
Secret Ballot law, 197
Segregation, 138–39
Senter, DeWitt C., 37–38, 81
Settle, Thomas: (1831–1888), 48, 50; (1865–1919), 148, 162, 164, 191
Sherman, John, 97, 116
Sherman, William T., 22, 69
Sherman Silver Purchase Act, 155
Sevier County, 18, 78
Simmons, Furnifold, 195
Simpson, Mathew, 36
Sketches of the Rise, Progress, and Decline of Secession, 33
Skinner, Harry, 190
Slavery, 4, 13, 17, 21, 27, 34

Slemp, C. Bascom, 199–201
Slemp, Campbell, 177, 199
Smith, G. P., 17
Smyth County, 217
Southern Baptists, 219
Southern Claims Commission, 84
Southeastern Kentucky. *See* Eastern Kentucky
Southwestern Virginia: 14, 18–19, 56, 60, 69, 74, 99, 188–90, 199, 214, 217, 219–20; State of, 26; Civil War in, 26, 28; Readjuster party in, 101–8; race relations in, 129–31, 134, 139; new Republican leadership in, 176–77, 179–82. *See also* Virginia
Sperry, C. A., 43
Stahlman, E. B., 84
State debt, 100, 105, 219
State Guard, 20
States-Rights party, 18
Spanish-American War, 187
Stevenson, William E., 43
Stewart, William M., 157
Stokes, William, 37–38, 81
Stone, George S., 173–74
Sturgiss, George C., 153, 155–56
Sumner, Charles, 32

T
Taft, William H., 200
Tate, Dick, 95
Taulbee, William P., 242 (n. 23)
Tariff: issue of, 5, 29, 91, 107, 121, 128, 142, 144, 146, 151, 155–56, 158, 160, 163, 172, 176–77, 180, 216–17, 221
Taylor, Alfred A., 111–12, 136–37, 144, 184–85, 244 (n. 72)
Taylor, Nathaniel G., 23
Taylor, Robert L., 184
Taylor, William, 198–99
Taylor, Zachary, 15
Temple, Oliver P., 82, 84–85
Tennessee: 16, 21, 28, 122, 124–25, 143–44, 146, 149, 153, 184–86, 197–98, 200, 206, 218; Reconstruction in, 31–35, 38–40, 44, 46, 49; party-army in, 63, 66, 71, 78–79, 84, 91; race relations in, 133, 135–37, 139, 141. *See also* Eastern Tennessee
Terry, William, 59
Test Oath: voters, 34, 41, 57–59
Thirteenth Amendment, 27
Thomas, Dorsey B., 40–41
Thomas, George M., 53, 95
Thornburgh, Jacob, 79, 81–82
Tonnies, Ferdinand, 127–28
Trout, Henry S., 130–31
Turner, Tom, 95

U

Unconditional Unionists, 28–31, 50
Union army. *See* Federal army
Union Association of Alexandria, 56
Union Democrats, 51–52. *See also* Conservative Union Democrats
Union Home Guards, 20
Union League, 35–36, 45, 52, 57
Union party: of 1864, 26–28, 33, 78
Unionists: 68–69, 96, 137, 150, 160, 221; during the secession crisis, 16–18, 20; in the Civil War, 22–28; during Reconstruction, 41, 44–47, 52, 56, 212–15, 254 (n. 5)
Urbanization, 10, 216, 218, 221

V

Van Buren, Martin, 14
Vance, Zebulon, 25, 44–45, 50, 75, 120, 164
Van Winkle, Peter, 27
Veterans: 5; in the Confederate army, 34, 39, 41, 44–45, 50–51, 56–59, 63, 69–70, 96, 180, 213; Federal army, 34, 41, 43, 63, 69, 76, 78, 80, 84–85, 87, 89, 92, 95, 146, 151, 155, 168, 172, 185, 187, 194
Virginia: 13, 22, 124, 129–31, 137, 155, 196–97, 199–200, 202, 214, 219–21; Reconstruction in, 31–32, 56–60; the party-army in, 63–72; and the Readjuster party, 100–8, 114–17, 119; and business Republicans, 176–82. *See also* Northwestern Virginia; Southwestern Virginia

W

Walker, Gilbert C., 58–59
Walker, James A., 139, 177, 179–82, 188–90, 197, 216, 243 (n. 23)
Walton Law, 179, 197
Washington County: Tenn., 37; Va., 18, 20
Watkins, Albert G., 82
Watterson, Henry, 53
Wells, Henry H., 57–59
West Virginia: 12–13, 21, 124–26, 146, 188, 206–7, 213; Civil War in, 24, 27–28; Reconstruction in, 31–32, 41–44, 46, 49, 56; party-army in, 63, 65, 67, 70, 74, 86–91, 112–14, 119, 121–22; race relations in, 132–33, 136, 138; and the Elkins machine, 150–60, 191–94, 196, 198, 200. *See also* Northwestern Virginia; Northwestern West Virginia
West Virginia Central Railroad, 151
Western North Carolina: 13–14, 18–19, 129, 134, 136, 160–65, 172, 175, 188, 191, 201, 213, 215, 217, 219; Civil War in, 24–26, 28; Reconstruction in, 44, 47–49; party-army in, 69, 74, 96–97, 114, 120. *See also* North Carolina
Wetzel County, 17
Wheeling, 17, 20, 113, 152–53, 206
Wheeling convention: 1861, 21
Wheeling Intelligencer, 27, 113, 152
Whig party, 12, 14–15, 18, 40
White, John D.: 54–55, 167, 173–75, 187–88, 221; creates a party-army, 63–64, 91–96, 109, 117–19
White Government Unions, 195
Whitley County, 27, 168
Wickham, William C., 102–3, 105, 107
Wiebe, Robert H., 127–28
Wilkes County, 46
Willey, Waitman T., 21, 27–28, 44, 75
Willey Amendment, 21
Williams, John, 80
Willson, Augustus E., 93
Wilson, Ben, 88
Wilson, John H., 167–72, 175
Wilson, William L., 121, 153–55
Wise, John, 70, 105, 115–16
Wisener, William H., 39
Withers, R. E., 58–59
Wood, Andrew T., 95, 169
Wood, Henry C., 178
Woodruff, W. W., 146
Worth, Jonathan, 45

Y

Yardley, William, 40–41, 86, 133
York, Tyre, 99

Z

Zollicoffer, Felix K., 22

THE AUTHOR

Gordon B. McKinney is associate professor of history at Western Carolina University, Cullowhee, North Carolina.

THE BOOK

Typeface: Mergenthaler VIP Palatino

Design and composition: The University of North Carolina Press

Paper: 60# Warren's Olde Style

Binding cloth: Roxite Linen B 53540 by The Holliston Mills, Incorporated

Printer and binder: Thomson-Shore, Incorporated, Dexter, Michigan

Published by The University of North Carolina Press